Dialogue is never easy when there are core differences that make conversation difficult. It takes a patient and kind heart to be open and learn from others. The benefit for this labor is always a richer and more complex engagement with reality, but for most, the fear exceeds the promise of goodness. Rabbi Eckstein and Dr. Longman offer immense and practical wisdom about the holy text of Scripture and also paint a beautiful portrait of how different perspectives of Scripture can refract, inform, and bless one another. This devotional guide will intrigue and instruct—and, far more, will invigorate your engagement with God.

DAN B. ALLENDER, PH.D.
Professor of Counseling Psychology and Founding President,
Seattle School of Theology and Psychology

Rabbi Eckstein and Professor Longman have teamed up in a wonderful act of partnership that will mean rich gifts to all who become their readers. This devotional has a unique capacity to feed the mind with lessons from the roots of our faith and keep our souls rooted in spiritual nourishment.

JOHN ORTBERG
Senior Pastor, Menlo Park Presbyterian Church, and author of *Who Is This Man?*

*Inspiring Reflections on Scripture
from a Jewish Rabbi and a Christian Theologian*

❖   ❖   ❖

THE ONE YEAR
HOLY LAND
MOMENTS
DEVOTIONAL

❖   ❖   ❖

RABBI YECHIEL ECKSTEIN
& DR. TREMPER LONGMAN III

TYNDALE
MOMENTUM

*An Imprint of
Tyndale House Publishers, Inc.*

Visit Tyndale online at www.tyndale.com.

Visit Tyndale Momentum online at www.tyndalemomentum.com.

TYNDALE, *The One Year*, and *One Year* are registered trademarks of Tyndale House Publishers, Inc. *Tyndale Momentum*, the Tyndale Momentum logo, and The One Year logo are trademarks of Tyndale House Publishers, Inc. Tyndale Momentum is an imprint of Tyndale House Publishers, Inc.

The One Year Holy Land Moments Devotional

Cover designed by Erik Peterson

Interior designed by Dean H. Renninger

Unless otherwise indicated, all Scripture quotations are from the *Holy Bible*, New Living Translation, copyright © 1996, 2004, 2007 by Tyndale House Foundation. Used by permission of Tyndale House Publishers, Inc., Carol Stream, Illinois 60188. All rights reserved.

Scripture quotations marked NIV are taken from the Holy Bible, *New International Version,*® NIV.® Copyright © 1973, 1978, 1984, 2011 by Biblica, Inc.™ Used by permission of Zondervan. All rights reserved worldwide. www.zondervan.com.

Scripture quotations marked KJV are taken from the *Holy Bible*, King James Version.

Scripture quotations marked NKJV are taken from the New King James Version.® Copyright © 1982 by Thomas Nelson, Inc. Used by permission. All rights reserved.

Scripture quotations marked ESV are taken from *The Holy Bible*, English Standard Version® (ESV®), copyright © 2001 by Crossway, a publishing ministry of Good News Publishers. Used by permission. All rights reserved.

Scripture quotations marked NASB are taken from the New American Standard Bible,® copyright © 1960, 1962, 1963, 1968, 1971, 1972, 1973, 1975, 1977, 1995 by The Lockman Foundation. Used by permission.

ISBN 978-1-4143-7021-7 Softcover

Printed in the United States of America

19   18   17   16   15   14   13
7   6   5   4   3   2   1

Introduction

*How wonderful and pleasant it is when
brothers live together in harmony!*
❖ PSALM 133:1

Welcome to the *One Year Holy Land Moments Devotional*!

I am delighted that you have selected this devotional guide, an
investment for the new year that will not only deepen your faith but
also help you discover the profound Jewish roots of Christianity and
the rich, shared biblical heritage of our ancient faiths. These devotions are written for anyone with a heart for God's people who is
interested in the stories, teachings, and traditions that the Jewish
boy Jesus grew up learning and observing—traditions that are still
very much a part of Judaism today.

As an Orthodox Jew and ordained rabbi, I have devoted my life
to building bridges of understanding between Christians and Jews.
In 1983, I founded the International Fellowship of Christians and
Jews to foster cooperation between our two great faith communities
and to build support for Israel and her people in need throughout
the world. With the help of our Christian friends, we have raised
more than three-quarters of a billion dollars to support this criti-
cally important work.

For two thousand years, relations between Christians and Jews
have been marked by distrust and animosity. This troubled history
has kept us from working together and recognizing the many things
we have in common. I have spent the past three decades finding
places of healing, forging connections, and improving relationships
between members of our faiths. The book you hold in your hands is
a fruit of this calling.

These devotions are based on *Holy Land Moments*, my daily radio
program now in its fourth year, which is heard, in English and
Spanish, on more than one thousand radio outlets by over nine
million listeners on five continents. The material I have written is

tied to my teachings on Jewish faith, observance, and tradition; the history of the Jewish people and the Jewish state; and current issues and challenges facing Israel today.

While the devotions reflect the Jewish perspective, for this book I have worked alongside Tremper Longman III, a Christian author and a scholar of the Old Testament (which Jews know as the Hebrew Bible). Professor Longman offers a Christian view on these teachings to help you clearly see what we share in common, as well as our differences. It is our hope that this collaboration will help Christian and Jewish brothers and sisters to "live together in unity," as the psalmist puts it so beautifully in Psalm 133.

That is my heart, and I believe deeply that it is also our God's heart. I fervently hope that, after exploring our great faith heritage through these devotions, it will be your heart as well.

With prayers for *shalom*, peace,
Rabbi Yechiel Eckstein

How to Use
This Devotional

This devotional is organized into fifty-two weeks, with each week centered on a theme or topic. Though the Jewish calendar varies from year to year as to when feast days and observances fall, we attempted to place devotions tied to the holy days and other events, such as Passover, *Rosh Hashanah*, *Yom Kippur*, and others, closest to the time of year they typically occur.

At the end of each week, on the Sabbath day, you will find a space for reflection and questions to prompt you to record a new truth, a new understanding, or a different perspective that you have learned from discovering the Jewish roots of your faith. Our hope is that this will help you to consider more thoroughly and thoughtfully what you have gleaned during the week's reading.

If you miss a day's reading here and there, don't become discouraged! Just pick up where you are and continue the journey. As with any discipline, persistence will be its own reward.

THE SECRET TO SUCCESS

Oh, the joys of those who do not follow the advice of the wicked, or stand around with sinners, or join in with mockers. ❖ PSALM 1:1

With so many ads bombarding us daily—through TV, the radio, our smartphones, pop-ups on our computers—we can become immune to the myriad claims of prosperity, health, and success. But when it comes to God's Word and the promises *he* makes, we need to readjust the lens of our cynicism. When God tells us what we must do in order to be successful, we need to pay attention.

Psalm 1 offers us just this type of advice. It is a beautiful contrast of two paths set before us—the life of the faithful person and the life of the unfaithful person. We can choose to obey and follow God, or we can choose a path of rebellion and disobedience.

Clearly, if we want to prosper in whatever we do, we will choose to be guided by God's wisdom. We will avoid being with people who tear down our faith rather than encourage us. We will spend time in God's Word and know his will for us.

In the Scriptures, God says, "See, I am setting before you today a blessing and a curse—the blessing if you obey the commands of the LORD your God" (Deuteronomy 11:26-27, NIV). The Sages teach that the word *today* is used in this passage to emphasize that God speaks to us every single day—not just when he gave us the Bible. When we attune our hearts to his voice and do his will, we will live blessed lives.

Does that mean we will never suffer disappointment, tragedy, or difficulty? No. Does it mean we are guaranteed health, wealth, and happiness? Absolutely not. But it does mean that as we live according to God's commands, whatever "fruit" we produce will be blessed, and we will receive God's approval. As we apply God's Word to our lives, we will adopt actions and attitudes that honor him.

That is the secret to success in God's eyes.

A Christian Reflection on Living Wisely

In his letter to the new Christians in Jerusalem, James offers some good advice about living wisely. First, he says, if we lack wisdom (specifically, the ability to make good decisions), we should ask God, "who gives generously to all without finding fault, and it will be given" (James 1:5, NIV). Such wisdom begins with respect for God, leads to right living, and results in the ability to tell right from wrong. Further, James says, as we understand God's will for our lives by spending time in his Word and through obedience, we will live lives reflected by our good deeds. This type of "wisdom that comes from heaven is first of all pure; then peace-loving, considerate, submissive, full of mercy and good fruit, impartial and sincere" (James 3:17, NIV).

ROOTED IN LOVE

I will make you my wife forever, showing you righteousness and justice, unfailing love and compassion. I will be faithful to you and make you mine, and you will finally know me as the LORD. ❖ HOSEA 2:19-20

At times, it is difficult to read the words of the prophets. Repeatedly, they convey messages of warning and dire consequences if God's people do not turn from their sinful ways. Sometimes, such harsh messages obscure the very reason God sent prophets to warn his people—because of his deep love for them.

When we talk about the covenant that exists between God and his people, Israel, it is more than a formal, legal agreement between two parties. It is a pact rooted in love.

Jewish literature often portrays the covenant between God and Israel as a marriage—established through vows and built on a foundation of mutual love and commitment. Through the prophet Hosea, for example, God addresses Israel as a husband would address his intended wife: "I will make you my wife forever. . . . I will be faithful to you and make you mine" (Hosea 2:19-20).

This covenantal relationship between God and Israel is a powerful force in Jewish life. Observant Jews renew their commitment to God daily by observing his commandments and by linking themselves to the chain of Jewish tradition. They acknowledge their personal relationship with God and spend time nurturing it.

Every morning, Jewish worshipers don ritual objects called *tefillin*, which consist of black leather straps and boxes containing biblical verses. Worshipers fasten the *tefillin* to themselves as an outward expression of their being bound to God. As they wrap the *tefillin* around their fingers, they recite today's verses from Hosea. Wearing the *tefillin* is like putting on a wedding band; it daily reaffirms their love for God.

Christians and Jews differ on many points of theology, but we share this powerful bond—that we are called into an intimate, mutual, and loving relationship with God that requires us to seek his face daily in prayer, listen to his voice by studying his Word, and obey him.

A Christian Reflection on Our Intimate Relationship with God

The Hebrew Bible's teaching that our covenant relationship with God is more than a legal arrangement is continued in the New Testament's depiction of our relationship with Jesus as a marriage. In Ephesians 5:31-32, Paul quotes from Genesis 2:24—"A man leaves his father and mother and is joined to his wife, and the two are united into one"—and then applies this verse to our relationship with Christ: "This is a great mystery, but it is an illustration of the way Christ and the church are one." Knowing we have such an intimate relationship with God should lead us to respond with prayer, listening to his Word, and obedience.

NEVER AGAIN!

God told Noah and his sons, . . . "Yes, I am confirming my covenant with you. Never again will floodwaters kill all living creatures; never again will a flood destroy the earth." ❖ GENESIS 9:8, 11

Covenants, or agreements, between two people or groups of people have a long history in the ancient world. However, the Bible radically transforms this idea by introducing the concept of God in covenant with humankind. After the great Flood, God promised never again to destroy all living creatures in that manner.

According to the *Talmud* (Judaism's oral tradition), Noah promised in return to uphold six moral laws prescribed at the time of Adam and Eve, including prohibitions against murder, theft, cruelty to animals, idol worship, blasphemy, and illicit sexual relations, as well as a seventh—positive—command, added at the time of Noah, to set up a system of justice so that society could be ruled fairly.

This interpretation of the Noahite covenant represents one of the foundational differences between Judaism and Christianity. In the Jewish view, these laws apply to all of Noah's descendants, not just to the Jews. This means *all* humanity. Jews believe that non-Jews who obey these laws deserve a place in the eternal world. Christians, on the other hand, believe that faith in Jesus is the only path to eternal life.

Despite this fundamental—and critical—difference between our two faiths, we can agree on God's faithfulness, based on his covenant with Noah. After the Flood, God says, "I have set my rainbow in the clouds, and it will be the sign of the covenant between me and the earth" (Genesis 9:13, NIV).

Jewish tradition teaches that a rainbow mimics an archer's bow pointed away from the ground as a sign that God will never again rain down arrows on the earth. And just as God promised, the earth has never again experienced a flood of the magnitude of Noah's day. The seasons come one after another, and God's rainbow can still be seen in the sky—an eternal representation of his graciousness to the world.

A Christian Reflection on the Noahite Covenant

Christians agree that God's covenant with Noah encompasses all of humanity and even Creation itself. But as Rabbi Eckstein indicates, Christians respectfully disagree that obedience to seven moral laws can earn one a place in eternity. For one thing, the apostle Paul cites the *Tanakh* (a Jewish term for the Hebrew Bible) itself to point out that no one is worthy. In Romans 3, after quoting from the Psalms, Isaiah, and Ecclesiastes, Paul concludes that "no one will be declared righteous in God's sight by the works of the law" (Romans 3:20, NIV), a reference to the Mosaic law, which also applies to the seven moral laws associated with the Noahite covenant. Paul maintains that "a person is justified by faith apart from the works of the law" (Romans 3:28, NIV) when that faith is placed in Jesus as the one who rescues us from sin and death.

OUR FATHER KNOWS BEST

I command you this day to love the LORD your God and to keep his commands, decrees, and regulations by walking in his ways. If you do this, you will live and multiply, and the LORD your God will bless you and the land you are about to enter and occupy. But if your heart turns away and you refuse to listen, and if you are drawn away to serve and worship other gods, then I warn you now that you will certainly be destroyed. ❖ DEUTERONOMY 30:16-18

If you're a parent, your children have probably expressed displeasure when you've given them a curfew or told them certain events were off-limits. They probably thought you were just being mean and didn't want them to have any fun, right?

What they didn't understand was *why* you made those decisions. You knew that getting enough sleep is better than staying out late. You knew the potential dangers of an unknown situation. You made rules based on what is best for your children.

It's often like that in our relationship with God, isn't it?

This is perhaps most clear in the covenant God made with the nation of Israel at Mount Sinai, called the Sinaitic covenant. God promised to bless and reward the Israelites, and they promised to obey God's Word and the commandments contained in the *Torah*, the first five books of the Hebrew Bible.

According to Jewish belief, God gave his people 613 commandments at Mount Sinai. That's a lot of rules! But each one was designed by our heavenly Father for our own good—just as our parental rules are designed for our children's well-being. God did not give us his commandments to make our lives difficult, burden us, or punish us. Rather, he established his law to enhance our relationship with him.

The Sages point out that *mitzvah*, the Hebrew word for "commandment," comes from the word *tzav*, which means "to connect." Instead of seeing the 613 laws as 613 obligations, the Sages urge us to see them as 613 opportunities to connect with our Creator.

God knows better than we do that our ultimate happiness and deepest satisfaction are found when we act in harmony with his will. Our disobedience causes us *and* God sorrow and pain. Thus, the Sinaitic covenant (also known as the Mosaic covenant) teaches us to keep God's commandments not as a chore but as a privilege.

A Christian Reflection on God's Law

The Hebrew Bible and the New Testament agree that our relationship with God is based on grace, not law. Notice, for instance, how the giving of the Ten Commandments is preceded by the statement that God brought the nation of Israel out of the land of Egypt. Their salvation did not depend on their obedience to the law. Some Christians wrongly believe that the Mosaic law is no longer relevant. However, the law is an expression of God's will for how his human creatures should behave in order to live life happily. God knows that we flourish in our relationship with him when we keep his commandments.

A CHOOSING PEOPLE

Now listen! Today I am giving you a choice between life and death, between prosperity and disaster. ❖ DEUTERONOMY 30:15

We make choices every day. Most of our choices are rather innocuous: what to wear, what to eat, what to do with our free time. Other choices carry more importance: whom we will marry, where we will live, and which job opportunities we will pursue.

Our ability to choose is something we treasure, particularly if we are blessed to live in a democracy such as Israel or America. We have the ability to choose who will govern us, how we will worship, and what principles will govern our lives.

We are a choosing people.

God created us this way, and he incorporated our ability to choose as part of our covenantal relationship with him. In the case of the Abrahamic and Mosaic covenants, God reached out to his people, Israel, who in turn responded to his divine initiative by accepting and obeying his Word. In this way, Israel is both the *chosen* people of God and the *choosing* people of God. A covenant relationship is not based simply on God's extending his promises; we also must respond with our reciprocal commitment.

Moses Maimonides, a preeminent Jewish thinker in medieval Spain during the Middle Ages, listed the fundamental principles of the Jewish faith, among which is the belief that God gives us free will to choose him or deny him. Judaism is based on choice, because God doesn't want spiritual robots. He isn't interested in a forced relationship and lackluster obedience. God chooses us, and though he deeply desires that we choose him in return, he will never force us to do so.

Ultimately, the choice to obey God rests with each of us. This is clear in Moses' address in Deuteronomy 30:15: "Today I am giving you a choice between life and death, between prosperity and disaster." Moses challenged the people: Obey, and God will bless you; disobey, and you will face certain disaster. The better choice may be obvious, but it is yours alone to make.

A Christian Reflection on the Ultimate Choice

"Look! I stand at the door and knock. If you hear my voice and open the door, I will come in, and we will share a meal together as friends" (Revelation 3:20). The picture of Jesus at the door requesting entry is one of the most familiar images of the New Testament. Sharing a meal represents the development of an intimate relationship. The passage suggests that we have a choice. Will we open the door to relationship with Jesus or shut him out? As John indicates in Revelation, those who choose to open the door will receive victory and honor (see Revelation 3:20-21).

FATHER ABRAHAM

The LORD had said to Abram, "Leave your native country, your relatives, and your father's family, and go to the land that I will show you. . . ." So Abram departed as the LORD had instructed. ❖ GENESIS 12:1, 4

When God commanded Abraham (then known as Abram) to leave his country and go to a distant land, Abraham responded immediately and "departed as the LORD had instructed" (Genesis 12:4). We often overlook what a remarkable response this was.

Abraham grew up in a society where multiple gods and idols were worshiped. In fact, his father, Terah, not only worshiped idols—he *made* idols. As the eldest son, Abraham more than likely was expected to follow in the family business and become an idol producer himself.

According to rabbinic tradition, Abraham came to realize that there was only one true God and that idols weren't the answer. He wanted his father to understand this as well. So when Terah was out of the workshop, Abraham destroyed all the idols, except the largest one, putting a stick next to it.

As the story goes, when Terah returned and saw the damage, he was furious and asked his son, "What happened?" Abraham replied, "Well, the big idol got angry at all the other idols, and he destroyed them." To which his father answered, "That's impossible. He doesn't move. It's just stone."

"Exactly, Father," Abraham said. "There is but one true God."

Because of his faith and his willingness to stand against the cultural norms of his day, Abraham has been credited as the founder of monotheism. He became the first person to be called a Hebrew (see Genesis 14:13). How did he get that name? The word *Hebrew* comes from a word that means "side." The whole world was on one side, and Abraham was on the other. The whole world believed one thing, but Abraham steadfastly believed something entirely different.

Abraham's bedrock faith in the one true God is the very foundation upon which Jews and Christians alike have built their faith traditions. His willingness to stand against the culture is a model for us all.

A Christian Reflection on Father Abraham

God's call to Abraham to leave his idolatrous background and worship God alone is recognized by the New Testament authors as a momentous decision. Paul reminds his readers that Abraham was "the founder of our Jewish nation" (Romans 4:1) and that Abraham serves as an example of how faith is the key to a relationship with God. Paul argues that Abraham was accepted by God even before he was circumcised, citing God's pronouncement: "Abraham believed God, and God counted him as righteous because of his faith" (Romans 4:3, citing Genesis 15:6). This message, according to Paul, is a blessing for Jews as well as for Gentiles (see Romans 4:9).

Sabbath Reflections

What new truth about our covenantal relationship with God did you learn from this week's devotions?

How has this truth affected your faith?

How will you apply this truth to your daily life?

Your Key Verse for the Week:

❖ OTHER REFLECTIONS

TRUE FREEDOM

Why are the nations so angry? Why do they waste their time with futile plans?
The kings of the earth prepare for battle; the rulers plot together against the LORD
and against his anointed one. ❖ PSALM 2:1-2

King David wrote Psalm 2 as he faced a conspiracy against Israel by her surrounding enemies. Even so, David remained confident. Why? Because he knew that God was in total control and would fulfill his promises to David as his "anointed one."

Do we have that same confidence?

The truth is, despite what we see and hear happening around us, God is in control. He alone is all-powerful. He alone created the world. God knew about every empire then, and he knows about every world power today—he knew them before they even came into being (see Daniel 2:26-45). Yet, throughout history and even today, the world and its leaders shake their fists at God—and his people—and declare their autonomy from him.

And what does God do? As David tells us in Psalm 2:4, "The one who rules in heaven laughs. The Lord scoffs at them."

God laughs at the nations in much the same way as a parent laughs at a three-year-old who stomps his feet and declares that he can "do it myself." Just as a parent knows the child's boundaries and what he can—and cannot—do, God knows us thoroughly. He knows what a nation can or cannot do, because *he* has set the boundaries.

We, too, can be tempted to believe we are in control and free of God's "fetters" and rule. Yet inevitably we all serve someone—whether it's an organization, another leader, or even our own selfish desires. We can be truly free only when we wholeheartedly serve and follow the one who created us in the first place. When we do that, we can have the same confidence that David had and enjoy God's blessing on us.

A Christian Reflection on Freedom

The New Testament teaches that we are no longer slaves to earthly masters but are now "servants of Christ." We find this phrase, or "servant of the Lord," peppered throughout its pages. Freedom and being a servant of God go hand in hand, because it is in a relationship with God that we are fully human, as he created us to be. And our service for God extends to other people as well. As Paul writes, "You have been called to live in freedom. . . . But don't use your freedom to satisfy your sinful nature. Instead, use your freedom to serve one another in love" (Galatians 5:13).

SITTING ON THE FENCE

Elijah stood in front of them and said, "How much longer will you waver, hobbling between two opinions? If the LORD is God, follow him! But if Baal is God, then follow him!" But the people were completely silent. ❖ 1 KINGS 18:21

Mount Carmel is one of the most beautiful sites in Israel. From atop its peak, you can see the broad expanse of the Israeli countryside and the glistening waters of the Mediterranean. Because of abundant rainfall, the slopes and summit are green year-round. No wonder in Hebrew the name *Carmel* means "vineyard of God."

Mount Carmel has an even greater significance beyond its breathtaking beauty. It was on this mountaintop that Elijah confronted the 850 pagan prophets of King Ahab and challenged the Israelites to choose between God and Baal.

And the people said nothing. They were content to stay where they were, straddling the fence. They refused to make a choice.

Now, some may argue that sitting on the fence is not necessarily a bad thing—that it's good to look at both sides of an argument; choosing sides can lead to division, confrontation, and general messiness. But sitting on the fence has never been an option for the people of God.

God demands that we make a choice. Moses did too: "Look, today I am giving you the *choice* between a blessing and a curse!" (Deuteronomy 11:26, emphasis added). And Joshua in his farewell address to the leaders of Israel issued a similar exhortation: "If you refuse to serve the LORD, then *choose* today whom you will serve. . . . As for me and my family, we will serve the LORD" (Joshua 24:15, emphasis added). So Elijah demanded that the people choose sides.

Daily we have opportunities to choose to represent God where we live, where we work, and where we go to school. For the people of God, remaining on the fence is not an option.

A Christian Reflection on Fence-Sitting

In the letters to the seven churches in Revelation, Jesus charges the Laodiceans with being lukewarm—neither hot nor cold. This reference would have resonated with the people of Laodicea, whose natural water supply was lukewarm, in contrast to that of their neighbors at Hierapolis, who had hot springs famous for their healing power, and those in Colossae, whose cold water springs were refreshing to drink. Jesus says that their lack of commitment to him is like drinking lukewarm water, and as a result, he says, "I will spit you out of my mouth!" (Revelation 3:16). In this way, he warns the Laodiceans (and us) to be consistent and bold in our commitment to him.

MAKE NO LITTLE PLANS

I know that you can do anything, and no one can stop you. ❖ JOB 42:2

One of the many miracles associated with the birth of the State of Israel was the revival of the Hebrew language. For thousands of years, Hebrew was deemed a dead language, existing only in the ancient writings of the rabbinic scholars and Jewish liturgy.

But in the late 1800s, when a young Jew named Eliezer Ben-Yehuda began dreaming of his people's return to their ancestral soil, he realized they would need a common language. So began his lifelong pursuit of reviving Hebrew as the language to unite all Jews in their historic homeland.

Ben-Yehuda devoted his lifework to creating the *Complete Dictionary of Ancient and Modern Hebrew*. In 1910, he published the first of six volumes. After Ben-Yehuda died in 1922, his widow and son continued his work, and by 1959, a complete set of seventeen volumes had been published.

Thanks to Ben-Yehuda's vision and passion, Hebrew was adopted as Israel's official language in 1948. It's amazing how one person could have such a lasting impact on a country, the Jewish people, and the world.

God often gives his children challenging tasks to accomplish. Moses was told to deliver a people from oppression. Joshua was told to conquer the land of Canaan; young David was given the job of defeating the giant Goliath. But God also provides the means to accomplish those tasks.

David writes, "Some nations boast of their chariots and horses, but we boast in the name of the LORD our God" (Psalm 20:7). Some people rely on power and influence; others, on their talents and possessions. But David drew his strength from the Lord—because he knew that, with God, anything is possible. Both giant warriors and monumental tasks are surmountable with God's help.

What task has God given you today? What passion has he stirred in your heart? Remember, God is able to do all things; he will enable you to complete his purposes.

A Christian Reflection on Making the Impossible Possible

"With God everything is possible" (Matthew 19:26). This was Jesus' conclusion following his conversation with the rich young ruler, who idolized his wealth. Challenged to sell all his possessions in order to enter God's Kingdom, the man refused. When Jesus observed that "it is easier for a camel to go through the eye of a needle than for a rich person to enter the Kingdom of God" (Matthew 19:24), his disciples wondered who could enter God's Kingdom. Jesus pointed out that while many things are impossible for humans on their own resources, everything is possible for God. Christians should live in that knowledge, confident that God will bring their hopes to realization in conformity to his great purposes.

HOMECOMING

Give them this message from the Sovereign LORD: *I will gather the people of Israel from among the nations. I will bring them home to their own land from the places where they have been scattered.* ❖ EZEKIEL 37:21

The fact that I call Israel home is a miracle. Each time I encounter the grandeur of Jerusalem, I am moved to tears. I also realize that the privilege I enjoy of living in my biblical homeland was built on the hard work and sacrifice of others.

I refer to those courageous men in the late 1800s who concluded that the Jews would never be fully accepted by the Gentiles. Their solution was to create a Jewish state in their ancient homeland.

Theodor Herzl, regarded as the father of Zionism, was one of the first to call for the establishment of a Jewish homeland. In 1897, at the first Zionist Congress, hundreds of delegates from around the world supported Herzl's resolution for the formation of a Jewish state.

Tragically, Herzl died before his dream was realized. His work appeared prophetic, however, as Israel was declared a nation one year after Herzl's prediction.

That Israel exists today is a testament to God's faithfulness and to those who kept alive the hope of a Jewish home. As far back as the exile of the Jews to Babylon—2,600 years ago—God promised to bring his children home. But until the last century, that return seemed highly implausible.

The miracle of the rebirth of Israel is most powerfully described in the book of Ezekiel, when God shows the prophet a valley full of bones and asks, "Can these bones become living people again?" (Ezekiel 37:3). Then God explains that the bones represent the people of Israel, who said, "We have become old, dry bones—all hope is gone. Our nation is finished" (Ezekiel 37:11). But God promises them that they "will live again and return home" (Ezekiel 37:14).

God's plans will not be thwarted—then or now. He is still in the business of bringing his children home, and together with the help of Christians around the world, we have been partners in the Jewish homecoming.

A Christian Reflection on Homecoming

When the Babylonians defeated Israel, destroyed Jerusalem, and exiled its leading citizens to Babylon in 586 BC, many probably thought it was the end of Israel as a nation. God's people, however, knew differently. The prophets, after all, along with their announcements of judgment, spoke of a promised restoration. God's promised homecoming continues today. It is good to be reminded of God's faithfulness. Jesus told his followers that his Father had a home with many rooms. "If this were not so, would I have told you that I am going to prepare a place for you?" (John 14:2). We now wait with confidence for Jesus to return so he can bring us home.

GOD'S ARTISTIC DESIGN

*The LORD said to Moses, "Look, I have specifically chosen Bezalel son of Uri, grandson
of Hur, of the tribe of Judah. I have filled him with the Spirit of God, giving him great
wisdom, ability, and expertise in all kinds of crafts. He is a master craftsman, expert
in working with gold, silver, and bronze."* ❖ EXODUS 31:1-4

In building the Tabernacle, God commanded that only the finest materials be used.
When it came time to select the craftsmen to design the objects for the Tabernacle,
God handpicked Bezalel and his assistant, Oholiab. These men were "filled . . . with
the Spirit of God" and given the needed skills to create these beautiful items.

As we read about the curtains that were hung in the Tabernacle, the utensils, the
Ark of the Covenant, the lampstands, and even the priests' clothing, we begin to
appreciate how ornate and elaborate the designs were for each object. This was not
a haphazard project; the beauty of each object was intended to enhance worship and
reflect God's glory.

When the Israelites left Egypt, they said, "I will sing to the LORD, for he . . . is my
God, and I will praise him" (Exodus 15:1-2, NIV). Jewish tradition teaches that the people
wanted to *glorify* God. How is it possible for humans to add glory to their Creator? The
Sages answer that we can glorify God by beautifying our service of him. The tradition of
adorning ritual objects and places of worship was born from this verse.

The exquisitely crafted items in the Tabernacle were among the earliest expressions of Jewish art. The craft of adorning objects of worship—*menorahs*, spice boxes,
wine goblets, and other objects—has evolved and been cultivated through the years.

Today, Israel has produced a new generation of artisans who work within this biblical framework and in obedience to the second commandment: "You must not make
for yourself an idol of any kind or an image of anything in the heavens or on the earth
or in the sea" (Exodus 20:4).

Though some may feel that this commandment inhibits artistic expression, Jewish
artists and craftsmen through each century have discovered ways to create art that
honors God and his call to excellence. In so doing, they glorify God.

A Christian Reflection on the Arts and Worship

The Tabernacle was a magnificent, divinely commissioned symbol of God's presence
among his people. After King David firmly established the people of God in the
Promised Land by subduing their enemies, his son Solomon built the Temple, a permanent house for God. For Christians, Jesus represents the presence of God. Because
God's presence fills the church, the New Testament speaks of the church (as well
as the individual Christian) as the temple of God (see 1 Corinthians 3:16-17; 6:19;
2 Corinthians 6:16). The beauty and excellence of the Tabernacle and Temple serve as
reminders that Christian worship, music, liturgy, architecture, and art should also be
characterized by excellence in order to honor God.

A SPIRITUAL FOCUS

Jacob gave Esau some bread and some lentil stew. He ate and drank, and then got up and left. So Esau despised his birthright. ❖ GENESIS 25:34, NIV

Undoubtedly, you remember the story of Esau and Jacob, when Esau sold his birthright to his twin brother for a bowl of stew.

The birthright, bestowed on the firstborn son, meant a double portion of the father's estate and considerable authority. More important, the firstborn son was in line for his father's blessing, which subsequently led to a close and favored relationship with God.

The birthright was more than a material reward; it was a spiritual reward and blessing of great value. So how could Esau sell it for a bowl of soup?

At first glance, it appears that Esau was forced into the deal, as he begs his brother, "Look, I am about to die" (Genesis 25:32, NIV). It seems that Esau made his choice under duress. But the Sages explain that Esau wasn't really dying. Rather, they say, he was making known his philosophy of life: *Life is short, so eat, drink, and be merry. What good will a promise of some future reward do for me now? Now, I am hungry. Now, I want soup.* That's why the Bible records, "So Esau despised his birthright" (Genesis 25:34, NIV).

Esau's willingness to trade a spiritual inheritance of immeasurable value to satisfy his hunger reveals a lot about his character. He appears to have been a person who reacted to his immediate situation, without considering the consequences. Indeed, his life was filled with choices that he must have bitterly regretted later.

On the other hand, his brother, Jacob, obviously valued the birthright blessings and future rewards. Through this interaction, we clearly see Jacob's hunger for spiritual blessings as opposed to Esau's desire for immediate gratification.

The story of Jacob and Esau teaches us that while living in the moment, as Esau did, we need to keep our focus on God. When we do that, we'll be more like Jacob, doing whatever it takes to pursue spiritual matters.

A Christian Reflection on Seeking First the Kingdom of God

We all are tempted to pursue the things that make us happy now, like Esau did. God knows that is part of our human nature. So when Jesus instructed his followers on Kingdom living, he told them to put spiritual matters first and that everything else would fall into place: "Don't worry about these things, saying, 'What will we eat? What will we drink? What will we wear?' These things dominate the thoughts of unbelievers, but your heavenly Father already knows all your needs. Seek the Kingdom of God above all else, and live righteously, and he will give you everything you need" (Matthew 6:31-33).

Sabbath Reflections

What new truth about worshiping and pursuing God did you learn from this week's devotions?

How has this truth affected your faith?

How will you apply this truth to your daily life?

Your Key Verse for the Week:

❖ OTHER REFLECTIONS

SWEET DREAMS

I lay down and slept, yet I woke up in safety, for the LORD was watching over me.
❖ PSALM 3:5

What keeps you up at night? Worries over your family? Your marriage? Your job? We all have experienced sleepless nights when we can't stop those nagging worries from filling our thoughts.

That's why David's words in Psalm 3:5 are so striking: "I lay down and slept." David wrote Psalm 3 not from his bed within the palace, under the watchful eyes of his guard. David wrote those words while he was on the run from his son Absalom, who had organized a rebellion and was attempting to overthrow him.

David was running for his life. As many as ten thousand soldiers were surrounding him (see Psalm 3:6). The odds were against him, and David had every reason to believe that all was lost. So what did he do? He turned to God.

David reminds us in this psalm that even when everything is going wrong and it seems there is no hope at all, God is still there. He cries out to the one who is "a shield around me" and "who holds my head high" (Psalm 3:3).

David could sleep peacefully in the midst of his crisis because he knew that God had heard his prayers: "I cried out to the LORD, and he answered me from his holy mountain" (Psalm 3:4). David could sleep because he knew that God was in control of his circumstances and he didn't need to worry.

Sleeping is an act of great faith. We surrender—both body and spirit—and become vulnerable to everything around us. In Jewish tradition, a special prayer is said just before going to sleep. It ends with these words: "Into his hand I shall entrust my spirit when I go to sleep. . . . God is with me, I shall not fear." We can sleep peacefully because we know that we are in good hands.

When we find ourselves tossing and turning at night, we can remember David. Cry out to God, because he hears us, too.

A Christian Reflection on Calm in the Midst of Storm

Remember the story in Luke 8:22-25 when Jesus slept during the storm that threatened to capsize the boat that he and his disciples were using to cross the Sea of Galilee? Although this storm was real, raging waters in the Bible often symbolize the threats of life. Though Jesus could sleep through the storm, his disciples could not, and they woke him in desperation. How did he respond? He quieted the storm, eliciting the disciples' amazement: "When he gives a command, even the wind and waves obey him!" (Luke 8:25). Faithful people can sleep well, knowing that God is the one who stills the storms of life. God is a Redeemer and a Protector who is working to set things right and who will care for his people.

HEAVEN ON EARTH

I was glad when they said to me, "Let us go to the house of the LORD."
❖ PSALM 122:1

If you were to imagine heaven on earth, what would it look like? A tropical paradise? A mountaintop hideaway? A place where it is always the Sabbath?

In the Jewish faith, life in heaven is described as a time when it is always the Sabbath, a time when the beauty and tranquillity of *Shabbat* are continuously experienced. For Jews, observance of *Shabbat* enables us to experience a taste of the world to come and gives us a glimpse of the ideal state of Creation experienced by Adam and Eve in the Garden of Eden.

The concept of Sabbath is central to the Jewish faith and life. More Jewish literature—legal, mystical, and homiletic—has been written on this topic than on any other. It is described by the rabbis as *shekulah kineged kol hamitzvot*, "of equal import to all the rest of the commandments put together." Those who observe the Sabbath are regarded as if they have observed the entire *Torah*.

Everything we do points to *Shabbat*. It is a day that rejuvenates our spirits, replenishes our strength, and revitalizes us so that we can face another week. But it has a deeper meaning as the epitome of sanctified living. The Sabbath is observed not for the sake of the rest of the week, but rather, the rest of the week is the prologue for the arrival of *Shabbat*. We live each day in anticipation of the Sabbath.

What would it look like if you spent your week anticipating your time with God? If you carved out time each week when no work was done, phones were turned off, the TV was silent? How might this refresh and rejuvenate you? How might it change your relationship with God?

A Christian Reflection on the Sabbath

The importance of the Sabbath in the *Tanakh* is indisputable. In the New Testament, however, Christ's coming transformed his followers' attitude toward the Sabbath. The apostle Paul puts it this way: "These rules are only shadows of the reality yet to come. And Christ himself is that reality" (Colossians 2:17). For this reason, Paul advises that there should be liberty in how one observes these days. That said, it has been common Christian practice to treat the first day of the week as a Sabbath, or Lord's Day (see Acts 20:7; 1 Corinthians 16:2). There is also a deep awareness that we look forward to that final, eternal Sabbath Day (see Hebrews 4:1-2, 9, 11).

THE PRICE OF FREEDOM

I will walk in freedom, for I have devoted myself to your commandments.
❖ PSALM 119:45

Irish dramatist George Bernard Shaw once penned these words: "Liberty means responsibility. That is why most men dread it." Many equate freedom with the absence of responsibility and the opportunity to do whatever we please. But for Jews, *true* freedom includes responsibility—a responsibility to serve God. This concept of freedom is rooted in our celebration and observance of the Sabbath.

When God gave the people of Israel the Ten Commandments, he instructed them, "Remember that you were once slaves in Egypt, but the LORD your God brought you out with his strong hand and powerful arm. That is why the LORD your God has commanded you to rest on the Sabbath day" (Deuteronomy 5:15). The Sabbath is a sacred day set aside for us by God to remind us of the Jews' slavery in, and Exodus from, Egypt.

However, the freedom gained when the Israelites left Egypt was not intended to be total independence from all authority. This freedom—*true* freedom—meant voluntary servitude *to* God. We see this clearly in God's instructions to Moses: "Go to Pharaoh and say to him, 'Thus says the LORD: "Let My people go, that they may serve Me"'" (Exodus 8:1, NKJV). The people were to stop serving Pharaoh as slaves so that they could serve God freely.

Moses understood that freedom from slavery does not mean we can do whatever we please. Rather, freedom from slavery is only true freedom if it leads to the acceptance of serving God.

By recalling the Exodus motif on *Shabbat*, we are reminded of the true nature of slavery and freedom—and of our duty to bring spiritual purpose and meaning into our lives.

A Christian Reflection on True Freedom

Christians understand that Jesus has freed us from sin and death and given us a true freedom—which means we have become servants of God. Paul makes this point in his letter to the Romans when he says, "When you were slaves to sin, you were free from the obligation to do right. And what was the result? You are now ashamed of the things you used to do, things that end in eternal doom. But now you are free from the power of sin and have become slaves of God. Now you do those things that lead to holiness and result in eternal life" (Romans 6:20-22). The choice is ours: Will we serve sin, which leads to death, or serve God, who leads us to eternal life?

GOD'S STOP SIGN

On the seventh day God had finished his work of creation, so he rested from all his work. And God blessed the seventh day and declared it holy, because it was the day when he rested from all his work of creation. ❖ GENESIS 2:2-3

One of the main misconceptions about the Jewish observance of the Sabbath is the prohibition about working on that day. How do we define work? Are we able to do anything at all? Many view prohibitions such as lighting a fire or cooking on the Sabbath as antiquated, because today these activities involve so little effort that they can hardly be considered work.

For answers, we turn to God's Word. In Exodus 35:3, the Lord clearly prohibits *milechet machashevet*, which means "creative work" in Hebrew. For six days, we are permitted—even commanded—to work and subdue nature. In this capacity, we serve as God's copartners in the creation of the world. But on the seventh day, we are commanded to take a break from our own creative work so we can focus on the true Creator: God.

You see, God knows us all too well. He recognized and anticipated that our intelligence and creativity might lead us to forget the *source* of our creative power. As human beings, we can easily get caught up in what we do and how much we accomplish, neglect the spiritual side of life, and turn away from God. (Doubt that's true? Flip a few pages in your Bible from Genesis 2 to Genesis 11 and read the story of the Tower of Babel.)

When we refrain from all creative activities on the Sabbath—including cooking—we acknowledge that God is the ultimate source of creation and our being. We affirm that the earth belongs to the Lord and that we are not God.

Consider how you might change your attitudes and behaviors on the Sabbath to keep your focus on God. In what ways can you affirm God as creator?

A *Christian Reflection on Changing Behaviors*

As we saw in the preceding meditation, Sabbath keeping is a matter of wisdom according to the principles of the New Testament. Jesus taught that "the Sabbath was made to meet the needs of people" (Mark 2:27), including our need for time set apart to keep our focus on God as we head into a busy and distracting week. Not that we should forget about God during the rest of the week, but we should develop behaviors on Sunday that help us keep our eyes on God as the center of our lives. Give careful thought to how you spend your Sabbath or Lord's Day. Invest your time in ways that will renew and deepen your devotion to God.

BE PREPARED

The LORD told Moses, "Go down and prepare the people for my arrival. Consecrate them today and tomorrow, and have them wash their clothing. Be sure they are ready on the third day, for on that day the LORD will come down on Mount Sinai as all the people watch." ❖ EXODUS 19:10-11

In Exodus, as God is about to appear to the people of Israel at the foot of Mount Sinai, he instructs Moses to have the people get ready for that occasion. In the book of Numbers, the Hebrew word for *prepare* appears more than thirty times as God gives his people detailed instructions for how they are to ready the sacrifices and themselves for worship. Clearly, being prepared is important to God.

For the Jews, the extensive, detailed preparations for the Sabbath, and our anticipation of this special day, are essential parts of its observance. Just as the Israelites prepared themselves physically and spiritually before receiving the Ten Commandments at Mount Sinai, so we undergo a physical and spiritual preparation before experiencing *Shabbat*.

Listen to the word of the Lord through Moses: "You have six days each week for your ordinary work" (Exodus 20:9). Physically, we should plan to finish all our work in six days. If we embrace this mind-set and plan for the week, then we are physically and mentally ready for *Shabbat*. Then "the seventh day is a Sabbath day of rest dedicated to the LORD your God" (Exodus 20:10).

The Sages teach that "he who cooks for *Shabbat* will eat on *Shabbat*." The rabbis are not just stating the obvious here; they are making a philosophical statement. Just as we must prepare our food before the Sabbath in order to eat on the Sabbath, we must prepare our whole lives for the afterlife.

In Jewish tradition, the Sabbath is considered "a taste of the world to come." It is the one day each week that we spend totally focused on God, just as the afterlife will be a time when we delight in his presence. The weekdays are like the years of our lives. Just as we spend our weeks hard at work, we need to spend our lives working hard in preparation for meeting our Creator.

A Christian Reflection on Being Prepared to Meet God

Hebrews 4 describes the future, final Sabbath, which is the goal of each believer's life. The writer speaks of the "promise of entering [God's] rest" (Hebrews 4:1), clearly referring to heaven, where we will meet God. At the same time, he warns his readers that they must be ready for that day. Accordingly, he encourages us by saying, "Let us do our best to enter that rest. But if we disobey God, as the people of Israel did, we will fall" (Hebrews 4:11). On the Sabbath, we can recalibrate and energize ourselves by worshiping God, and so prepare our hearts for the coming week—and our future rest.

THE SABBATH EXPERIENCE

Those who live in the shelter of the Most High will find rest in the shadow of the Almighty. ❖ PSALM 91:1

If you have ever been on a spiritual retreat, you know how difficult it can be to reenter the daily routine. Those closing moments are bittersweet as we savor the time we have spent with God and with others, knowing that it will soon be over.

In many respects, that sentiment parallels our experience as the Sabbath comes to a close each week. The Sabbath is to be experienced as "an island in time"—we are to live fully in the moment and find the pleasure and holiness that comes from relaxing, studying the *Torah*, and having fellowship with family and friends. If we fully partake of the Sabbath experience—rest, study, and fellowship—we have achieved our spiritual goal.

As the Sabbath draws to a close, we formally conclude our time with an evening prayer service and the *Havdalah*, or "separation ceremony." During that time, we reaffirm our belief in the coming Messiah and the redemption of the world. We acknowledge again our duty to sanctify life every day and to fill it with holiness. Then, we light a long, braided candle, drink from an overflowing cup of wine, and deeply inhale the fragrance of spices.

Each step of this ceremony is very important. The light of the braided candle symbolizes the intertwining of the Eternal One and the divine spirit in humanity. The overflowing cup of wine symbolizes our uncontainable optimism and hope for the coming week. And the aromatic spices refresh our souls and dispel the emptiness we feel at the conclusion of *Shabbat*.

Observing the Sabbath is intentional, purposeful, and spiritual—involving all our senses and affecting all aspects of our lives. As you reflect on your own spiritual encounters with God, both daily and weekly, consider what you might add—or subtract—to make your experience more meaningful.

A Christian Reflection on Reentering the Daily Routine

On the Lord's Day, the opportunity for a more focused, intimate communion with God refreshes us so that we can face the distractions, struggles, and difficulties of the rest of the week. That said, of course God is with us all the time and everywhere we go. While appreciating the blessings of a day set apart to reflect on God's presence in our lives, we need to cultivate a sensitivity and gratitude for his presence in the ordinary activities of our lives. After all, at the very end of the Gospel of Matthew, Jesus assures his followers, "I am with you always, even to the end of the age" (Matthew 28:20).

Sabbath Reflections

What new truth about observing the Sabbath did you learn from this week's devotions?

How has this truth affected your faith?

How will you apply this truth to your daily life?

Your Key Verse for the Week:

❖ OTHER REFLECTIONS

ARE YOU SURE?

You can be sure of this: The LORD set apart the godly for himself.
The LORD will answer when I call to him. ❖ PSALM 4:3

As Ben Franklin once noted, "In this world nothing can be said to be certain, except death and taxes." Truly, we live in an uncertain world. Leaders and nations change; our economy changes; technology changes how we live and operate, on an almost daily basis. The list of what we can count on is rather short.

But as King David writes in Psalm 4, there is something we can absolutely bank on: "You can be sure of this: The LORD set apart the godly for himself. The LORD will answer when I call to him."

As God's faithful and obedient follower, David had total confidence that God would hear his prayers when he called. The same is true for us. There may be times when we feel as if God isn't listening to our prayers because we have fallen short of his standard. We feel we are unworthy, so therefore, God doesn't hear us. But David assures us—God hears *all* the prayers of his children and answers them.

We see this assurance repeated elsewhere in the Psalms: "The LORD has heard my plea; the LORD will answer my prayer" (Psalm 6:9); and, "I am praying to you because I know you will answer, O God. Bend down and listen as I pray" (Psalm 17:6). David took his every concern to God because he knew without a doubt that God would not only hear him but also answer him.

Does this mean God will give us exactly what we are praying for? Not at all. But he will answer us according to his grace, his wisdom, his love, and his mercy.

You can be sure of that.

A Christian Reflection on Certainty in Prayer

The New Testament also teaches that God hears his people's prayers. The author of Hebrews presents a picture of Jesus as "a great High Priest who has entered heaven" (Hebrews 4:14). As our High Priest, Jesus intercedes on our behalf, and therefore, we can "come boldly to the throne of our gracious God. There we will receive his mercy, and we will find grace to help us when we need it most" (Hebrews 4:16). As we offer our specific requests, God will answer them accordingly. We might not get what we ask for—even Jesus did not get all he asked for in prayer (see Luke 22:41-44)—but God will respond according to his grace and mercy.

THE DEW OF MOUNT HERMON

Harmony is as refreshing as the dew from Mount Hermon that falls on the mountains of Zion. And there the LORD has pronounced his blessing, even life everlasting.
❖ PSALM 133:3

I have a special place in my heart for Mount Hermon, known as the "gray-haired mountain" for its beautiful, snow-covered peaks. At 9,200 feet, it is the highest point in Israel. But neither its height nor its beauty is what inspires me. Rather, it is the psalm that David wrote about this majestic peak.

In Psalm 133, David writes, "How wonderful and pleasant it is when brothers live together in harmony!" Several lines later, he compares the fruits of this harmony to the dew of Hermon falling on Mount Zion. This very passage served as my inspiration in founding the bridge-building ministry of The Fellowship.

To fully understand what David is talking about, you need to know the geography of Mount Hermon. The runoff from the mountain's western and southern bases feeds several streams and rivers. These then merge to become the Jordan River, the main source of water for Israel. The runoff also makes possible the fertile plant life below the snow line, where vineyards flourish and pine, oak, and poplar trees are abundant.

I believe that this image of the dew of Hermon flowing down the mountain for thousands of years into springs that feed the river is an apt representation of The Fellowship's ministry. It is the harmony and understanding that come from our bridge-building efforts—Christians and Jews working together—and flow into the lives of those most in need.

Christians throughout the world continue to pray and support the people of Israel through the many programs and ministries that The Fellowship supports. When I think of the abundant blessings poured out on Zion by our Christian friends, I can only humbly echo King David's heartfelt words: "How wonderful and pleasant it is when brothers live together in harmony!"

A Christian Reflection on Brothers and Sisters in Unity

Psalm 133 presents a powerful and beautiful picture of people who live in harmony with one another. The New Testament also describes people from different backgrounds who come together in God. Jesus speaks of himself as the Good Shepherd, whose sheep "listen to my voice, and there will be one flock with one shepherd" (John 10:16). Paul talks about how Jews and Gentiles were once separate but now "have been brought near to [God] through the blood of Christ" (Ephesians 2:13). The message of the Bible is clear: God's work brings diverse people together in harmony and love.

OVERCOMING OBSTACLES

*There once was a man named Job who lived in the land of Uz. He was blameless—
a man of complete integrity. He feared God and stayed away from evil.*
❖ JOB 1:1

Israel's Moran Samuel made her country proud when she recently won a gold medal at an international rowing competition in Italy. She made us even prouder when she sang Israel's national anthem, the *Hatikvah*, on her own.

Apparently, the event organizers did not have a recording of the *Hatikvah* to play. When Samuel realized that, she asked for the microphone and began singing the song *a cappella*.

Afterward, Samuel said, "If you look at an obstacle as an obstacle, there's a good chance it will knock you down. If you look at an obstacle as a challenge, then you'll do the maximum to overcome it. There can be small challenges, like the anthem and my taking the mic and singing, and there can be bigger challenges."[1]

Moran Samuel should know. She has been paralyzed from the chest down since she was twenty-four.

Life comes with plenty of challenges, and how we view them is critical. In the book of Job, Job and his friends spend much time and energy asking, "Why? Why is Job being punished?"

The Bible makes it clear that Job was not being punished; he was being tested. Job and his friends had the wrong perspective, and it cost Job dearly. He could have experienced his suffering with the humility, composure, and empowerment of faith. Instead he felt helpless, hopeless, and abandoned.

Jewish tradition teaches that the correct response to challenging times is to ask, "What?" not "Why?" What can I do to be a better person? What can I do to overcome this challenge? What does God want from me now? These questions are empowering.

Asking "why?" traps us in our sorrow and self-pity. Asking "what?" helps us move on.

A Christian Reflection on Moving beyond Obstacles

Rabbi Eckstein has beautifully captured an important teaching of the book of Job. Many people look at Job's questioning of God and consider it an ideal reaction to suffering. Certainly, God honors our faithful questioning of his ways, as we see in many of the Psalms. But, though our questions may be appropriate, they are not where God wants us to end up. He wants us to respond like Job did, not complaining but submitting to God, trusting him, and moving on with our lives. Paul suffered an unidentified but serious physical problem that he called a "thorn in my flesh" (2 Corinthians 12:1-10). Like Job, he begged God to take it away, but God did not. Eventually, Paul accepted his suffering and even saw a benefit in that it kept him from becoming proud (see 2 Corinthians 12:7).

NOTHING TO LOSE

Job stood up and tore his robe in grief. Then he shaved his head and fell to the ground to worship. He said, "I came naked from my mother's womb, and I will be naked when I leave. The LORD gave me what I had, and the LORD has taken it away. Praise the name of the LORD!" ❖ JOB 1:20-21

The book of Job provides us with a stunning example of courage in the midst of adversity. Who is not touched by Job's faith in response to unfathomable tragedy? Just as he was discovering that he had lost all his worldly possessions, Job learned that he had also lost all his children.

His response is startling. He does not curse God, and he does not doubt him. Instead he says, "I came naked from my mother's womb, and I will be naked when I leave. The LORD gave me what I had, and the LORD has taken it away. Praise the name of the LORD!"

Job realized that he never really had anything to lose in the first place. Every human being enters this world with nothing and will leave with nothing. Anything acquired in the meantime is a gift.

Thousands of years later, Job's words were echoed by Steve Jobs, the late CEO and cofounder of Apple, during a commencement speech at Stanford University. Jobs told the graduates, "All external expectations, all pride, all fear of embarrassment or failure, these things just fall away in the face of death, leaving only what is truly important. Remembering that you are going to die is the best way I know to avoid the trap of thinking you have something to lose. You are already naked. There is no reason not to follow your heart."[2]

Job and Jobs are making the same point. We come into this world with nothing, and we leave with nothing. But that's not depressing; it's empowering! The moment we let go of our physical attachments and petty concerns, we are free to focus on what really matters. We are free to try new things and to risk failure. Failure is not nearly as scary when we have nothing on the line.

A Christian Reflection on What Really Matters

Steve Jobs was right that death strips away things that we have a tendency to think are important: wealth, status, and power. God's people need to remember that only one thing is truly important: our relationship with the Lord. In the parable of the rich fool (see Luke 12:13-21), Jesus talks about the folly of someone who spent all his life amassing a large fortune, only to hear from God, "You fool! You will die this very night. Then who will get everything you worked for?" (Luke 12:20). We should listen to Jesus' teaching from this parable: "Yes, a person is a fool to store up earthly wealth but not have a rich relationship with God" (Luke 12:21).

MINISTRY OF PRESENCE

They sat on the ground with him for seven days and nights. No one said a word to Job,
for they saw that his suffering was too great for words. ❖ JOB 2:13

Just about everyone can tell you exactly where they were when the Twin Towers came
down on September 11, 2001. I remember watching the TV in utter shock at what
was unfolding.

One story that caught my attention was an interview with a minister who came
to Ground Zero daily to console the families of the deceased. The reporter asked him
what words of comfort he offered to the bereaved families. The minister replied with
wisdom that deeply resonated with me: "I don't actually say anything. It is merely a
ministry of presence. I just stand by their side, hold their hand, and cry with them."

All too often, when people hear about their friends' suffering, they are reluctant to
call. They simply don't know what to say, so they don't do anything. In truth, like Job's
friends, nothing needs to be said. The closeness of another person, the warmth of the
human touch, simply being present is all it takes.

According to Jewish law, when we experience the loss of a close relative, we are
required to sit in mourning for seven days. During this time, friends and family visit
and offer comfort. Interestingly, Jewish law dictates that the visitors must sit quietly.
Any conversation must be initiated by the mourners. Jewish law is sensitive to the
needs of those who grieve and understands that they just need to know that they
have the closeness and support of friends.

Do not underestimate the value of your presence. In tragic moments—and in good
times—we give our friends and family so much simply by being present with them.
There is a time for conversation and a time for silence. And there are moments in life
when silence says so much more than words ever could.

A Christian Reflection on Weeping with Those Who Weep

We often revile Job's three friends because they made Job's miserable life unbearable
by blaming him for all the horrible things that happened to him. But that was only
when they began to talk! For seven days, they sat with him silently in support. Sitting
in silence was the appropriate response to this unexplainable tragedy. What advice
does the New Testament give for us to be authentically and helpfully present with
people, regardless of the circumstances? "Be happy with those who are happy, and
weep with those who weep. . . . And don't think you know it all!" (Romans 12:15-16).

A QUESTION WITH NO ANSWER

You asked, "Who is this that questions my wisdom with such ignorance?" It is I—
and I was talking about things I knew nothing about, things far too wonderful for me.
❖ JOB 42:3

When tragedy struck, Job, like everyone else, tried to understand God's ways. Why do bad things happen to good people? Why do the wicked experience so much prosperity and comfort?

Most of the book of Job is dedicated to Job and his friends trying to answer these questions for which no answer has been found.

Finally, God himself answers Job's question with another question: "Where were you when I laid the foundations of the earth? Tell me, if you know so much" (Job 38:4). Translation: "Why in the world would you expect to understand my ways? I am the Creator; you are the creation." Confronted with the majesty of the Almighty, Job concedes his limited knowledge: "Surely I spoke of things I did not understand, things too wonderful for me to know" (Job 42:3, NIV). And with these words, Job found comfort.

It is natural and human to try to understand the world around us. But there are many times when we just can't make sense of it. In our generation, one of the hardest things to come to terms with is the Holocaust.

Rabbi Israel Meir Lau, the former chief rabbi of Israel, is a survivor of the Holocaust. In his recently published memoirs he writes, "I am a believer—and I will remain so until my dying day. . . . The question for which I have not found an answer remains the question of why. Why did it have to happen? . . . I will never know, but this will not diminish my faith."

Sometimes we can't understand. But that's okay. Just because we don't understand God doesn't mean that we can't have faith in him. We trust that the Creator knows what he is doing.

Comfort is not found in knowing all the answers. It is found in knowing that we don't have to.

A Christian Reflection on Mystery

When we suffer, we want to know why. The book of Job informs us that we can't always know the reason why we suffer. It remains a mystery to us. The New Testament affirms the message of Job. Suffering is not always the result of sin, and often we can't see a reason for it. Jesus made that point to his disciples when he asked them, "What about the eighteen people who died when the tower in Siloam fell on them? Were they the worst sinners in Jerusalem? No" (Luke 13:4-5). The Gospels do not give us answers to why we suffer, but they describe how God enters into our suffering and comforts us in the person of Jesus.

Sabbath Reflections

What new truth about the life of Job did you learn from this week's devotions?

How has this truth affected your faith?

How will you apply this truth to your daily life?

Your Key Verse for the Week:

✦ OTHER REFLECTIONS

AFTER GOD'S OWN HEART

*Listen to my voice in the morning, L*ORD*. Each morning I bring my requests to you and wait expectantly.* ✦ PSALM 5:3

I have always admired King David's close relationship with God. Despite his many failings, David maintained an intimate connection with God throughout his life. In fact, God called him "a man after [my] own heart" (1 Samuel 13:14).

How did David earn such high esteem from God?

Part of the answer lies in the opening verses of Psalm 5, written during a difficult period in David's life. In verse 1, David pleads with God to "pay attention to my groaning." As he cries out, David reaffirms God as his King, the only one to whom he prays. David reveals his total dependence on God. David knew without a doubt that God alone could help him.

David's confidence is further revealed in verse 3: "Listen to my voice in the morning, LORD. Each morning I bring my requests to you and wait expectantly." We see two important lessons here. First, David prayed *expecting* God to answer him. For David, praying wasn't wishful thinking or an exercise in futility. It was a real exchange between David and God rooted in mutual love and faithfulness.

Second, we see that David consistently spent time in prayer *each morning*. Prayer was woven into David's daily routine; it wasn't a once-in-a-while occurrence. David habitually found time to lay his requests before God.

In rabbinic writings, prayer is called "the work of the heart." The word *work* implies that prayer is something we are obligated to do consistently. Just as we work our bodies regularly to maintain good physical health, we have to constantly work our hearts to maintain good spiritual health. The word *heart* reminds us that our prayers need to be sincere and authentic. Our hearts must truly yearn for God.

Want to be known as a person after God's own heart? Acknowledge God as your Helper and King, come before him in total dependence and expectation, and spend time with him as part of your daily routine.

A Christian Reflection on the Importance of Prayer

If we never, or rarely, talk to a person, we won't have much of a relationship. Prayer is talking to God and listening for his answer. If God is important in our lives, we should desire to speak with him. Jesus' prayer life provides a model for ours. Whenever he faced an important decision or a crisis, Jesus turned to his heavenly Father in prayer (see Luke 6:12-13). Jesus teaches that we "should always pray and never give up" (Luke 18:1). And like David, Jesus was known to begin the day with prayer (see Mark 1:35). We should follow Jesus' example of constant communication through prayer with our heavenly Father.

THE DARKEST VALLEY

Even when I walk through the darkest valley, I will not be afraid, for you are close beside me. Your rod and your staff protect and comfort me. ❖ PSALM 23:4

Natan Sharansky, head of the Jewish Agency for Israel (JAFI) and a partner in ministry with The Fellowship, has helped hundreds of thousands of Jews from around the world make *aliyah*—emigration to Israel. Mr. Sharansky is a bold and persuasive defender of Israel and an eloquent champion of freedom because his own freedom was denied for many years.

In 1977, Sharansky was arrested by the KGB in Russia on a false espionage charge for his role in pressuring Communist authorities to allow Soviet Jews to emigrate to Israel. He was convicted and placed in a Soviet prison, confined to a damp, cold, concrete room barely larger than an oversize box.

What helped Sharansky through this dark time was a small book of Psalms that his wife gave to him days before his arrest.

Although the book was confiscated at first by his captors, Sharansky fought for three years to get it back. When he finally succeeded, he began reading the Psalms, even though his knowledge of Hebrew was limited. He said, "The first phrase which I understood fully was . . . from Psalm 23, 'And when I go through the land of death, I will fear no evil because you are with me.'

"There are small words, short words, which I understood, . . . and that was very powerful. [It was as if] God, [the] Jewish people, my wife, the State of Israel, all together came to me to say, 'Don't be afraid; we are with you.' And that was [a] big encouragement."[3]

Small words, short words, yes. Yet powerful enough to sustain a man through imprisonment and isolation. And powerful enough to sustain you in whatever dark valleys you may be walking through today.

A Christian Reflection on the Dark Valleys

In reading Psalm 23, Christians cannot help but think of Jesus' words: "I am the good shepherd" (John 10:11). Like the shepherd in Psalm 23, Jesus leads us to the right places and in the right ways. He is our Protector, our Guide, and our Provider. He willingly "sacrifices his life for the sheep," and he knows each and every one of his flock and cares for them (John 10:11). Ultimately, through faith in Jesus, we find fulfillment of David's words written thousands of years ago: "Surely your goodness and unfailing love will pursue me all the days of my life, and I will live in the house of the LORD forever" (Psalm 23:6).

A VOTE OF CONFIDENCE

The LORD told Joshua, "Today I will begin to make you a great leader in the eyes of all the Israelites. They will know that I am with you, just as I was with Moses."
❖ JOSHUA 3:7

After forty years of wandering in the desert, the people of Israel stood at the border of the Promised Land. As before, they faced obstacles in reaching their goal. Before them stood the raging waters of the Jordan River.

In addition, they were now following Joshua, a new, untried leader. How would the people respond? How would Joshua know if he had earned their respect?

God understood these doubts, and he gave Joshua the same promises he had given to Moses—he would be with him and help him. God knew that the people needed assurance as well. So he promised Joshua one more thing: "Today I will begin to make you a great leader in the eyes of all the Israelites. They will know that I am with you" (Joshua 3:7).

As the people stood on the banks of the Jordan, God told Joshua to instruct the priests carrying the Ark of the Covenant to step into the fast-moving waters. The people had a choice. They could choose to obey Joshua's instructions and trust in God. Or they could trust in their own wisdom and wait until the waters receded.

The people stepped out in faith, the water stopped, and they crossed into the Promised Land.

King David writes, "I have chosen to be faithful; I have determined to live by your regulations" (Psalm 119:30). In every situation, we have a choice: We can trust in our human strength, or we can put our faith in God. And though choosing God may not always be the easiest decision, it is always the most fruitful. As the prophet Jeremiah tells us, "Blessed are those who trust in the LORD and have made the LORD their hope and confidence" (Jeremiah 17:7).

What obstacles are you facing today? Where is your confidence—in your own ability or in God's? We may not witness a spectacular miracle; however, we do have God's Word to guide us.

A Christian Reflection on Confidence in God's Word

The parable of the rich man and Lazarus (see Luke 16:19-31) makes it clear that God's Word is a much better foundation for our confidence than a spectacular event. The rich man, who is suffering in the place of the dead, asks Abraham to send a warning to his brothers so they could avoid his fate. He tells the patriarch, "If someone is sent to them from the dead, then they will repent of their sins and turn to God" (Luke 16:30). Notice Abraham's response: "If they won't listen to Moses and the prophets [the Bible], they won't listen even if someone rises from the dead" (Luke 16:31). The message is clear. All we need is God's Word to find the wisdom and guidance necessary to face life's obstacles.

SURPRISE!

The LORD delights in his people; he crowns the humble with victory.
❖ PSALM 149:4

God delights in surprising us. Certainly Abraham and Sarah were surprised by the news that they would have a child when Sarah was ninety and Abraham ninety-nine! In fact, they chose to immortalize their moment of surprise by giving their child the name Isaac, which comes from a Hebrew word that means "to laugh." As Sarah says, "God has brought me laughter" (Genesis 21:6). Humor is often based on the element of surprise. That's why when Abraham and Sarah heard the unexpected news about the pending arrival of their son, they laughed.

The Bible is filled with many such surprises, and I think God delights in bestowing every single one of them. So I had to chuckle when I read about the "surprising" discovery of an ancient boat that had been buried in the shores of the Sea of Galilee for nearly two thousand years. It was a miracle that the boat was even discovered.

In 1986, following a drought, the water levels of the lake had dropped. Two brothers were walking along the exposed shoreline and stumbled upon some old Roman and Jewish coins. Spurred on by their discovery, the brothers continued searching the area and soon found a handful of nails and some wood. Then came the most incredible find of all—a boat!

Antiquities experts were brought in, and the boat was examined—it was found to be two thousand years old, a boat likely used during the time when Jesus lived and traveled on the Sea of Galilee. The boat has since been dubbed the "Jesus Boat" and is one of the most significant archaeological finds of modern times.

And in case we missed how surprising it was to find this boat preserved for two millennia, the two brothers told of how, at the very moment they found the boat, a brilliant double rainbow appeared over the Sea of Galilee!

As the psalm writer noted, our God takes delight in us. He enjoys giving good gifts to his children.

A Christian Reflection on Divine Surprises

When it comes to God surprising his people, I think of the two disciples on the road to Emmaus. They were confused and dismayed at the crucifixion of Jesus. Imagine their surprise when "suddenly, their eyes were opened, and they recognized him. And at that moment he disappeared!" (Luke 24:31). Yet Jesus reminded them they should not have been surprised, because the Scriptures "clearly predicted that the Messiah would have to suffer all these things before entering his glory" (Luke 24:26). Indeed, we should remember this when the New Testament tells us not to be surprised on the day the Lord comes again (see 1 Thessalonians 5:4). Because he will come suddenly and without previous announcement, we need to always be ready.

A TIME FOR EVERYTHING

There is a time for everything, and a season for every activity under the heavens.
❖ ECCLESIASTES 3:1, NIV

Did you know that Jews measure days, months, and years differently than Christians—and most of the world—do? And though Jewish holidays occur on the same day each year on the Jewish calendar, the dates change every year on the Gregorian calendar—the one most people use.

The major difference is that the Jewish calendar is based on lunar cycles while the Gregorian is based on solar cycles. Each month in the Jewish calendar begins with the appearance of the new moon. In biblical times, that day was set by the Jewish council after hearing testimony from two separate witnesses who had observed the new moon.

Because the solar year equates to approximately 12.4 lunar months, adjustments have to be made every so often to the Jewish calendar. Otherwise *Pesach* (Passover), which is typically celebrated in the spring, would eventually occur in the winter.

You may also notice that the Jewish calendar is more than 3,500 years ahead of the Gregorian calendar. The year on the Jewish calendar represents the number of years since creation—a number that was determined by adding up the ages of people in the Bible back to the time of creation.

Even with all these differences in measuring time, the one truth about time that Christians and Jews can agree on is that God has created a time and a season for everything. This is noted most eloquently in the verses King Solomon wrote in the book of Ecclesiastes. God has appointed a time for all the cycles of our lives.

Interestingly, the first commandment ever given to the children of Israel after the Exodus was to celebrate time. Just before the people left Egypt, God gave them the commandment to commemorate every new moon (see Exodus 12:2). God wants us to celebrate every stage in the yearly cycle and to recognize that it is he alone who powers the clock of the world. When we accept God's perfect timing in our lives, no matter which calendar we may follow, we will find peace.

A Christian Reflection on God's Timing

Solomon insists rightly that God has established a time for everything. Why did Jesus come when he did? John the Baptist's answer was simply "the time has come" (Mark 1:15, NIV). It was the right time. Was the time and circumstance of Jesus' death a result of happenstance? Did he just get caught up in the events of the day? No, Jesus himself referred to the time of his upcoming crucifixion as an "appointed time" (Matthew 26:18, NIV). When is the right time to accept the "marvelous gift of God's kindness"? Listen to Paul, who tells us that "the 'right time' is now. Today is the day of salvation" (2 Corinthians 6:1-2).

HIS STORY

Tell your children about it in the years to come, and let your children tell their children.
Pass the story down from generation to generation. ❖ JOEL 1:3

Tel Megiddo is one of the most important archaeological sites in Israel—and an object lesson of historic and biblical proportions. Located near the entrance of the Jezreel Valley and along the Via Maris, antiquity's superhighway, this ancient site reveals the story of twenty-five civilizations that were built upon the ruins of one another.

Because of Megiddo's strategic location, historians believe it was the site of more battles than any other place in history. The citizens of Megiddo, at different times in its history, battled against the armies of Assyria, Canaan, Egypt, Greece, Persia, Philistia, and Rome. Even as late as World War I, a decisive battle between English and Ottoman forces occurred near Megiddo.

Megiddo is mentioned in six different books of the Hebrew Bible. The king of Megiddo was one of many rulers that Joshua killed during the conquest of the Promised Land (see Joshua 12:7, 21). It's where Deborah and Barak led the people of Israel to victory over the Canaanites (see Judges 5:19-20). Solomon made Megiddo one of his district capitals, as well as one of the three main fortress cities of his kingdom (see 1 Kings 4:12; 9:15).

Why is this little history lesson important? Because it underscores that history is God's story. These places are not of value just to historians but to people of faith. Sites such as Tel Megiddo help us understand that the stories of the Bible are real and that God's story continues to unfold today.

We can play a part in God's story. Referring to the coming of the Messiah, God says, "In its time I will do this swiftly" (Isaiah 60:22, NIV). The Sages teach that this means that the End Days will either come at a predetermined time—that is, "in its time"—or, if humanity is deserving, God will "do this swiftly" and bring in the Messianic era sooner.

Most of history is already written, but we can help write the final chapter.

A Christian Reflection on Armageddon

The New Testament speaks of Armageddon as the location of the last battle between the forces of evil and God: "The demonic spirits gathered all the rulers and their armies to a place with the Hebrew name *Armageddon*" (Revelation 16:16). *Armageddon* means "mountain of Megiddo," and though Megiddo is located on a plain, there are mountains nearby. Thus it is near the city of Megiddo where the last battle is pictured. Some Christians believe this will be a literal battle, while others interpret the passage symbolically in reference to the final judgment. Whether it's literal or symbolic, one thing is perfectly clear: God will surely defeat the forces of evil. What a wonderful picture of hope for God's people.

Sabbath Reflections

What new truth about God's control of all things—from history to time—did you learn from this week's devotions?

How has this truth affected your faith?

How will you apply this truth to your daily life?

Your Key Verse for the Week:

❖ OTHER REFLECTIONS

POUR OUT YOUR HEART

I am worn out from sobbing. All night I flood my bed with weeping,
drenching it with my tears. ❖ PSALM 6:6

When we are at our lowest moments, we tend to withdraw from others. It's hard to admit that we're struggling. So we put on a brave face and do our best to carry on.

During those times, we need to remember that there is someone with whom we can be completely honest: God. We can bring to him our anger, our despair, our doubts, and our weaknesses, without fear of rejection or judgment.

David models this for us in Psalm 6. As he comes before God, David pours out his heart. He is weary from groaning, and his bed is drenched in tears. In anguish, David cries out, "Have compassion on me, LORD, for I am weak" (Psalm 6:2).

Because David is completely honest with God, he is able to turn his inward grief toward God. He concludes his prayer by stating, "The LORD has heard my plea; the LORD will answer my prayer" (Psalm 6:9). David knew that God would take care of him.

We, too, can be honest with God, even when we're filled with anger or despair, because God knows us thoroughly and desires the very best for us. He knows our situation, and he alone can guide us.

The prophet Jeremiah says, "Pour out your hearts like water to the Lord" (Lamentations 2:19). The Sages explain that on the second day of creation, when God separated the waters above from the waters below, the waters below began to "cry." They longed to be higher and closer to their Creator, like a child who wants to be close to his or her parent. That's the way we need to pour out our hearts to God—like the waters of creation that yearned desperately for the closeness of their Father.

As we pour out our hearts to God, we will find, as David did, that our focus shifts from our earthly problems to our all-powerful, all-loving Father in heaven.

A Christian Reflection on Total Honesty with God

I have observed over the years that Christians struggle more than others—including our Jewish brothers and sisters—with an honest expression of our difficult emotions. When we pray, we find it hard to express disappointment, frustration, even anger toward God. Perhaps we feel that since Jesus "won the victory" on the cross, we are not permitted to cry or yell at God when we suffer. But the truth is that we still feel pain in this life, and as Rabbi Eckstein notes, the Psalms—particularly laments such as Psalm 6—are models to us of honest prayer, revealing our hearts to God. The key is to direct our sorrows and our complaints to God as the psalmists did. God invites us to bring our every emotion to him.

WEEK 6 // DAY 2

SING A NEW SONG!

Sing a new song to the LORD! Let the whole earth sing to the LORD!
❖ PSALM 96:1

One of my great joys is music and singing, so I connect with David when I read the words of Psalm 96: "Sing a new song to the LORD!" I imagine David as a shepherd boy, harp in hand, strumming softly to calm his flock with praise notes to God.

I'm struck by the great joy David demonstrates when praising God. Remember when David danced in front of the Ark of the Covenant as it was brought back to Jerusalem? Although his wife looked upon him with disdain, David could not contain himself. His joy broke out in music.

The Bible records the scene: "David and all the people of Israel were celebrating before the LORD, singing songs and playing all kinds of musical instruments" (2 Samuel 6:5). David wasn't content to watch from the sidelines. No, he was leading the songs. He danced before the Lord with all his might.

What I look forward to the most, however, is when the new song of praise will be played on the ten-string harp during the reign of the Messiah. According to rabbinic literature, the harp is a symbol of that time—a time when all humanity will live together in harmony.

Jewish tradition teaches that in Messianic times an eighth note will be added to our current musical scale. This means that we will be able to make all kinds of new music and symbolizes the new ways in which we will live and serve God. The Messianic era will usher in a whole new world!

At that time we will come into God's presence, and it won't be a quiet, stately procession. No, it's going to be a joyous, raucous, rowdy affair. As it says in Psalm 100, "Shout for joy to the LORD, all the earth. Worship the LORD with gladness; come before him with joyful songs" (Psalm 100:1-2, NIV).

Like David, we won't be able to contain ourselves!

A Christian Reflection on Singing a New Song

The book of Revelation pictures God entering the world at the end of the age to usher in the New Jerusalem, a symbol of heaven, marking the final victory over evil in the world. Just as Israel's victories were followed by joyful song, so this great, final victory will be celebrated with singing when God's people are brought into his presence. Indeed, the phrase "new song" found throughout the Psalms and Isaiah in the Hebrew Bible is found only in Revelation (5:9; 14:3) in the New Testament. The purpose of Revelation is to remind God's people that, in spite of their present struggles, God will come again and rescue them from the travails of this life. That will be cause for singing!

SHIRAY DOROT: SONGS OF GENERATIONS

I will sing to the LORD as long as I live. I will praise my God to my last breath!
❖ PSALM 104:33

Music has always been an integral part of my life. I cherish the memories of sitting around the table with my parents and siblings on *Shabbat*, singing praise songs to God. Songs of faith and inspiration are part of my spiritual heritage—a vital part that I have sought to pass on to my three daughters.

Remember what Moses and the Israelites did after the miraculous crossing of the Red Sea? They broke into song. First, Moses led the people in a song of deliverance, called the "Song of the Sea." Then Miriam grabbed a tambourine and led all the women in song and dance.

In *Torah* scrolls, where the Word of God is handwritten in a traditionally prescribed manner, the "Song of the Sea" is recorded in an unusual way. Its phrases are separated by vast empty spaces. That spacing is deliberate. It teaches us that when it comes to songs, there is so much more than mere words. Music allows us to convey our deepest emotions, far beyond what words can express.

Music has always played an important role in Israel's worship and celebration. Singing is an expression of love and thanksgiving and also a way to pass along the stories of faith and oral tradition from generation to generation. David, one of the most prolific and greatest songwriters of the Bible, composed songs of thanksgiving, praise, prayer, and supplication in what we now treasure as the Psalms. He even organized musical worship by appointing a choir of Levites to "sing joyful songs" (1 Chronicles 15:16).

I believe that music, especially songs inspired by the Psalms and other Scripture, is a common bond that Christians and Jews share. It is one avenue that has been so important to me in building bridges of understanding between our two faith communities and introducing Christians to the rich Jewish roots of their faith.

Whether we are musically talented or not doesn't matter to God—only our joyful and thanks-filled sounds!

A Christian Reflection on Songs of Praise

The musical heritage of the Hebrew Bible continues in the New Testament and in the church today. Paul encourages the Ephesian church to "be filled with the Holy Spirit, singing psalms and hymns and spiritual songs among yourselves, and making music to the Lord in your hearts" (Ephesians 5:18-19; see also Colossians 3:16). The grace of God overwhelms us, so we must express our gratitude. Song is one important way we can proclaim our thanks to God—not only with our minds but also with our hearts. We can sing as individuals and together as people of God. "Let everything that breathes sing praises to the LORD!" (Psalm 150:6).

FACE TO FACE

There has never been another prophet in Israel like Moses, whom the LORD knew face to face. ❖ DEUTERONOMY 34:10

In our world of instant communication via text, e-mail, and Internet, it is not uncommon to have a relationship with another person without ever seeing him or her. When you finally meet, it's always good to put a face to the name.

This was true in biblical times as well. Israel had many great prophets—Isaiah, Jeremiah, Ezekiel, and others—but none met God face to face. That level of intimacy was achieved by only one human in the entire Hebrew Bible: Moses.

That's why the Jewish faith distinguishes between the revelation given to Moses—the *Torah*—and that given to the other prophets. We consider the *Torah* (the first five books of the Hebrew Bible) as divine *revelation*, God's exact words given directly to Moses. The prophecies given to men such as Isaiah and Jeremiah, though divinely *inspired*, were not God's direct words but general themes recorded in each prophet's own words.

In Jewish tradition, Moses is considered the greatest prophet to ever live. But he also stands out in another way. The Bible calls Moses "more humble than any other person" (Numbers 12:3). It's not coincidental that Moses, who mastered humility, also achieved the greatest intimacy with God. It was because of his humility that he was so honored by God.

Imagine knowing God face to face! God was able to transform Moses from a stuttering shepherd into a national leader. Throughout Moses' life, his love and respect for God grew daily. Because of that, God was pleased to call Moses his *friend*: "Inside the Tent of Meeting, the LORD would speak to Moses face to face, as one speaks to a friend" (Exodus 33:11).

While on earth, we will never see God face to face. But we can know him through his Word. We can speak to him through prayer. And we can experience his love as we come before him humbly, seeking his will for our lives.

A Christian Reflection on Moses

Moses is like none other in the Hebrew Bible. He enjoyed a relationship of intimacy with God that surpassed all others. Yet for Christians, one person not only enjoyed an intimate relationship with God but *was God* (see John 1:1). For this reason, the author of Hebrews, while extolling Moses' important place in the Bible, tells us that "Jesus deserves far more glory than Moses" (Hebrews 3:3). However—and here Christians often err—this statement does not render the words of Moses (or the other prophets) any less authoritative. Christians should be avid students of the *Torah* and the Prophets because God speaks to us through these sacred pages.

FOLLOW MY INSTRUCTIONS!

Obey the terms of this covenant so that you will prosper in everything you do.
❖ DEUTERONOMY 29:9

When you receive a new appliance, do you try to figure out how it works on your own? Or do you read through the instruction manual and learn how to operate it? If you skip the instructions, you may learn to use your appliance, but only after much frustration. If you want to operate your appliance successfully, it's best to consult the manual.

That's true, too, when it comes to knowing how to operate our lives successfully. God has given us plenty of instructions to help us. First, he gave us the rules to live by through direct revelation to Moses. Then he gave us tips through his prophets.

That was the role of God's prophets. They were instruments of God, used for both education and discipline. They alternately instructed people on how to live in accordance with God's Word and roused people to repentance.

Sometimes the instructions were simple, such as when to conduct the annual feast days, as in Exodus 23. Other times, God's anger is clearly evident, as in Isaiah 58, when the prophet chastises the people for conducting fasts that end in quarrels. Often, dire circumstances were spelled out if the people ignored a prophet's message.

While those messages were often specific to the circumstances of the times, we know that God still communicates to us through Scripture. Like the people of Israel, we have a clear choice: Either we can listen to God's instructions, or we can choose to figure things out on our own—and suffer the consequences.

In the book of Deuteronomy, God says, "Today I have given you the choice between life and death" (30:19). God gives us the choice, every day, to follow his life-giving instructions: "You can make this choice by loving the LORD your God, obeying him, and committing yourself firmly to him. This is the key to your life" (Deuteronomy 30:20). Following God's law is the key to a successful life.

A Christian Reflection on God's Instructions

Jesus clearly emphasized the importance of God's law: "I tell you the truth, until heaven and earth disappear, not even the smallest detail of God's law will disappear until its purpose is achieved" (Matthew 5:18). True, the purpose of some laws was achieved with Jesus' coming. For this reason, Christians don't observe the food laws of Leviticus, which served the purpose of differentiating Jews from Gentiles. Christians also understand Jesus' death on the cross as fulfillment of the sacrificial system, so they stopped offering sacrifices even before the Temple was destroyed. For Christians, the moral law is an expression of God's will for how we should live. These laws are God's instructions, and we ignore them at our own peril.

THE RIGHTEOUS PATH

The LORD watches over the path of the godly, but the path of the wicked leads to destruction. ❖ PSALM 1:6

In a man-on-the-street survey a few years ago, media personality Dennis Prager approached random people and asked, "Are you a good person?" Just about everyone said yes. When he asked why, most told him because they didn't steal or cheat on their taxes or kill anyone.

So, the question for us is this: Is that enough? Can one be considered good by avoiding evil?

The psalmist lists what a person should not do in order to be blessed: Don't walk with the wicked, don't stand with the sinners, and don't sit with the mockers (see Psalm 1:1). The next logical step would be to tell us what we *should* be doing, but that line never comes.

Many people feel that righteousness is unattainable. Yet the book of Psalms begins by teaching us that it is totally within reach. We only need to stop ourselves from doing evil. Really? Can that possibly be enough?

Psalm 1 begins, "Blessed is the '*ish*.'" *Ish* is the Hebrew word for "man." In other words, God expects us to be human, not saints. "Just be human," says God, "and the rest will follow." By the end of the psalm, the "man" is called righteous because a person who refrains from evil will naturally engage in goodness.

Oskar Schindler, made famous by the movie *Schindler's List*, saved almost twelve hundred Jewish lives during the Holocaust. Schindler was no saint. At the beginning, he was just a guy out to make a buck when he hired more than one thousand Jewish laborers to work in his factory. But with time, Schindler started to protect his workers and save their lives.

Schindler never considered himself a hero. He was quoted as saying, "When you know people, you have to behave toward them like human beings." Just by acting like a human being, though, Schindler became one.

Imagine what the world would look like if everyone took one step toward doing less evil and, therefore, doing more good.

A Christian Reflection on a Life of Obedience

Jesus echoes the teaching of Psalm 1. At the end of his Sermon on the Mount, he announces that "anyone who listens to my teaching and follows it is wise, like a person who builds a house on solid rock" (Matthew 7:24), whereas "anyone who hears my teaching and doesn't obey it is foolish, like a person who builds a house on sand" (Matthew 7:26). Of course, while the house on the sand crumbles in a storm, the one built on a rock endures. Jesus' teaching here (as well as Psalm 1) urges us to obey God and live meaningful and profitable lives.

Sabbath Reflections

What new truth about obeying God and worshiping him did you learn from this week's devotions?

How has this truth affected your faith?

How will you apply this truth to your daily life?

Your Key Verse for the Week:

❖ OTHER REFLECTIONS

THE GOD WHO SEES ME

End the evil of those who are wicked, and defend the righteous. For you look deep within the mind and heart, O righteous God. ❖ PSALM 7:9

Throughout the Hebrew Bible, we discover that God has many different names, which reveal different aspects of his nature. One such name is *El-roi*, Hebrew for "the God who sees me." This was the name that Hagar, Sarah's maidservant, gave to the Lord after her encounter with him in Genesis 16.

You may remember the story—uncertain as to how God would fulfill the promise of offspring through his wife, Sarah, Abraham fathered a child with Hagar. Sarah, despite her role in arranging this, was unhappy with the situation and "treated Hagar so harshly that she finally ran away" (Genesis 16:6). It was as Hagar was despairing in the wilderness that "the angel of the LORD" came to her and comforted her, telling Hagar that God, indeed, had seen her misery.

When you feel alone or troubled, remember Hagar. Remember *El-roi*. Remember that God sees you, knows you, and understands exactly what you are going through. King David reminds us again in Psalm 7 that God searches our hearts and our minds. He knows our every thought. Nothing is hidden from him.

The *Talmud* teaches, "An eye is watching, an ear is listening, and everything that we do is recorded in a book." This means that God is always paying attention and taking notes. As King Solomon puts it, God is "gazing through the windows, peering through the lattice" (Song of Songs 2:9, NIV). He is constantly checking up and checking in.

This may be a terrifying thought for some, but it can also be a great comfort. It's true that we can't hide our thoughts or our true motives from God, but it also means we don't have to impress him. He is the God who sees us, and because he does, he can be the God who comforts us, who guides us, who protects us, who loves us, and who will help us in our misery.

A *Christian Reflection on* El-roi

The story of Hagar powerfully illustrates that God knows our hearts. Jesus reminded his followers of this important truth to encourage them. First, he told them that they should not help others in order to receive the praise of people, but they should do so privately, so that "your Father, who sees everything, will reward you" (Matthew 6:4). He went on to talk about prayer, warning them not to pray publicly with the hope that people will think they are pious, but rather to "pray to your Father in private. Then your Father, who sees everything, will reward you" (Matthew 6:6). Finally, he instructs them to fast in private as well, and says once again, "Your Father, who sees everything, will reward you" (Matthew 6:18).

FIRST IMPRESSIONS

The LORD said to Samuel, "Don't judge by his appearance or height, for I have rejected him. The LORD doesn't see things the way you see them. People judge by outward appearance, but the LORD looks at the heart." ❖ 1 SAMUEL 16:7

Making a good first impression can be critical. Often we will look at people, and based on how they look, we will make judgments about the type of people they are, how much they earn, and whether we want to meet them.

In God's economy, however, our outward appearance means nothing. What matters most to God is what's on the inside—our hearts and our character. We see this illustrated as Samuel is sent to Jesse's home to anoint one of his sons as the next king of Israel. As the first son is brought to him, Samuel says, "Surely this is the LORD's anointed!" (1 Samuel 16:6). But he was not the one, nor were his six brothers who were brought after him.

Finally, God, in essence, says, "Don't look at their height or appearance. I don't look at the same things that you do. You may look at the outward appearance, but I look at the heart!"

Eventually, Jesse summons his youngest son, David, and God tells Samuel, "Yes, this is the one" (1 Samuel 16:12). Though it was not evident from looking at David, God knew that this young man would one day have the courage to defeat Israel's enemies, the faith to be obedient despite hardships, and a desire to follow God throughout his entire life. David was beautiful on the inside.

Once, an unattractive rabbi said something very wise to Caesar's daughter. She exclaimed, "How can such wisdom come out of such an ugly container?" He challenged her, "Why don't you pour your father's good wine out of its clay bottles and into gold ones?" Thinking the rabbi was serious, she transferred the wine into gold bottles, where it soon spoiled. Thus she learned that the ugly clay bottles were superior for storing wine. That's why the Sages say, "Don't look at the container, only at its contents." It's the inside that matters most.

God is not swayed by appearances. If we want to make a good impression in God's world, we need to check our hearts first.

A *Christian Reflection on the Heart*

The New Testament joins the Hebrew Bible in focusing on a person's heart. Jesus warned that it is what comes "from within, out of a person's heart" that defiles, naming evil thoughts, sexual immorality, and theft, among other things (Mark 7:20-23, NIV). God told Samuel not to look at outward appearance (as Israel had with Saul; see 1 Samuel 10:23-24) but at the heart. So Paul told the Corinthians not to be amazed by those who have "a spectacular ministry" but rather those who have "a sincere heart" (2 Corinthians 5:12). May God grant us all pure hearts and eyes that see behind the glitz and hype that permeate our world.

MALIGNED AND MISUNDERSTOOD

David continued to succeed in everything he did, for the LORD was with him. When Saul recognized this, he became even more afraid of him. But all Israel and Judah loved David because he was so successful at leading his troops into battle.

❖ I SAMUEL 18:14-16

When others perceive our honest efforts as an attempt to undermine them, we can respond in a number of ways: We could confront them; we could give up; we could complain. Or we could say nothing and just continue to do our best.

That's what David did. Despite growing opposition, he continued to do his best. As a result, King Saul became increasingly jealous of David with each new success—whether it was on the battlefield or within his own household, where David was much loved by Saul's son Jonathan and daughter Michal. In Saul's eyes, David was using his successes as stepping-stones to the throne.

Nothing David could say or do would persuade Saul otherwise. Unfortunately, the consequences were far worse than just having an angry boss; Saul wanted David dead. David was forced to run for his life, becoming Israel's most famous fugitive.

Despite having the popular support of the people and a sizable army that remained loyal to him, David did not press his advantage against Saul. He did not allow his successes to color his perception of his own importance, nor did he demand the throne.

Why? Because David knew that God was in control and would work out the situation according to his plan.

When God parted the Red Sea for the children of Israel, Scripture tells us that they walked through "with a wall of water on their right and on their left" (Exodus 14:22, NIV). The Sages teach that this is often the path we must also take. We need to have walls on either side of us that block out what people say—both bad and good—so that we stay focused on our goal and do what we must.

When we are unfairly maligned or misunderstood, we must stay focused and continue to do our best. Like David, we can have faith and carry on with our mission.

A Christian Reflection on Blessing Those Who Persecute You

Jesus is clear about how we should respond to those who persecute us. He instructs his followers to rejoice when others hate them because of their belief in him, and to "love your enemies! Do good to those who hate you. Bless those who curse you. Pray for those who hurt you" (Luke 6:27-29). Likewise, Paul advises the church in Rome to ask God to bless those who persecute them. He urges them to "never pay back evil with more evil" and to "live in peace with everyone" (Romans 12:17-18). In this way, Paul continues Jesus' own teaching to "turn the other cheek" to those who assault us (see Luke 6:29).

REVENGE IS SWEET?

The LORD forbid that I should do this to my lord the king and attack the LORD's anointed one, for the LORD himself has chosen him. ❖ 1 SAMUEL 24:6

Revenge is sweet—or so it seems in the movies when the bad guys are finally defeated. There's something satisfying about seeing people who are obviously in the wrong finally get what they deserve.

So, when we come to a passage such as 1 Samuel 24, it gives us pause. Hiding in a cave with his men, David is given a golden opportunity to defeat his archenemy as Saul unknowingly enters the cave. David's men have revenge on their minds, and they urge David to kill the unsuspecting king.

Instead, David crept forward and cut off a piece of the king's robe. As Saul left the cave, David ran after him, bowed before him, and showed him the piece of cut robe. Then he said, "May the LORD judge between us. Perhaps the LORD will punish you for what you are trying to do to me, but I will never harm you" (1 Samuel 24:12). Saul was "the LORD's anointed"—and regardless of his behavior, David knew he had no right to harm him.

At a moment when many would have followed their human desire to exact revenge, David showed compassion, sparing Saul's life. In response, Saul's hardened heart finally relented, and he wept aloud, recognizing that David was "surely going to be king, and that the kingdom of Israel will flourish under your rule" (1 Samuel 24:20).

Scripture instructs, "Do not seek revenge" (Leviticus 19:18). But as the Sages point out, the punitive system is full of revenge. The Sages clarify that there is a difference between our reaction to criminal behavior and how we treat offensive behavior. Though it is true that society cannot properly function if crime is tolerated, it is also true that society cannot function if every hurtful word or action is *not* tolerated. Tolerance is necessary for peace.

Revenge may appear to be sweet, but allowing God to work out the situation is sweeter still.

A Christian Reflection on Revenge

Paul is adamant: "Dear friends, never take revenge" (Romans 12:19). More than that, Paul tells his readers to bless their enemies. We have seen that David modeled this attitude in his relationship with Saul. We have a greater example in Jesus. As he hung on the cross, receiving abuse from the Roman soldiers who were crucifying him, Jesus prayed, "Father, forgive them, for they don't know what they are doing" (Luke 23:34). Does this mean that evil people will get away with their wicked actions? Not according to Paul. Those who deserve punishment will indeed receive it—not from human hands but from God himself (see Romans 12:19-21).

OUR ROCK OF REFUGE

Be my rock of safety where I can always hide. Give the order to save me, for you are my rock and my fortress. ❖ PSALM 71:3

Finally, David and King Saul came to an understanding. Saul acknowledged David as God's anointed king and recognized David's compassion toward him. At this point, you might think that David's troubles were over.

Not so.

David and his men returned home, only to discover that enemy raiders had plundered their homes, taken their wives and children, and burned their homes to the ground. As the Bible records it, "They wept until they could weep no more" (1 Samuel 30:4).

Faced with such loss, David's men turned on him. They blamed David for their circumstances and threatened to kill him. David, however, did what he had always done when facing difficult situations; he "found strength in the LORD his God" (1 Samuel 30:6).

David inquired of God, "Should I chase after this band of raiders?" And the Lord answered him, "Yes, go after them. You will surely recover everything that was taken from you!" (1 Samuel 30:8). So David and his men pursued the enemy until they found them celebrating their plunder. David and his men destroyed the raiders and regained everything that had been taken.

David was successful in defeating his enemies and defusing a volatile situation because he had a lifelong habit of not panicking in difficult situations but instead looking for help from God, his "rock of safety" (Psalm 71:3).

Later, as recorded in Psalm 121, David says, "I look up to the mountains—does my help come from there?" David wonders if the natural strength of nature is what would grant him success. He answers, "My help comes from the LORD, who made heaven and earth!" Why rely on the things of Creation when we can lean on the one who created everything?

Is this how we approach difficulties in life? Do we look to God, or do we look for scapegoats? Better to be like David and cultivate a habit of going to God first and seeking his guidance.

A Christian Reflection on Seeking God First

When trouble comes into our lives, our first reaction is often to worry: What will we do? Perhaps, like David's men, we blame others for our trouble. Perhaps we find ourselves paralyzed by anxiety. Jesus addressed our propensity to worry by pointing out that such worry is characteristic of unbelievers, not of those who have a heavenly Father who "knows all your needs" (Matthew 6:32). What should the reaction of God's people be when trouble inevitably comes into their lives? "Seek the Kingdom of God above all else, and live righteously" (Matthew 6:33). Our Father in heaven will take care of us.

FRAILTY OF LIFE

Teach us to realize the brevity of life, so that we may grow in wisdom.
❖ PSALM 90:12

Considered one of the oldest psalms, Psalm 90 offers words that are as applicable today as when they were written. They speak to people in every generation, powerfully contrasting the frailty of human life with the eternal existence of God. The Bible is unfailingly honest in portraying life as a moment in which we make a brief appearance, a mere footnote in history, and then are gone.

The psalmist helps us to recognize that transience is an undeniable fact of our existence, and it serves as a lesson that we need to make the right choices in light of life's fleeting nature. The psalmist points out that, as imperfect beings, we spend our days under the shadow of God's wrath. However, the wrath of the Lord is not an outburst of capricious anger. Rather, because God's wrath is brought to those who flout his law and disobey him, it is an expression of his righteous character.

It is the brevity of life that makes our faith in God—living in accordance to his law, following his righteous path—even more urgent and necessary. Psalm 90 may seem pessimistic at first glance. But closer study reveals that it encourages us to live under God's direction and blessing. We can ask God for his mercy each day, confident that he will answer our prayers. And because he does hear our prayers—because he is merciful and compassionate—we can enjoy his unfailing love and spend our days in his favor.

The *Talmud* shares with us an exchange between a teacher and his students. Rabbi Eliezer told his students, "Repent one day before your death." His students asked, "Does a person know when he will die?" The rabbi replied, "Then he should repent today. Maybe he will die tomorrow." Rabbi Eliezer taught his students that it is best to live every day as if it could be our last.

Life *is* short, so embrace the wisdom of God and live it to the fullest by living a life of righteousness.

A Christian Reflection on the Brevity of Life

The New Testament writers pick up the theme that we must come to terms with the brevity of life: "Your life is like the morning fog—it's here a little while, then it's gone" (James 4:14). James makes the point that we should not be overly self-confident about our plans but rather submit to God's will for our lives. While there will inevitably be struggles in this life, Jesus proclaimed that his purpose was to give his people "a rich and satisfying life" (John 10:10). Of course, the New Testament is also very clear in its teaching that this brief life is not the end of the story, but rather the beginning of a relationship with God that lasts forever.

Sabbath Reflections

What new truth about David's life did you learn from this week's devotions?

How has this truth affected your faith?

How will you apply this truth to your daily life?

Your Key Verse for the Week:

❖ OTHER REFLECTIONS

LIKE LITTLE CHILDREN

O LORD, our Lord, your majestic name fills the earth! Your glory is higher than the heavens. ❖ PSALM 8:1

One of the joys of being a parent is experiencing the world through the eyes of your children. Everything they come across—whether it's a rock, a feather, or a tiny bug skittering across the sidewalk—is an object of fascination. Their world is an amazing place.

No wonder the psalmist says, "From the lips of children and infants, you have ordained praise" (Psalm 8:2, NIV 1984). Children have an incredible capacity to trust God and thoroughly enjoy his Creation. They don't come with the same baggage of doubts and past hurts that often taint an adult's relationship with God and hinder the ability to praise him.

This psalm begins and ends with the declaration: "O LORD, our Lord, your majestic name fills the earth!" In this psalm, King David uses the personal name that God gave to Moses at the burning bush—that is, *Yah-weh*, the God of Israel's covenant (Psalm 8:1, 9). Though God is majestic and transcendent, he is also personal in his interactions with us. We are more than God's creations; we are his children, and he invites us to delight in his world.

Through various word pictures, the psalmist encourages us to consider God's majesty and glory as expressed in "the moon and the stars," "the flocks and the herds," "the birds in the sky, the fish in the sea,"—indeed, all "the work of [his] fingers" (Psalm 8:3, 7-8). We should have a childlike sense of awe when it comes to all that God has done—and continues to do—for us, his beloved children.

Scripture teaches that whenever Moses spoke with the Lord, "he heard the voice speaking to him from between the two cherubim above the Ark's cover" (Numbers 7:89). Jewish tradition explains that the cherubim were child-faced angels, and that only from between them could God's voice be heard. From this we learn that if we want an intimate relationship with God, we, too, need to be childlike—full of awe and faith.

A Christian Reflection on the Faith of Children

In Mark 10, Jesus grows angry with his disciples for preventing children from coming to him for a blessing. He uses this occasion to teach that "the Kingdom of God belongs to those who are like these children. I tell you the truth, anyone who doesn't receive the Kingdom of God like a child will never enter it" (Mark 10:14-15). What does it mean to receive the Kingdom like a child? Though the passage does not make it explicit, Jesus surely means that we should receive the gospel humbly but with excitement.

BITTER OR BETTER?

"Don't call me Naomi," she responded. "Instead, call me Mara, for the Almighty has made life very bitter for me. I went away full, but the LORD has brought me home empty." ❖ RUTH 1:20-21

As the book of Ruth opens, we quickly discover Naomi's dire situation. Widowed and now without any sons to care for her, Naomi plans to return to her hometown of Bethlehem. Her daughters-in-law, Orpah and Ruth, want to accompany her, but after Naomi explains that there is no future for them there, Orpah returns to her family.

Ruth, however, proclaims, "Don't ask me to leave you and turn back. Wherever you go, I will go; wherever you live, I will live. Your people will be my people, and your God will be my God" (Ruth 1:16).

Apparently, Ruth had become acquainted with the God of Israel and had become a devoted follower. She was determined to live among his people. In Ruth's eyes, such a future was better than remaining in Moab with people who did not know the Lord.

Contrast Ruth's response to tragedy with Naomi's. Upon returning to Bethlehem, Naomi announces that her name is now Mara, which means "bitter" in Hebrew. As she tells everyone, "I went away full, but the LORD has brought me home empty" (Ruth 1:21).

Certainly, Naomi had experienced great hardship. As a widow, she had no means to care for herself, and her future looked bleak. However, Naomi overlooked the rich relationships she had in Ruth and in God. Her bitterness blinded her to the opportunities and resources that were still available to her.

God may allow hardship into our lives not to punish us but to test us. The book of Job expresses this beautifully: "Blessed is the one whom God corrects; so do not despise the discipline of the Almighty" (Job 5:17, NIV). The difficulties that God sends us are a lot like bad-tasting medicine; they may *taste* bitter, but they make us better.

When hardships come into our lives, as they surely will, either we can blame God or others (or even ourselves), or we can look for the opportunities to grow from those experiences.

A Christian Reflection on the Redemptive Side of Hardship

We can grow bitter like Naomi as we struggle with the hardships that God brings into our lives. The Bible, though, is clear. God's people do not escape the pain of a sinful world. The difference is that we can experience joy in the midst of suffering. We must understand that suffering can be redemptive. As James writes, "Dear brothers and sisters, when troubles come your way, consider it an opportunity for great joy. For you know that when your faith is tested, your endurance has a chance to grow. So let it grow, for when your endurance is fully developed, you will be perfect and complete, needing nothing" (James 1:2-4).

CHARACTER STUDY

[Boaz said,] "But I also know about everything you have done for your mother-in-law since the death of your husband. I have heard how you left your father and mother and your own land to live here among complete strangers. May the LORD, the God of Israel, under whose wings you have come to take refuge, reward you fully for what you have done." ✦ RUTH 2:11-12

It's evident from the Bible that others knew a lot about Ruth's character just by watching her. After arriving in Bethlehem, widowed and with no means of support, Ruth went out into the fields to pick up the leftover grain—a practice known as gleaning.

As Ruth was gleaning, the owner of the field, Boaz, noticed Ruth and asked the workers, "Who is that young woman?" The workers replied, "She is the young woman from Moab who came back with Naomi. She asked this morning if she could gather the grain behind the harvesters, and she's been hard at work ever since" (see Ruth 2:5-7).

Impressed, Boaz told Ruth that she could glean in his fields as long as she wanted. Then, he invited her to eat with the harvesters. Additionally, Boaz told his workers to drop even more grain for her to gather.

Ruth was overwhelmed and asked Boaz, "Why are you so kind to me? I'm just a foreigner." And Boaz said, "Yes, I know. But I have heard all about you—about how kind you have been to Naomi and how you left your country and family to be with her."

Ruth's character was obviously the talk of Bethlehem. Even though she was a stranger, people knew she was a kind woman—just by watching her actions.

Ruth's life exhibited admirable qualities. She was hardworking, loving, and faithful. She had gained a reputation for these qualities because she demonstrated them consistently.

In Ecclesiastes 7:1, King Solomon writes, "A good reputation is more valuable than costly perfume." A good name is better than all the money in the world because we are not here to make a living; we are here to make a life. Only our reputation will remain once we are gone.

What do our actions say about us? A good reputation is something we earn when we consistently live out the principles we believe in.

A Christian Reflection on Reputation

What are we known for as God's people? Before his death, Jesus prayed that his disciples then and in the future would be characterized by "perfect unity" (John 17:23): "I pray that they will all be one, just as you and I are one—as you are in me, Father, and I am in you. And may they be in us so that the world will believe you sent me" (John 17:21). This unity is achieved through our love for one another. "Just as I have loved you, you should love each other. Your love for one another will prove to the world that you are my disciples" (John 13:34-35). What does our reputation as the people of God say to the world?

THE MARK OF A HERO

[Boaz said,] "But while it's true that I am one of your family redeemers, there is another man who is more closely related to you than I am. . . . If he is willing to redeem you, very well. Let him marry you. But if he is not willing, then as surely as the LORD lives, I will redeem you myself!" ❖ RUTH 3:12-13

The great heroes of the Bible—men such as Abraham, Moses, Joshua, and David—accomplished great things for God. So it might be easy to overlook Boaz as a hero. After all, he didn't go to a foreign land, deliver people from enslavement, win great battles, or kill a giant.

Throughout the story of Ruth, however, Boaz quietly exhibits heroic qualities. He puts the needs of others before his own, and when faced with a difficult choice, Boaz makes the right one, not necessarily the easy one.

We see this demonstrated when Ruth approaches Boaz to be her kinsman-redeemer—a relative who volunteers to take responsibility for the extended family by marrying the widow in the event of a husband's death. The relative did not have to marry the widow. If he chose not to, the next nearest relative could take his place.

Boaz was a close relative, and it is clear that he was attracted to Ruth and agreeable to marrying her. But he was *not* the kinsman-redeemer. Unbeknownst to Naomi and Ruth, there was a closer relative who had to be given the option to marry Ruth first.

In seeking out that other relative, Boaz acted in Ruth's best interest. Above all else, he wanted to see Ruth provided for according to the Mosaic law—even if it meant that Ruth would marry someone else. Boaz put aside his personal feelings to do the right thing and, ultimately, bring honor to God.

The *Talmud* asks, "Who is a hero?" Is it the strongest person? The most powerful? The most famous? No. The *Talmud* answers, "He who conquers his own desires." The greatest accomplishment is to become a master over one's own self.

We often are faced with difficult decisions: choosing to do what is easiest and most expedient for *us*, or choosing to do what is right and follow God. Making the right choice is the mark of a real hero.

A Christian Reflection on Redemption

God used Boaz to redeem the lives of Ruth and Naomi by becoming their family redeemer according to the Mosaic law. During the period of the Hebrew Bible, the kinsman-redeemer was the one who came to the defense of family members during times of need to save them. The Gospels also present a story of redemption. In the New Testament, Jesus is the Redeemer who saves his people from sin and death. As Paul writes in Galatians, "Christ has rescued [the word has the legal sense of "redeemed"] us from the curse pronounced by the law" (Galatians 3:13).

A REVERSAL OF FORTUNE

The women of the town said to Naomi, "Praise the LORD, who has now provided a redeemer for your family! May this child be famous in Israel. May he restore your youth and care for you in your old age. For he is the son of your daughter-in-law who loves you and has been better to you than seven sons!" ❖ RUTH 4:14-15

The story of Ruth ends with her marriage to Boaz and blessings from Bethlehem's elders. The greatest joy, however, belonged to Naomi.

Not only was Naomi blessed by the marriage of her daughter-in-law Ruth to Boaz, who would now care for her, but God also continued to bless her with the birth of her grandson, Obed.

God had brought great blessings out of Naomi's tragedies. Whereas once she had asked the women of Bethlehem to call her Mara, meaning "bitter," now Naomi's life was enriched by a son-in-law and grandson. Moreover, Naomi was blessed with a daughter-in-law who loved her and who had been "better to [her] than seven sons," meaning an abundance of heirs.

Even when Naomi was bitter about her circumstances, she never failed to trust God. She showed this by returning to Bethlehem and her people, by bringing Ruth with her, and by recognizing God's provision for them in Boaz's field. Naomi did what she could to guide Ruth to find a husband, even though Ruth's marriage would change their relationship.

Through it all, God was at the center of Naomi's and Ruth's lives. Ruth came to know the God of Israel through Naomi. And Naomi allowed Ruth to witness an honest relationship with God, in all its ups and downs, through tragedy to gratitude, through bitterness to blessing.

Naomi's story reminds us of a great truth: God loves us even in the midst of extreme hardship. He is able to bless us, despite our difficult circumstances, as long as we continue to turn to him and trust his plan for us.

Years later, Naomi's descendant, King David, would write, "You have turned my mourning into joyful dancing" (Psalm 30:11). Like his ancestors, David recognized that everything can turn around for the better. By maintaining our faith, we can see this manifested in *our* lives too.

A Christian Reflection on Reversal of Fortune

The Bible is full of stories of surprising reversals of fortune. Joseph was a slave in Egypt, but God put him in a position of power in order to save the lives of his family, preserving Israel. David, a shepherd boy, became a mighty king. For Christians, the most dramatic reversal of fortune was Jesus, who "appeared in human form, . . . humbled himself in obedience to God and died a criminal's death on a cross. Therefore, God elevated him to the place of highest honor and gave him the name above all other names, that at the name of Jesus every knee should bow, . . . to the glory of God the Father" (Philippians 2:7-11).

THE BEST FOR LAST

Boaz took Ruth and she became his wife. When he made love to her, the LORD enabled her to conceive, and she gave birth to a son. ❖ RUTH 4:13, NIV

By the final chapter of the book of Ruth, Naomi and Ruth's situation has changed dramatically from one of hardship to one of abundant blessings.

Look at all the blessings God bestowed upon these two faithful widows: He provided them with sustenance. He provided them with a protector, in Boaz. He provided Ruth with a husband and legal standing within the community. He restored Naomi's name and erased her feelings of bitterness.

But God saved his best blessing for last: "The LORD enabled [Ruth] to conceive, and she gave birth to a son." This child was assurance for both Naomi and Ruth that they would never be without someone to care for them.

As if that weren't enough, God had one more blessing to bestow upon Ruth. Through her son, Obed, she was eternally grafted into the family line that would bless the world. Obed would have a son named Jesse, who would have a son named David. And from David's line would eventually come the Messiah.

Because of Ruth's faithfulness, God was able to use her life for a greater purpose than she could have ever imagined. Each choice that Ruth made with humility, love, and compassion led her into a life and legacy that she could not have foreseen.

King Solomon, also a descendant of Ruth's, wrote a song about a "woman of valor." In it he says, "She is clothed with strength and dignity, and she laughs without fear of the future" (Proverbs 31:25). The Sages explain that because this woman acts with strength and dignity, she can laugh without fear of the future. Ruth's greatest blessing may have come last; but as we know, she who laughs last, laughs best.

When we live faithfully before God, he will ultimately reward us with great blessings and imbue our lives with significance far beyond what we could ask or think.

A Christian Reflection on the Line of David

For Christians, the significance of Ruth's reversal of fortune is expressed by the genealogy that begins the Gospel of Matthew. Ruth is among the few women mentioned in this genealogy (see Matthew 1:5), which culminates when "Mary gave birth to Jesus, who is called the Messiah" (Matthew 1:16). Just as Ruth, a non-Jew, was grafted into the family line of David, Christians are similarly grafted into "God's special olive tree"—his people, Israel (see Romans 11:13-18).

Sabbath Reflections

What new truth about the life of Ruth did you learn from this week's devotions?

How has this truth affected your faith?

How will you apply this truth to your daily life?

Your Key Verse for the Week:

❖ OTHER REFLECTIONS

JUSTICE WILL BE SERVED

You have upheld my right and my cause, sitting enthroned as the righteous judge.
❖ PSALM 9:4, NIV

The Innocence Project is an organization dedicated to proving—through the science of DNA testing—the innocence of prisoners who have been wrongly convicted. Since the beginning of the project, hundreds of people have been exonerated of serious crimes.

That such a group exists underscores the fact that injustice is part of our human experience. At some time in our lives, we have all felt, to some extent, as if we've been treated unfairly.

David certainly was. Although he did nothing but advance King Saul's kingdom by securing victories on the battlefield, his success threatened Saul, who ordered David killed. For years, David was a fugitive.

David might have doubted God's promise that he would one day be king of Israel. He could have become angry about the situation. Certainly, David had opportunities to harm King Saul. But David never wavered in his faith in God. Nor did he ever take justice into his own hands.

Why? Part of the answer lies in Psalm 9:4, where David affirms that God has "upheld my right and my cause, sitting enthroned as the righteous judge." David trusted completely that God saw his good deeds and would bring justice.

In a later psalm, David criticizes anyone who would doubt God. He writes, "Think again, you fools! . . . Is he deaf—the one who made your ears? Is he blind—the one who formed your eyes?" (Psalm 94:8-9). God knows exactly what is happening. David adds, "God will turn the sins of evil people back on them" (Psalm 94:23). Justice will be served.

This is a good lesson to remember when we have been wronged and feel the sting of injustice. Rather than take revenge or allow feelings of hatred or pity to wash over us, we need to trust in God. Only then will we be able to experience his peace and be free from the worry of how others perceive us.

A Christian Reflection on God's Justice

Jesus famously said, "Love your enemies! Do good to those who hate you. Bless those who curse you. Pray for those who hurt you. If someone slaps you on one cheek, offer the other cheek also" (Luke 6:27-29). Jesus modeled this attitude when he prayed for those who were crucifying him. Paul later reinforced this teaching in his letter to the Romans: "Bless those who persecute you. Don't curse them; pray that God will bless them" (Romans 12:14). Noting that it is God who works ultimate justice on our behalf, Paul encourages us by saying, "Don't let evil conquer you, but conquer evil by doing good" (Romans 12:21).

FOR YOUR OWN GOOD

The LORD God said, "It is not good for the man to be alone. I will make a helper who is just right for him." ✦ GENESIS 2:18

In the Jewish faith, marriage is viewed as a sacred institution. That's because marriage was ordained by God from the very beginning.

In Genesis, God considers each act of creation as "good"—from the sea and sky, to the sun and moon, to the entire animal kingdom. It's all good. But when it comes to humans, God deems his creation "very good."

Yet, after God gives Adam a place to live and food to eat, God recognizes that something is *not* good: "It is not good for the man to be alone." So God creates woman as the best partner for man. And when Adam sees her, he totally agrees!

Marriage was given as a gift to Adam and Eve and to all their descendants. Marriage was not meant as an institution of convenience; it was ordained by God. Through marriage, we are able to fulfill our scriptural obligation to procreate and fill the earth. Marriage represents the biblical ideal for men and women—providing a source of love, intimacy, and companionship.

But, as we all recognize, strong and successful marriages are not easily achieved. One thing we can do to strengthen and protect our marriages is to include God as part of that bond. As Jewish literature suggests, God himself helps in the selection of mates and then dwells amid married couples who share a common devotion to him.

The Sages point out an interesting phenomenon regarding the Hebrew words for "man" and "woman." If we remove the letters of God's name from the two words, both words become the word *esh*, which means "fire." The Sages explain that when God is removed from a marriage relationship, the man and woman become like fire—in their fury and passion, they could potentially destroy each other.

If you have been given the gift of marriage, consider how you might strengthen and protect it by inviting God to be part of your union.

A Christian Reflection on the Goodness of Marriage

For some people, as Paul points out, remaining single allows them to "spend [their] time doing the Lord's work and thinking how to please him" (1 Corinthians 7:32). Marriage, though, is a gift from God, and the marriage relationship is used as a metaphor of the divine/human relationship (see Revelation 19:7-9). As such, the relationship must be nurtured, as husbands and wives are called to love and respect each other (see Ephesians 5:21-33). The author of Hebrews urges his readers to "give honor to marriage, and remain faithful to one another in marriage" (Hebrews 13:4).

THE SECRET TO A STRONG MARRIAGE

Who can find a virtuous and capable wife? She is more precious than rubies.
Her husband can trust her, and she will greatly enrich his life.
❖ PROVERBS 31:10-11

What makes one marriage succeed and another fail?

Certainly, viewing marriage as ordained by God and including him at the center of a marriage will strengthen those bonds. Another clue for a successful marriage can be found in the Hebrew word for marriage—*kiddushin*, meaning "sanctification." It comes from the root word *kadosh*, or "holy," which means "separateness." In the Jewish faith, men and women consecrate each other through marriage by setting themselves apart from all others.

To be holy, or set apart, is something God commanded his people to do when they left Egypt as former slaves. All the laws given to the people of Israel at Mount Sinai were designed to help them become a holy nation. Holiness was developed through the daily practices of sanctified living.

In a marriage, we express our "set apartness" for each other by acting with respect and consideration for the other's needs. In the Jewish faith, the husband has a biblical obligation not only to provide for his wife's physical needs—food, clothing, and intimacy—but also to respect her.

Another Jewish tradition that underscores this respect is the blessing the husband offers to his wife during each Sabbath meal. Reciting Proverbs 31, the husband extolls his wife's noble character. Imagine how a wife must feel when her husband praises her as "more precious than rubies," as someone whose words are wise, and as one who brings honor to the entire household.

Certainly, a marriage built on a foundation of honor and respect, acknowledged as being "set apart" from all other relationships, has a better chance of surviving the odds.

A Christian Reflection on Nurturing a Strong Marriage

In his letter to the Ephesians, Paul points to the relationship between Jesus and the church as a model for marriage. He begins by talking about *submission*, a word that many find distasteful. Truth be told, mutual submission is a key to marital happiness. First, while wives in particular are called to submit to their husbands (see Ephesians 5:22), it is within a framework in which both spouses "submit to one another out of reverence for Christ" (Ephesians 5:21). Second, submission is not blind obedience but an ordering of one's self-interest. In the words of Philippians 2:4, "Don't look out only for your own interests, but take an interest in others, too."

HOW TO "IMPRESS" YOUR CHILDREN

You must commit yourselves wholeheartedly to these commands that I am giving you today. Repeat them again and again to your children. Talk about them when you are at home and when you are on the road, when you are going to bed and when you are getting up. ❖ DEUTERONOMY 6:6-7

When it comes to rearing children, the Bible is clear that parents' primary duty is to teach their children God's commandments. Other translations render this command as "teach diligently" or "repeat to your children," or even "impress" upon them.

We are to teach our children when we get up, when we lie down, when we are walking on the road, when we are sitting down. Obviously, teaching our children about God's laws is a full-time endeavor.

How do we do this? The most effective way is by serving as role models of holiness for our children and creating a home atmosphere that is conducive to spirituality. We can be proactive in surrounding our children with the proper environment and eliminating ungodly influences wherever possible.

In addition, teaching our children about God should be life oriented. Formal religious education, even family devotional time, has its place, but often our children learn best within the context of everyday life.

Do you want your children to know what it means to be honest? Let them see you return a lost wallet. Want them to learn about compassion? Let them see you take groceries to an elderly neighbor.

Remember the story about Joseph and Potiphar's wife, who tried to ensnare him in sin? The Sages ask how Joseph was able to refrain from sinning. They answer that, when Joseph was about to succumb, he saw his father's face. When Joseph remembered how Jacob lived his life, he remembered how he should live his own.

As you make God a part of your everyday experience, your children will be "impressed" with how to follow and love God.

A Christian Reflection on Raising Children

When Peter preached the gospel, he urged his listeners to repent and be baptized in the name of Jesus. If they did, then they would receive the gift of the Holy Spirit. Further, "this promise is to you, and to your children" (Acts 2:39). Children need to be told about God and instructed to live in a way that pleases him. In 2 Corinthians 12:14, Paul states, "Children don't provide for their parents. Rather, parents provide for their children." That this is true in spiritual matters as well becomes clear in the book of Ephesians, where Paul says, "Bring them up in the training and instruction of the Lord" (Ephesians 6:4, NIV).

COMING OF AGE

Direct your children onto the right path, and when they are older, they will not leave it.
❖ PROVERBS 22:6

In the Jewish tradition, girls become adults at age twelve, boys at age thirteen. Through the *bar mitzvah* ceremony for boys and *bat mitzvah* for girls, Jewish sons and daughters are initiated into the faith community and become obligated to observe the commandments in the Bible.

Does this mean our young teenage children are fully adult, capable of making their way in the world? No, not at all.

It does mean, however, that our children are now full members of the congregation and responsible for their own behavior. It is a time when they affirm their commitment to follow God and obey his commandments.

For parents, it is a time when we need to step back and allow our children to become adults spiritually.

That doesn't mean our responsibility to guide our children has ended. Rather, it means introducing them to a lifetime of spiritual discovery and providing them with opportunities to express their own faith. It's a time to keep the doors of communication open and discuss issues of morality, faith, and God.

Proverbs 22:6 charges parents with the responsibility to place their kids on the right path. But if we translate the original Hebrew literally, the verse reads, "Direct your children onto *their* path." The Sages explain that we need to identify our children's unique character and encourage them to serve God accordingly.

As parents, we don't need to have all the answers. But as we address these issues and answer questions honestly, out of our experiences, we continue to teach our children about faith.

Unlike the early years, when we supervised every aspect of their growth, now we are more like coaches, helping our children along, suggesting ways they can strengthen their faith. We're the cheering section as well, supporting the unique paths that each of our children will take.

A Christian Reflection on Parenting Older Children

In one sense, we never stop being parents to our children. However, the nature of our relationship with them changes as they grow older and more independent. Be careful, though, not to "provoke your children to anger by the way you treat them" (Ephesians 6:4). This warning is appropriate no matter the age of the child. As our children make their own professions of faith, as they go off to college, as they get married, the nature of our spiritual relationship with them changes, but it never becomes unimportant. While respecting their maturity, we can still be a healthy influence in their lives.

A SIGN OF THE COVENANT

This is the covenant that you and your descendants must keep: Each male among you must be circumcised. ❖ GENESIS 17:10

Did you know that circumcision was the first commandment given by God to Abraham, the first Jew? In establishing the covenant with Abraham, God promised to make Abraham into a great nation. Abraham would be the father of not only one nation but of a "multitude of nations." God would give Abraham millions of descendants (see Genesis 17:1-6).

For his part, Abraham was required to follow the terms of the covenant, which included circumcision. So at age ninety-nine, Abraham was circumcised, as were all males in his household. It is a sign of the covenant that has become central to Judaism.

Circumcision was an act of total obedience. More than anything else, circumcision set apart God's people from their pagan neighbors. It was the sign of belonging to the covenantal people.

The act of circumcision itself does not make a person Jewish. Rather, it gives testimony that, through obedience of the parents, the child is now covenanted with all the children of Israel—past, present, and future—and with God. It is a sign that the Lord who called Abraham also calls us and bids us to accept the covenant for ourselves and for our children. It is a sign of the partnership between God and Israel.

At *Brit Milah* ceremonies, we give God the gift of our sons, and we give our sons the promise and hope of God. As Rabbi Shai Held, a noted lecturer and adult educator, writes, "Circumcisions are still painful to watch. But perhaps that is as it should be. If we succeed in raising our children to love what is good and just, and to pursue what is holy and of ultimate value, then we will undoubtedly see them hurt and disappointed time and again."

A Christian Reflection on Baptism

For Christians, baptism functions much like circumcision as a ritual of entering into a covenantal relationship with God. It is considered a sacrament, an outward sign of an inward act, in this case becoming a member of the covenant community. Christians disagree over when baptism should be administered—some believing that infants of believing parents should be baptized, while others assert that only adult believers should be baptized. In either case, however, like circumcision in Judaism, baptism does not make a person a Christian; though if a person has authentically entered into a relationship with God, it symbolizes the reality of a changed life and warns, like circumcision, against denying that relationship in the future.

Sabbath Reflections

What new truth about marriage or child-rearing did you learn from this week's devotions?

How has this truth affected your faith?

How will you apply this truth to your daily life?

Your Key Verse for the Week:

❖ OTHER REFLECTIONS

WHO GETS THE CREDIT?

You gave me victory over my accusers. You appointed me ruler over nations; people I don't even know now serve me. ❖ PSALM 18:43

David's life is truly a rags-to-riches story. From his humble beginnings as a lowly shepherd boy, David became a giant-slayer, an accomplished musician, a champion on the battlefield, and the anointed king of Israel.

But David's life was not without its struggles. In fact, he spent much of his adult life running from his enemies. Yet through it all, he ultimately triumphed.

At the time David wrote Psalm 18, his power had become legendary. Already he had defeated the Jebusites, the Philistines, the Arameans, the Edomites, and the Ammonites. His reputation on the battlefield was such that, "As soon as they hear of me, they submit; foreign nations cringe before me. They all lose their courage and come trembling from their strongholds" (Psalm 18:44-45). Apparently, all David needed to do was show up, and the battle was over!

Yet David never forgot the source of his victories. Throughout Psalm 18, David praises God for protecting him, for rescuing him, and for defeating his enemies. In verse 29, David writes, "In your strength I can crush an army; with my God I can scale any wall." Psalm 18 is David's victory song, but all the credit goes to God.

David knew why God had allowed him such success. It wasn't so that David could amass wealth, power, and fame for himself. David knew that God had done these things for him on behalf of God's children, Israel: "David realized that the LORD had confirmed him as king over Israel and had greatly blessed his kingdom for the sake of his people Israel" (1 Chronicles 14:2).

As we reflect on the victories and successes in our lives, remember David's victory song. Let us give God the credit and thanks for what he has done for us.

A Christian Reflection on Life's Battles

As Christians, we recognize that we are also fighting a battle, but ours is against spiritual forces. Paul writes, "We are not fighting against flesh-and-blood enemies, but against evil rulers and authorities of the unseen world" (Ephesians 6:12). Though invisible, these are quite formidable enemies. Paul reminds us that God has provided the weapons we need to engage these enemies, including "the belt of truth and the body armor of God's righteousness," "shoes" that are "the peace that comes from the Good News," "the shield of faith," "salvation as [a] helmet," and "the sword of the Spirit, which is the word of God" (Ephesians 6:14-17). With these God-given weapons, we can face life's hardships with full confidence in final victory.

THE "HAMANS" OF THIS WORLD

Haman approached King Xerxes and said, "There is a certain race of people scattered through all the provinces of your empire who keep themselves separate from everyone else. Their laws are different from those of any other people, and they refuse to obey the laws of the king. So it is not in the king's interest to let them live."
❖ ESTHER 3:8

The Jewish holiday of *Purim* celebrates the inspiring story of Queen Esther, who took a bold stand against injustice. Yet it is also a sobering account of evil, hate, and prejudice in this world, as represented by Haman, the Persian king's prime minister.

Haman was in the top echelon of leaders and was obviously one of the king's favorites. This allowed Haman to amass a huge amount of wealth and great influence. When Mordecai, a Jew, refused to bow to him, Haman sought to wipe out all the Jews.

So why did Haman want to destroy *all* the Jews because of one man's actions? The Bible tells us that Haman was an Amalekite, one of the ancient enemies of the Israelites. Therefore, Haman's hatred went beyond Mordecai to all the Jews. As the rabbis teach, Amalek represents all who embody evil, not just physical descendants such as Haman.

As second in command, Haman enjoyed his power and authority. The Jews, however, looked to God as their final authority, not to any man, and certainly not to Haman. Haman realized that the only way to fulfill his selfish desires was to kill those who disregarded his authority.

Haman is more than just a historical figure—he is as alive today as he was in biblical times. We feel Haman's presence when we read the news of terrorists who make murderous attacks on Jews and Jewish institutions around the world. We hear Haman in the hateful words of radical Muslim clerics who preach that Jews are the descendants of apes and pigs.

One of the messages of *Purim* is that, in a world with no shortage of "Hamans," we need more "Esthers" committed to standing humbly before God and seeking to defend his people.

A Christian Reflection on the "Hamans" of the World

The story of Esther informs us that evil will not be ultimately victorious, no matter how many "Hamans" are out there who want to destroy or undermine the people of God. While nations have a right, even a duty, to defend their citizens against violent attacks, the people of God have at their disposal not physical but spiritual weapons to combat evil in the world (see Ephesians 6:10-18). The apostle Paul writes, "Bless those who persecute you. . . . Pray that God will bless them. . . . Never take revenge. Leave that to the righteous anger of God" (Romans 12:14, 19).

TAKING A STAND

Esther sent this reply to Mordecai, "Go and gather together all the Jews of Susa and fast for me. Do not eat or drink for three days, night or day. My maids and I will do the same. And then, though it is against the law, I will go in to see the king. If I must die, I must die." ❖ ESTHER 4:15-16

We might have expected that Esther, as queen of Persia, had one of the most secure positions in the empire. But Queen Esther enjoyed the privileges that came with her position only as long as she obeyed the king. Her "security" teetered on a delicate balance that could easily tip if she made the wrong move.

So when her cousin Mordecai informed her of a plot to kill all the Jews in the empire and begged her to intervene on her people's behalf, Esther was faced with a difficult choice: either remain silent and hope the king would not discover her secret identity as a Jew; or risk death by appearing before the king, revealing her identity, and seeking relief for her people.

Mordecai's words surely must have guided her decision: "Don't think for a moment that because you're in the palace you will escape when all other Jews are killed. If you keep quiet at a time like this, deliverance and relief for the Jews will arise from some other place, but you and your relatives will die. Who knows if perhaps you were made queen for just such a time as this?" (Esther 4:13-14).

Esther must have realized that her security did not rest on her position or her possessions or even her husband, the king, but in God, though his name is not even mentioned in the book. Her decision was made, and as she told Mordecai, "If I must die, I must die."

God has placed each of us in a unique situation and position. We all have a choice to make: remain silent in the face of injustice and suffering to "save" our reputation; or, like Esther, take a stand, no matter what.

A Christian Reflection on Taking a Stand

After the resurrection and ascension of Jesus, the apostles shared their newfound faith in God in the face of considerable opposition. In fact, Peter and others were arrested and threatened with death. Rather than retreat from this persecution, Peter exclaimed, "We must obey God rather than any human authority" (Acts 5:29). Even today, many Christians around the world are willing to publicly declare their faith despite the risk of imprisonment, or even death. May God grant his people the courage to choose what is right in the face of any kind of threat.

A REASON TO CELEBRATE

[Mordecai] told them to celebrate these days with feasting and gladness and by giving gifts of food to each other and presents to the poor. This would commemorate a time when the Jews gained relief from their enemies, when their sorrow was turned into gladness and their mourning into joy. ❖ ESTHER 9:22

The great victory that Esther and Mordecai won in Persia many centuries ago is still celebrated today by Jews during the Festival of *Purim*. It commemorates a time when the Jews' "sorrow was turned into gladness and their mourning into joy."

Instead of losing their families and their lives, the Jews of Persia gathered together to celebrate God's deliverance. Instead of losing their property, they gave gifts to one another. But Mordecai realized that people tend to have short memories when it comes to God's faithfulness. Both Esther and Mordecai felt so strongly about the observance of *Purim* that they made it a decree and sent it throughout the empire with the king's full authority behind it. Mordecai became such an important figure in Persia that his story was recorded in the annals of King Xerxes.

The book of Esther was a tremendous encouragement to Jews who had returned to the land of Israel from foreign captivity and who also faced many obstacles and enemies. Imagine the inspiration, comfort, and strength they must have received from this thrilling story of God's watchful care over his people. We can take comfort as well, knowing that God is still watching over us and all his people today.

Purim is also a reminder of the importance of taking time to recall God's blessings and expressing praise and thanksgiving to him for these gifts. Celebrations of feasting, gladness, and gift-giving are important ways to remember God's specific acts.

When we pause in our daily routines to participate in such celebrations and retell these stories, we pass along the legacy of faith from one generation to the next. We instill in those who follow us a calling to become the "Esthers" and "Mordecais" of their generation.

A Christian Reflection on Celebrating Deliverance

The story of Esther is a source of encouragement to all God's people. The book is full of reversals—from certain destruction to rescue and judgment on God's enemies. No wonder *Purim* is such a joyful celebration. Christians, too, rejoice in the story of Esther. God's people and his promise continue on. Further, we see in the core events of our faith—the crucifixion and resurrection of Jesus—the same kind of reversal from death to life, which we celebrate in the Lord's Supper. In the stories of both Esther and Jesus, God had an amazing and unexpected plan of rescue and redemption, just when it seemed as if all were lost.

THE FINGERPRINTS OF GOD

The LORD keeps you from all harm and watches over your life. The LORD keeps watch over you as you come and go, both now and forever. ❖ PSALM 121:7-8

One of the most significant features of the book of Esther is what it lacks—the name of God. Nevertheless, the sovereign, concealed hand of God is seen in the unfolding dramatic story of deliverance from certain annihilation.

We see God's fingerprints all over this story—from the beginning, as Esther wins the "beauty contest" to replace Queen Vashti, to Mordecai's exposure of a plot to kill the king, to the king's inability to sleep one night, which led to the discovery that Mordecai had never been rewarded for his heroic deed. Coincidence after coincidence piles up until we must acknowledge the benevolent Master behind the scenes.

Certainly, God answered the prayers of the Jews as they fasted and prayed for Esther before she went before the king. Not only did King Xerxes welcome her into his presence, but he offered her whatever she wanted! Esther received an open invitation—not a death sentence.

Finally, we see God's hand as Haman justly receives the punishment he deserves: death on the same gallows he had built for Mordecai. When the time came for the decreed attack against the Jews, no one dared to harm them. It was a total victory for God's people.

The rabbis of the *Talmud* find God's concealed presence hinted at in the very name of Queen Esther. The rabbis explain that the name Esther is derived from the word *hester*, which means "hidden." Esther, therefore, represents the book of the hidden God.

The story of Esther reminds us that God—though often hidden—quietly works in the world. Although we may question certain circumstances in our lives, we must have faith that God is in control, working through both the pleasant and the difficult times so that we can serve him effectively.

A Christian Reflection on God's Hidden Providence

When life seems out of control, God can seem absent. From a human point of view, the situation in Persia at the time of Esther and Mordecai would seem to be such a time. But God was working behind the scenes. What else explains all the ironic reversals in the book? Even today, when we wonder where God is in the midst of our troubles, we should remember Esther's story and God's hidden providence to bring life out of death. As Paul reminds us, "God causes everything to work together for the good of those who love God and are called according to his purpose for them" (Romans 8:28).

LIVING WATER

My people have done two evil things: They have abandoned me—the fountain of living water. And they have dug for themselves cracked cisterns that can hold no water at all!
❖ JEREMIAH 2:13

Water featured significantly in the lives of the people during Bible times. Consequently, the symbol of water took on many meanings. Droughts were understood as God's punishment, and rainfall as God's favor. Yet water also signified death and destruction, as in the stories of the Flood and the drowning of the Egyptians in the Red Sea.

The rabbis teach us that water's goodness—like fire's—depends on how we use it. The rabbis also teach that the Bible is like water in that it bestows life on those who read and obey it; but it can also drown a person when used improperly. Yet the most abiding symbol of water is as the purifying and calming caress of the Almighty. In Psalm 23:2 we read, "He lets me rest in green meadows; he leads me beside peaceful streams."

In Jeremiah 2:13, this imagery is taken a step further as God refers to himself as living water, the only source of truth, spiritual refreshment, and renewal. God chastises his people for turning from him, the fountain of living water, and instead embracing empty, broken cisterns, by worshiping idols.

Whether we are in the middle of a spiritual drought or have turned to broken cisterns in misusing God's gifts to us—such as money, possessions, or our jobs—we must remember that the remedy is close at hand. God will refresh us, as he promises in Isaiah 41:17-18: "When the poor and needy search for water and there is none, and their tongues are parched from thirst, then I, the LORD, will answer them. . . . I will open up rivers for them on the high plateaus. I will give them fountains of water in the valleys. I will fill the desert with pools of water. Rivers fed by springs will flow across the parched ground."

A Christian Reflection on Finding Spiritual Refreshment

In reflecting on God as "living water," we are drawn to the story of the Samaritan woman at the well (see John 4:1-42). Jesus tells the woman, "If you only knew the gift God has for you and who you are speaking to, you would ask me, and I would give you living water" (John 4:10). Later, during the last day of the Festival of Shelters, Jesus proclaimed, "Anyone who believes in me may come and drink! For the Scriptures declare, 'Rivers of living water will flow from his heart'" (John 7:38).

Sabbath Reflections

What new truth about the Jewish celebration of Purim did you learn from this week's devotions?

How has this truth affected your faith?

How will you apply this truth to your daily life?

Your Key Verse for the Week:

✦ OTHER REFLECTIONS

PANIC ATTACK?

I trust in the LORD for protection. So why do you say to me, "Fly like a bird to the mountains for safety!" ❖ PSALM 11:1

In Psalm 11, David faces a personal crisis. Perhaps he wrote the psalm in reaction to being hunted down, either by King Saul or by his own son Absalom. Regardless, it appears that those around David advised him to run and hide from his enemies. And David's answer? "I trust in the LORD for protection. So why do you say to me, 'Fly like a bird to the mountains for safety!'"

In fact, David did flee from his enemies, for his own safety—but not in panic, not in fear. He never lost sight of who controlled his life. He never forgot who shaped his circumstances. And it was this faith in God that kept David from succumbing to the fear and panic that engulfed his advisors. While they could see only the alarming circumstances, David focused instead on the God whom he called "my shield" (Psalm 7:10) and "my rock and my fortress" (Psalm 31:3).

David was not immune to life's troubles and difficulties. Neither are we. But we can learn from David's life and be encouraged by his example. Rather than hit the panic button, we need to remember the examples of Abraham, Isaac, Jacob, and David. As the *Talmud* teaches us from Psalm 91:15 (NIV)—"He will call on me, and I will answer him; I will be with him in trouble"—God is not only with us in these moments, but it was in these moments that our forefathers found their deepest connection to him.

In good times and times of plenty, we can easily forget about God's presence; but in times of loss and suffering, if we turn to God, he serves as our last and only refuge. Family and friends can leave, but God stays by our side. When life's circumstances tempt you to hide, turn to God instead. Remember, as David did, that "the LORD is near to all who call on him, to all who call on him in truth" (Psalm 145:18, NIV). His line is always open.

A Christian Reflection on Anxiety

The world presents many challenges to our confidence. We may be anxious about our physical or mental safety or that of our loved ones. We may worry about finances or the security of our jobs. These are the times when we need to remember that "all who are led by the Spirit of God are children of God" (Romans 8:14). Paul reminds us that "you have not received a spirit that makes you fearful slaves. Instead, you received God's Spirit when he adopted you as his own children. Now we call him, 'Abba, Father'" (Romans 8:15). What an encouragement when we are anxious! Our Father is the God who created us and sustains all things.

OUR GOD OF ORDER

God is not a God of disorder but of peace—as in all the congregations of the Lord's people. ❖ 1 CORINTHIANS 14:33, NIV

Anyone reading the book of Leviticus—essentially a manual on sacrifices, offerings, and observing the feast days—cannot miss the fact that our God is a God of order. In great detail, God instructs his people on how to worship him and how to live so that his holiness is reflected through them.

Later, even before the First Temple was built, King David began planning the administration and the structure of the worship service. In 1 Chronicles 23–26, David outlines the various duties of the Levites, assigning them as priests, musicians, officials, judges, and gatekeepers.

The Temple service was highly structured, not to hinder worship or God's Spirit, but rather to allow worshipers and members of the congregation the freedom to respond to God because *they* didn't have to think about all those details. Their worship was not hampered by disorganization.

This same sense of order is reflected today in the formal, structured prayers that are part of every Jewish worship service. These prayers are rooted in our faith heritage, essentially the same prayers that were used in worship during the times of Ezra and Nehemiah. Jesus, too, would have recited these prayers in his boyhood synagogue.

So when a Jew prays today, he recites the same prayers recited by Jews worldwide for centuries. These prayers connect us with God, our fellow Jews, our shared history, and our ancient culture. Though the melodies might differ from one synagogue to the next, Jews can attend prayer services in any city throughout the world and feel comfortable.

Rather than stifling spontaneity and freedom in worship, the established prayers and liturgies give us boundaries so that we may worship, obey, and honor our Creator effectively. Order brings glory to God so that we can fully experience the joy, peace, and freedom that come from being in his presence.

A Christian Reflection on Order and Spontaneity in Worship

The apostle Paul advocates order in our worship of God (1 Corinthians 11). Of course, preserving order does not remove spontaneity and emotional expression in worship. Think of David dancing in front of the Ark of the Covenant, expressing his joy that this potent symbol of God's presence had returned to Jerusalem (see 2 Samuel 6:16-23). David's dance was a God-focused celebration of joy. The psalmist often urges his hearers to worship God with singing, dancing, or clapping. These imperatives in the book of Psalms encourage us to an enthusiastic and participatory, but orderly, worship of God.

MAKING AN IMPACT

*Instruct the wise, and they will be even wiser. Teach the righteous,
and they will learn even more.* ❖ PROVERBS 9:9

How can we affect someone's life in a way that would make a real difference? One way that the Bible talks about is by *instruction*—teaching the pathway of wisdom and righteous living.

The book of Proverbs was written to guide its readers toward wise, godly living and away from the pitfalls of unwise, ungodly behavior. Indeed, the short, pithy writings of this book were to help the Israelites understand how faith in God and his Word should affect their daily lives.

Another way we can influence others is by equipping them with the proper tools to help them in their endeavors. For example, although God chose Solomon rather than King David to build his Temple, David did all he could to help his son accomplish this task. He gathered all the materials; he assigned tasks to the various workers; he laid the groundwork for the administration of the Temple. Through his many victories on the battlefield, David even ensured that Israel would be at peace with its neighbors so that Solomon could concentrate solely on building God's Temple.

The Fellowship, through its scholarship program, instructs and equips immigrants to Israel and underprivileged former Israeli combat soldiers. The program, appropriately called IMPACT Scholarships, provides these young men and women with funds to pay for their education after they have served Israel. In doing so, we are not only helping to instruct these young people but also equipping them with the means to study, thereby removing their financial burden and worry.

It truly is a blessing to help these young men and women who have served in the Israeli military and who now want to give back and make a contribution to Israel's future.

A Christian Reflection on the Importance of Teaching

Teachers pass on their wisdom to others. In Romans, Paul warns that if no one teaches the gospel, no one will believe: "How can they believe in [the Lord] if they have never heard about him? And how can they hear about him unless someone tells them?" (Romans 10:14). Mature Christians should pursue opportunities to teach others who are younger in the faith. But with this task comes great responsibility to seek the wisdom that comes from above (see James 3:17). Such teaching will surely have an impact on others' lives.

AN ABUNDANCE OF BLESSINGS

Taste and see that the LORD *is good. Oh, the joys of those who take refuge in him!*
✦ PSALM 34:8

One of Jesus' most beloved teachings is known as the Sermon on the Mount, or the Beatitudes, from the Latin word for "blessings." These verses, found in the books of Matthew and Luke, describe how to receive the blessings of God—to be poor in spirit, to mourn, to be meek, to hunger and thirst for justice, to be merciful, to be pure in heart, to be a peacemaker.

But did you know that these values are as much a part of the Jewish tradition? In fact, the Hebrew Bible expresses many of these same ideals. We read in Isaiah 57:15: "I live in the high and holy place with those whose spirits are contrite and humble." *Blessed are the poor in spirit!* Or we find in Psalm 37:11: "The lowly will possess the land and will live in peace and prosperity." *Blessed are the meek!*

Furthermore, the rabbis write, "Such is the way of Bible study: Bread with salt you shall eat, water in small measure you shall drink, and upon the ground you shall sleep to toil in the Bible." Though this is not a commandment to live ascetic lives, the rabbis understand that we must be willing to sacrifice our most basic needs to our devotion to God. In the potential to sacrifice for God lies the root of our blessings.

Both Christian and Jewish traditions emphasize the need to humble ourselves as a condition to the blessings of abundance. In our willingness to give up our most prized possessions to the service of the Almighty, God responds with a surplus of reward. As we take that first step to follow him, we will experience all the good he plans for us. Or as the psalmist writes, "Taste and see that the LORD is good."

A Christian Reflection on Jesus and the Hebrew Bible

Jesus fully embraced the Scriptures, so it is surprising that some Christians read the Sermon on the Mount as if Jesus were saying something radically new. Perhaps this idea arises from the times when Jesus prefaced a teaching by saying, "You have heard it said," thinking that Jesus was contrasting his teaching with that of the Old Testament. However, a closer look at these teachings shows that he is not rejecting the Old Testament teaching but reaffirming—or perhaps even *intensifying*—that teaching. Rabbi Eckstein has appropriately reminded us that the profound teaching of the Sermon on the Mount finds roots deep in the Hebrew Bible, and this should encourage Christians to study the Old Testament.

THE POWER OF STORY

*O my people, listen to my instructions. Open your ears to what I am saying, for I will
speak to you in a parable. I will teach you hidden lessons from our past—stories we have
heard and known, stories our ancestors handed down to us.*
❖ PSALM 78:1-3

When God sent Nathan to confront David about his sin with Bathsheba, Nathan
wisely chose to tell a story about a rich man who, though he lacked for nothing, stole
a poor neighbor's only sheep to provide a feast for a guest.

Upon hearing the story, David declared that any man who would do such a thing
deserved death and must repay quadruple what he had stolen. After David passed
this harsh judgment on himself, Nathan dropped the bombshell: "You are that man!"
(2 Samuel 12:7).

Stories help us see ourselves more clearly. The ancient Jewish teachers understood
this and used stories called parables, or *midrashim*, to teach important faith lessons.
Jesus, educated in the local synagogue, was trained in this method and often used
stories in his teachings.

The *midrashim* served many purposes. The rabbis understood that a story could
often instruct more powerfully than a direct lesson. They used these stories to fill
in gaps in the stories of the Bible in ways that would provide moral lessons. Often,
they used explanations that were rooted in examples from their contemporary times,
thereby making the Bible eternally relevant.

When Jesus told the parable of the good Samaritan—about a man robbed, beaten,
and left to die alongside a desolate road—his listeners knew exactly what he was
describing. They could imagine themselves in a similar predicament. From that parable, they understood what it meant to love their neighbor—and, in obeying that command, to love God.

When we come to God's Word, we need to put ourselves into the story and ask
what lesson God has for us to learn. That's the true power of story.

A Christian Reflection on the Power of Story

Christian theology often speaks of Jesus as prophet, priest, and king. To that list we
can add sage. In the Hebrew Bible, God spoke through wise teachers (Sages) who
taught using proverbs. Interestingly, when the Hebrew Bible was translated into
Greek, the word *parabole* (from which we get our English word *parable*) was chosen to
render the word *proverb* (*mashal*). Jesus used parables as his main teaching tool, not only
to teach us how to obey and love God but also to reveal the nature of God's Kingdom.
According to Paul, the people were amazed with Jesus' teaching because "in him lie
hidden all the treasures of wisdom and knowledge" (Colossians 2:3).

GOD'S BATTLE PLAN

The LORD said to Gideon, "You have too many warriors with you. If I let all of you fight the Midianites, the Israelites will boast to me that they saved themselves by their own strength." ✤ JUDGES 7:2

When faced with a difficult challenge, it helps to have a plan. When God called Gideon to rescue the Israelites from the massive armies of Midian and Amalek, Gideon planned as a veteran general. First, he summoned troops; then he sent messengers to other tribes to garner warriors for battle. When thirty-two thousand men answered the call, Gideon developed a battle plan with this number in mind.

But God envisioned a different plan, which didn't include thirty-two thousand men. In fact, by the time God finished winnowing out those not fit for this battle, he left Gideon with only three hundred men to face an army the Bible describes as "a swarm of locusts" (Judges 7:12).

Facing such overwhelming odds, Gideon was understandably afraid. But God sent Gideon into the enemy's camp, where he overheard a conversation that provided courage for battle (see Judges 7:9-15). Trusting in God's plan, Gideon and his three hundred men marched against the enemy, armed with only torches, horns, and jars. In the end, Gideon's army stood by as God threw the enemy into such panic and confusion that they began to fight one another.

Certainly, that was *not* the battle plan Gideon had in mind. But because of his trust in and obedience to God, Gideon and the Israelites completely routed the enemy.

Yet the rabbis also teach us not to rely on miracles. God demands that we do the most we can, given our circumstances. Only when we try our best will God intervene. Only after Gideon took the most practical route did God act in a miraculous way.

Though we must rely on the grace and goodness of the Almighty, God also seeks our independent effort. Take your challenges and problems to him, and ask for his guidance and his wisdom. But remember that God gives us the strength to strive with him, not just depend on him.

A Christian Reflection on Planning

Planning is often an important key to success, but only if the plans are held tentatively, subject to God's approval. In the words of the sage, "Commit your actions to the LORD, and your plans will succeed" (Proverbs 16:3). Likewise, James chastises people who make definite plans that don't rely on God's wisdom: "How do you know what your life will be like tomorrow?" (James 4:14). James says that we ought to say, "If the Lord wants us to, we will live and do this or that" (James 4:15). We need to live conscious of the fact that we are not the masters of our own destiny, but rather we are in the hands of a God who loves us.

Sabbath Reflections

What new truth about the Jewish roots of the Beatitudes and parables did you learn from this week's devotions?

How has this truth affected your faith?

How will you apply this truth to your daily life?

Your Key Verse for the Week:

❖ OTHER REFLECTIONS

A RARE FIND

The LORD's promises are pure, like silver refined in a furnace,
purified seven times over. ❖ PSALM 12:6

Diamonds, although expensive, are not rare. In fact, worldwide there are more than sixty million diamonds produced annually. But colored diamonds—called fancies—are quite rare, and red fancies are the rarest of all. Worldwide there are only thirty-five red diamonds, with an asking price between $800,000 and $1.9 million—per carat!

What makes red diamonds more valuable, and more expensive, is obviously their scarcity. We appreciate items that aren't easily found. The rarer an object, the more its value rises in our eyes.

So when David writes that God's promises are "pure, like silver refined in a furnace, purified seven times over," he means that God's words are extremely valuable. What makes them so valuable is that truth and sincerity were as hard to find in David's court as they are in our society today.

David would certainly know about that. As king, he undoubtedly encountered people on a daily basis who used lies, flattery, and deception to get what they wanted from him. In fact, he complained of neighbors lying to one another, speaking with flattering lips and insincere hearts (see Psalm 12:2).

Sound familiar? We all encounter lies, flattery, and people out to deceive us. And if we are honest with ourselves, we will admit to using some of those same tactics to get what we want.

But David also knew that the antidote for falsehood is relying on God's Word. God is, was, and always will be completely trustworthy, completely true, and valuable above all else. The *Talmud* tells us that God's stamp—his signature—is truth. In a world of lies, in a world of ambiguity and uncertainty, we take heart in our most treasured possession: the Bible, a book full of God's truth.

A Christian Reflection on the Certainty and Power of God's Word

Though we can't always count on people's words to be reliable, we can always be sure that God's Word is true and trustworthy. God can't lie and won't mislead us. Even more, God's Word is effective and powerful, according to the author of Hebrews: "The word of God is alive and powerful. It is sharper than the sharpest two-edged sword, cutting between soul and spirit, between joint and marrow. It exposes our innermost thoughts and desires" (Hebrews 4:12). In other words, it can reveal to us who we really are and transform our lives.

THE JOURNEY HOME

*On that day I will gather you together and bring you home again. I will give you
a good name, a name of distinction, among all the nations of the earth, as I restore
your fortunes before their very eyes. I, the LORD, have spoken!*

❖ ZEPHANIAH 3:20

A visit to the Holy Land differs from any other trip. You walk in the footsteps of the
patriarchs, prophets, apostles, and Jesus himself. Each place is imbued with significance and holiness. Atop Mount Carmel, you imagine the prophets of Baal urging
their god to light the altar. Walking among the ruins at Capernaum, you envision the
crowds clamoring after Jesus to heal and preach. The Bible stories come alive.

Even enjoying the local dish, St. Peter's fish, at a restaurant along the Sea of Galilee
evokes the dish's namesake, who, on Jesus' instructions, caught such a fish and found a
coin in its mouth—enough to pay the owed taxes! (See Matthew 17:24-27.) Eating this
dish anywhere else is just another fish fry.

Many Christians who visit Israel have a love for her already. But even those who
are just "along for the ride" can't help but be swept up in emotion as they catch their
first glimpse of the Holy City, or as they walk around the area near the Southern
Wall and hear the tour guide say, "Jesus, in all likelihood, walked on these very steps."
I believe that few who make the journey return unchanged.

It is a joy, an honor, and a God-given privilege to see a group in awe as they walk in
the footsteps of the Bible, to see the tears of joy in their eyes. Throughout history, the
rabbis have exuded constant love for the waters, the countryside, and even the dirt of
the land of Israel. They explain that every four steps taken in the land count as a good
deed. The *Talmud* abounds with stories of rabbis who, as they entered the land of Israel,
bent down to kiss the hallowed ground.

My prayer is that all people of faith will be able to make the journey to Israel and
experience God's holy place for themselves.

A Christian Reflection on Seeing the Holy Land

I can honestly say that nothing deepened my understanding of the Bible and strengthened my confidence in it more than a visit to Israel. I made my first trip there in 1976.
Afterward, I could picture with a new level of accuracy events such as David's confrontation with Goliath "near the valley of Elah" (1 Samuel 17:2) or the Temple setting
in Jerusalem. After visiting the beautiful oasis called Ein Gedi near the barren Dead
Sea, I have a new appreciation of the compliment the woman gives the man when she
says, "He is like a bouquet of sweet henna blossoms from the vineyards of En-gedi"
(Song of Solomon 1:14). I hope and pray that everyone gets the opportunity to visit
the place where Judaism and Christianity were born.

MY HIDING PLACE

You are my hiding place; you protect me from trouble. You surround me
with songs of victory. ❖ PSALM 32:7

For many years, David roamed the rocky hills outside Ein Gedi and hid in numerous caves from the murderous intent of King Saul. This was his hiding place, where he felt safe and protected—at least until he had to move on to the next haven. Although the caves and hills provided a physical place to hide, David knew their safety was only temporary.

Ultimately, David knew that his true hiding place, the place where he would find complete protection and safekeeping, was with God. In Psalm 32:7 he writes, "You are my hiding place; you protect me from trouble. You surround me with songs of victory."

It is a theme repeated throughout the Psalms: "Keep me safe, O God, for I have come to you for refuge" (Psalm 16:1); "He will conceal me there when troubles come; he will hide me in his sanctuary. He will place me out of reach on a high rock" (Psalm 27:5); and, "God is our refuge and strength, always ready to help in times of trouble" (Psalm 46:1).

David knew that the true source of his security was God. Wherever David was, he was confident that God would provide him with comfort and the courage to withstand whatever trials or circumstances he faced.

In our own difficulties, in those moments when we wish we could hide from our troubles, we can be encouraged that God offers us the same place of protection, the same shelter, and the same help as he did for David. As we trust in him and come to him with our troubles, God promises to be our safe hiding place as well.

A Christian Reflection on God's Protection

During the time that the New Testament was written, the early followers of Christ were often persecuted for their faith. In some parts of the world, violent persecution continues today. However, no matter where we live, difficulties—even tragedies— come into our lives. People of faith do not escape such troubles. Still, the author of Hebrews reminds us that God does not break his promises to his people. Thus, "we who have fled to him for refuge can have great confidence as we hold to the hope that lies before us" (Hebrews 6:18).

GOD'S UNCHANGING WORD

Your eternal word, O LORD, stands firm in heaven. ❖ PSALM 119:89

In 1947, when a young bedouin shepherd followed an errant goat into a cave in the hill country around the Dead Sea, he did more than recover his lost animal—he unearthed a treasure that would substantiate the accuracy of the Hebrew Bible, or what Christians call the Old Testament.

The Dead Sea Scrolls are a collection of more than nine hundred pieces of parchment upon which manuscripts from every book of the Hebrew Bible, except for Esther, were recorded and preserved. The most complete of these scrolls is the entire book of Isaiah.

Until this discovery, the Hebrew Bible in use today was translated from what is called the Masoretic Text. The Masoretes were Jewish scholars who, between AD 500 and AD 950, gave the Hebrew Bible its form. With the discovery of the scrolls, scholars now had in their hands manuscripts that predated the Masoretic Text by one thousand years!

The present-day Hebrew Bible had long been criticized for being corrupted over time and not well preserved. Now here was an opportunity to see how well the Dead Sea documents would match up with the Masoretic Text. The book of Isaiah was used as the test. After years of careful study, the results were nothing less than amazing: Scholars found that the two texts were practically identical. Most variations were minor spelling differences, and none affected the meaning of the text.

The discovery of the scrolls affirmed for students of the Bible everywhere that "your eternal word, O LORD, stands firm in heaven."

We can come to the Bible assured of God's promises, assured that what the patriarchs and the prophets recorded is as true today as it was then. In the words of the prophet Isaiah, "The grass withers and the flowers fade, but the word of our God stands forever" (Isaiah 40:8).

A Christian Reflection on Our Confidence in God's Word

As Rabbi Eckstein points out, the Dead Sea Scrolls confirmed the accuracy of the texts that we use in our study and translation. We can thank God for the Masoretes, and the scribes who preceded them, for their very careful transmission of his Word. They, after all, recognized that they were dealing with God's revelation to his people, and they acted with requisite care—even counting all the letters of a book to make sure none were missing or added! We should approach our reading and study of God's Word with the same devotion and care.

ROOTS OF OUR FAITH

You Gentiles, who were branches from a wild olive tree, have been grafted in. So now you also receive the blessing God has promised Abraham and his children, sharing in the rich nourishment from the root of God's special olive tree. But you must not brag about being grafted in to replace the branches that were broken off. You are just a branch, not the root. ❖ ROMANS 11:17-18

Several years ago a book was published covering a subject near and dear to my heart: bridge-building between Christians and Jews. *The Sistine Secrets: Michelangelo's Forbidden Messages in the Heart of the Vatican* shows how, five hundred years ago, the renowned artist embedded images that appeal for Jewish-Christian understanding in one of his greatest works: the ceiling of the Sistine Chapel in the Vatican.

In 1508, Pope Julius II commissioned Michelangelo to paint the crumbling chapel ceiling in a very simple fashion—a demeaning job for such a great artist, particularly one who considered himself primarily a sculptor. Instead, Michelangelo threw his full creative energies into the task. The result is a masterpiece adorned primarily with images of heroes and heroines of the Hebrew Bible, full of subtle reminders of the Jewish roots of the Christian faith—a stunning visual appeal for a revolutionary change in the relationship between Christians and Jews.

Indeed, the apostle Paul, in his letter to the emerging church in Rome, makes it very clear that Gentiles—"branches from a wild olive tree"—have been grafted into Abraham's tree. Therefore, "now you also receive the blessing God has promised Abraham and his children. . . . But you must not brag about being grafted in to replace the branches that were broken off. You are just a branch, not the root" (Romans 11:17-18).

Only when we begin to understand each other—what it means to be a Christian, what it means to be a Jew—can we truly love each other as God intends. God calls us to lead lives of *imitatio Dei*, imitating him by loving people. Though it is often difficult to love *real* people, that is what God calls each one of us to do.

A Christian Reflection on Jewish-Christian Relationships

Christians have much to ask for forgiveness for over the centuries in terms of our relationship with our Jewish friends. We must move forward in love to bridge the gap between our two communities. Of course, it would be mere illusion to suggest that Jews and Christians are in total agreement with each other, and it would be wrong to repress discussion of those differences. Even so, these discussions should be carried out with deep respect, mindful that we have so much in common.

HEAL OUR LAND

If my people who are called by my name will humble themselves and pray and seek my face and turn from their wicked ways, I will hear from heaven and will forgive their sins and restore their land. ❖ 2 CHRONICLES 7:14

At first glance, the geography of Israel does not lend itself naturally to agriculture. More than half the land is desert, and the climate and lack of water resources do not favor farming. Yet Israel is a major exporter of fresh produce and a world leader in agricultural technologies.

How did the people of Israel accomplish this? Since Jews began returning to Israel and settling there in the late nineteenth century, they worked hard to restore the land. They cleared rocky fields, constructed terraces for farming, drained swampland, refor-ested certain areas, and took steps to counteract soil erosion. As a result, the total area of land now under cultivation has increased from 408,000 acres to slightly more than one million acres since Israel became an independent state in 1948.

While the people of Israel were successful in restoring their land physically, 2 Chronicles 7:14 reminds us that there is also a need to restore our land spiritually. In this account, the people of Israel are summoned to Jerusalem for the dedication of the Temple. King Solomon prays, asking God to remember his promises to the people; to hear and forgive the people; and to protect the people from crime, war, and enemy attacks, and the land from famine and drought.

In verse 14, God replies, telling Solomon what is required for forgiveness for the people and for healing of the land. The people must (1) humble themselves before God; (2) pray for forgiveness; (3) continually seek God; and (4) turn from sinful behavior.

The same is true for us today. Whether we are dealing with individual sin or the sins of a group, or even a nation, God will forgive and bring healing to all who seek him earnestly in prayer and come humbly before him.

A Christian Reflection on Restoration

God is in the business of restoration, and this theme is certainly continued in the New Testament teachings. In his letter to the Romans, Paul writes, "Since our friend-ship with God was restored by the death of his Son while we were still his enemies, we will certainly be saved through the life of his Son" (Romans 5:10). Peter encour-aged the early church with these words: "In his kindness God called you to share in his eternal glory by means of Christ Jesus. So after you have suffered a little while, he will restore, support, and strengthen you, and he will place you on a firm foundation" (1 Peter 5:10).

Sabbath Reflections

What new truth about God's care for his land and his people did you learn from this week's devotions?

How has this truth affected your faith?

How will you apply this truth to your daily life?

Your Key Verse for the Week:

❖ OTHER REFLECTIONS

HOW LONG?

O Lord, how long will you forget me? Forever? How long will you look the other way? How long must I struggle with anguish in my soul, with sorrow in my heart every day? How long will my enemy have the upper hand? ❖ PSALM 13:1-2

Read aloud the first two verses from Psalm 13. Four times, King David cries out, "How long . . . ? How long . . . ? How long . . . ? How long . . . ?" Honestly, haven't we all had times when we cried out, "How long?"

Like David, we often feel impatient with God. *Why hasn't he acted yet? Has he even heard my prayer?* Though David claimed that God was slow to act, even in his lowest moments he affirmed his abiding trust in God.

We see David's wonderful affirmation at the end of his lament: "But I trust in your unfailing love. I will rejoice because you have rescued me. I will sing to the Lord because he is good to me" (Psalm 13:5-6). How could David's thoughts change so quickly?

The answer lies in David's steadfast faith in God, even at his lowest points. This came from a lifetime of trusting God, of taking every thought, care, anxiety, and thanksgiving to him. In turning outward to God, David didn't focus inward and allow self-pity or negativity to spiral out of control. Rather, he conversed with God about his feelings—and in doing so gained a new perspective on suffering.

For David, suffering became an opportunity to talk to God. But we are always encouraged to talk with God. One of the great rabbis of the 1800s, Rabbi Nachman of Breslov, encouraged his followers to converse with God even on the most mundane matters. He did so to remind them that God is always listening, regardless of the situation.

When we are prone to despair, when we are crying out, "How long?" we should remember David. Talk to God, and before long you will be singing praises to God because of his goodness to you. Whenever we turn to God in our despair, in that dialogue there are already hints of salvation.

A Christian Reflection on Divine Abandonment

More than a thousand years after David cried out to God, "How long?" his descendant Jesus experienced God's abandonment like no one ever had, as he hung on the cross. He articulated his distress using David's words from Psalm 22:1: "My God, my God, why have you abandoned me?" (Matthew 27:46). Even so, Jesus maintained his confidence in God to the end. According to Luke 23:46, his last words were, "Father, I entrust my spirit into your hands!" From both Jesus and David, we can learn to maintain our confidence in God in the midst of our struggles.

A DEAD END

The LORD will guide you continually, giving you water when you are dry and restoring your strength. You will be like a well-watered garden, like an ever-flowing spring.
❖ ISAIAH 58:11

The Dead Sea is one of Israel's most remarkable and most visited geological sites. Situated some thirteen hundred feet below sea level, it is the lowest point on Earth and also one of the saltiest places. Because of its harsh conditions, no animal or marine life can survive in its salty waters—hence, the name.

But do you know why the Dead Sea is so salty? It's a terminal lake with no outlet. Water from the Jordan River and its tributaries flows into the Dead Sea, bringing along all sorts of minerals, including salts. Because there is no outlet for the water, and because temperatures routinely soar over 100 degrees in that region, the water evaporates, leaving behind the dissolved minerals. As the minerals have accumulated and become concentrated in the water, they've made the Dead Sea uninhabitable for any type of life.

The Dead Sea can teach us an important life lesson. We may immerse ourselves in good biblical teaching that is truly enriching, but if we allow that knowledge to merely accumulate, without a practical outlet in our daily lives, we can become just like the Dead Sea—stagnant, brackish, and unable to sustain life.

The blessings that God has poured on us—whether in material wealth, talent, or wisdom—are not meant only for our own benefit. As God's Word says in Deuteronomy 15, we are not to be tightfisted but openhanded, giving freely. What flows into our lives through the grace and blessing of God needs to flow outward to those around us. That's what pleases and honors him.

The prophet Isaiah told the people of Israel that if they looked to the interests of others, their lives would be "like a well-watered garden, like an ever-flowing spring" (Isaiah 58:11).

And that's far better than a dead sea.

A Christian Reflection on Living Water

Jesus offered himself as "living water." To the Samaritan woman at the well, he said, "Anyone who drinks this water will soon become thirsty again. But those who drink the water I give will never be thirsty again. It becomes a fresh, bubbling spring within them, giving them eternal life" (John 4:13-14). Later, on the occasion of the Festival of Shelters, he said, "Anyone who is thirsty may come to me! Anyone who believes in me may come and drink! For the Scriptures declare, 'Rivers of living water will flow from his heart'" (John 7:37-38). People who are filled with living water will naturally want it to flow through them to others and will not allow those waters to grow stagnant.

RESTORING HOPE, REBUILDING LIVES

Some of you will rebuild the deserted ruins of your cities. Then you will be known as a rebuilder of walls and a restorer of homes. ❖ ISAIAH 58:12

I watched an elderly man wearing a tattered wool coat as he waited outside a food box distribution center in the former Soviet Union. The man wore the hard years of his life on his stooped shoulders. His eyes betrayed the hopelessness he felt. He shuffled his feet as he moved forward in line to receive a bowl of soup. I saw him again later, holding a box of food to take home, and I immediately noticed the twinkle in his eyes.

Hope had been restored to this man's life.

The people of Isaiah's day needed hope too. After warning the Israelites about God's impending judgment, Isaiah spoke words of comfort to the people. Isaiah looked forward to a day when the people of Israel would be restored to their former relationship with God. They would rebuild the ancient ruins of their cities. God would guide his people and supply their needs so that they would be able to restore the cities.

Hope would be renewed.

In Isaiah 58:6-12, the prophet explains that as God's people extend justice and mercy to the hungry and oppressed, God will bless them by bringing about the restoration of lives as well as of the ancient ruins. Today, we also have the opportunity to demonstrate mercy to those who need it, and in so doing, we help restore lives.

Wherever we are, we can be restorers of hope, rebuilders of lives. As we go through our days, we must consider the various ways we can offer hope and encouragement to those around us. Taking a moment to speak a word of affirmation to someone could begin to rebuild a life or instill hope.

A Christian Reflection on Encouraging Others

God's people should be agents of encouragement to those who are discouraged in life. Paul writes, "If your gift is to encourage others, be encouraging" (Romans 12:8). However, it will not do to say, "That's not my gift," because in Ephesians 4:29, Paul tells his readers, "Let everything you say be good and helpful, so that your words will be an encouragement to those who hear them." Of course, encouragement comes in many forms. Sometimes it is an uplifting word; other times it is a tangible gift, such as food for the hungry or money for the poor. When we encourage others, we imitate God, "who encourages those who are discouraged" (2 Corinthians 7:6).

TENT OF MEETING

*It was Moses' practice to take the Tent of Meeting and set it up some distance from
the camp. Everyone who wanted to make a request of the LORD would go to the Tent
of Meeting outside the camp. . . . Inside the Tent of Meeting, the LORD would speak
to Moses face to face, as one speaks to a friend.* ❖ EXODUS 33:7, 11

If you have ever seen photos of or visited the Western Wall in Jerusalem, you will have
noticed hundreds of men standing near the wall, praying with shawls draped over their
heads, enfolding their entire bodies.

This garment, known as a *talith*, is a prayer shawl. Observant Jews wear a *talith* at
morning prayer services, in obedience to God's command in Numbers 15:37-39, where
God instructs the people to attach blue tassels on the corners of their garments as
a physical reminder to obey his commandments. That garment became the prayer
shawl. Even today, we wrap ourselves in the prayer shawl to symbolize that our entire
being is devoted to fulfilling and following God's Word.

The word *talith* comes from two Hebrew words: *tal*, meaning "tent," and *ith*, meaning "little"—literally, "little tent." Interestingly, this is exactly how Moses approached
God while the people were encamped at the foot of Mount Sinai.

In Exodus 33, we discover how Moses set up a tent outside the camp where
he would go to meet with God. As he went out, the people stood in the entrances
of their own tents, watching, worshiping, and waiting to hear what God spoke
to Moses.

Later, that small "Tent of Meeting" Moses used was transformed into the large
movable tent of worship, the Tabernacle, where God's presence rested while the
people journeyed to the Promised Land. Since there were so many people in the
camp, not everyone could fit into the Tabernacle to meet with God. So the prayer
shawl became their personal prayer closet. Each man would pull the shawl up over
his head, forming a tent where he could worship God privately and intimately.

No matter our situation, we can envision being inside a "little tent" and meeting with God in prayer, just as Moses did. God will be there.

A Christian Reflection on Meeting with God

The Tent of Meeting and the Tabernacle represented God's presence on earth, and
Moses went to the tent to meet with God "face to face." The Gospel of John announces,
in reference to Jesus, that "the Word became human and made his home among us"
(John 1:14). A more literal rendition of "made his home" (from the Greek word *shenoo*) is
"pitched his tent" or "tabernacled" among us. The idea is that Jesus made God's presence
real among humanity. Now, because God fills us with his Spirit, we are "the temple of
the living God," and God "will live in [us] and walk among [us]" (2 Corinthians 6:16).

A CLOSE CALL

The LORD is close to all who call on him, yes, to all who call on him in truth.
❖ PSALM 145:18

As the people of Israel stood at the border of the Promised Land, Moses encouraged the Israelites to obey God's laws and commands. Doing so, he said, would cause the other nations surrounding them to marvel at their wisdom and understanding. Moses asked them, "What great nation has a god as near to them as the LORD our God is near to us whenever we call on him?" (Deuteronomy 4:7).

Prayer—the ability to talk to God and the assurance that he hears us—is one of the hallmarks of our faith. Prayer connects us to God. Through prayer, we draw near to the personal, infinite, loving God of Israel, the Almighty Father who hears our cries and cares for us.

Prayer uplifts us; it cleanses us. Prayer gives expression to our natural longing for what the Jewish mystics described as "union with the divine" and what Christians define as "a personal relationship with God."

For devout Jews, prayer is an integral part of everyday life. Though our prayers may take on many forms—asking for our needs, seeking forgiveness, offering thanksgiving or praise—two elements must always be present. First, true prayer always involves a time of looking inward, an element of personal introspection and self-assessment. The very term "to pray" in Hebrew (*lehitpallel*) is derived from a word that means "to judge oneself."

The second key element is a sincere heart. Devout Jews seek a right mind-set and a right heart before God when entering into prayer. In the words of the rabbis, "The All Merciful One desires the heart."

God will indeed hear us if we come before him in truth, in introspection, and with the right heart. Come now—he is near to you.

A Christian Reflection on Self-Assessment and Sincerity in Prayer

Jesus both taught and modeled prayer for his disciples. Perhaps the most famous lesson is recorded in the sixth chapter of Matthew. Jesus warns the disciples that they should not be "like the hypocrites who love to pray publicly on street corners . . . where everyone can see them" (Matthew 6:5). Jesus even gives them a model prayer, which we know as the Lord's Prayer (Matthew 6:9-13). Read this prayer aloud, and notice how it combines glorification of God, submission to his will for our lives, request for provision, and a healthy introspection that asks for forgiveness and help so that we do not fall into temptation.

IT'S HABIT-FORMING

Never stop praying. ❖ 1 THESSALONIANS 5:17

How often do you pray each day? Once a day? Twice? Three or more times, if you include grace before meals? How about one hundred prayers or more each day? For observant Jews, that's exactly how often we pray on a daily basis!

In biblical times, prayer was most certainly offered independently, as a spontaneous emotional outburst of thanks or a petition to God, such as Hannah's repeated, anguished prayers for a son in 1 Samuel. Generally, though, prayers in biblical times were offered at the Temple in conjunction with the animal and grain sacrifices.

When the Temple was destroyed and sacrificial worship ceased, prayers were substituted entirely for the sacrificial offerings. Subsequently, we Jews hold three daily prayer services—morning, afternoon, and evening—which correspond to the daily Temple sacrifices that they replaced.

This does not mean that Jews pray only in the synagogue or during the three formal worship services. Ideally, personal prayer occurs throughout the day. In fact, observant Jews usually recite at least one hundred mini-prayers or blessings in the course of each day.

For example, we recite blessings in the morning to give thanks for our eyesight, intelligence, and strength. We offer blessings before and after enjoying food and drink—even just a snack—and when we hear thunder or see lightning, comets, mountains, or rivers. Both good and bad news will elicit a blessing, as will wearing new clothes or purchasing a new home.

The idea is not about getting down on our knees or closing our eyes whenever we pray. Rather, it's about cultivating a prayerful attitude throughout the day. As we share our mundane thoughts and events with God, it solidifies our relationship with him, and our day's activities become sanctified, imbued with profound spiritual significance.

That's a habit worth forming.

A Christian Reflection on Constant Prayer

Today's verse, 1 Thessalonians 5:17, demonstrates that the New Testament also encourages constant prayer. Prayer is talking to God, and we should be in constant communication with our heavenly Father. At the end of his letter to the Ephesians, Paul encourages the church to "pray in the Spirit at all times and on every occasion. Stay alert and be persistent in your prayers for all believers everywhere" (Ephesians 6:18). Start by praying that God will give you a spirit of prayer in order to help you stay in close touch with him and receive guidance for how you should live your life.

Sabbath Reflections

What new truth about prayer and meeting with God did you learn from this week's devotions?

How has this truth affected your faith?

How will you apply this truth to your daily life?

Your Key Verse for the Week:

❖ OTHER REFLECTIONS

WHAT A FOOL (DIS)BELIEVES

Only fools say in their hearts, "There is no God." ❖ PSALM 14:1

We may think of a fool as a silly person who does juvenile, typically harmless things. But in the Bible a fool is a person who lacks sense, judgment, or understanding. And a fool's actions can result in serious consequences.

Throughout the book of Proverbs, fools are contrasted with the wise. We learn that fools (among other characteristics) lack common sense (10:21), are gullible (14:15), refuse wise advice (23:9), and repeat their foolish actions (26:11). Because of their foolishness, these people choose the wrong path (14:2). Their words cause them trouble and lead to fights (18:6-7). They receive no respect or honor (26:1).

But a fool's worst characteristic is that he or she denies the very existence of God. In Psalm 14:1, David writes, "Only fools say in their hearts, 'There is no God.'" David describes such a person as corrupt, someone whose actions are evil. This is not a person with a *mental* deficiency but a *moral* deficiency. In fact, the Hebrew words for fool in the Psalms denote one who is morally deficient.

Fools may say there is no God, in order to cover up their sinful ways or to continue living immorally. Perhaps they believe they can escape judgment by ignoring the Judge. They ignore the evidence that God exists, and they refuse to live by his rules and commands. Fools reject the only one who can truly help them.

As people of faith, we would never deny the existence of God, but we sometimes act like fools when we persist in living by our own rules—when we act as if God will look the other way when we sin, or when we rely on ourselves rather than on him. When we do act like fools, the good news is that God will forgive us and restore us if we confess our wayward behavior.

A Christian Reflection on Acting Like Fools

James echoes the warning in the Psalms that God's people can act like fools even when they believe that he exists: "You say you have faith, for you believe that there is one God. Good for you! Even the demons believe this, and they tremble in terror. How foolish! Can't you see that faith without good deeds is useless?" (James 2:19-20). Even the demons believe that God exists! But they keep living by their own standards, not God's. We need to believe *and* obey. When we fail, we must repent and turn to God for help and forgiveness.

THE RIGHT THING TO DO

[The Lord said,] "I have singled him out so that he will direct his sons and their families to keep the way of the LORD by doing what is right and just. Then I will do for Abraham all that I have promised." ❖ GENESIS 18:19

In Jewish homes, charity begins in the kitchen. The homes of most observant Jews have a charity box—or *tzedakah* box—in the kitchen as a physical reminder of our obligation to give to others. Throughout the week, parents and children drop coins in the box to help the less fortunate.

This custom of placing the charity box in such a prominent place in the home reinforces the Jewish concept of charity—that it should be practiced constantly and that it is more than just a good deed or act of generosity. It is the right thing to do.

The Hebrew word for charity, *tzedakah*, has a different connotation from the typical meaning of charity—that is, benevolence and generosity, or magnanimous acts by the wealthy and powerful for the benefit of the needy and poor. The Hebrew word also carries with it the idea of *righteousness, justice,* and *fairness.*

This idea of charity can be traced back to when God told Abraham that he had chosen him so that Abraham would "direct his sons and their families to keep the way of the LORD by doing what is right and just." Other translations say "doing righteousness and justice"—which is *tzedakah.*

Giving to the poor in Judaism is an obligation, a duty that can't be forsaken even by those in need themselves. According to Jewish law, we are required to give one-tenth of our income to the poor—a practice that many Christians also exercise.

Some Jewish Sages have suggested that *tzedakah* is the highest of all commandments—one that includes all the others. Indeed, the apostle Paul writes, "Now abideth faith, hope, charity, these three; but the greatest of these is charity" (1 Corinthians 13:13, KJV).

Consider ways that you can begin practicing charity in your home.

A Christian Reflection on Charity

Most modern translations of 1 Corinthians 13:13 conclude with the words "The greatest of these is love." But the word *charity,* from the King James Version, reminds us that love is not just an abstract concept; it is an *action.* If we love someone in need, we will do what we can to help that person. As the apostle John writes in his first epistle, "We know what real love is because Jesus gave up his life for us. . . . If someone has enough money to live well and sees a brother or sister in need but shows no compassion—how can God's love be in that person?" (1 John 3:16-17).

A GIVING HEART

Give generously to the poor, not grudgingly, for the LORD your God will bless you in everything you do. There will always be some in the land who are poor. That is why I am commanding you to share freely with the poor and with other Israelites in need.
✦ DEUTERONOMY 15:10-11

In Judaism, charity—or giving to others—is our duty and obligation. But when it comes to acts of charity, we acknowledge that there can be a difference in our heart attitude. In fact, Judaism identifies eight levels of charity, depending on *how* we give.

For example, at the very lowest level of charity is one who gives but gives begrudgingly. The next level is one who doesn't give enough but does so gladly and with a smile. Next is the person who gives to the poor *after* being asked, followed by someone who gives to the poor *before* being asked. Other levels of charity have to do with whether the recipient knows his or her benefactor, or whether the benefactor knows the recipient.

The highest form of charity in the Jewish tradition, however, is giving people in need the means of supporting themselves. This could mean endowing them with a loan or gift, entering into a partnership, or providing employment—basically equipping them to take care of themselves and their families.

This is the type of giving that The Fellowship has been able to do for needy Jews and others around the world through the generosity of our donors. I know from the letters we receive from our donors that this giving is done not only sacrificially but also willingly and lovingly. It is indeed the highest form of charity.

As Moses reminded the people, the poor will always be with us. It is up to each one of us to decide how we will respond. As God's Word commands us, we are to be openhanded when it comes to the less fortunate and give what we can in response to their needs.

A Christian Reflection on the Poor Always Being with Us

Jesus famously said, "You will always have the poor among you," in rebuking Judas for accusing Mary of squandering money that could have gone to the poor when she poured precious ointment on his feet and wiped it with her hair (see John 12:1-11). Far from demeaning generosity to the poor, Jesus assumed that his followers would normally be generous. Indeed, Jesus taught that only those who feed the hungry, give water to the thirsty, show hospitality to strangers, and clothe the naked will inherit the Kingdom (see Matthew 25:31-46).

THE POWER TO ACT

Do not withhold good from those who deserve it when it's in your power to help them.
If you can help your neighbor now, don't say, "Come back tomorrow, and then I'll
help you." ❖ PROVERBS 3:27-28

Ronald Dimaline from Ransom, Kentucky, has always had a heart for Israel and a
desire to bless the descendants of Abraham. Initially, he sent a gift to The Fellowship
to help one Jew emigrate to Israel via our On Wings of Eagles program.

But that wasn't enough for Mr. Dimaline. He began sending money each quarter,
from the proceeds of his business, to bring another person back to Israel. But, he said,
he still had "this burning in me" to do something more. That's when he met Sister
Emma, a woman who had devised a unique way of raising money for Wings. She took
an old box her grandfather had made for her, put it in her church, and challenged the
people to give one dollar a week to help persecuted Jews emigrate to Israel.

The idea hit home for Mr. Dimaline. He began making small boxes, calling them
"Abraham boxes," and placed them in churches around the country, asking people to
donate one dollar a week to help bring needy Jews home. From this, New Mount Zion
Ministries was born.

What a beautiful illustration of fulfilling Proverbs 3:27: "Do not withhold good from
those who deserve it when it's in your power to help them." Not only did Mr. Dimaline
act out of his own heart, but he also saw a way to get others involved in giving.

We are all called to respond in whatever way we can when we see a need. Maybe that
means volunteering at the local food pantry or opening your wallet to help a homeless
person on the street. It may mean helping out an elderly neighbor with grocery shopping
or other chores. Or it may mean, as it did for Mr. Dimaline, beginning a ministry to help
others.

A Christian Reflection on Not Withholding Good

Even donating a dollar a week brings enormous help to other people, and the more
God has blessed us, the more we should give to others. Hear the words of Paul to
Timothy: "Teach those who are rich in this world not to be proud and not to trust in
their money, which is so unreliable. . . . Tell them to use their money to do good. They
should be rich in good works and generous to those in need, always being ready to
share with others. By doing this they will be storing up their treasure as a good foundation for the future so that they may experience true life" (1 Timothy 6:17-19). In
response, we must ask, "What can I share with others?"

GOD'S HEART

Those who oppress the poor insult their Maker, but helping the poor honors him.
✧ PROVERBS 14:31

One of the blessings of leading an organization like The Fellowship is seeing firsthand the impact of our ministries. I meet people like Nina and her granddaughter Tanya from the former Soviet Union, whose lives have been greatly improved thanks to the generosity of our donors and supporters. I witness Jews from Ethiopia landing at Ben Gurion International Airport and stepping out onto Israeli soil—and into freedom— for the first time. I talk with countless orphans, elderly men and women, and families who have been helped with medicine, food, heat for the winter, and other necessities of life.

I see how hundreds of thousands of needy people, Jews and others, have been blessed—and I know that God is pleased. You see, as Proverbs 14:31 tells us, God has a special place in his heart for the poor. In the words of the psalmist, "He lifts the poor from the dust and the needy from the garbage dump. He sets them among princes, even the princes of his own people!" (Psalm 113:7-8).

God repeatedly insists that we use our resources generously to provide for those less fortunate. And these are not just suggestions—these are God's very commands. In Leviticus 23:22, God instructs the people to leave some of the grain behind for the poor when harvesting their fields. Isaiah 58 tells us that the true nature of a fast is to feed the hungry, clothe the naked, and provide shelter for the homeless.

Opportunities to help others are all around us. We just need to be aware of those needs and be willing to respond. And when we do, we know that our Father in heaven is pleased. "Blessed are those who help the poor" (Proverbs 14:21).

A Christian Reflection on Honoring God by Providing for the Poor

Jesus described the final judgment as a separation of the "sheep" and the "goats" (see Matthew 25:31-46). To the sheep, he announces that they will "inherit the Kingdom prepared for [them] from the creation of the world" (Matthew 25:34), but the goats will "go away into eternal punishment" (Matthew 25:46). What distinguishes the sheep from the goats? The sheep, Jesus says, fed him, gave him something to drink, clothed him, and cared for him when he was sick and in prison. When the sheep asked about these things, Jesus responded, "When you did it to one of the least of these my brothers and sisters, you were doing it to me!" (Matthew 25:40). The message is clear: When we provide for the poor, we honor our Lord.

SHINING YOUR LIGHT

Feed the hungry, and help those in trouble. Then your light will shine out
from the darkness, and the darkness around you will be as bright as noon.
❖ ISAIAH 58:10

From the very foundation of the nation of Israel, God instructed the people on caring for those less fortunate in their midst. The people were to use their tithe every third year for those who were needy, and they were to leave behind, as a source of food for the poor, any grain that dropped during the harvest.

Caring for the poor was more than just a government concern; it was an integral part of religious life. This is what God addresses in Isaiah 58. After chastising the people, through the prophet, for their "show" of righteousness, he tells them what true faith looks like—helping the poor, feeding the hungry, visiting the sick and impris-oned, clothing the naked, offering justice to the oppressed.

These instructions also come with a promise: "Feed the hungry, and help those in trouble. Then your light will shine out from the darkness, and the darkness around you will be as bright as noon" (Isaiah 58:10). How can we honor God? By serving and helping others.

Jewish tradition teaches that the formative moment in the life of Moses was when he noticed the suffering of the Hebrews "and he saw how hard they were forced to work" (Exodus 2:11). Moses paid attention and then took action—he killed an Egyptian who was unjustly beating a Hebrew man. Following Moses' example, a prominent rabbi once said, "The physical needs of another are the obligation of my spiritual life."

God counts on us to provide for the needy and to use what he has given us to help the less fortunate. In that way, we show our regard for God as creator of all people, share his goodness with others, and draw others to him.

How can we make a difference in someone's life today? What can we do to reach out to other people? A simple act of kindness or word of encouragement might help shine our light and bring honor to God.

A Christian Reflection on Helping Others

The Bible is clear that we should help those in need. It is also clear about the attitude with which we should give. We shouldn't give in order to receive the praise of people, but rather we should give out of selfless motives. In his Sermon on the Mount, Jesus teaches, "When you give to the needy, do not let your left hand know what your right hand is doing, so that your giving may be in secret. Then your Father, who sees what is done in secret, will reward you" (Matthew 6:3-4, NIV). I don't think this instruction means that we have to give gifts anonymously, but it does mean that our gifts should not be given for the purpose of gaining praise.

Sabbath Reflections

What new truth about giving did you learn from this week's devotions?

How has this truth affected your faith?

How will you apply this truth to your daily life?

Your Key Verse for the Week:

❖ OTHER REFLECTIONS

THIS HOLY SEASON

The LORD is my rock, my fortress, and my savior; my God is my rock, in whom I find protection. He is my shield, the power that saves me, and my place of safety.
❖ PSALM 18:2

The observance of *Pesach* (Passover) is rich in spiritual lessons for Jews and Christians alike. In fact, the spiritual roots of many aspects of Christian worship can be traced directly to the Jewish faith and the early history of Israel.

Such is the case with the term *Paschal lamb*, or "Lamb of God," which in the Christian tradition refers to Jesus. From the Jewish perspective, the term *Korban Pesach*, or "sacrifice of Passover," dates back to the first Exodus. The blood of a sacrificed lamb, smeared on the doorframes of each Jewish household, served as sign of deliverance from death. The lamb's blood was the only path to salvation—without it, the firstborn among the people would die, along with those of the Egyptians.

During the time of Temple worship, Jews obeyed God's command to remember the first Passover by sacrificing a lamb on that day. This lamb had to be male, one year old, and, most important, without blemish. Only then would it suffice to serve as the perfect Passover sacrifice (see Exodus 12:5).

Jesus, as an observant Jew, and his disciples were celebrating *Pesach* on the very night that he foretold his coming death. As he broke bread with his disciples, Jesus followed the same divine instructions that were given to Moses. Later, the apostle Paul wrote instructing the Corinthians to "keep the Festival" (that is, Passover or the Lord's Supper) with unleavened bread (1 Corinthians 5:8, NIV).

Indeed, the Christian observance of Easter calls to mind the story of the Jews' escape and deliverance from Egyptian bondage. Understanding the story of *Pesach* and the rich symbolism of the *Seder* meal gives a new depth to many of the worship traditions at Christian churches around the world.

A Christian Reflection on Recognizing Our Ancient Roots

Unfortunately, many Christians believe—or at least act as if—our religion began in the first century of the Common Era. They rarely read the Old Testament and don't understand that our beliefs and our practices find deep roots in Judaism. Rabbi Eckstein does us a great service by reminding us of our connections to the practices of the Jewish faith. Make a commitment today to read and study the portion of God's Word delivered *before* the coming of Christ. Otherwise, how can we understand New Testament teaching such as Paul's happy announcement that "Christ, our Passover Lamb, has been sacrificed for us" (1 Corinthians 5:7)?

A STORY OF REDEMPTION

The LORD told [Moses], "I have certainly seen the oppression of my people in Egypt.
I have heard their cries of distress because of their harsh slave drivers. Yes, I am aware
of their suffering. So I have come down to rescue them from the power of the Egyptians
and lead them out of Egypt into their own fertile and spacious land. It is a land flowing
with milk and honey." ❖ EXODUS 3:7-8

Pesach (Passover) commemorates the seminal event in Jewish history—the Exodus of the people of Israel from bondage in Egypt. It was at that particular juncture some 3,200 years ago that the national Jewish identity was shaped, and from this event, some of the most profound affirmations of the Jewish faith were drawn.

Primary among these is the notion that God is not some distant power, uninterested in his Creation. The story of *Pesach* affirms for us that God is present in human life, that he hears the cries of his people, and that he intervenes in human history to deliver his people from affliction and redeem them from oppression.

By retelling the story of the Exodus and symbolically reliving the events, we are meant to feel as if we ourselves were just delivered from Egyptian bondage. Judaism maintains that God's act of liberation is not a one-time-only event, but an ongoing and repeated one. In the words of the *Haggadah*, the text read during the *Seder* meal to retell the Exodus story, "God did not redeem our ancestors alone, but us, as well."

Today, many Christians celebrate Passover in their own way, motivated by a desire to reclaim the Jewish roots of their faith and Jesus' Jewish heritage. Certainly, the links between suffering and joy, or death and resurrection, are familiar to both faith traditions. Like the Jews, Christians affirm that darkness will be followed by light, oppression by redemption, and death by resurrection.

We all can reflect on the story of the Exodus, of a people brought from slavery into freedom because of a God who cared so deeply about them that he intervened in human history to deliver them.

A Christian Reflection on Our Passover Lamb

Like the Jews, Christians look back on the Exodus as evidence that God can—and does—save his people from the most formidable enemies. Indeed, it is not a stretch to say that the Exodus was the salvation event *par excellence* in the Hebrew Bible. Perhaps it is not surprising, then, that the Gospel writers highlight many connections between the Exodus and the ministry of Jesus. After passing through the water (during his baptism), Jesus experienced temptations for forty days and forty nights, which may symbolize Israel's forty years in the wilderness. It is no coincidence that Jesus' crucifixion took place on the eve of the Passover. In Paul's words, Jesus is "our Passover Lamb" (1 Corinthians 5:7).

ATTITUDE OF SERVITUDE (FOR *PESACH*)

*The L*ORD *said to Moses, "Go to Pharaoh and say to him, 'This is what the L*ORD, *the God of the Hebrews, says: "Let my people go, so that they may worship me."'"*
❖ EXODUS 9:1, NIV

"Let my people go" is probably the most famous line in the entire Exodus story. However, "let my people go" is only half of the line, and it represents only half of the story.

The verse continues, "so that they may worship me." God wanted the Israelites to be free . . . so they could serve him! So why is *Pesach* (Passover) celebrated as the holiday of *freedom* when the whole point of leaving Egypt was for the Israelites to become *slaves* again?

What is slavery? Slavery means living a life without choices. You are not the master of your own life. Someone else tells you what to do and when to do it. What is freedom? Freedom is the chance to choose your own life. You decide how you spend your time, your money, and your energy.

Now here's the key: A person can be physically free and yet live completely in bondage. Pharaohs come in all shapes and sizes. Slavery is still alive and well.

Every time you don't make a conscious decision, you experience slavery. The Exodus story is not just about a bunch of Jews in ancient Egypt. Every person experiences slavery in some form. Yet we can all experience redemption.

Here's how: No one can tell me what to do when I listen only to God. Nothing can force me to do anything when I do only what God tells me to do. And what does God tell us to do? He tells us to rise above money. He teaches us to transcend popular opinion. He asks us to become masters of our desires. Everything that we do in service to God puts *choice* back in our hands.

That, my friends, is why only a servant of God is truly free.

A Christian Reflection on Freedom

Paul informs us that "Christ has truly set us free" (Galatians 5:1). The context specifically speaks of freedom from the law and its condemnation. It's not that the law is bad; after all, it is God's law and expresses his will for how we live. Paul understands that no one can fully keep the law, and so he rejoices that Jesus stands in our place and removes the penalty of sin. Thus, God's people are free from guilt and death. However, this freedom is not to be exploited for selfish reasons. Paul tells us, "Use your freedom to serve one another in love" (Galatians 5:13). How can you use your freedom to serve others today?

TAKING THE PLUNGE

*Moses raised his hand over the sea, and the LORD opened up a path through the water
with a strong east wind. The wind blew all that night, turning the seabed into dry land.
So the people of Israel walked through the middle of the sea on dry ground, with walls
of water on each side!* ❖ EXODUS 14:21-22

We know the scene: After the children of Israel leave Egypt, Pharaoh changes his
mind and pursues the Israelites until they are cornered at the Red Sea. Moses
stretches his arms out to the sea and one of the greatest miracles of all time occurs.
The waters part! The Israelites cross safely on dry land.

Now rewind that scene and pause it before the parting of the Red Sea. Jewish
tradition teaches us a very powerful story about what occurred right before the
waters parted.

The story features Nahshon, from the tribe of Judah. The people were panicking.
Behind them was the Egyptian army. In front of them was the sea—the only barrier
between them and freedom. Egypt was warm and familiar. The sea was cold and
unknown. It was decision time.

The people stood paralyzed with fear. Should they return to Egypt, or should they
follow God into the sea? Nahshon alone takes the plunge. Literally. He steps into the
sea—but nothing happens. Undeterred, he continues up to his ankles, and then his
knees, but the sea does not split.

Nahshon continues onward. The sea covers his chest and approaches his mouth.
Finally, when the sea reaches Nahshon's nostrils, at the last second, it parts! The children of Israel witness the great miracle and follow after Nahshon just in the nick
of time.

Nahshon teaches us a powerful lesson about faith. There are times in our lives
when we have to choose between something new and unknown and something old
and familiar. The new opportunity seems like the better choice, yet there are no guarantees it will work out. The familiar option is clearly less than ideal, but we know
exactly what to expect. Do we take the plunge, or stay dry and safe on land?

Sometimes, like Nahshon, we need to take the first steps with courage and faith.

A Christian Reflection on Taking Another Sort of Plunge

In 1 Corinthians 10:1-2, Paul says that the Israelites "were guided by a cloud that
moved ahead of them, and all of them walked through the sea on dry ground. In the
cloud and in the sea, all of them were baptized as followers of Moses." The experience of crossing the sea appears as an initiation into Israel's becoming a nation.
Likewise, Jesus began his ministry with an initiation through water baptism. Clearly,
for Christians and Jews, baptism signifies initiation into community. Have you taken
the plunge?

OUR CREATOR AND SAVIOR

I am the LORD your God, who rescued you from the land of Egypt,
the place of your slavery. ❖ EXODUS 20:2

When God introduces himself to the world at large, by revealing himself at Sinai and handing down the Ten Commandments, he says: "I am the LORD your God, who rescued you from the land of Egypt, the place of your slavery."

What does God want us to know about him? Not just that he created the world. God wants humanity to know him as the one who took the nation of Israel out of Egypt.

The Lord performed amazing miracles when he freed the Israelites from Egyptian bondage. No one can argue with that. But doesn't parting the Red Sea pale in comparison with having created it in the first place?

Many years ago, I was discussing the existence of God with some teens. One girl raised her hand and said, "Rabbi, I don't believe in God. But I do believe in a creator." Huh?

It sounds ridiculous, but this girl was really saying that she believes that some infinite being created the universe, but is no longer involved in it. That's why, for her, there is no God. In her mind, thousands of years after creation, God has no idea that cars and computers have been invented, that nations are engaged in war, or that I had pizza for dinner last night. He did his job and moved on.

But God wants us to know this: "I'm still here! I always have been and always will be!"

This is why the Almighty wants to be known as the one who saved Israel. In other words, not only did he create the world, he runs it too! God hears our prayers, just as he heard the prayers of the Israelites. Just as he saved them, God will come through for us, too.

A Christian Reflection on Our Creator and Savior

The Gospel of John famously introduces Jesus in dramatic fashion: "In the beginning the Word already existed. The Word was with God, and the Word was God. He existed in the beginning with God. God created everything through him, and nothing was created except through him" (John 1:1-3). In other words, Jesus was integrally involved in creation. As John points out, God did not stay uninvolved with his Creation. Rather, "the Word became human and made his home among us" (John 1:14). Throughout the Gospels, we see God intimately involved in his Creation through his Son's life, death, and resurrection.

A MATZAH BY ANY OTHER NAME

Eat it with bread made without yeast. For seven days the bread you eat must be made without yeast, as when you escaped from Egypt in such a hurry. Eat this bread—the bread of suffering—so that as long as you live you will remember the day you departed from Egypt. ❖ DEUTERONOMY 16:3

For seven days out of every year, Jews around the world trade in their regular bread for the unleavened bread we call *matzah*. If you've ever tasted it, it's no wonder the Bible refers to it as "the bread of suffering." Tasteless and flimsy, *matzah* is a poor man's bread containing nothing but flour and water.

Curiously, *matzah* is also known as "the bread of freedom." *Matzah* was born out of the Exodus narrative, when the children of Israel were told to leave Egypt in such a hurry that their bread didn't have time to rise. What they ended up with is the *matzah* that we eat today in remembrance of their freedom from slavery.

How is it that the same item represents both suffering and redemption? One symbolizes our pain, the other our greatest pleasure. The discrepancy is reconciled by a third term for *matzah*. Jewish mysticism refers to *matzah* as "the bread of faith."

Pain and pleasure are not opposites. Rather, they are two sides of the same coin. The source of our greatest pain is often the source of our greatest pleasure. Take parenting, for example. Most parents will affirm that their children have given them the most grief and also the most joy in their lives. The key to joining the two is faith.

So, when my child is painfully stubborn, I have faith that he will turn out to be a very successful and persistent adult. Along those same lines, when we find ourselves in painful situations, we need to have faith that they are part of greater things yet to come.

Matzah reminds us that, no matter where we find ourselves on our journey—whether it's all uphill or we're enjoying a smooth ride down the other side—it's all part of the story of redemption.

A Christian Reflection on Opportunity in Our Troubles

How true it is that pain and pleasure are not opposites. James, the brother of Jesus, teaches that suffering should lead to joy. On what grounds does he believe this? His surprising argument goes like this: "Dear brothers and sisters, when troubles come your way, consider it an opportunity for great joy. For you know that when your faith is tested, your endurance has a chance to grow. So let it grow, for when your endurance is fully developed, you will be perfect and complete, needing nothing" (James 1:2-4). Suffering produces faith, and faith gives us the strength to endure suffering. And that leads to joy!

Sabbath Reflections

What new truth about the story of Pesach *(Passover) did you learn from this week's devotions?*

How has this truth affected your faith?

How will you apply this truth to your daily life?

Your Key Verse for the Week:

❖ OTHER REFLECTIONS

MY HERO

The godly people in the land are my true heroes! I take pleasure in them!
❖ PSALM 16:3

We live in a hero-worshiping culture. We're attracted to people who are the richest, most attractive, or most successful. We want to know all about them.

But as so frequently happens, we are disappointed when our heroes fall in disgrace because of some scandal or personal indiscretion. And so, we wait for the next hero to come along so we can delight in him or her.

In Psalm 16, look at the people David admires most: "The godly people in the land are my true heroes" (Psalm 16:3). They were the ones who didn't run after other gods but put their trust in the one true God. And for good reason. As David puts it, "Every good thing I have comes from [God]" (Psalm 16:2).

God provided many good things for David—he made his lot secure; he gave David a "wonderful inheritance." God counseled David at night, and with God at his side, David was never shaken. David was filled with joy—joy that sustained him even in the darkest of times because it was not tied to something fleeting but to the eternal God.

Trusting in God was the secret to David's success from the very beginning. When David was young, there was a great enemy war hero named Goliath. He was a fierce giant whom no one could defeat. But David wasn't afraid to try. Why? Because he had the greatest hero of all by his side. As he said to Goliath, "You come to me with sword, spear, and javelin, but I come to you in the name of the LORD" (1 Samuel 17:45).

God is our ultimate hero. He will never disappoint us. He will never let us down. He will never abandon us.

With God as our hero, we can say wholeheartedly, "You will show me the way of life, granting me the joy of your presence and the pleasures of living with you forever" (Psalm 16:11).

A Christian Reflection on Celebrity

Like David, we should look to the godly as our role models; but even then, we have the tendency to turn the godly into celebrities. Many have favorite ministers or authors. We hang on their every word; we believe what they believe, and we reject what they reject. While such guidance from a truly godly person can be beneficial, we must be careful not to put these people on a pedestal. Paul addressed this issue when he noted that people tended to turn him and others into celebrities, saying, "I am a follower of Paul" or "I follow Apollos" in ways that were unhealthy (1 Corinthians 1:12). Paul said that such attitudes are wrong and that Christians are to remember that we "belong to Christ, and Christ belongs to God" (1 Corinthians 3:23).

A PLACE TO CALL HOME

Have the people of Israel build me a holy sanctuary so I can live among them.
You must build this Tabernacle and its furnishings exactly according to the pattern
I will show you. ✤ EXODUS 25:8-9

After the Ten Commandments were given, God summoned Moses to meet with him atop Mount Sinai again. This time, God told Moses to have the people build him a place where he could dwell among them.

This Tabernacle, meaning "tent" or "sanctuary," would be the sacred place where God would meet his people and accept their worship. Located at the very heart of their camp, the Tabernacle would be a constant reminder of God's presence.

Just as his presence was visible as a pillar of cloud by day and a pillar of fire at night during the Exodus, God knew his people needed continual visual evidence. This movable tent would help them sense his guidance as they journeyed to the Promised Land.

The Tabernacle was also an object lesson in God's relationship with his people. He gave precise instructions for how to create the Tabernacle: "You must build this Tabernacle and its furnishings exactly according to the pattern I will show you." The lengthy instructions were not intended to burden the people. They were meant to remind them that they could come to God only on his terms—not on their own.

We also learn that God desires to be close to his people. God says, "Build me a holy sanctuary so I can live among them," but in the original Hebrew, the verse literally reads "so I can live inside them." The Sages explain that God wants to live not only in the Temple but also inside us. When we build a holy sanctuary, God will live inside it. When we become a holy people, God will dwell inside us.

The fact that God desired to reside among his people should be an encouragement for us all. God is not a disinterested caretaker of his Creation. No, the God of the Bible shows over and over his desire for a deep, intimate relationship with his people.

A Christian Reflection on Our Tabernacle

From Moses through the time of David, God made his presence known through the Tabernacle, because Israel was not yet established in the land. After David completed the conquest of Israel's enemies within the Promised Land, the Temple was built by his son Solomon. In the New Testament, God chose to make his presence known in the person of his divine Son, Jesus, who "made his home among us" (John 1:14). When Jesus died, he sent the Holy Spirit, who dwells in individual Christians so that we are "the living stones that God is building into his spiritual temple" (1 Peter 2:5).

A LOVELY DWELLING PLACE

How lovely is your dwelling place, O LORD of Heaven's Armies!
❖ PSALM 84:1

In biblical times, no place was more beautiful or awe-inspiring—or more holy—than the Temple. This was where God's presence, *Shekhinah*, was evident more than any other place in the world. Even today, the holiest place in Israel is the Western Wall—the only remaining vestige of where the Temple once stood. When Jews around the world pray, they face toward Jerusalem; and in Jerusalem, we face toward the Western Wall.

In its time, the Temple that Solomon built was unrivaled in its beauty. It was a magnificent building containing the finest materials of gold, silver, and cedar. We get a sense of how the Temple must have inspired all who saw it from the psalmist who wrote, "How lovely is your dwelling place. . . . I long, yes, I faint with longing to enter the courts of the LORD" (Psalm 84:1-2).

For the psalmist, being in God's house was better than being anywhere else. Why? It wasn't simply the grandeur. The Temple was the place where the psalmist felt God's presence. It was here he met with God and experienced him through worship.

In Psalm 27:4, King David reveals his deepest desire: "The thing I seek most . . . is to live in the house of the LORD all the days of my life." The Sages ask, Was David shirking his responsibilities by seeking a life inside the Temple? They explain that David wasn't looking to stay put; he wanted to take God's sanctuary with him. Whether he was on his throne or on the battlefield, David wanted that closeness with God in all aspects of his life.

While it's true that we can meet with God anytime and anywhere, it's also helpful to have a place where we can go to step aside from our busy lives and focus on God. Where is that place for you? How can you make your time with God something that you long for?

A Christian Reflection on God's Presence

When the Tabernacle was completed, a cloud settled down over it (see Exodus 40:34-35). When the Temple was built, "a thick cloud filled" it (1 Kings 8:10). This cloud represented "the glorious presence of the LORD" (1 Kings 8:11). Against this backdrop, we read that on the Day of Pentecost, after the death and resurrection of Jesus, "what looked like flames or tongues of fire appeared and settled on each of [the disciples]. And everyone present was filled with the Holy Spirit" (Acts 2:3-4, fulfilling the prophecy in Joel 2:28-32). In other words, God's people are continuously in the intimate presence of God.

COMMUNITY CENTER

*This is what the LORD says: "Heaven is my throne, and the earth is my footstool. Could
you build me a temple as good as that? Could you build me such a resting place?"*
❖ ISAIAH 66:1

Community is important for people of faith. We keep each other accountable, support
each other in faith, and inspire one another to better serve God. In biblical times, the
Temple was the center of community for the Jewish people.

When the Temple was destroyed and the people were exiled to Babylon in the
sixth century BC, the Jewish people began gathering in what eventually became the
synagogue. By New Testament times, there were hundreds of synagogues throughout
Israel. In fact, Jesus did much of his teaching in the local synagogues.

The synagogue became even more important after the Second Temple was destroyed
in AD 70 and the Jewish people were dispersed throughout the world. Since then, the
synagogue has become the place where Jews celebrate life's joyous occasions and gather
in times of sorrow. It is where we assemble to pray and study the Bible.

A look inside a synagogue reveals its connection to the Temples that once stood
in Jerusalem. Indeed, the *Talmud* calls synagogues "miniature Temples." Just as there
was an eternal flame burning in the Temple, every synagogue has a light that shines
continuously. Just as there was the Ark in the Temple, every synagogue has an ark that
holds the *Torah*. There are many more similarities. They remind us that the synagogue
is the epicenter of our faith community, just as the Temple once was.

For Jews and Christians alike, our primary responsibilities have always been to
God—obeying his commands, worshiping him, and studying his Word. God knew
that, in order to fulfill those responsibilities, we needed a "house" where we could
gather and meet with him. For the Jews, that place is the synagogue; for Christians,
it is the church.

These places are more than just buildings—they are where we live out our faith
and values together, in community. In both faith traditions, we need one another to
offer support and encouragement throughout life's challenges.

A Christian Reflection on Meeting Together

Hillary Clinton made famous the African proverb, "It takes a village to raise a child."
It's also true that it takes a community to raise a person of faith. For this reason, the
author of Hebrews urges, "Let us not neglect our meeting together, as some people do,
but encourage one another, especially now that the day of his return is drawing near"
(Hebrews 10:25). It's often a fatal mistake to think that we can make it on our own.
We need the encouragement and help of others in our faith communities to weather
the storms of life and the challenges to our beliefs.

GOD'S ETERNAL LIGHT

Command the people of Israel to bring you pure oil of pressed olives for the light, to keep the lamps burning continually. The lampstand will stand in the Tabernacle, in front of the inner curtain that shields the Ark of the Covenant. Aaron and his sons must keep the lamps burning in the LORD's presence all night. This is a permanent law for the people of Israel, and it must be observed from generation to generation.

❖ EXODUS 27:20-21

Throughout the world, the eternal light, or flame, is universally recognized as a symbol to honor noble people. In the Arlington National Cemetery in Virginia, eternal flames can be found at the Tomb of the Unknown Soldier and at President John F. Kennedy's gravesite. In Israel, an eternal flame at *Yad Vashem*, Israel's official memorial to the Holocaust, honors those who perished during that horrific time.

The symbol of light is part of our faith language as well. In Psalm 18:28, the psalmist rejoices in God's light: "You light a lamp for me. The LORD, my God, lights up my darkness." God's light is seen as our guide: "Send out your light and your truth; let them guide me" (Psalm 43:3).

Since biblical times, an eternal flame was lit before the altar, first in the Tabernacle and then in the Temple, as a sign of God's eternal presence. Today, in synagogues worldwide, you will find the sanctuary lamp, or *ner tamid*, representing the continuously burning light in the Temple.

Even if the *ner tamid* is just a lightbulb, these lights are never allowed to dim or go out. In the event of a power outage, alternate emergency sources are often used to prevent the light from going out. As God commanded, "This is a permanent law for the people of Israel, and it must be observed from generation to generation" (Exodus 27:21).

The eternal light is a wonderful reminder not only of God's presence with us always but also of our call as people of faith to be God's light in the world. King Solomon writes, "The human spirit is the lamp of the LORD" (Proverbs 20:27, NIV). Just as God is an everlasting source of light, human beings can also give off eternal light. We can bring God's love and grace to those around us through acts of kindness, compassion, and charity. As we do so, we share God's presence and light up even the darkest places in the world.

A Christian Reflection on the Light of the World

In the magnificent prologue to his Gospel, John speaks of Jesus as the Word who existed already "in the beginning with God" (John 1:2). He was the one through whom all was created (see John 1:3). Indeed, "the Word gave life to everything that was created, and his life brought light to everyone. The light shines in the darkness, and the darkness can never extinguish it" (John 1:4-5). Later in the Gospel, we read Jesus' bold claim: "I am the light of the world. If you follow me, you won't have to walk in darkness, because you will have the light that leads to life" (John 8:12).

WHERE ARE YOUR ROOTS?

If I forget you, O Jerusalem, let my right hand forget how to play the harp.
❖ PSALM 137:5

Remembering our history and roots is important to us, not only individually but also as a people. We see this in the places we designate as historical monuments, in the holidays we celebrate collectively, and in the stories we pass down from one generation to the next.

So when Israel began life as a new state in 1948, the fledgling nation turned to its roots in the Bible as a source of inspiration. The Knesset, Israel's national parliament, is a wonderful tribute to her spiritual heritage. The Knesset takes its name and fixed its number of members based on a model from the Bible. The term *knesset* is derived from the ancient Great Assembly, consisting of 120 Sages, initially convened in Jerusalem by Ezra and Nehemiah in the fifth century BC.

Much of the artwork in the Knesset also reflects Israel's spiritual roots. The Chagall State Hall, where receptions and state dinners are held, is decorated with tapestries and mosaics depicting biblical motifs. Scenes such as the sacrifice of Isaac, Jacob's dream, and Moses receiving the Ten Commandments cover the walls.

One of the mosaics designed by famed Jewish artist Marc Chagall illustrates the words of Psalm 137:1, 5: "Beside the rivers of Babylon, we sat and wept as we thought of Jerusalem. . . . If I forget you, O Jerusalem, let my right hand forget how to play the harp." The words of the psalmist describe the longing of the exiled Jewish people for their homeland and appropriately reflect the deep bond that the Jewish people have to their homeland today.

About 2,600 years ago, the prophet Jeremiah warned: "Remember the LORD, though you are in a far-off land, and think about your home in Jerusalem" (Jeremiah 51:50). And for more than two millennia the Jewish people proclaimed, "Next year in Jerusalem!" They remembered their roots, and God remembered them; he has indeed brought them back to Jerusalem.

A Christian Reflection on the Roots of Our Faith

Paul twice uses the metaphor of a plant to describe the roots of our faith. In his letter to the Ephesians, he speaks about how our spiritual growth is empowered by God's love: "Christ will make his home in your hearts as you trust in him. Your roots will grow down into God's love and keep you strong" (Ephesians 3:17). In Colossians, also speaking of our spiritual growth, he instructs his readers: "Let your roots grow down into [Christ Jesus], and let your lives be built on him. Then your faith will grow strong in the truth you were taught, and you will overflow with thankfulness" (Colossians 2:7). Where have you planted the roots of your faith?

Sabbath Reflections

What new truth about the places where we worship God did you learn from this week's devotions?

How has this truth affected your faith?

How will you apply this truth to your daily life?

Your Key Verse for the Week:

❖ OTHER REFLECTIONS

OUR COVERED SINS

You forgave the guilt of your people—yes, you covered all their sins.
❖ PSALM 85:2

When Adam and Eve sinned, they covered themselves with fig leaves (see Genesis 3:7). When we sin, we often try to cover it up too. Yes, we are foolish enough to think that we can hide our sins from God.

In Psalm 32, David shares his experience of trying to hide his sin. When he kept silent about his sin, he felt sick—until he admitted his sin to God (Psalm 32:3-5). That's why David proclaims there is great joy for those who live in complete honesty.

Confessing his sin was such a relief that David urged others to confess their sins immediately, rather than trying to hide them. The *Tanakh* translation of Psalm 32:6 reads, "Therefore, let every faithful man pray to You upon discovering [his sin]."

David uses three Hebrew verbs in relation to forgiveness. The first is *nesuy*, literally "carried away." This speaks of the removal of sin. The second is *kesuy*, meaning "are covered." When sin is covered, God doesn't look upon it anymore. The third is *lo'yahshob*, which is translated "does not count." Once God forgives a sin, it no longer counts against you.

The Sages liken sin to a stain on a white garment. We can cover it up all we want, but it's still there, and we know it. When we confess our sins, it's as if we uncover the stain and show it to God. If we repent, God washes our stain away as only he can. "Though your sins are like scarlet, I will make them as white as snow. Though they are red like crimson, I will make them as white as wool" (Isaiah 1:18).

Whenever we are tempted to cover up our sins, we should remember that if we confess them to God, he will carry them away, as if they never happened. This is cause for great joy.

A Christian Reflection on Confessing Sin

Why are we so quick to hide our sin, not only from other people but also from God? Shame, I suspect. But listen to the teaching of John: "If we claim we have no sin, we are only fooling ourselves and not living in the truth. But if we confess our sins to him, he is faithful and just to forgive us our sins and to cleanse us from all wickedness. If we claim we have not sinned, we are calling God a liar and showing that his word has no place in our hearts" (1 John 1:8-10). John lays it all out for us and calls us to a life of daily repentance and cleansing from our guilt and sin. The good news for Christians is that because of Jesus' sacrificial death on the cross, our sins have been completely removed and forgiven.

WELCOME HOME!

*He will raise a flag among the nations and assemble the exiles of Israel. He will gather
the scattered people of Judah from the ends of the earth.* ❖ ISAIAH 11:12

As a people, the Jews were homeless for centuries, driven out of their biblical homeland by invaders on multiple occasions throughout their history. The term created for
this phenomenon is *diaspora*, meaning "dispersion" or "scattering." The *Diaspora* Jews
were dispersed across the globe.

After centuries of longing for their homeland, the Jews experienced the darkest
hour and deepest hopelessness during the Holocaust. Then, as an affirmation from
God that he had not abandoned his people, God fulfilled his promise in Isaiah 11:12 to
"gather the scattered people of Judah from the ends of the earth."

In 1948, Israel officially became an independent nation. This was more than the
realization of a centuries-long dream; it was the fulfillment of biblical prophecy. Both
Jews and Bible-believing Christians point to the theological significance of this event.

Many displaced Jews began returning to Israel. In 1948, Jewish inhabitants in
Israel numbered a little more than six hundred thousand. Within three years, that
number had nearly doubled, as Jews living in the Arab world returned and more
Holocaust survivors were brought to Israel. The Jewish people were coming home!

Homecomings always give us the opportunity to appreciate our home. But it is
much more than that each time a Jew sets foot onto Israeli soil and calls it his or her
home. It is a celebration of God's great provision for his people and the fulfillment
of ancient prophecies.

As Zechariah prophesied, "Once again old men and women will walk Jerusalem's
streets with their canes and will sit together in the city squares. And the streets of the
city will be filled with boys and girls at play" (Zechariah 8:4-5). Even less than a century ago, what Jew would have believed they would ever see this?

Yet today, if you walk the streets of Jerusalem, you will see Jewish children playing
and Jewish elders walking by. The children of Israel have indeed come home!

A Christian Reflection on God Keeping His Promises

When we say that God fulfills prophecy, we are claiming that he keeps his promises. The
Bible is filled with examples of God doing exactly what he said he would do. Sometimes
he fulfills his promises quickly, and sometimes, in his wisdom, God does so after a long
period of time. Our temptation is often to think that God has forgotten us, and then we
neglect him. Christians wait in expectation of Christ's second return and being brought
home to God in heaven. Peter reminds us that we are "temporary residents and foreigners" (1 Peter 2:11; see also Hebrews 3:7–4:11). If you begin to doubt that God will fulfill
his promises to us, remember that he has a perfect track record.

A DREAM COME TRUE

Ezra was a scribe who was well versed in the Law of Moses, which the LORD, the God of Israel, had given to the people of Israel. He came up to Jerusalem from Babylon, and the king gave him everything he asked for, because the gracious hand of the LORD his God was on him. ❖ EZRA 7:6

Theodor Herzl, a Jewish journalist from Austria, came to France in 1894 to cover the trial of Alfred Dreyfus, a Jewish captain in the French army. Herzl was shocked to find French mobs shouting, "Death to the Jews!" After witnessing such hateful displays of anti-Semitism, Herzl committed his life to the formation of a Jewish state.

In 1897, Herzl convened a Zionist convention in Switzerland, which brought together delegates from around the world. Herzl boldly predicted that within fifty years, a Jewish state would exist. His words were immortalized: "If you will it, it is no dream." Herzl believed that, with enough determination, the dream of a Jewish state would become real.

Herzl died in 1904; forty-four years later, his vision was realized.

The biblical priest Ezra had a dream too. Having grown up during the seventy-year exile of the Jewish people to Babylon, he dreamed of returning to Jerusalem and teaching in the Temple. As part of the priestly line, Ezra had studied the *Torah*, the law of Moses, and wanted "to teach those decrees and regulations to the people of Israel" (Ezra 7:10).

Finally, when the Temple had been rebuilt in Jerusalem, Ezra had the privilege of teaching God's law to the people of Israel. Jewish tradition teaches that as Ezra and his followers went to Jerusalem, they composed the words of Psalm 126:1: "When the LORD brought back his exiles to Jerusalem, it was like a dream!" A dream come true.

Both the prophet Ezra and Theodor Herzl had grand visions for the future of Israel. Each one stepped into the void during times when the Jews had nearly lost hope. Today, the nation of Israel looks back on both men with gratitude for helping preserve Israel's identity as a nation and as God's chosen people.

As we step forward in trust and obedience to pursue the dream God has given us, he will keep his promises to help us.

A Christian Reflection on Paul's Dreams

The apostle Paul played a key role in spreading the gospel throughout the world. Like Ezra, Paul had a passion to serve God and a clear purpose. One cannot help but be impressed with his determination to share the Good News about Jesus in the light of opposition, imprisonment, and outright persecution (see 2 Corinthians 6:3-10). After God made it clear to Paul that Jesus had come and died for all people, Paul desired more than anything to share his faith with others. Not all of us are called to be evangelists like Paul or teach Scripture like Ezra, but all of us are to devote our lives and use our gifts for the purposes of God's Kingdom.

HOPE DEFERRED

Hope deferred makes the heart sick, but a dream fulfilled is a tree of life.
❖ PROVERBS 13:12

We all know the pain of broken promises. These situations break our hearts. The book of Proverbs explains that "hope deferred makes the heart sick" (Proverbs 13:12). With hope aroused, the disappointment is greater than if the promise had never been made.

In 1917, Lord Arthur James Balfour, the British foreign secretary, wrote a letter stating that the British government would help to facilitate the creation of a Jewish homeland in Palestine. This letter, known as the Balfour Declaration, was approved by the League of Nations in 1922.

It was a statement that elicited great hope among the Jewish people. But in 1939, the British government reversed its position, stating that it did not endorse turning Palestine into a Jewish state. Imagine the great disappointment caused by this reversal.

Nonetheless, events had already been set in motion. The hope of a Jewish homeland was kindled, and the Jewish people pursued it with fiery passion. The United Nations approved the creation of the State of Israel on November 29, 1947. Six months later, the British withdrew from Palestine and Israel was reborn on May 14, 1948. This marked a dream fulfilled for Jews everywhere.

The prophet Jeremiah warns us, "Cursed are those who put their trust in mere humans, who rely on human strength. . . . But blessed are those who trust in the LORD and have made the LORD their hope and confidence" (Jeremiah 17:5, 7). While mortal humans can lie and let us down, the infinite God never breaks his promises—with one exception, as the rabbis explain: A prophecy of redemption will always come true, but a prophecy of doom can be undone through repentance. And that is good news for all.

The history of our lives will inevitably contain broken promises, but we can place our faith in the unswerving promises of redemption as we turn to God.

A Christian Reflection on Sure Hope

In light of the frustration and disappointment of broken promises, we often abandon hope. Whom can we trust to follow through on their promises? Even those who love us and are close to us will let us down at least on occasion. There is only one on whom we can rely with unwavering certainty—God himself. In him we can rightly place our faith. As the author of Hebrews tells us, "Faith is the confidence that what we hope for will actually happen" (Hebrews 11:1). It is not wishful thinking or pie-in-the-sky dreaming. It is hope built on the one who never fails us.

AGAINST ALL ODDS

When Sanballat and Tobiah and the Arabs, Ammonites, and Ashdodites heard that the work was going ahead and that the gaps in the wall of Jerusalem were being repaired, they were furious. They all made plans to come and fight against Jerusalem and throw us into confusion. ❖ NEHEMIAH 4:7-8

At 8 a.m. on May 14, 1948, the British rule of Palestine ended. Within hours, six Arab nations invaded the brand-new State of Israel. By 4 p.m., when David Ben-Gurion read the Proclamation of Independence over the radio, the citizens of Jerusalem could not hear the broadcast, having lost electricity in the siege. Yet, despite being outnumbered, Israel defeated her united foes.

Facing opposition from enemies is nothing new for God's people. Nehemiah met with similar opposition when he led a group of Jews to rebuild Jerusalem's war-torn walls. When their enemies heard that the Jews were repairing the walls, they "made plans to come and fight against Jerusalem and throw us into confusion" (Nehemiah 4:8).

Undaunted, Nehemiah instructed his people to work "with one hand supporting their load and one hand holding a weapon" (4:17), and they took turns serving as guards by night and workmen by day (see 4:22). Despite the opposition, the people completed the repairs in a record fifty-two days (see 6:15)!

During the difficult work, amid attacks from their enemies, Nehemiah's people became discouraged. But he reminded them, "Don't be afraid of the enemy! Remember the Lord, who is great and glorious, and fight for your brothers, your sons, your daughters, your wives, and your homes!" (4:14).

We all face enemies in life, whether internal or external. We all, at some point, want to give up, but the Bible constantly reminds us that those who push forward in their faith overcome every adversity. God, the rabbis remind us, considers us his children. We know personally what we would do for our own children. In fact, like God, there is nothing we wouldn't do to protect them.

In times of adversity, remember that God, our Eternal Father, will always support and defend us against any type of enemy.

A Christian Reflection on Facing Overwhelming Odds

Life comes at us from many different directions. We struggle against other people as well as with ourselves (see Romans 7:14-25). Ultimately, the battle is spiritual. Paul points out that "we are not fighting against flesh-and-blood enemies, but against evil rulers and authorities of the unseen world, against mighty powers in this dark world and against evil spirits in the heavenly places" (Ephesians 6:12). Thus, "we don't wage war as humans do" (2 Corinthians 10:3), but rather with spiritual weapons such as "the belt of truth and the body armor of God's righteousness," shoes of peace, the shield of faith, and the helmet of salvation (Ephesians 6:14-17). Thus armed, we are ready for battle, already ensured victory through Christ.

PLOWSHARES AND PRUNING HOOKS

The LORD will mediate between nations and will settle international disputes. They
will hammer their swords into plowshares and their spears into pruning hooks. Nation
will no longer fight against nation, nor train for war anymore. ❖ ISAIAH 2:4

Even though peace in the Middle East is in the best interests of the entire world, the conflict persists. Continued terrorist attacks and the barrage of missiles fired at Israel on an almost daily basis by her enemies make the prospect of peace seem remote.

The prophets envisioned a future age when peace would prevail. Both Isaiah and Micah looked forward to the time when Jerusalem would be a place of peace instead of war, with God judging disputes between nations (see Isaiah 2:4; Micah 4:3). Conflict might still arise, but it would be resolved peacefully with God as arbitrator and the nations in compliance with his will.

In this future age, nations will not "train for war anymore"; their weapons will become useless. Their tools of war will become tools of agriculture: "They will hammer their swords into plowshares and their spears into pruning hooks" (Isaiah 2:4).

Today, we hope for peace; we pray for peace; and yet a world without war seems inconceivable to us. War sows destruction and reaps death, but Isaiah looked forward to a time when God "will swallow up death forever! The Sovereign LORD will wipe away all tears" (Isaiah 25:8).

Jews and Christians alike continue to look forward to the future age when peace will be a reality. Until then, we must remember the value that God places on peace. In fact, peace represents one of God's ultimate values. As the rabbis explain, most of the Jewish prayers end with a call for universal peace. Maimonides, the renowned Jewish philosopher, penned this: "Great indeed is peace, forasmuch as the purpose for which the whole of the Law was given is to bring peace upon the world."

Wishes cannot solve historical problems, but we must always remember the prevailing and eternal value of true peace.

A Christian Reflection on Praying for Peace

Christians join others in praying for "peace in Jerusalem." What is impossible for people is not impossible for God. After all, our God is a God who opened the Red Sea to save his people as they fled from Egypt. Our God is a God who raised Jesus from the dead. Christians join others in praying for the end of all conflict in the world, though the New Testament does acknowledge that there will be "wars and rumors of wars" up to the very end of history (Mark 13:7, NIV). Even so, the New Testament continues the vision of a world without warfare, particularly in its picture of the New Jerusalem, where there will be "no more death or sorrow or crying or pain" (Revelation 21:4).

Sabbath Reflections

*What new truth about God's promises and care for his people did you learn
from this week's devotions?*

How has this truth affected your faith?

How will you apply this truth to your daily life?

Your Key Verse for the Week:

❖ OTHER REFLECTIONS

MY ROCK OF PROTECTION

O LORD, I have come to you for protection; don't let me be disgraced. Save me, for you do what is right. Turn your ear to listen to me; rescue me quickly. Be my rock of protection, a fortress where I will be safe. ◆ PSALM 31:1-2

Lies and false accusations can cause great anguish, can't they? Slander is an attempt to turn others against us, and when it seems as if everyone is conspiring against us, it feels as if there is nowhere left to go.

At the time David penned Psalm 31, he apparently was the target of a severe verbal assault that included rumors and plots (see 31:13), "lying lips" (31:18), and "accusing tongues" (31:20). The rabbis refer to slander as *lashon hara*, literally "evil speech." As the rabbis explain, there is no antidote for evil speech. Once unleashed, it spreads like fire, consuming and burning everything in its path.

When faced with such an unbeatable foe, David looked to God as his "rock of protection" and "fortress." He trusted "the God of truth" (Psalm 31:5, NASB) to counter all lies, and he knew that the God of righteousness was able to right every wrong.

David portrays God as a strong fortress in which to wait out the verbal assaults: "He kept me safe when my city was under attack" (Psalm 31:21). Inhabitants of a city under siege could wait out the attack in safety. Fiery darts and stones hurled by attackers could not penetrate the fortifications around the city. Likewise, we can take refuge in God when others hurl insults and accusations against us.

There is no evidence that David tried to set the record straight with his accusers. Instead, he left it up to God. David was able to do this because of his ongoing relationship with God. Like David, those who know God and know his character are able to seek him confidently and know that he will deliver his people. We can handle adversity better when we recognize our true relationship with the sovereign God, as David did.

A Christian Reflection on God's Help When under Assault

David found encouragement in the midst of persecution because he knew that God was with him to protect him. Jesus warned his disciples that those who followed him would be the object of hate and persecution (see John 15:18-25). It's in this context that Jesus spoke of the Advocate, the Holy Spirit, who would come after Jesus left. The "Spirit of truth" (John 15:26) would give them—and us—the courage to endure and the words to speak in the midst of persecution. God never leaves his faithful people alone in the midst of their struggles.

NEVER FORGET

Let this be recorded for future generations, so that a people not yet born will praise the Lord. ❖ PSALM 102:18

Human nature avoids unpleasant topics. The more serious the topic, the more discomfort it provokes. So it makes sense that when we attempt to discuss the Holocaust, words escape us. We would rather not talk about it.

Yet it is the most uncomfortable topics that need the most discussion. We can never forget the atrocities of history. All Jews consider themselves Holocaust survivors. Because Hitler planned to eradicate the entire Jewish nation, all Jews bear the awesome responsibility of telling the painful story of that dark time. If we fail to convey the horrors of the Holocaust, we risk allowing history to repeat itself. That's why eyewitness accounts are so important.

These are the stories we cannot afford to forget, not for ourselves and not for future generations. They convey the extent to which humanity had fallen into the depths of evil. But stories do not merely convey history; they convey moral values as well. They are stories of hope, courage, heroism, and devotion. A Jewish woman who survived Auschwitz recalls that whenever Allied planes flew overhead, she and the other Jewish prisoners prayed that the pilots would bomb the gas chambers, "even if it meant we might be killed." They were willing to give their lives to save others.

The rabbis, time and again, convey the importance of cultural memory. We are told to remember the Exodus, the revelation at Mount Sinai, and other important historical events. Memory informs our current identities as we see ourselves as part of a long chain of courageous, dedicated believers. We take heart and courage from the deeds of our predecessors.

History, the rabbis explain, does not stay in the past. It infuses our present and creates a guidebook for our future. As God commands, "Be careful never to forget what you yourself have seen. Do not let these memories escape from your mind as long as you live! And be sure to pass them on to your children and grandchildren" (Deuteronomy 4:9).

A Christian Reflection on the Holocaust

Christians must never forget the Holocaust. Oh, that there would have been more Christians like Corrie ten Boom or the people of the French village of Le Chambon-sur-Lignon, who aided and sheltered Jews during this horrific time. The sad fact is that many Christians stood by silently and some even participated in the atrocities. Nothing like the Holocaust must ever be allowed to happen again. Forgetting opens up the possibility of repetition. For this reason, it is important for Christians to know about the Holocaust. As difficult as it is, read the stories, listen to the survivors, and pray that God would shatter the plans of all who intend violence against the Jews even today.

MY BROTHER'S KEEPER

Rescue those who are unjustly sentenced to die; save them as they stagger to their death. Don't excuse yourself by saying, "Look, we didn't know." For God understands all hearts, and he sees you. He who guards your soul knows you knew. He will repay all people as their actions deserve. ❖ PROVERBS 24:11-12

Raoul Wallenberg came from a wealthy and famous Swedish family. When the Nazis started rounding up Jews in Hungary, Wallenberg went to Budapest as a diplomat to hand out Swedish citizenship papers to thousands of Jews.

Because of Wallenberg's decisive actions, he saved as many as one hundred thousand Jews from certain death.

Wallenberg's willingness to act, at great personal cost and risk, is a model for us today. Too often, we see something and think, *That doesn't affect me;* but the principle of accountability for our fellow human beings reaches as far back as Genesis. After Cain killed Abel, God asked Cain, "Where is your brother? Where is Abel?" "I don't know," Cain responded. "Am I my brother's guardian?" (Genesis 4:9).

The answer to Cain's question is, of course, *yes*, we are our brother's keeper. God desires that we serve as guardians for one another.

People tend to ask, "Where was God during the Holocaust?" but we must also ask, "Where was man?" More than six million Jews perished in the Holocaust, not only at the hands of perpetrators but also because of silent bystanders.

We must do more than just remember the atrocities of the past. We must also accept responsibility for preventing such tragedies in the future. The rabbis tell us that God created the first man *alone* to convey that one life is equivalent to the whole world. From this they derive that one who saves even a single life is the same as one who saves the entire world. Conversely, the loss of one life is tantamount to the loss of an entire world.

In realizing the value of even one human life, no matter the life, we can realize the importance of accepting personal responsibility to prevent injustices and atrocities against others, wherever they may occur.

A Christian Reflection on Defending the Vulnerable

Jesus was serious about caring for the vulnerable. In Matthew, he tells his disciples that "when the Son of Man comes in his glory" (Matthew 25:31), he will separate humankind into two groups, the "sheep" and the "goats." The sheep "will go into eternal life" while the goats "will go away into eternal punishment" (Matthew 25:46). What separates the sheep from the goats? The sheep, according to Jesus, are the ones who showed compassion for the hungry, the poor, the sick, the imprisoned. When did they do these things? Jesus says, "When you did it to one of the least of these my brothers and sisters, you were doing it to me!" (Matthew 25:40). Lord, give us the grace to help those in need.

TREATED LIKE A LADY

Learn to do good. Seek justice. Help the oppressed. Defend the cause of orphans.
Fight for the rights of widows. ❖ ISAIAH 1:17

Holocaust survivor Gerda Weissmann Klein describes how the actions of a US soldier restored her dignity after several dehumanizing years in forced-labor camps during World War II. Toward the end of the war, following a death march, a group of women prisoners had been abandoned in a warehouse to die. While standing outside, Gerda saw a strange car approaching. It wasn't bearing a swastika, but a white star. Two soldiers jumped out of the jeep, and one asked her, "Does anybody here speak German or English?"

"I speak German," replied Gerda. Though afraid to reveal her Jewishness, she added, "We are Jewish, you know."

The soldier didn't answer right away, and then his own voice betrayed his emotion as he said, "So am I." He then asked, "May I see the other ladies?" *What an incredible question*, thought Gerda. At the time, she weighed sixty-eight pounds, her hair was white, and she hadn't bathed properly in six years—and he asked for "the other ladies"?

She told him the other girls were inside, too weak and ill to walk. He said, "Won't you come with me?" Gerda recalled, "He held the door open for me and let me precede him, and in that gesture, restored me to humanity. And that young American today is my husband."

Treating other people with honor lifts them from shame and restores a sense of worth and dignity. When King David granted Jonathan's disabled son, Mephibosheth, a seat at the king's table and treated him like a son, he restored to life a man ashamed of his disability. Isn't that how we all should treat one another?

The rabbis explain that if someone embarrasses another person, it's as if he or she killed that person. Conversely, we learn that one who restores a person's dignity restores that person to life. Day in and day out, small acts of kindness can restore others to life; we need to remember the power of dignity.

A *Christian Reflection on Treating Others with Respect*

Most early Christians were the down-and-outers of their day, but not all. The apostle James had to remind his readers not to favor the rich over the poor (see James 2:1-13). Apparently, some in the church had a tendency to give preferential treatment to rich people, but James told them they were "breaking the law" (James 2:9). We learn as early as Genesis 1 that every person is equally valuable, created in God's image, reflecting his glory. Everyone deserves our respect as someone whom God has created.

SHARING YOUR STORY

I will not die; instead, I will live to tell what the LORD has done.
❖ PSALM 118:17

Eva Mozes Kor and her twin sister were one of fifteen hundred sets of twins on whom Nazi doctor Josef Mengele performed unspeakable genetic experiments. Miraculously, they were among the two hundred, of those three thousand individuals, who survived.

In Eva's case, she was given injections that caused a high fever and severe swelling to her legs and arms. Despite the doctors' prognosis that she had only two weeks to live, Eva and her twin, Miriam, survived. As a Holocaust survivor, Eva has lived by the motto "There are two choices in life when we face tragedy. Give in to despair, or triumph over it."

She has devoted her life to telling her story and shedding light on the destructive effects of hatred and prejudice. She founded CANDLES—Children of Auschwitz Nazi Deadly Lab Experiments Survivors—and the CANDLES Holocaust Museum and Education Center in Terre Haute, Indiana, to help educate others about the Holocaust and the need for forgiveness.

At seventy-nine, Eva continues to speak at schools, synagogues, and civic groups to share a message of forgiveness. She says that everyone has the power to forgive and that once she was able to forgive, she was able to overcome the psychological damage: "I was no longer a victim of Auschwitz. I was no longer a victim of my tragic past."

The rabbis of the *Talmud* explain that the extent to which we can forgive others, God will forgive us. The rabbis explain that anger will only lead us into further sin. Forgiveness will lead us into the presence of God in our imitation of his all-forgiving ways. Of course, we must always remember the horrors of the past; but, like Eva, we also must learn forgiveness so we can move on into the loving and forgiving embrace of God.

A Christian Reflection on Sharing Our Stories

God works in the lives of all his people—sometimes dramatically, as in the life of Eva Mozes Kor, and sometimes in what we might think are the ordinary events of life. Consider the life of Tabitha, a follower of Jesus in the early church (Acts 9:32-42). She had devoted her life to "doing kind things for others and helping the poor." When she died, many gathered to mourn, and when Peter came to the deathbed and ordered her to get up, many more believed because of what God did through her and for her, raising her from the dead. Think about the course of your life. Where do you see the hand of God working in a special way? Find opportunities to share your life story. By doing so, you will encourage others and give praise to God.

AN AMERICAN TRADITION

Listen to my prayer and my plea, O LORD my God. Hear the cry and the prayer
that your servant is making to you. ❖ 2 CHRONICLES 6:19

Since 1775, when the Continental Congress asked the colonies to pray for wisdom in forming a nation, the call to prayer has been a continual thread in US history.

The National Day of Prayer, which President Harry S. Truman signed into law in 1952, has great significance for us as people of faith, but also for us as a nation. It helps us recall that our founding fathers sought God's wisdom in making critical decisions about the formation of our country. It stands as a call for us to humbly come before God and seek his guidance for our leaders and his grace for our nation.

The call to prayer not only signifies our faith in God but also symbolizes our relationship to the nation we live in. People of all religions see themselves as both Jewish and American, or both Christian and American, and so forth. Though these dual identities often clash, our prayer for the government constantly illustrates our allegiance to our country, though ultimately to our country *under* God.

As Jews looking back on our history, we tend to take a wary approach toward government. We've previously placed our trust in governments rather than God, with disastrous results. Yet in America, rabbi after rabbi, decade after decade, has referred to America as a "kingdom of kindness." We will never forget the one who truly governs the world, but we also value and pay tribute to a government devoted to the principles of life, liberty, and the pursuit of happiness, under the loving gaze of God.

Jewish tradition abounds with prayers for governments, but none loftier than King Solomon's beautiful prayer in his dedication of the Holy Temple (see 2 Chronicles 6:14-42), in which he reminds the children of Israel to pray for peace among the nations, humility in our leaders, and for all to acknowledge the sovereignty of God.

It still serves as a wonderful model for us today as we lift our nation in prayer.

A Christian Reflection on Prayer for the Nations

Jews and Christians live in many different nations, but each individual lives in one nation. While we should pray for all the nations of the world that they would come to know God, we should especially pray for the nation we live in. Paul exhorts his readers to pray "for kings and all who are in authority so that we can live peaceful and quiet lives marked by godliness and dignity" (1 Timothy 2:2). Those who live in America should seek the spiritual welfare of our nation. Solomon's prayer is a wonderful guide to how we should pray for it. While especially praying for our nation on the National Day of Prayer, every day is a good day to ask God to bless our nation.

Sabbath Reflections

What new truth about a Christian response to the Holocaust did you learn from this week's devotions?

How has this truth affected your faith?

How will you apply this truth to your daily life?

Your Key Verse for the Week:

❖ OTHER REFLECTIONS

GOD'S INHERITANCE

*The LORD's plans stand firm forever; his intentions can never be shaken. What joy
for the nation whose God is the LORD, whose people he has chosen as his inheritance.*
❖ PSALM 33:11-12

Among all the nations of the world, God chose one people as his "special treasure":
Israel (Exodus 19:5). It was for this very reason that God rescued them from Egypt.
Moses said, "Remember that the LORD rescued you from the iron-smelting furnace
of Egypt in order to make you his very own people and his special possession, which
is what you are today" (Deuteronomy 4:20).

Like anyone holding a treasured possession, God has always been protective of his
inheritance, Israel. The Lord spoke though the prophet Joel, saying, "I will gather the
armies of the world. . . . I will judge them for harming my people, my special possession,
for scattering my people among the nations, and for dividing up my land" (Joel 3:2).

Even though God judges the nations for their treatment of Israel, his love and
protection do not mean that Israel is immune from war. At times, God also "gave
his people over to be butchered by the sword, because he was so angry with his own
people—his special possession" (Psalm 78:62). But God has never allowed Israel to
be completely destroyed by her enemies.

We see evidence of this throughout history. The people of Israel have been war-
torn, exiled, scattered around the globe, faced with almost certain annihilation, and
seemingly forgotten. Yet Israel as a people, as a nation, and as God's treasured possession has persevered. Despite all the threats she has faced and continues to face, God
has seen fit to restore her.

That God sees fit to restore and revive the nation of Israel time and time again
should not only move us to feel thankful for and pray for God's gift, the land of Israel,
but also remind us that God's "chosen-ness" is a responsibility, a call to action to live
lives befitting God's treasure.

A Christian Reflection on God's Treasured Possession

Israel is indeed God's treasured possession, and we should pray for that nation, which
God uses in the accomplishment of his purposes to reach the whole world. Indeed, in
the promises given to Abraham, God tells Abraham that he will make him into a great
nation. Not only will he bless that nation, but through it, he will bless "all the families on earth" (Genesis 12:3). The apostle Peter recognized God's blessings when he
addressed Christians living in "the provinces of Pontus, Galatia, Cappadocia, Asia, and
Bithynia" (1 Peter 1:1) using the language of Exodus 19: "You are a chosen people. You
are royal priests, a holy nation, God's very own possession" (1 Peter 2:9). We are God's
treasured possession.

AN IRRATIONAL HATRED

They wear pride like a jeweled necklace and clothe themselves with cruelty. These fat cats have everything their hearts could ever wish for! They scoff and speak only evil; in their pride they seek to crush others. ❖ PSALM 73:6-8

Throughout history, Jews have often found themselves the object of irrational hatred. For example, Jews have been accused of being too poor or too wealthy; too politically domineering or too politically uninvolved. We've been accused of being too spiritual or too secular; unambitious or overly aggressive; too separated from others or too assimilated.

How can that be possible?

Anti-Semitism, like other forms of racism, is a condition of the heart. It reflects a callous heart that has lost sensitivity to others. As the writer of Psalm 73 says, "These fat cats have everything their hearts could ever wish for!" A hardened heart that has lost sensitivity to others is a breeding ground for evil.

In addition to a callous heart, anti-Semitism forms in a conceited mind. At the base of racism is the belief that one person or group is better than another, and "in their pride they seek to crush others." Rather than listening to reason, irrational thoughts prevail, driven by passionate hatred. For those who promote anti-Semitism, their hatred is without justification and leads to inconsistent accusations against the Jews—such as those above—because these charges are not based on logic or merit but on hate.

Finally, the psalmist says that those with callous hearts and conceited minds also have threatening lips, for "they scoff and speak only evil." Anti-Semitism often expresses itself in threats, intimidation, and oppression. Acts of terrorism against Jews and Jewish icons are an attempt to instill fear in the lives of Jews.

As the psalm writer concludes, when faced with unreasonable and unmerited prejudice, there is only one place to find hope: "Yet I still belong to you; you hold my right hand. You guide me with your counsel, leading me to a glorious destiny. Whom have I in heaven but you?" (Psalm 73:23-25).

We can have confidence in God's presence and guidance no matter what circumstances or difficulties we face.

A Christian Reflection on Irrational Hatred

Christians must stand fast with our Jewish friends and denounce anti-Semitism, especially if that perverse hatred comes from another Christian. No one should stand silent in the face of anti-Semitic talk, attitudes, or actions. Christians in the West should also remember that our Christian brothers and sisters around the world face irrational hatred that results in harassment, imprisonment, and even death. Prejudice in all forms must be resisted and attitudes changed.

PRIDE AND PREJUDICE

Do not twist justice in legal matters by favoring the poor or being partial to the rich and powerful. Always judge people fairly. Do not spread slanderous gossip among your people. ❖ LEVITICUS 19:15-16

How we think about others affects how we treat them. When we *think* we are better than others, we often act that way. For example, we may dismiss a person as beneath us even before we understand his or her situation. Our tone of voice may be brusque, or our smile forced. Without realizing it, we may act differently around those people we think inferior.

This inclination of human beings to make assumptions about other people is at the root of prejudice and anti-Semitism. Like a virus, these hateful ideas, thoughts, and values can be passed on to others.

The passage in Leviticus 19 teaches that it is a corruption of justice to favor one person or group over another. It is only natural to favor one group over others or a friend over a stranger, but God commands us to rise above our natural impulses. Rather, we are to judge others fairly and treat everyone as equal with universal values based on a loving God.

We might think ourselves above this favoritism, but the rabbis teach us that even Moses and Aaron could not testify together in a case because they were brothers and subject to the possibility of bias. We must remember that no one is above the natural inclination to judge others—and judge them harshly.

Though gossip is everywhere, we must not spread slander. Words are powerful. If you've ever been hurt by someone's words, you know how painful untrue words can be. God's standard is clear: "Do not seek revenge or bear a grudge against a fellow Israelite, but love your neighbor as yourself. I am the LORD" (Leviticus 19:18). Imagine what our world would be like if we all obeyed this one simple command.

A Christian Reflection on Favoritism

The Bible could not be clearer: "God has no favorites" (Colossians 3:25; Galatians 2:6; see also Romans 2:11; 1 Peter 1:17). The religious leaders of Jesus' day, in spite of their differences with him, knew that Jesus was impartial and did not play favorites (Matthew 22:16; Mark 12:14). Since God shows no favorites, neither should his people. As Paul said, "I solemnly command you in the presence of God and Christ Jesus and the highest angels to obey these instructions without taking sides or showing favoritism to anyone" (1 Timothy 5:21).

A TIME TO SPEAK UP

If I warn the wicked, saying, "You are under the penalty of death," but you fail to deliver the warning, they will die in their sins. And I will hold you responsible for their deaths. If you warn them and they refuse to repent and keep on sinning, they will die in their sins. But you will have saved yourself because you obeyed me.

❖ EZEKIEL 3:18-19

More than thirty years ago, as a newly ordained rabbi, I was sent by the Anti-Defamation League to raise community support to protest a proposed march of a neo-Nazi group in Skokie, Illinois, a Chicago suburb where a large number of Holocaust survivors lived. Do you know who were the most willing to stand against this march? The Christian community. Why? Because of their love for the Jewish people and their sense of responsibility to stand against anti-Semitism.

One of the best ways to combat anti-Semitism—or any form of prejudice—is with love. A loving attitude toward others ensures that we will think the best of them and treat them well. But what if we don't harbor any ill thoughts toward others, but we encounter someone who does? Again, love is the best response.

Oftentimes, a loving but straightforward reply is all that is needed. People might not realize that what they have said is offensive unless someone tells them. And sometimes people will stop speaking hatefully if they know that such remarks do not gain them approval. Leviticus 19:17 reminds us to "confront people directly so you will not be held guilty for their sin."

But why should we share in the guilt of someone who harbors anti-Semitic attitudes?

By doing nothing to stop it, we bear the responsibility. God says that if we do not warn a wicked man, "I will hold you responsible for their deaths" (Ezekiel 3:18).

It may be difficult or uncomfortable to speak up against hatred, and it may take some courage. But it is our God-given duty to defend those who cannot defend themselves. If we all made a loving but firm response to anti-Semitism, we could make great strides toward eliminating this harmful attitude.

A Christian Reflection on Speaking Up

Anti-Semitic comments, attitudes, and actions are sinful and should be confronted. Sometimes Christians avoid confrontations by citing Jesus' words, "Do not judge others, and you will not be judged" (Luke 6:37), but Jesus clearly wants his people to confront others' sins. After all, he instructed, "If another believer sins, rebuke that person" (Luke 17:3). What Jesus wants is for his people to lovingly admonish each other with the purpose of restoring one another to the right path. Next time you hear an anti-Semitic comment, speak up, knowing that "an open rebuke is better than hidden love! Wounds from a sincere friend are better than many kisses from an enemy" (Proverbs 27:5-6).

WEEK 19 // DAY 5

THE BEGINNING OF WISDOM

Instruct the wise, and they will be even wiser. Teach the righteous, and they will learn even more. Fear of the LORD is the foundation of wisdom. Knowledge of the Holy One results in good judgment. ❖ PROVERBS 9:9-10

I am always thankful that Bible-believing Christians stand with Israel in the midst of terrorist attacks, Arab propaganda campaigns, and growing anti-Semitism. One of the most important ways Christians can support Israel is through knowledge.

Proverbs 9:9 says to "instruct the wise, and they will be even wiser." A wise person always looks to learn and gain more wisdom. The more you know about Israel, the more likely you are to follow current events and get involved where appropriate.

As you learn about Israel's history and current events, share them with others. Make an effort to "teach the righteous, and they will learn even more." Sharing your knowledge about Israel helps others to overcome apathy and dispel misinformation.

Along with knowledge comes understanding. Specifically, the proverb says that "knowledge of the Holy One results in good judgment." The more you learn about Israel and her people, the more you will understand the present problems they face. Knowing the facts provides an accurate context for current events. Sharing those facts dispels myths.

Most important, the proverb states that "fear of the LORD is the foundation of wisdom." The Sages warn against the danger of knowledge without a foundational fear of God. That type of knowledge can lead down a dangerous path of distortion. But, the Sages explain, if we fear God, he will guide us toward the truth. The situation in Israel is complex, but if we ground our understanding in the fear of God, we will not go astray.

Therefore, let your desire to honor God be the motivating factor in gaining knowledge of Israel's past and present. As Christians and Jews, we share a common heritage rooted in the land of Israel. Together we stand for Israel and the people God calls "my own special treasure" (Exodus 19:5).

A Christian Reflection on Our Common Heritage

How true it is that Jews and Christians share a common heritage in the land of Israel and that Christians should seek more knowledge about the land, both in the past and in the present. In order to learn how God used the land and its people in the past, Christians need to resist the temptation to avoid the Old Testament and read only the New. In order to learn about Israel today, read newspapers and books from different perspectives in order to learn the truth about what is going on there. And most of all, pray for Israel.

BAD BLOOD

*[Haman] had learned of Mordecai's nationality, so he decided it was not enough
to lay hands on Mordecai alone. Instead, he looked for a way to destroy all the Jews
throughout the entire empire of Xerxes.* ❖ E S T H E R 3 : 6

When two people have a history of not getting along, it is often said that "bad blood"
exists between them. But when prejudice is involved, people don't get along *because* of
"blood," or race.

Sadly, this kind of racial prejudice has often been displayed toward the Jews. Today,
we call it anti-Semitism, but hatred toward the Jews can be traced back to the Persian
Empire, when the Jews faced government-sanctioned extermination.

In the book of Esther, bad blood existed between two main characters—Haman and
Mordecai. Haman was an Agagite, a descendant of Agag, an Amalekite king. Mordecai
was a Jew. Their bad blood dated back to when the Amalekites attacked Israel as they
left Egypt (see Exodus 17:8-16). Over the centuries, it had escalated into hatred toward
an entire race of people—the Jews.

Haman's prejudice was characterized by broad generalizations, lies, and personal
pride. Haman hated the Jews because they had a different belief and culture from his.
He also falsely accused the Jews of being disloyal to the king, saying, "There is a certain
race of people . . . who keep themselves separate from everyone else. . . . They refuse to
obey the laws of the king" (Esther 3:8). However, Mordecai had already demonstrated
his loyalty to the king (see Esther 2:21-23), so this accusation was clearly untrue.

Additionally, Haman desired honor and public recognition, and he was willing to
destroy others in an attempt to elevate himself. In the end, Haman was punished for
his arrogance (see Esther 7:9-10), as will be all who look down on others because of a
difference in belief or culture, for God himself will judge.

The story of Mordecai and Haman has lessons for us all. As people of faith, we
must be vigilant in exposing prejudice wherever it may exist and bringing God's love
and truth into those situations.

A Christian Reflection on Prejudice

The Bible allows no room for prejudice among God's people toward others. After all,
everybody is God's creature and, according to Genesis 1:27, is made in God's image. To
mistreat or shun others because of their race or ethnicity is a sin not only against them
but against God their creator. Christians must remember that "God loved the world
so much that he gave his one and only Son, so that everyone who believes in him will
not perish but have eternal life" (John 3:16). How can we mistreat people based on
their race if Jesus died on the cross for them?

Sabbath Reflections

What new truth about our responsibility for standing up against prejudice and injustice did you learn from this week's devotions?

How has this truth affected your faith?

How will you apply this truth to your daily life?

Your Key Verse for the Week:

❖ OTHER REFLECTIONS

DISPELLING OUR FEARS

I prayed to the LORD, and he answered me. He freed me from all my fears.
❖ PSALM 34:4

In Psalm 34, David gives us an example of what we can do to combat our fears—whether it's fear of losing a job, fear of the future, or fear of a doctor's report. In the midst of his fears, David prayed—and God freed him from all his fears. But how does that work? As David explains, we need to have a greater "fear" that dispels the lesser fears of this world, meaning we need to "fear the Lord" (Psalm 34:9).

This doesn't mean that we are afraid of God. Rather, "fear of the LORD" involves reverence, respect, and awe. This produces a submissive and obedient posture toward God. In fact, the *Torah* equates the fear of the Lord with obedience: "Israel, what does the LORD your God require of you? He requires only that you fear the LORD your God, and live in a way that pleases him. . . . And you must always obey the LORD's commands and decrees that I am giving you today for your own good" (Deuteronomy 10:12-13). As we obey God, we learn to trust him in a variety of situations, and this frees us from our fears.

How can we develop this reverent type of fear? In Psalm 34:13-14, David lists several characteristics of the person who fears God: This person doesn't lie, does good, and promotes peace. Such obedience builds a foundation of trust in God. With such a foundation, we don't have to fear anything.

As we develop reverence for God and submissive obedience to his Word, we will experience the kind of trust in God's goodness and provision that will free us from fear.

A Christian Reflection on the Fear of God

Christians sometimes wrongly think that the call to "fear God" is an Old Testament, not a New Testament, command. After all, the apostle John says, "Love has no fear, because perfect love expels all fear" (1 John 4:18). However, a closer look at the teaching of the New Testament makes it clear that Christians indeed are to "fear God." Notice how the book of Acts depicts the maturity of the growing church in Judea, Galilee, and Samaria: "[Peace] became stronger as the believers lived in the fear of the Lord" (Acts 9:31; see also 10:35). What kind of fear does perfect love expel, then? Not the fear of the Lord but rather the "fear of punishment" (1 John 4:18). Put your fear in God, and all other fears will disappear.

THE SECOND EXODUS

Do not be afraid, for I am with you. I will gather you and your children from east and west. I will say to the north and south, "Bring my sons and daughters back to Israel from the distant corners of the earth." ❖ ISAIAH 43:5-6

In addressing the Provisional State Council in Tel Aviv eight hours before the end of British rule in Palestine, David Ben Gurion declared the establishment of the State of Israel based on "the historic right of the Jewish people in the Land of Israel" and the "natural right of the Jewish people to be masters of their own fate."

These ringing words of Jewish independence found their truest expression in a law passed two years later, the Law of Return. This law, which guarantees the right of all Jews to emigrate to Israel, put into practice the Zionist movement's desire to build a safe haven for all Jews. Since that law was enacted, more than three million Jews have returned to Israel.

But for many Jews, emigration to Israel, or *aliyah*, is more than just a legal enactment or realization of a political movement. It is the fulfillment of biblical prophecy and God's promise to the descendants of the patriarchs: Abraham, Isaac, and Jacob.

"*Aliyah* is the heart, the very ideal of Israel. The State of Israel is only a tool . . . to bring Jewish people, who have been scattered all over the world for thousands of years, back to the Holy Land," said Natan Sharansky, who heads the Jewish Agency for Israel (JAFI), a partner organization of The Fellowship to support *aliyah*.

For centuries, Jews have dreamed of returning to their homeland. It has been a recurring theme in our daily prayers, and our holiday services on *Pesach* (Passover) and *Yom Kippur* traditionally conclude with the words, "Next year in Jerusalem."

Today, this is taking place before our very eyes. By praying and supporting this "second exodus" of Jews from oppression to freedom, Christians can show their compassion and concern for the Jewish people and help fulfill the biblical prophecies that promise the return to Israel of Jewish exiles from "the distant corners of the earth."

A Christian Reflection on the Second Exodus

Christians should pray today for the Jews' exodus from oppression to freedom and show compassion and concern for the Jewish people. Christians should also understand that the New Testament applies the "second exodus" expectations to the gospel story. As Jews and Christians look back on the Exodus as God's dramatic rescue from enslavement to the Egyptians, so Christians look back to Jesus as the one who rescues us from enslavement to guilt, sin, and death.

STRANGERS IN THE LAND

"I will give you the land of Canaan as your special possession." [God] said this when they were few in number, a tiny group of strangers in Canaan. They wandered from nation to nation, from one kingdom to another. ❖ PSALM 105:11-13

For thousands of years, since the Jews were expelled from their land by the Romans in AD 70, God's "special possession" has wandered from one nation to another. As they tried to settle, raise their families, and live according to God's Word and law, they remained strangers, often facing persecution, opposition, and hardship.

By the mid-1800s, it became clear to many in the Jewish community that "the Jews have lived and labored among the nations for almost two thousand years, but nonetheless they cannot become rooted organically within them. . . . We shall always remain strangers among nations."[4]

With the birth of the State of Israel, the long-held dream of the Jewish people returning to their homeland—the land given to them by God—became a reality. And since that time, more than three million Jews have returned to Israel.

But for many Jews today, the dream of returning to the Holy Land has remained just that—a dream. That is why The Fellowship and our partner organizations, such as the Jewish Agency for Israel, have worked tirelessly over the years to bring persecuted Jews home from the four corners of the world.

Over the next several years, we will work to help the final group of Ethiopian Jews make *aliyah*, or emigrate to Israel. Despite centuries of anti-Semitism, physical destruction, land confiscation, and enslavement, these Jews have maintained their Jewish heritage and prayed for their return to Jerusalem.

The Ethiopian Jews have never lost hope that they will return home. They have tirelessly and continually held to God's promise of the portion of land that they will inherit.

With the prayers and support of Christians around the world, these Jews will no longer be strangers in a foreign land, but will be home at last.

A *Christian Reflection on Helping the Persecuted*

As we think about the plight of the Ethiopian Jews, we should remember what Jesus taught his followers in the Sermon on the Mount: "God blesses those who hunger and thirst for justice, for they will be satisfied. God blesses those who are merciful, for they will be shown mercy" (Matthew 5:6-7). Christians should stand on the side of those who have been persecuted and mistreated and help them find a place of safety from their oppressors. Christians should mobilize their resources and their prayers in support of those who experience injustice.

A CELEBRATION OF HERITAGE

*All the people assembled with a unified purpose at the square just inside the Water
Gate. They asked Ezra the scribe to bring out the Book of the Law of Moses, which
the LORD had given for Israel to obey.* ❖ NEHEMIAH 8:1

For centuries, Jews in Ethiopia have celebrated their Jewish faith and roots in a
unique holiday known as *Sigd*, which means "to prostrate oneself." The celebration is
believed to have started in the fifteenth century when the priests gathered *Beta Israel*,
the "House of Israel," as they called themselves, to strengthen their faith in the face
of great persecution.

The priests were inspired by the description in the book of Nehemiah of how the
Jews who had returned from Babylon after seventy years of exile dedicated themselves
to follow God: "All the people assembled with a unified purpose at the square just
inside the Water Gate. They asked Ezra the scribe to bring out the Book of the Law
of Moses, which the LORD had given for Israel to obey" (Nehemiah 8:1).

Prior to the mass *aliyah* (emigration to Israel) of *Beta Israel*, which began in the 1980s,
generations of Ethiopian Jews would walk for days to a mountaintop where thousands
would join in prayer and the reading of the *Torah*. Following the afternoon prayers and
blowing of the *shofar*, the entire community would descend from the mountain for a joyous feast.

In this way, the Ethiopian Jews celebrated and remembered their connection to
Jerusalem and renewed their commitment to Jewish unity.

Sigd is now an official holiday, celebrated by all Jews in Israel. Ethiopian Jews who
have made *aliyah* to Israel gather at the Western Wall in Jerusalem to commemorate
this day. It is truly an inspiring and spiritual experience.

The holiday of *Sigd* commemorates the struggles that all who resettle went through
to arrive in the Holy Land. It also reminds us about the love that God will always have
for his children, wherever they may be found.

A Christian Reflection on Recommitment

Similar to how the Ethiopian Jews renew their covenant commitment, Christians
celebrate the Lord's Supper. Taking the cup and eating the bread is a statement of
continued faithfulness to Jesus, who died on the cross to forgive our sins. Whether
the Lord's Supper is celebrated every Sunday or once a month, the sacrament is a
powerful reminder of the sacrifice of Jesus and an opportunity for us to express our
continued faith in him.

WAITING IN HOPE

I waited patiently for the LORD to help me, and he turned to me and heard my cry.
❖ PSALM 40:1

Hanok was only ten when he, his mother, and his two brothers left their rural village and set out for Addis Ababa, Ethiopia's capital. Belonging to *Beta Israel*, the "House of Israel," as the Ethiopian Jews call themselves, Hanok and his family dreamed of one day emigrating to Israel.

For seven years, they lived in a refugee camp, awaiting their chance to leave. Conditions in the camp were horrendous, with cramped living conditions, inadequate medical attention, and a lack of other basic necessities, such as food and clothing. Still, they waited hopefully and prayed for the day when they would be able to board a plane bound for Israel.

For Hanok and his brother Tadasa, that prayer was answered when the two received word that they were cleared for emigration by the Ethiopian government. With the help of The Fellowship's On Wings of Eagles program, which brings needy Jews from other countries to Israel, the two boarded a plane to begin their new life in the Holy Land.

It was a bittersweet occasion for the brothers. Because of government restrictions, their mother and other brother were prevented from joining them. Even more tragic, Hanok's mother was one of hundreds of Ethiopian Jews who died in the refugee camps while waiting. To this day, Hanok does not know what has happened to his other brother.

The story of the Ethiopian Jews is historical and prophetic, but it is also inspirational. Their story is the story of God's people throughout the ages as they waited on the promise of God: Abraham and Sarah for a son and heir; the enslaved people of Israel for a deliverer; and countless others.

Their story is the story of answered prayer, as God is in the midst of all who wait on him in hope.

A Christian Reflection on the Power of Prayer

Hanok's story is a story of perseverance and answered prayer. Indeed, he spent seven years in the refugee camp asking God to hear his request. Jesus said this about prayer: "I tell you, keep on asking, and you will receive what you ask for. Keep on seeking, and you will find. Keep on knocking, and the door will be opened to you. For everyone who asks, receives. Everyone who seeks, finds. And to everyone who knocks, the door will be opened" (Luke 11:9-10). What is your deepest desire? Stay steadfast in your prayers to God.

REUNITED!

The LORD is rebuilding Jerusalem and bringing the exiles back to Israel. He heals the brokenhearted and bandages their wounds. ❖ PSALM 147:2-3

Because I travel frequently between my home in Israel and the United States, where The Fellowship is headquartered, I am frequently away from my family for weeks at a time. I know firsthand how difficult being apart from family can be.

But what if you were separated from your family for decades? And what if you had little or no information about them? What if you believed they were suffering and you could do nothing to help them? It would be unbearable.

During the 1980s, when Jews in Ethiopia were treated poorly and suffered from a widespread famine, Israel quietly began smuggling Jews out of Ethiopia and into Israel. When journalists reported it, the Ethiopian government stopped the program, known as Operation Moses. With the abrupt end to the exodus, families were separated, some members in Israel and others left behind in Ethiopia. Family members in Israel feared for those left behind because the situation for Jews in Ethiopia remained very bad.

Over the years, through the combined efforts of The Fellowship's On Wings of Eagles ministry, the Jewish Agency for Israel, and the Israeli government, more Ethiopian Jews have been reunited with family in Israel. Still, more work needs to be done, and in the upcoming years, more than seven thousand Ethiopian Jews will be brought to Israel in an effort appropriately dubbed Completing the Journey.

Not only is this a historic occurrence, but it is also the completion of a biblical mission. God is, indeed, gathering the exiles of Israel: "The LORD builds up Jerusalem; he gathers the exiles of Israel" (Psalm 147:2, NIV).

We rejoice for those who are being reunited with family members, and we welcome them home with open arms and open hearts.

A Christian Reflection on "Completing the Journey"

We join our Jewish friends in supporting and celebrating the return of the Ethiopian Jews to Israel. Psalm 74 was composed in the aftermath of the destruction of Jerusalem and in the midst of the exile. The Ethiopian Jews, in a sense, continue to live in exile and desire to return to the land after many, many centuries. We can join with the psalmist in praying, "Don't let the downtrodden be humiliated again. Instead, let the poor and needy praise your name" (Psalm 74:21).

Sabbath Reflections

What new truth about hope and God's faithfulness did you learn from this week's devotions?

How has this truth affected your faith?

How will you apply this truth to your daily life?

Your Key Verse for the Week:

❖ OTHER REFLECTIONS

DELIGHT IN THE LORD

Take delight in the LORD, and he will give you your heart's desires.
❖ PSALM 37:4

To take delight in someone means we experience great pleasure in that person's presence. We come away from our time together uplifted, refreshed, and encouraged, wanting to spend more time with that person.

But delighting in someone requires that we truly know that person. So when David tells us to "take delight in the LORD," he means we need to take time to know God. We can do this through studying his Word, spending time in prayer, and worshiping him.

Maimonides, a renowned medieval philosopher and rabbi, in explaining the commandment to love God, said that God promises that the more we understand him intellectually, the more we will appreciate his ways. And the more we appreciate his ways, the more we will come to love him in our hearts. According to Maimonides, this sequence is written into the very code of the universe as a natural progression toward loving God.

As we come to understand God's great love for us, his never-failing mercy and grace, his everlasting arms of comfort, and his tender compassion for all his children, we will delight in him.

David says that as we delight in God, "he will give [us our] heart's desires." This doesn't mean that he will give us the new car we've been wanting, or whatever else our heart thinks it desires. Rather, as we spend time with God, take joy in his presence, and truly understand him, the desires of our heart will be transformed and made more pure.

We will discover, as David did, that God's concerns will be our concerns. We will reflect his love for others, his care for the poor and needy, his compassion for the downtrodden. In other words, we will want what he wants, and so he will give us that which is according to his will, his plan, and his purpose.

A Christian Reflection on Joy in Christ's Presence

Before Jesus was crucified, he instructed his disciples to cultivate an intimate and lasting relationship with him. In John, he teaches this point with the image of a grapevine: "I am the vine; you are the branches" (John 15:5). He told his disciples repeatedly to "remain" (or "abide") in him (John 15:4-7, 10). As David understood, those who spend time in God's presence experience transformation of desire and answered prayer. Jesus taught, "If you remain in me and my words remain in you, you may ask for anything you want, and it will be granted" (John 15:7). The result? Abundant joy (see John 15:11).

MAKING A DIFFERENCE

When I heard this, I sat down and wept. In fact, for days I mourned, fasted, and prayed to the God of heaven. ✦ NEHEMIAH 1:4

When Nehemiah received the disheartening news about the state of the Jewish exiles who had returned to Jerusalem, he cried, prayed, and then took action. Because of his willingness to get involved, Nehemiah is a true hero, a remarkable man who made a difference.

Nehemiah was a Jewish exile serving Artaxerxes, the king of Persia, as his wine tester. The Jews, who had been exiled by the Babylonians seventy years earlier, finally were allowed to return to Jerusalem. But things at first went badly. As Nehemiah's brother, Hanani, reported, "They are in great trouble and disgrace" (Nehemiah 1:3).

When Nehemiah heard this news, his heart broke. But while he grieved deeply, he didn't brood about it. Rather, after his initial grief, Nehemiah fasted and prayed to God. In fact, Nehemiah spent *four months* praying, planning, and preparing to appeal to the king.

One day, as Nehemiah was serving the king, Artaxerxes noticed that his servant was downcast. When the king asked Nehemiah what was wrong, Nehemiah—though badly frightened—was ready with his request. Because "the gracious hand of God" (Nehemiah 2:8) was upon Nehemiah, the king not only listened but granted all Nehemiah's requests.

Nehemiah made a difference. He saw a problem and he stepped up to the call. The Sages, in *Ethics of Our Fathers*, explain that in situations where no one else steps forward, we must act like Nehemiah and be the person to take responsibility. It takes initiative and courage to rise up when no one else will heed the call, but the Sages remind us not to rely on others to carry the responsibility, but to realize that—at every moment—we can stand up.

We can make a difference as we look for opportunities where God can use us. Then, like Nehemiah, ask God for the courage and wisdom to take action.

A Christian Reflection on Making a Difference

Nehemiah truly made a difference in the life of the Jewish community. God gifted him with the wisdom, leadership skills, and determination to return to Jerusalem, serve as the governor of Judah, and rebuild that city's walls. Though he lived many centuries before Paul, he is an illustration of someone who models the proper response to the apostle's charge: "Work hard to show the results of your salvation, obeying God with deep reverence and fear. For God is working in you, giving you the desire and the power to do what pleases him" (Philippians 2:12-13).

IN THE FACE OF OPPOSITION

*I replied, "The God of heaven will help us succeed. We, his servants, will start
rebuilding this wall. But you have no share, legal right, or historic claim in Jerusalem."*
❖ NEHEMIAH 2:20

When I began forming an organization devoted to building bridges of understanding
between Christians and Jews, the naysayers quickly emerged: "Why are you doing
this?" "This isn't going to work." "How can anyone repair two thousand years of animosity and discord between these two?"

If I had listened to my detractors, The Fellowship might never have been birthed.
But I trusted that an organization whose mission was to help "brothers live together
in harmony" (Psalm 133:1) was following God's heart and that he would guide me and
give me success. And he did!

Nehemiah faced his detractors as well. Even before he started to rebuild the ruined
walls of Jerusalem, his critics mocked him. "What are you doing? Are you rebelling
against the king?" (Nehemiah 2:19). Despite their ridicule, Nehemiah remained reso-
lute and believed God would help him.

Unfortunately, Nehemiah's enemies began attacking the people as they worked on
the walls. Still, Nehemiah didn't give up. He first prayed to God for protection and
then took action to position guards and arm the people in defense.

Prayer and action, prayer and action. Are you seeing a pattern here? Just as he had
when petitioning the king for favor, Nehemiah trusted God to protect him while he
remained focused on his goal: to rebuild the city walls of Jerusalem.

When you face criticism for doing what you know is right, remember Nehemiah.
Refuse to respond to your detractors in kind or become discouraged. Take your concerns to God and tell him how you feel.

Remember, God promises that he will be with you. And as you labor in his name,
God will reward your faith—just as he did for Nehemiah.

A Christian Reflection on Facing Opposition

How do we avoid disappointment when we run into obstacles and opposition in life?
Even more radically, how do we experience joy in the face of our problems? Paul asks us
to consider the following: "We can rejoice, too, when we run into problems and trials,
for we know that they help us develop endurance. And endurance develops strength of
character, and character strengthens our confident hope of salvation. And this hope will
not lead to disappointment" (Romans 5:3-5). Nehemiah is indeed a good example of this
attitude in the face of the most severe opposition. As we face trials, we can remember
that God is in control and will use these trials for our good.

CARING FOR THE POOR

When I heard their complaints, I was very angry. After thinking it over, I spoke out against these nobles and officials. I told them, "You are hurting your own relatives by charging interest when they borrow money!" Then I called a public meeting to deal with the problem. ❖ NEHEMIAH 5:6-7

Sometimes we get so involved in a project that we forget about the needs of others. Not Nehemiah. Even though he undertook a major rebuilding project, he still paid attention to the needs of those around him—particularly the poor.

In this instance, the strenuous job of wall building, plus the added stress of protecting themselves against enemy threats, prevented some people from cultivating their fields. This led to widespread famine and economic crisis.

As a result, many Jewish families sold everything they owned to pay the taxes on their land. To make matters worse, their fellow countrymen were charging exorbitant interest in violation of the law. Some of the poorer families were even forced to sell their children into slavery!

Nehemiah was furious when he learned of these abuses. He realized that the rebuilding of Jerusalem would be *useless* if the people didn't care for one another. Nehemiah called the leaders together and chastised them for their behavior. As a group, the leaders agreed to halt their unfair practices and give back the money they had extorted.

God's concern for the poor and oppressed is expressed in nearly every book of the Bible. In Psalm 41:1, we read, "Blessed are those who have regard for the weak; the LORD delivers them in times of trouble" (NIV). The word *regard* in Hebrew conveys the sense of "paying attention, or pondering." It captures the idea of focusing one's mind on something. Nehemiah clearly was pondering and paying attention to the needs of those around him.

Time and time again, the prophets and Sages addressed the inconsistency of those who expressed ritual piety but mistreated people. They explained that God first and foremost desires his people to show kindness to others before extravagant displays of righteousness.

Today, God still calls us to pay attention to the needs of others around us. Ponder how you might help.

A Christian Reflection on Concern for the Poor

In similar fashion to Nehemiah, James confronts Christians who favor the rich over the poor and challenges them by asking, "Hasn't God chosen the poor in this world to be rich in faith? Aren't they the ones who will inherit the Kingdom he promised to those who love him? But you dishonor the poor!" (James 2:5-6). The Jerusalem church affirmed Paul's ministry to the Gentiles; their only suggestion was to "keep on helping the poor" (Galatians 2:10). People of faith who have resources are called to be sensitive to the needs of the poor.

FINAL RESTORATION

The people responded, "In view of all this, we are making a solemn promise and putting it in writing. On this sealed document are the names of our leaders and Levites and priests." ❖ NEHEMIAH 9:38

Nehemiah and the people had completed rebuilding the walls of Jerusalem in an amazing fifty-two days, despite all the obstacles. It was obvious to everyone that the work had been done with the help of God. Now it was time to relax, right?

No. Nehemiah realized that restoring the walls of Jerusalem was the first step in helping the returned exiles. Now it was time to help restore the people spiritually.

The people gathered in the city square as Ezra the priest began reading the law of Moses. As the Levites walked among them, explaining the meaning of what was read, the people wept, for they realized how far they had strayed from obeying God.

While reading God's law, the people discovered that it was the time to celebrate the Jewish festival of *Sukkot*, the Feast of Shelters. So they set out to gather branches and build their shelters, as commanded in the law, to commemorate the wanderings of their ancestors during the Exodus. It was a wonderful reminder for the people of how God had faithfully protected them and guided them throughout their history to that very day.

This time of restoration concluded with a time of community confession and repentance. For three hours, the people took turns confessing their sins and worshiping the Lord. Finally, the people joined in prayer, retelling their history as God's people and his work on their behalf. As they recounted God's many promises and his faithfulness, the people solemnly vowed to recommit themselves to God.

What a beautiful illustration of the need for restoration in our lives as well. As you study God's Word, ask him to show you the areas where you might need to recommit yourself to obeying him.

A Christian Reflection on Spiritual Restoration

God used both Ezra and Nehemiah to restore Jerusalem spiritually and physically. How often through our lives do we find ourselves drifting into a kind of spiritual lethargy without even realizing it? In the book of Revelation, the church in the city of Laodicea is called "lukewarm," indicating their lack of passion in their relationship with God. How does God respond to those who are lukewarm? "I will spit [them] out of my mouth!" (Revelation 3:16). If that is where you find yourself today, turn to God in prayer and ask him to rekindle your affection for him and your desire to follow him.

A HAPPY ENDING?

Remember this good deed, O my God, and do not forget all that I have faithfully done for the Temple of my God and its services. ❖ NEHEMIAH 13:14

As the book of Nehemiah concludes, we might imagine that all is well—the walls have been restored and the people have recommitted themselves to following and obeying God. Israel was again a godly nation, trusting in God and living by the truth of his Word.

Unfortunately, after Nehemiah returned to Persia, he received news that the people had lapsed into disobedience. Imagine his dismay when he discovered that one of his old enemies, Tobiah, who had mocked his efforts, had his own room in the Temple.

Not only that, but the people had quit tithing, forcing the Levites to neglect their Temple responsibilities because they had to work in the fields to feed their families. People were even working on the Sabbath!

All this occurred despite the people's renewed vow to God and despite all that God had allowed them to accomplish. How quickly they had forgotten.

Nehemiah returned to Jerusalem and got to work again. He tossed out Tobiah, instructed the people to bring their proper tithes to the Temple, and stationed some of his own men at Jerusalem's gates to prevent desecration of any kind on the Sabbath. In short, Nehemiah's swift and firm leadership in the face of the crisis made it clear to the people that they must respect and submit to God's holy law at all times.

We all have a tendency to lapse into neglect of God's will and forget his goodness to us. Thankfully, God, in his infinite mercy, constantly waits for his people to repent—*teshuvah* in Hebrew. As we turn to God again, with confession and thanksgiving, we will find him waiting.

A Christian Reflection on Daily Repentance

It's important for people of faith to remember that our decision to follow God is not a one-time act, but rather a lifestyle of continual repentance and recommitment. The struggle with sin, wanting to live life our own way and not God's way, continues, and we need to draw on our faith to persist. Paul confesses his continuing struggle with sin in Romans 7, honestly stating, "I have discovered this principle of life—that when I want to do what is right, I inevitably do what is wrong" (Romans 7:21). But Paul does not despair; he goes on to ask, "Who will free me from this life that is dominated by sin and death? Thank God! The answer is Jesus Christ our Lord" (Romans 7:24-25). As you continue to struggle with sin, turn to Jesus, repent, and discover God's forgiveness.

Sabbath Reflections

What new truth about the life of Nehemiah did you learn from this week's devotions?

How has this truth affected your faith?

How will you apply this truth to your daily life?

Your Key Verse for the Week:

❖ OTHER REFLECTIONS

THE CONTENDER

O LORD, oppose those who oppose me. Fight those who fight against me.
❖ PSALM 35:1

As a young shepherd boy, David stepped into the role of the contender confidently.
He willingly volunteered to fight Goliath, the giant Philistine champion, because he
knew God would fight for him.

Do you remember what he said to his mighty opponent? "You come to me with
sword, spear, and javelin, but I come to you in the name of the LORD of Heaven's
Armies—the God of the armies of Israel, whom you have defied. Today the LORD will
conquer you" (1 Samuel 17:45-46).

Fast-forward to an older David when he wrote Psalm 35. David was being hunted
down by enemies who hated him without cause. And whom did David call upon? God,
his contender!

In Psalm 35, David addresses God as the contender who is able to fight on his
behalf against his enemies. He urges God to "put on your armor, and take up your
shield" (35:2), to "lift up your spear and javelin" (35:3)—to take up the full range
of offensive and defensive weaponry to engage the enemy. David exhorts God to
announce to his enemies, "I will give you victory!" (35:3).

David was completely confident that God would come to his rescue. He knew that
God comes to the aid of all who call upon him. Indeed, he writes, "LORD, who can com-
pare with you? Who else rescues the helpless from the strong?" (Psalm 35:10).

When facing opposition or wrongly accused by our enemies, we can have the same
confidence that God will be our Contender. With God on our side, we have a Mighty
Warrior prepared to fight on our behalf. We can pray along with David: "Wake up!
Rise to my defense! Take up my case, my God and my Lord." (Psalm 35:23).

A Christian Reflection on the Mighty Warrior

Paul was one who faced considerable opposition in his life and ministry. Like David,
he also had confidence in God's power to protect him. In 2 Corinthians, Paul responds
to those who thought he acted from human motives, saying: "We are human, but we
don't wage war as humans do. We use God's mighty weapons, not worldly weapons,
to knock down the strongholds of human reasoning and to destroy false arguments"
(2 Corinthians 10:3-4). As you face daily struggles in life, think of David facing
Goliath or Paul facing his detractors, and draw on the power of God.

A TIME TO REMEMBER

We have happy memories of the godly, but the name of a wicked person rots away.
❖ PROVERBS 10:7

If you've ever been to the Vietnam Veterans Memorial in Washington, DC, known as "The Wall," you probably have witnessed someone doing a rubbing of a name. It's a way for that person to honor and acknowledge the sacrifice of that soldier during the Vietnam War.

More than fifty-eight thousand names are etched on the polished black granite. There's LeRoy Tafoya, Jimmy Martinez, and Tom Gonzales, boyhood friends from Midvale, Utah, who were killed in a span of sixteen dark days in late 1967. There is Spec. 4 James T. Davis, the first battlefield casualty in Vietnam, and Kelton Rena Turner, an eighteen-year-old Marine, the final life lost. Behind each name is a story, a life, a loved one lost, and a sacrifice given for his or her country.

Memorial Day is a time to remember those who have died while fighting for the United States. Holidays such as Memorial Day and Veteran's Day are intended to focus our attention on the sacrifice others have made on our behalf. Many of these brave men and women made the ultimate sacrifice. On Memorial Day, we honor and remember them.

The Word of God says that "the memory of the righteous is a blessing" (Proverbs 10:7, ESV). For generations to come, people will remember the sacrifices made by those who died so that we could live in freedom and peace. God does not take such sacrifices lightly, and neither should we. "The LORD cares deeply when his loved ones die" (Psalm 116:15). The value of a human life cannot be measured; its loss cannot be replaced.

For those who are left behind—those who have lost loved ones in war—Memorial Day can be difficult. For those families, we thank you for the service and sacrifice of your loved ones. And in your grief remember that "the LORD is close to the broken-hearted; he rescues those whose spirits are crushed" (Psalm 34:18).

A Christian Reflection on a Soldier's Sacrifice

In America, our military protects our freedom, our rights, and even our very lives. Memorial Day and Veteran's Day are indeed special times for us to thank our military and their families for their service, and in particular, to remember those who have lost their lives. Jesus reminds us that his heavenly Father has a special place in his heart for those who suffer the ultimate sacrifice of a loved one: "God blesses those who mourn, for they will be comforted" (Matthew 5:4).

OUR HOPE

I will put my Spirit in you, and you will live again and return home to your own land.
Then you will know that I, the LORD, have spoken, and I have done what I said. Yes,
the LORD has spoken! ❖ EZEKIEL 37:14

Seventy years before Israel was declared a nation, Naphtali Herz Imber penned the words to a poem titled "*Tikvateynu*," which translates to "Our Hope." In this poem, Imber puts into words how he felt upon learning about the establishment of one of the first Jewish settlements in what was then Ottoman Palestine. Here are the first two stanzas:

> *As long as in the heart, within,*
> *A Jewish soul still yearns*
> *And onward, toward the ends of the east,*
> *An eye still gazes toward Zion;*
> *Our hope is not yet lost,*
> *The hope of two thousand years,*
> *To be a free people in our land,*
> *The land of Zion and Jerusalem.*

In 2004, this poem was officially adopted as the Israeli national anthem, "*Hatikvah*," which means "The Hope."

Some have linked the idea of hope to the biblical prophet Ezekiel and his vision of the dry bones. In this account, Ezekiel sees a valley filled with dry bones, and God commands him to prophesy to the bones to come to life. But the bones, which symbolize the exiled people of Israel, reply, "We have become old, dry bones—all hope is gone. Our nation is finished" (Ezekiel 37:11). But God replies, "I will put my Spirit in you, and you will live again and return home to your own land. Then you will know that I, the LORD, have spoken, and I have done what I said" (Ezekiel 37:14).

Our hope has been realized today, and we have been brought back to new life in Israel. We thank God for what he has done for us as his people and for what he will continue to do.

A Christian Reflection on Bringing Life to Dry Bones

What God has done for a nation, he can also do for individuals. As Paul writes in Ephesians 2:1, "Once you were dead because of your disobedience and your many sins." But he does not end the story there. Paul continues: "But God is so rich in mercy, and he loved us so much, that even though we were dead because of our sins, he gave us life when he raised Christ from the dead" (Ephesians 2:4-5). Even when we die, God will not allow the dry bones of his people to rot; rather, "our dying bodies must be transformed into bodies that will never die" (1 Corinthians 15:53). Praise God, who can turn dry bones into living ones!

SONGS OF PRAISE

Praise the LORD! Yes, give praise, O servants of the LORD. Praise the name of the LORD! Blessed be the name of the LORD now and forever. Everywhere—from east to west—praise the name of the LORD. ❖ PSALM 113:1-3

In the Jewish tradition, we have a collection of songs we sing or recite at our great festivals of Israel: *Pesach, Shavuot, Sukkot,* and *Hanukkah.* We also honor holidays such as Israel Independence Day and Jerusalem Day through song. In fact, we have a special collection of songs known as the *Hallel,* psalms of praise that we sing on just these special occasions. The *Hallel* actually consists of the words from Psalms 113–118. *Hallel,* meaning "praise," is an oft-repeated word in this collection of psalms.

By reciting these psalms on holidays, we remember that God is exalted over all the nations (Psalm 113:4); that he delivered us from Egypt (Psalm 114); that God is our help and shield (Psalm 115:9-11); and that he delivers us from trouble (Psalm 116).

We conclude by inviting the nations to join our songs of praise (Psalm 117) and by giving thanks to God for our continuing survival (Psalm 118). This thanksgiving is particularly appropriate for Israel Independence Day and Jerusalem Day because those are the days on which we celebrate God's sovereign authority: "Though hostile nations surrounded me, I destroyed them all with the authority of the LORD. Yes, they surrounded and attacked me, but I destroyed them all with the authority of the LORD" (Psalm 118:10-11).

Reciting the *Hallel* is a way to express our joy and praise for God's past miracles and affirm our faith in God's future miracles on our behalf. I invite you to read through these stirring and beautiful psalms of praise this week. Let the words of the psalmist inspire you to praise God for how he has delivered you and provided for you in the past, and for how he will work in your life in the days ahead.

A *Christian Reflection on Jesus and the* Hallel

"They sang a hymn and went out to the Mount of Olives" (Mark 14:26). After observing the Passover (*Pesach*) meal, Jesus and his disciples left the upper room to go to the Mount of Olives, specifically the olive grove called Gethsemane, where he would be arrested and ultimately crucified. What were they singing? The passage doesn't say, but it's likely they were singing the *Hallel,* because it was common for the Jews in the first century to sing Psalms 113–114 before the final Passover meal and 115–118 afterward. As you read through the *Hallel* yourself, think of Jesus singing these songs of thanksgiving, celebration, and redemption at this crucial moment in his life.

RESTORED TREASURE

Writhe and groan like a woman in labor, you people of Jerusalem, for now you must leave this city to live in the open country. You will soon be sent in exile to distant Babylon. But the LORD will rescue you there; he will redeem you from the grip of your enemies. ❖ MICAH 4:10

For the Jewish people, Jerusalem is one of our most treasured possessions. For centuries, we grieved the loss of Jerusalem and the Temple, until the city was finally restored to us—an event that we celebrate and honor on Jerusalem Day.

Even after Israel was declared a state in 1948, the United Nations designated the city of Jerusalem as an international city. Half of it, including the Western Wall, remained under Jordanian control. Even though there were stipulations allowing Jews to visit the Western Wall and other holy sites, the Jordanians never honored that agreement. For nearly two decades, Jews were denied access to these sacred sites.

During the Six-Day War in 1967, Israeli forces recaptured Jerusalem and reunited the city. One of the first people to reach the Western Wall was Israeli Defense Minister Moshe Dayan, who inserted a prayer into a crevice in the wall. His petition: that lasting peace would "descend upon the House of Israel."

We mark this momentous occasion by a mass pilgrimage to the Western Wall. The streets of Jerusalem are transformed into a festive, symbolic procession as we sing, dance, pray, and celebrate our restored treasure.

This tradition echoes the ritual manner of celebration of the Israelites in the time of the Temple. During the biblically mandated holy days, all Jews trekked from everywhere in Israel to celebrate in Jerusalem. They came to the Temple amid cheers and songs from the inhabitants of Jerusalem. On these occasions, Jerusalem became the center of the world, the source of all holiness.

On Jerusalem Day, we remember this tradition, God's faithfulness to his people, and his answer to our prayers that Jerusalem be restored as the center and capital of the Jewish homeland.

A Christian Reflection on Jerusalem

Jerusalem is an amazing city. God made his presence known there at the Temple on Mount Zion. Jesus walked its streets; his crucifixion, burial, and resurrection took place there. Indeed, when the book of Revelation describes our life forever with God, it speaks of the New Jerusalem (see Revelation 21–22). This Jerusalem has no Temple, because "the Lord God Almighty and the Lamb are its temple" (Revelation 21:22). This Jerusalem is made not of stone and mortar, but of pure gold and precious stones and jewels. And finally, there is a river that flows through the city, and on each side is a tree of life (Revelation 22:1-2). The earthly Jerusalem points to heaven and our life forever with God and attests to the greatness of that city for which we can thank God and pray for peace and prosperity.

WHOM WILL YOU SERVE?

Fear the LORD and serve him wholeheartedly. Put away forever the idols your ancestors worshiped when they lived beyond the Euphrates River and in Egypt. Serve the LORD alone. But if you refuse to serve the LORD, then choose today whom you will serve. . . . But as for me and my family, we will serve the LORD. ❖ JOSHUA 24:14-15

Apart from Jerusalem, the ruins of Masada are one of the most popular destinations for tourists visiting Israel. The events that took place atop this high rocky mountain have become a modern-day symbol of Jewish resistance and faith and a desire to serve the one true God.

The courageous and tragic story of the 960 Jews who killed themselves rather than submit to Roman capture in the first century has encouraged Jews for hundreds of years. Historians have credited this story with inspiring the Warsaw Ghetto uprising during World War II. Even today, Israeli soldiers pledge their loyalty to defend Israel atop Masada with the vow, "Masada shall not fall again."

It is the words of the Masada leader, Elazar ben Yair, that resonate with people of faith: "Since we long ago resolved never to be servants to the Romans, nor to any other than to God himself, Who alone is the true and just Lord of mankind, the time is now come that obliges us to make that resolution true in practice."

Throughout the Bible, men and women of faith have voiced their determination to choose God over idols, over foreign rule, over the culture. We hear it echoed in the words of Joshua: "Choose for yourselves this day whom you will serve. . . . But as for me and my household, we will serve the LORD" (Joshua 24:14-15, NIV).

We may never face the same circumstances as the Jews who lived atop Masada, but we each must make a choice daily whom we will serve. Whom will you choose today?

A Christian Reflection on Exclusive Loyalty

"Who sits on the throne of your life?" That was the question popularized by Bill Bright, the founder of a ministry to college students now known as Cru. In other words, *what* or *who* is most important to you? After searching for meaning in a variety of areas—money, wisdom, work, power—the author of Ecclesiastes realized the only meaningful response was to "fear God and obey his commands" (Ecclesiastes 12:13). In other words, choose God first, and then you will find meaning in your life. Jesus also taught his disciples about exclusive loyalty when he told them, "No one can serve two masters. For you will hate one and love the other; you will be devoted to one and despise the other" (Matthew 6:24). Choose today to put God first in your life.

Sabbath Reflections

What new truth about Israel's history and traditions did you learn from this week's devotions?

How has this truth affected your faith?

How will you apply this truth to your daily life?

Your Key Verse for the Week:

❖ OTHER REFLECTIONS

MY SHEPHERD

The LORD is my shepherd; I have all that I need. ❖ PSALM 23:1

The opening words of Psalm 23 are among the most well-known and beloved of Scripture: "The LORD is my shepherd." While the imagery of a shepherd may seem foreign to us, this was a familiar image for people in biblical times.

Shepherds are concerned with feeding their sheep, bringing them to good pasture, grooming them, leading them, protecting them, and oftentimes, going after the wandering lost ones. It is an all-encompassing job!

The job of shepherding often went to the children of the family, and David, the youngest of eight brothers, was given the task. According to Jewish tradition, David had such compassion for his sheep that when one was tired, he would carry that sheep on his shoulders. So when it came to describing his relationship with God, David relied on an example that came from his experience—and his heart.

David knew God as his shepherd. He knew God cared for him, protected him, and guided him. David trusted his shepherd to lead him through life's difficulties and to provide rest when he needed it. David had full confidence in his shepherd and obediently followed wherever God led.

During the holiest holidays on the Jewish calendar, *Rosh Hashanah* (the Jewish New Year) and *Yom Kippur* (Day of Atonement), we recite a prayer called the *Unetaneh Tokef*. The imagery in this prayer is that of a shepherd tending to his flock: "All mankind will pass before You like members of the flock." According to Jewish tradition, every single soul passes before God, one at a time, and he considers each person, determining their needs for the year to come with compassion, mercy, and love—just like a shepherd.

David found great comfort in knowing God as his shepherd. Just as God cared for David, we can trust that we, his people and his sheep, will be cared for also.

A Christian Reflection on the Good Shepherd

With Psalm 23 as background, consider Jesus' words in John 10:11, 14-16: "I am the good shepherd. The good shepherd sacrifices his life for the sheep. . . . I am the good shepherd; I know my own sheep, and they know me. . . . I sacrifice my life for the sheep. I have other sheep, too, that are not in this sheepfold. I must bring them also. They will listen to my voice, and there will be one flock with one shepherd." We look to Jesus as our Good Shepherd. He sacrificed himself for his sheep (the Jews) as well as for "other sheep" (Gentiles), making all who believe in him "one flock with one shepherd" (John 10:16).

A CELEBRATION OF UNITY

After breaking camp at Rephidim, they came to the wilderness of Sinai and set up camp there at the base of Mount Sinai. ❖ EXODUS 19:2

The Jewish celebration of *Shavuot*, also known as Pentecost, commemorates the giving of the *Torah* at Mount Sinai exactly fifty days after the Exodus from Egypt. Jews around the world spend all night studying the *Torah*, after which, at morning prayers, we read the climactic story of the giving of the Ten Commandments.

We're always excited to hear the Ten Commandments, but it's important not to overlook the verses that immediately precede them. Oftentimes, the deepest parts of Scripture are found in the places we don't immediately look. We're taught to look for little clues—and we find one at the very beginning of Exodus 19: "They had departed from Rephidim, had come to the Wilderness of Sinai, and camped in the wilderness. So Israel camped there before the mountain" (Exodus 19:2, NKJV).

Why does the *Torah* repeat that seemingly meaningless detail about the encampment at Sinai? The very same verse tells us twice that the people camped. Why the repetition?

Rashi, the great eleventh-century Jewish Sage, notices a telling bit of grammar in the text. When the sentence first uses the word *camped* (Hebrew, *vayachanu*), the subject is plural—*they* camped. In the second part of the verse, *camped* (*vayichan*) is singular—*he* camped. The Jews arrived at Sinai as many—individuals, families, and tribes. But the experience at Sinai made them one—a single people with a single heart worshiping the one God.

In this simple, easily overlooked verse, the *Torah* reminds us to find unity in joy and gratitude. Be like the Israelites at Sinai—gather together around the fountain of faith and learning, and come away with a single heart for a single purpose: to do God's will in the world.

A Christian Reflection on Unity

When we study the church, we cannot miss the sad fact that there are many, many divisions and denominations. Even within denominations there are divisions. Notwithstanding some good reasons for different denominations, we should be sad that the church has experienced this type of fragmentation. Even in light of our present situation, we must hear Paul when he encourages his readers to "make every effort to keep yourselves united in the Spirit, binding yourselves together with peace. For there is one body and one Spirit, just as you have been called to one glorious hope for the future. There is one Lord, one faith, one baptism, and one God and Father, who is over all and in all and living through all" (Ephesians 4:3-6).

ETERNAL REVELATION

Count off seven weeks from when you first begin to cut the grain at the time of harvest. Then celebrate the Festival of Harvest to honor the LORD your God. Bring him a voluntary offering in proportion to the blessings you have received from him.
❖ DEUTERONOMY 16:9-10

Shavuot, or Pentecost, is associated with the giving of the *Torah* and the revelation of God at Mount Sinai, and yet neither the date of the revelation nor the precise date of the holiday is written in the Scriptures.

All we are told is that the festival occurs seven weeks from the time that we "first begin to cut the grain at the time of harvest." In addition, no one knows for sure where this momentous event occurred. Different theories abound, but God has made it so that no one can point to the precise location of Mount Sinai with complete certainty.

What we don't know tells us a lot. The details that are absent from the story of the revelation point to a profound truth about the *Torah*: It is absolutely and unequivocally eternal. No date is given because the Word of God is beyond time. It was, is, and always will be true.

The location of the revelation is unknown because God's Word is also beyond space. It holds true in every corner of the earth and is accessible no matter where we live. By deliberately leaving us without the exact knowledge of where and when this revelation took place, God tells us that exactly where and when are irrelevant.

What we do know is that the *Torah* was given in the desert. Had the *Torah* been given in a lush, bountiful land, we could have argued that obeying it depended on easy circumstances. The *Torah* was given in a place known for harsh conditions and scarcity in order to teach us that there are no conditions under which God's Word does not apply.

No matter where you are or what your circumstances may be, God has a message for you right now that is timeless, relevant, wise, and good.

A Christian Reflection on God's Eternal Word

The New Testament joins the *Tanakh* in praising and commending God's Word as always and everywhere relevant to our lives. According to Peter, quoting Isaiah 40:6-8, the Word of God transforms our lives: "You have been born again, but not to a life that will quickly end. Your new life will last forever because it comes from the eternal, living word of God. As the Scriptures say, 'People are like grass; their beauty is like a flower in the field. The grass withers and the flower fades. But the word of the Lord remains forever.' And that word is the Good News that was preached to you" (1 Peter 1:23-25).

DIVINE TIME

When the people saw how long it was taking Moses to come back down the mountain, they gathered around Aaron. "Come on," they said, "make us some gods who can lead us. We don't know what happened to this fellow Moses, who brought us here from the land of Egypt." ❖ EXODUS 32:1

The Festival of Weeks—*Shavuot*, or Pentecost—celebrates the giving of the *Torah*, God's Word, to humanity. But it didn't go smoothly.

Moses went up on Mount Sinai to receive the tablets, promising to return forty days later. The children of Israel miscalculated, and when Moses didn't show up when they expected, they assumed he had died. Although they had witnessed the hand of God just seven weeks earlier during their Exodus from Egypt, the Israelites turned to idolatry and created the infamous golden calf.

When Moses came down from the mountain with the tablets in his hands and saw the horrible thing the people had done, he threw the tablets down and smashed them. The relationship between God and Israel was tainted, three thousand men were executed, and the opportunity to receive the greatest gift from God was nearly lost altogether. It took many months and prayers before Israel was forgiven.

All this because the Israelites thought that Moses was late! He wasn't a week late or even a day late. He was only six hours late. But that was enough for the Israelites to give up and walk away from something that, only moments earlier, they had believed in so deeply!

One of life's greatest challenges is waiting. Waiting to find your soul mate. Waiting for children. Waiting for a good job. Waiting for things to get better. The challenge is to keep our faith even when we feel abandoned, forgotten, and alone.

There are two kinds of time in life. There is "my time" and "divine time." "My time" is when I think things should happen. "Divine time" is the *right time* for things to happen. There is no time like the right time—and only the Master of the world knows exactly when that should be.

A Christian Reflection on Patience

The Bible emphasizes repeatedly that God keeps his promises. However, sometimes he does not do so according to our timetable. Even after Jesus' death, resurrection, and ascension, the early church grew impatient concerning Jesus' promised return, and some even left the faith. What does James counsel people who think God is slow to fulfill his promises? Patience. "Dear brothers and sisters, be patient as you wait for the Lord's return. Consider the farmers who patiently wait for the rains in the fall and in the spring. They eagerly look for the valuable harvest to ripen. You, too, must be patient. Take courage, for the coming of the Lord is near" (James 5:7-8).

THE FIFTY-DAY CLIMB

Keep counting until the day after the seventh Sabbath, fifty days later. Then present an offering of new grain to the LORD. ✦ LEVITICUS 23:16

We're used to counting down the days when we have something exciting to look forward to. But when it comes to the festival of *Shavuot*, we count up. Why?

On *Shavuot*, or Pentecost, we celebrate the revelation of God and the giving of the *Torah* to humanity. Surely it would make more sense to say, "forty-nine days left until the big day; now forty-eight," and so on. Yet the Bible commands us to start at *one* and count aloud every day until we reach fifty.

The practice of counting the days between *Pesach* (Passover) and *Shavuot* is known as "counting the *omer*." It is named for the barley sacrifice that was brought during this time period when the Temple stood. At the end of these seven weeks, a new and different offering was brought—one of "new grain."

Something changes in these intermediate weeks. They are intended to be introspective and transformational, so much so that what a person can offer God in the beginning is profoundly different by the end. At the beginning of the fifty days, a journey starts. By the end, we are ready to receive the Word of God.

That's why we count up, and not down. As each day passes, we become more, not less. *Pesach* celebrates our physical redemption, but it takes seven weeks until we are able to experience our spiritual redemption on *Shavuot*.

Counting the *omer* lends us a paradigm that can be used year-round. When tackling the big goals in life, it's easy to feel overwhelmed. How will we cross such a great distance? How can we accomplish such lofty tasks? Maybe it's better to not even start! But the message of the *omer* is to take the journey one step at a time. At the completion, you will not be the same person as when you started.

A Christian Reflection on Becoming Like Jesus

In the language of the Bible, when people turn to God through faith in Jesus, they experience a new birth (see John 3:7; 1 Peter 1:23). A birth, of course, is a beginning, not an ending; it initiates a life journey—in this case, a journey of faith. What is the goal? To be like Jesus. This cannot be accomplished in a day, but is a long, step-by-step process. Fortunately, according to Paul, God helps us on this journey: "The Lord—who is the Spirit—makes us more and more like him as we are changed into his glorious image" (2 Corinthians 3:18).

TORAH IN ACTION

"The LORD bless you, my daughter!" Boaz exclaimed. "You are showing even more family loyalty now than you did before, for you have not gone after a younger man, whether rich or poor." ❖ RUTH 3:10

Why is it the Jewish tradition to read the book of Ruth on the holiday of *Shavuot*?

One answer explains that Ruth and *Shavuot* are two sides of the same coin. While Shavuot celebrates the giving of the *Torah*, the book of Ruth describes *Torah* in action. *Shavuot* is about the theory; Ruth is about the application.

The goal of the *Torah* is not spiritual transcendence. It's not about sitting on a mountain deep in meditation or experiencing great miracles. The *Torah* is about everyday life. When Hillel the elder was asked to sum up the whole of the *Torah*, he said, "That which is hateful to you, don't do to someone else."

In other words, *be nice*. Kindness is what it's all about. It's the simple things we do daily, when no one else is looking, that bring the *Torah* to life. Appropriately, that's the central theme of the book of Ruth.

When we look into the story of Ruth, we find kindness in the way the harvesters leave behind grain for the poor, and in the way Ruth works all day in the hot sun to collect the precious sustenance for Naomi. We witness the kindness of Boaz to Ruth before he even knows her, and we see the great reward that is given to Ruth and Boaz for their kind actions. They become the great-grandparents of King David, from whom the Messiah will come. The book of Ruth is about the small acts of kindness and the huge impact they have for eternity.

Every year on *Shavuot*, we accept the Bible all over again. One way to do this is to reaffirm its central theme and make it a goal to do one extra act of kindness each day for one month. That's what the *Torah* is all about.

A Christian Reflection on Doing Torah

When Jesus asks an expert in the religious law to summarize the Law, he applauds the man's answer: "'You must love the LORD your God with all your heart, all your soul, all your strength, and all your mind.' And, 'Love your neighbor as yourself'" (Luke 10:27). Ruth is a marvelous example of loving one's neighbor. God's people today should reflect this kind of character in their relationships with other people. It is, after all, a fruit, or consequence, of following God: "The Holy Spirit produces this kind of fruit in our lives: love, joy, peace, patience, kindness, goodness, faithfulness, gentleness, and self-control" (Galatians 5:22-23).

Sabbath Reflections

What new truth about the Jewish holy day of Shavuot (Pentecost) did you learn from this week's devotions?

How has this truth affected your faith?

How will you apply this truth to your daily life?

Your Key Verse for the Week:

❖ OTHER REFLECTIONS

TURNING A DEAF EAR

I am deaf to all their threats. I am silent before them as one who cannot speak. I choose to hear nothing, and I make no reply. For I am waiting for you, O LORD. You must answer for me, O Lord my God. ❖ PSALM 38:13-15

When someone criticizes us unfairly, the hardest thing to do is walk away. Human nature demands that we defend ourselves from wrongful accusations.

In Psalm 38, David finds himself in a dire situation, and he expresses great anguish over his sin. Indeed, David sees his suffering as punishment for his sin: "Because of your anger, my whole body is sick; my health is broken because of my sins" (Psalm 38:3).

Even David's friends abandoned him because of his condition (see Psalm 38:11), making him feel utterly alone. Moreover, David's enemies were on the prowl, plotting to harm him (see Psalm 38:12).

Not many of us would have blamed David for lashing out at his detractors. But that's not what he did. Instead, he turned a deaf ear toward the evil words of his enemies (see Psalm 38:13-14). He made no reply: "I am silent before them as one who cannot speak." David would not respond to his enemies. Instead, he turned his case over to God.

In Psalm 38:15, David writes, "For I am waiting for you, O LORD. You must answer for me." Despite his dire circumstances, David still trusted in God to uphold him and his reputation. Rather than going on the attack, he looked to God to defend him against his enemies.

In the *Talmud*, the Sage Shimon writes, "All my life I have been raised among the wise, and I have found that nothing is better for a person than silence." Shimon must have learned many wise and witty sayings from all of the Sages that he grew up around. But from their wisdom he learned that oftentimes the most powerful thing to say is nothing at all.

When you are tempted to defend yourself against unfounded gossip or unfair criticism, take a deep breath and walk away. As David did, leave your defense in God's hands and allow him to make your case.

A Christian Reflection on Silence in the Face of Accusation

"But Jesus remained silent." With these words, Matthew records Jesus' response to the high priest's accusation that Jesus had claimed he would destroy the Temple and build it in three days (Matthew 26:63). Jesus had the same silent response as he was charged before Pilate (Matthew 27:12-14). Like David, from whose family line he came, Jesus also stood silent before his accusers and put his trust in God to answer these charges. Although Jesus remained silent and did not defend himself, God vindicated him through his resurrection from the dead. Remember this when you are tempted to attack those who attack you.

A MOTHER OF FAITH

The woman became pregnant and gave birth to a son. She saw that he was a special baby and kept him hidden for three months. ❖ EXODUS 2:2

When children leave home as young adults, it's a moment filled with mixed emotions—sadness at their leaving, pride in what they have accomplished, and hope that they will remember the lessons instilled in them.

Imagine if you had only half that time to teach them important lessons of faith. In all likelihood, Jochebed, Moses' mother, had roughly seven years to impart her knowledge and love for God into her son.

The story of Moses' mother hiding her baby from certain death decreed by Pharaoh is a familiar one. We know how Jochebed placed her son in a waterproof basket and set it alongside the Nile. We remember how her daughter, Miriam, waited nearby and watched.

We know that when the pharaoh's daughter discovered the baby, Miriam bravely offered to get a Hebrew woman to care for the child, which Jochebed did until Moses was about seven, when he was sent back to Pharaoh's daughter. And for the brief time Jochebed had with Moses, we know that she raised him well.

How do we know that? We see the results of her influence on all three of her children. Moses became one of Israel's greatest leaders of all time; Aaron became Israel's first high priest; and Miriam was a prophet who turned the hearts of a nation toward the Lord.

In the Jewish tradition, when we put our children to bed, we recite the *Shema* prayer: "Listen, O Israel! The LORD is our God, the LORD alone" (Deuteronomy 6:4). We put our children to bed with faith. When they wake up, we say the *Modeh Ani* prayer, which begins, "I am thankful to the LORD, the living King." We begin their day with faith.

By beginning and ending every day with words of faith, every parent—Jewish or Christian—can continue Jochebed's legacy.

A Christian Reflection on a Mother's Faith

As Proverbs 22:6 states, "Direct your children onto the right path, and when they are older, they will not leave it." Proverbs reminds mothers and fathers alike that they are responsible to teach the faith to their children. We see this in the New Testament as Paul writes about Timothy's faith: "I remember your genuine faith, for you share the faith that first filled your grandmother Lois and your mother, Eunice" (2 Timothy 1:5). We don't know anything else about Lois and Eunice, but we know that Paul recognized their instrumental role in young Timothy's faith, which prepared him for an important role in the growth of the early church. Not every mother's child will be a Moses or a Timothy, but God will use all children of faith to grow his Kingdom on earth.

THE POET AND PROPHET OF ISRAEL

Miriam the prophet, Aaron's sister, took a tambourine and led all the women as they played their tambourines and danced. ❖ EXODUS 15:20

As Moses, Aaron, and Miriam led the people of Israel, discord rose among them and Miriam became resentful of Moses' leadership.

As a child, Miriam had played a key role in the rescue of her brother. Eighty years later, she was deemed a prophet, one to whom the Lord spoke. Along with Moses, Miriam led the song of victory after crossing the Red Sea (see Exodus 15).

Few women in the Bible have the distinction of being a prophet. But this distinction became a point of pride for Miriam. Years later, she pulled her brother Aaron aside and said, "Has the LORD spoken only through Moses? Hasn't he spoken through us, too?" (Numbers 12:2).

Her rejection of Moses' leadership caused the Lord to punish her. She was stricken with leprosy, but Moses prayed for her, and after seven days of separation from the camp, she was healed.

This jealous prophet was humbled with a contagious disease. Whereas Miriam once led people in triumphant procession, they now fled from her. She was undoubtedly repentant during her seven days of separation, but she faded into obscurity and did not live long thereafter.

In the *Talmud*, the Sages say, "Jealousy, lust, and the pursuit of honor remove a person from the world." Being "removed from the world" is not a punishment per se. It's the natural consequence. People who embody these traits are not able to enjoy what they have, and moreover, people aren't able to enjoy them.

When we are discontent with the level of influence that God has given us, we risk damaging our character and reputation by aspiring to a higher place of honor. Thank God for the sphere of influence he has given you, rather than being jealous of the responsibilities he has assigned to someone else.

A Christian Reflection on Our Place in God's Work

How often have jealousies and conflicts harmed and even destroyed churches and synagogues? Paul reminds his audience that everyone has different tasks in God's Kingdom. Though not all receive the same notoriety, they are all important. The church is like a body. Not everyone is a head or a hand or a foot: each has his or her own special place. If you think your place in the community is beneath you, remember that "some parts of the body that seem weakest and least important are actually the most necessary" (1 Corinthians 12:22). What is important is that we are a body, and for the body to function properly, it must have harmony between its different parts.

IN BARREN TIMES

Go in peace! May the God of Israel grant the request you have asked of him.
❖ I SAMUEL I:I7

For anyone who has faced the heartbreak of repeated disappointment—whether it's an inability to have children, find employment, or foster a lasting relationship—the story of Hannah provides a much-needed balm.

Hannah, as you may remember, was barren—a condition considered a curse in ancient Israel. Moreover, as was the custom, Hannah's husband took another wife, and this woman continually insulted Hannah. Even when Hannah prayed fervently to God for a son, Eli the priest mistakenly thought she was drunk!

Hannah had more than enough reasons to give up. But she didn't. Instead, she brought her problem to God and prayed that he would "look upon my sorrow and answer my prayer and give me a son" (I Samuel I:II). In return for God's favor, Hannah vowed to dedicate her son in lifelong service to God.

After pouring out her heart, Hannah was able to leave in peace, entrusting her problem to God and having faith that he would answer her prayer.

When Hannah finally gave birth to Samuel, she joyfully brought him to serve Eli because she knew that this son had been given to her by God and that she was returning him to God for his purposes.

Hannah was not the first barren mother and certainly not the last. The Sages teach that three of the Matriarchs—Sarah, Rebekah, and Rachel—were barren because God desires "the prayers of the righteous" (Proverbs 15:29). Sometimes God doesn't give us what we ask for right away because he wants to give us an additional gift—himself. When we recognize our dependence on God through prayer, we greatly enhance our relationship with him.

As Hannah discovered, continued prayer opened the door for God to work. Let Hannah's story encourage you in facing the disappointments and barren times of this life.

A Christian Reflection on Persistent Prayer

Jesus taught about the power of prayer by using the parable of the persistent widow (see Luke 18:1-8). In the parable, Jesus describes a judge who ignored a request for justice from a widow. He neither feared God nor cared about the people. But the woman came so often to present her petition before him that he finally gave up and granted her request. If such a godless and negligent judge would respond to a repeated request, Jesus points out, how much more will God hear our requests? Let this be an encouragement to bring your needs and desires to God in prayer daily.

A WORTHY ROLE MODEL

Israel's leaders took charge, and the people gladly followed. Praise the LORD!
❖ JUDGES 5:2

As the father of three daughters, I knew how important it was to provide them with strong female role models growing up. Thankfully, the Bible provides us with many outstanding examples who can inspire women of all ages. Among those notable women is Deborah. Her story is found in Judges 4–5.

As a prophet and judge, Deborah had a unique role in the story of Israel. She was known for holding court "under the Palm of Deborah" (Judges 4:5), where people came to her to resolve their disputes. In addition to dispensing justice, Deborah had been appointed by God to deliver his people from bondage. At the time of Deborah's leadership, the people had been oppressed for twenty years by the Canaanites.

Deborah's leadership in the face of this challenge stands in stark contrast to her second-in-command, Barak. Whereas Deborah took charge when God ordered Barak to face Sisera on the battlefield, Barak refused to go without Deborah. Even when Deborah told him that God would grant victory, Barak needed more assurance.

Barak's response shows that he trusted human strength rather than God's promise. As a person of true faith, Deborah was willing to heed God's call, no matter what the circumstances. Because of her faith, Deborah was able to lead—and succeed—when others hesitated.

We see this same type of courage and faith in the Exodus story. The Sages say, "Our forefathers were redeemed from Egypt because of the righteous women." During the harsh slavery, the men decided that they didn't want to bring more children into the world. But the women, who had faith that God would save them, went to their husbands and insisted. Because of their faith, generations were born and eventually redeemed.

Like those righteous women in Egypt, Deborah is an inspiration to all who are committed to following God. Her story challenges us to be willing to take charge and obediently follow what God has called us to do.

A Christian Reflection on Godly Women Leaders

"Many women who had come from Galilee with Jesus to care for him were watching from a distance" (Matthew 27:55-56). So reads Matthew's account of the Crucifixion. Note who was with Jesus when he died on the cross. Not the crowds who had welcomed him warmly into Jerusalem a short while before. Not the disciples who had deserted Jesus after his arrest. It was his female followers who stayed by his side. Indeed, they were the ones who were the first to learn the good news that he had been raised from the dead. Because of their faithfulness, they received the honor of announcing the empty tomb to his disciples.

BLESSED ARE THE PEACEMAKERS

This man's name was Nabal, and his wife, Abigail, was a sensible and beautiful woman.
But Nabal, a descendant of Caleb, was crude and mean in all his dealings.
❖ 1 SAMUEL 25:3

No doubt we all have encountered a person whom we term "difficult." No matter what we do to extend kindness, this person rebuffs our efforts.

Abigail, another notable woman of the Bible, knew such a person—her husband, Nabal. Whereas Abigail is described as "sensible and beautiful," her husband is described as "crude and mean in all his dealings." His name, in fact, means "fool."

No doubt, Abigail had to smooth over situations that her husband had caused through his rudeness. Her diplomacy skills were well honed. So when Abigail found out that Nabal had snubbed David's men and their request for provisions—even after they had provided an armed escort for Nabal's flocks—she acted quickly.

Before the situation could escalate, Abigail loaded donkeys with food and set out to meet David. She apologized for her husband's behavior and encouraged David to forgive him.

Thankfully, Abigail's entreaties had the intended result. David responded, "Praise the LORD, the God of Israel, who has sent you to meet me today! Thank God for your good sense! Bless you for keeping me from murder and from carrying out vengeance with my own hands" (1 Samuel 25:32-33).

Abigail was indeed a woman of physical beauty, but it was her inner beauty that gave her the ability to quell intense emotional reactions in others. She used her skills to keep the peace and didn't allow her circumstances to stop her.

Hillel the Elder said, "Be a student of Aaron; love peace and pursue it." Tradition teaches that Aaron, the brother of Moses, would do almost anything to make peace between people. To be like Aaron, it is not enough to love peace; one must be willing to pursue it—to take action, make sacrifices, and actively seek out peaceful solutions.

Abigail was a true student of Aaron. What an excellent role model for us in dealing with the "difficult" people in our lives!

A Christian Reflection on Peacemaking

Abigail truly illustrated Jesus' saying, "God blesses those who work for peace, for they will be called the children of God" (Matthew 5:9). This work is not easy. Abigail had to deal with an unreasonable husband who offended a powerful man who had helped him. Her actions brought peace and saved Nabal's life. But it is so tempting for us to pay back evil with more evil, which is why Paul has to urge the Roman church to "do all that you can to live in peace with everyone" (Romans 12:18).

Sabbath Reflections

*What new truth about the lives of the women of the Bible did you learn
from this week's devotions?*

How has this truth affected your faith?

How will you apply this truth to your daily life?

Your Key Verse for the Week:

❖ OTHER REFLECTIONS

THE ANTIDOTE TO DESPAIR

Your unfailing love, O LORD, is as vast as the heavens; your faithfulness reaches beyond the clouds. Your righteousness is like the mighty mountains, your justice like the ocean depths. You care for people and animals alike, O LORD. ❖ PSALM 36:5-6

In Psalm 36:3, David writes about evildoers: "Everything they say is crooked and deceitful. They refuse to act wisely or do good." Sound familiar?

Certainly, the existence of evil and those who reject God have been part of the human experience since Adam and Eve. And if our thoughts remain fixed and focused on the wicked, we can easily fall into despair and lose hope.

Thankfully, David offers us a remedy by focusing instead on the attributes of God.

In verse 5, David reflects on God's love, faithfulness, righteousness, and justice. God's love and faithfulness are as vast as the skies above. Because of God's faithfulness, we can rely on the constancy of his love. And because of God's righteousness, we can know that God's justice is delivered equitably.

Even when it appears as if the wicked prosper, God's justice ensures that, ultimately, the righteous will experience God's deliverance and salvation, while the wicked will experience God's judgment. Everything God has created, from heaven to earth, reflects the constancy of his love, faithfulness, righteousness, and justice.

In the book of Nahum, the prophet addresses God's judgment *and* his mercy: "The LORD is slow to anger but great in power; the LORD will not leave the guilty unpunished" (Nahum 1:3, NIV). God doesn't strike the wicked right away. Rather, he is patient and gives them the chance to repent. But that doesn't mean he will wait around forever or that evil will remain unpunished. God may be "slow to anger," but he is also "great in power." In time, justice will be served. The righteous will be rewarded greatly, and the wicked will be punished harshly.

At times, when the evil of this world threatens to overwhelm us, we must remember that God is faithful, righteous, and just. We need not despair because of evil people, because God loves us, judges evil, and will care for us forever.

A Christian Reflection on God's Victory over Evil

We can often despair when it seems as if the wicked are in control. Yet we only have to look to the Bible to realize God's ultimate victory over evil. The book of Daniel, in its four visions of the future (Daniel 7–12), makes it clear that God is in control and will have the victory. Though God's final and complete victory over evil awaits the end of time, according to the book of Revelation, even today we can see God prevail in our own life situations. When you feel overwhelmed, know that God "causes everything to work together for the good of those who love God and are called according to his purpose for them" (Romans 8:28).

ADVICE FROM A WISE GUY

*It is a good thing to receive wealth from God and the good health to enjoy it. To enjoy
your work and accept your lot in life—this is indeed a gift from God. God keeps such
people so busy enjoying life that they take no time to brood over the past.*
❖ ECCLESIASTES 5:19-20

What would you wish for if you were granted three wishes? Would you wish for
money? Romance? Healing?

After Solomon became king, God said, "What do you want? Ask, and I will give
it to you!" (1 Kings 3:5). Humbled by the responsibility of governing God's people,
Solomon asked for *wisdom*—so he could rule Israel wisely (1 Kings 3:6-15).

Solomon's great wisdom gave him a curious mind. He explored everything and
analyzed it. But he also became frustrated because he was not easily fooled. He saw
beyond the things people said and did and realized that those pursuits, in and of
themselves, were meaningless.

That's also true for us today. Without God, the things we do have no lasting value.
Nothing we pursue, nothing we attain, means anything apart from him. Solomon's
repeated refrain throughout Ecclesiastes is that, without God, everything is meaningless.

Solomon's final conclusion? He wrote in the book of Ecclesiastes, "I decided there
is nothing better than to enjoy food and drink and to find satisfaction in work. Then I
realized that these pleasures are from the hand of God. For who can eat or enjoy anything apart from him?" (Ecclesiastes 2:24-25). In God alone can we find true enjoyment.

In Leviticus 19:2, we are commanded to "be holy." But what does it mean to be holy?
Interestingly, *kadosh,* the Hebrew word for "holy," is also the name for marriage. *Kadosh*
means to be consecrated or designated for someone. In marriage, the partners are dedicated exclusively to each other. To be holy means to live a life totally dedicated to God.
In that way, everything we do is meaningful.

We all want to have a life filled with meaning and significance. And it's possible.
We can find true meaning in life each day by dedicating ourselves to God in all we do.

A Christian Reflection on the Ultimate Meaning of Life

The Teacher in the book of Ecclesiastes exposes what happens when we try to make
anything—wealth, work, pleasure, status—other than God the most important thing
in our lives. Life becomes meaningless! Likewise, Paul tells us that God subjected
everything to "God's curse" (using the same Greek word, *mataiotes,* used to translate the
word *meaningless* [*hebel*] in Ecclesiastes), but in hope of redemption (Romans 8:18-25).
The "good news" of the gospel is that Jesus, whom Christians believe is God himself,
subjected himself to the fallen world and even experienced death itself in order to
break death's grip through his resurrection. Thus, the only meaningful life is a life
that puts God first.

HOW ARE YOU SPENDING YOURSELF?

Remove the heavy yoke of oppression. Stop pointing your finger and spreading vicious
rumors! Feed the hungry, and help those in trouble. Then your light will shine out from
the darkness, and the darkness around you will be as bright as noon.
❖ ISAIAH 58:9-10

When it comes to investing your life, what do you spend yourself on? One of the best ways we can "spend ourselves" is by investing ourselves in others.

For hundreds of thousands of needy Jews in Israel and throughout the world, the investments of Christians in their lives, through ministries such as The Fellowship, have been life-giving and lifesaving. Hungry people are fed, elderly people receive money to heat their homes in the winter, sick people receive the medication they so desperately need, and children without parents are given a loving and safe place to live.

It is quite possibly the most powerful expression of love that Christians can show to their Jewish brothers and sisters. And such love and generosity do not go unnoticed—from the single mom waiting in line for a much-needed food box during *Pesach* (Passover) or *Rosh Hashanah*, to the gracious expression of thanks from political and religious leaders from around the world.

Former Israeli Prime Minister Ariel Sharon wrote to The Fellowship: "This great show of solidarity and support for Israel from . . . Christians offers great encouragement to me, my government, and most importantly, the Israeli people. [The Fellowship's] programs and visit to Israel are a source of inspiration and confidence to all of us in these difficult times."

Practical expressions of love reassure Jews that Christians care about them and that they, as Jews, are genuinely accepted by their Christian neighbors. These acts are seen by Jews as sincere and sacrificial. Moreover, these practical acts help to "remove the heavy yoke of oppression" (Isaiah 58:9), such as the hateful sting of anti-Semitism and the stigma of poverty.

Consider how you are "spending yourself," and how you might use your resources to invest in others so that "your light will shine out from the darkness" (Isaiah 58:10).

A Christian Reflection on Helping Those in Need

When people who were worried about their relationship with God asked, "What should we do?" John the Baptist responded, "If you have two shirts, give one to the poor. If you have food, share it with those who are hungry" (Luke 3:10-11). Jesus will welcome into the Kingdom those who fed and clothed the hungry (see Matthew 25:31-46). Christians should "excel also in this gracious act of giving" (2 Corinthians 8:7). Reflect on your giving patterns. Pray that God will give you the resources and the desire to help those who are poor.

I PLEDGE MY ALLEGIANCE

Listen, O Israel! The LORD is our God, the LORD alone. And you must love the LORD
your God with all your heart, all your soul, and all your strength.
❖ DEUTERONOMY 6:4-5

Just as American schoolchildren recite the Pledge of Allegiance before class, we Jews
recite the *Shema* every morning and evening. *Shema*, the Hebrew word for "hear," is the
first word in the basic confession of faith in Judaism: "Hear, O Israel: The LORD our
God, the LORD is one" (Deuteronomy 6:4, NIV). This is Judaism's defining statement,
and we make sure to speak it daily as a witness to others.

In speaking the *Shema*, we join our voices with Jews throughout the world to assert
that there is one God and to affirm that he is our God. We look forward to the fulfillment of this theological truth in the messianic age, when "the LORD will be king over
all the earth. On that day there will be one LORD—his name alone will be worshiped"
(Zechariah 14:9).

Jesus, as a Jew, affirmed the value and significance of the *Shema*. When a Jewish
teacher asked Jesus which commandment was the most important, he replied by reciting the *Shema*: "The most important commandment is this: 'Listen, O Israel! The LORD
our God is the one and only LORD. And you must love the LORD your God with all
your heart, all your soul, all your mind, and all your strength'" (Mark 12:29-30). In these
words, Christians and Jews share and express a common confession of faith and love.

When Moses first spoke these words, the Israelites were surrounded by the false
gods of other nations. God's people needed this daily reminder of whom they served
and to whom they belonged. That is still true today. We also hear the competing
claims of false gods, and we, too, need to affirm our loyalty and devotion to the one
true God.

A Christian Reflection on the One God

In Jesus' response to the teachers of religious law who asked him, "Of all the commandments, which is the most important?" (Mark 12:28), he affirmed the *Shema* and
the first four commandments, which address the divine-human relationship. Based
on Jesus' and the apostles' teaching, Christians believe that God is "three in one," the
Father, Son, and Holy Spirit, and that the triune God deserves our exclusive adoration. In the same context, Jesus also affirmed the other six of the Ten Commandments
when he said that "love your neighbor as yourself" is "equally important" (Mark 12:31).

LET IT BE A REMINDER

Commit yourselves wholeheartedly to these words of mine. Tie them to your hands and wear them on your forehead as reminders. ❖ DEUTERONOMY 11:18

Throughout history, Jews have remembered the most important commandments of the *Torah* by literally wearing them on their arms and their heads. Called *tefillin* or *phylacteries*, these small cube-shaped, black leather boxes are "attachments" to the body and serve to distinguish Jews as people who keep God's precepts constantly in mind.

Contained in these two leather boxes are four sections of Scriptures that include the *Shema* (see Deuteronomy 6:4-5); God's promise of reward for all who obey the precepts of the *Torah* (see Deuteronomy 11:13-21); the duty of all Jews to remember the Exodus (see Exodus 13:1-10); and the obligation to teach our children about these matters (see Exodus 13:8-16).

The *tefillin* remind us to dedicate ourselves in service to God in all that we think, feel, and do. They also signify for us the submission of mind, heart, and actions to God. In the words of the great Jewish theologian and philosopher Maimonides, "Great is the sanctity of *tefillin*, for as long as the *tefillin* are upon man's head and arm, he is humble and God-fearing and is not drawn after frivolity and idle talk, and does not have evil thoughts, but directs his heart to words of truth and righteousness."

Truly, at the heart of this observance is a powerful reminder to submit every part of our lives—heart, mind, and actions—to the Lord. Jews and Christians alike share the same desire to love the Lord with all our heart, soul, and strength.

A *Christian Reflection on the* Shema

Though Christians don't wear the *tefillin*, Jesus affirmed the continuing significance of the *Shema* for his followers: "The most important commandment is this: 'Listen, O Israel! The LORD our God is the one and only LORD. And you must love the LORD your God with all your heart, all your soul, all your mind, and all your strength'" (Mark 12:29-30). We share with our Jewish brothers and sisters both a belief in the one true God of the universe and a passion to love him as fully as we can. Make this your prayer that God would create in your heart, mind, and soul a burning desire to love him.

NO PLACE LIKE HOME

Write them on the doorposts of your house and on your gates.
❖ DEUTERONOMY 6:9

Jewish homes for centuries have been distinguished by the placement on the doorpost of a *mezuzah*, a small, often ornately designed box that contains a piece of parchment on which is written the *Shema*. On the other side of the parchment is the name for God, *Shaddai*, from an acronym for "Guardian of the Doors of Israel."

The *mezuzah* recalls the Exodus from Egypt, when lamb's blood was smeared on the doorposts to identify Jewish households so the angel of death would pass over them. From that day forward, the *mezuzah* has identified a home as being Jewish. We find the command to post a *mezuzah* on our doorframes in Deuteronomy 6:9: "Write them on the doorposts of your house and on your gates," and again in Deuteronomy 11:20.

In Israel, all public buildings—restaurants, government offices, hotels—have a *mezuzah* on every door (except bathrooms). In the home, the custom is to put a *mezuzah* not only by the main entrance but also on the doors that people typically use—bedrooms, living rooms, laundry rooms, kitchens, dens, and so forth.

For Jews, the *mezuzah* not only identifies our homes as Jewish but also serves as a public affirmation that we trust God to guard and protect our homes. The rabbis point out that, unlike an earthly king who dwells inside his house and surrounds it with guards to protect him, God, the true King, surrounds the house of his children, Israel, and protects them.

How could you distinguish your home as a household that worships and serves God? Whether or not we have a visual reminder, our lives can bear witness of our love for God through our words and actions. The way we live honors God's Word. And that is the point of the *mezuzah*.

A Christian Reflection on Reminders

What signs around your home indicate that those who live there are faithful followers of God? What things remind you that you are a follower of God and that you live in obedience to him? Christians typically don't mark doorways with the *mezuzah*, but are there Bibles around, pictures of religious subjects, or Scripture sayings hung on the walls? Though none of these things are necessary, the point is that we all need to be mindful that we are followers of God. Ask yourself, *What would focus my attention on God daily, even hourly?*

Sabbath Reflections

What new truth about the Jewish tradition of mezuzahs, tefillin, or reciting the Shema did you learn from this week's devotions?

How has this truth affected your faith?

How will you apply this truth to your daily life?

Your Key Verse for the Week:

❖ OTHER REFLECTIONS

COUNT YOUR BLESSINGS

Oh, the joys of those who are kind to the poor! The LORD rescues them when they are in trouble. The LORD protects them and keeps them alive. He gives them prosperity in the land and rescues them from their enemies. ❖ PSALM 41:1-2

The Bible is filled with countless verses about blessings and curses—blessings for obedience, and curses for disobedience. We all desire God's blessings; yet often we focus on material blessings—a surprise check in the mail, a bigger house, perhaps a nicer car.

God may choose to bless us in these ways. But his blessings may also come to us in healing; in peace that passes all understanding; in community among believers; in forgiveness, mercy, companionship, love, and everlasting salvation. Truly, God's blessings are vast, at times even surprising, and nearly always undeserved!

In Psalm 41:1, David writes about those who care for the needy: "Oh, the joys of those who are kind to the poor!" As God cares for the poor, the oppressed, and the vulnerable, he delights when we demonstrate concern for them too. When God's concerns become our concerns, he promises to bless us.

Those blessings, according to David, may take many forms: namely, that the Lord "rescues," "protects," "keeps . . . alive," and "gives . . . prosperity." These promises harmonize with those found in God's list of blessings for obedience found in Deuteronomy 28. God promises, "You will experience all these blessings if you obey the LORD your God" (Deuteronomy 28:2).

As we strive to live in obedience to God and care about what concerns him, such as loving others—especially the weak—God will cause his blessings to fill our lives. There's no telling how or when he may respond with blessings in our lives, but he will.

A Christian Reflection on God's Blessing

How true that the most important blessings God bestows on his people are spiritual, not material. God will sometimes give us material blessings, but he always offers to bless us with a good relationship with him—the most important blessing of all. This leads to other nonmaterial blessings, such as peace of mind in the midst of trials or good relationships with other people. We know that the full blessing of God will not be experienced in this life but in the next. Jesus promised that his Father has a home for us, in which Jesus himself has prepared a place where "you will always be with me" (John 14:3). What greater blessing can we imagine than living with Jesus in heaven forever?

HONORING GOD'S ANOINTED

"Why were you not afraid to kill the LORD's anointed one?" David asked.
❖ 2 SAMUEL 1:14

If anyone was justified in attacking an opponent and celebrating his demise, David surely was that person. Although anointed as the next king of Israel, David spent years running from King Saul, knowing that, if caught, he surely would be killed.

Despite this, David did not respond in kind. Even when he had opportunities to take revenge on King Saul, David refrained (see 1 Samuel 24:1-5; 26:9). Why? Because until it was his time to take the throne, he knew that Saul was God's anointed king. David respected the authority that God had given to Saul as leader of the nation of Israel.

So when a young man came to David, bragging that he had killed King Saul, David responded, "Why were you not afraid to kill the LORD's anointed one?" David did not rejoice that Saul had been defeated and he could finally take the throne. Instead, David mourned for Saul.

In a beautiful expression of grief and love for Saul and Jonathan, his beloved friend, David writes, "How beloved and gracious were Saul and Jonathan! They were together in life and in death" (2 Samuel 1:23). Even though David had every reason to hate Saul, he chose not to. Instead, he remembered the good that Saul had done for Israel.

It takes great courage and fortitude to put aside hatred and hurt in order to respect the positive side of a person—particularly an enemy. But that's what David did. And that is what the Bible calls us to do as well—to treat others with love and respect, for they, too, are created in the image of God.

A Christian Reflection on Loving One's Enemies

David's relationship with Saul is a marvelous example of treating an enemy with respect. David models the proper response to Jesus' command to his followers: "Love your enemies! Do good to them. Lend to them without expecting to be repaid" (Luke 6:35). God's people need to cultivate this type of attitude toward their enemies—or simply those people with whom we do not see eye to eye. Why should we love our enemies? Jesus tells us that "you will truly be acting as children of the Most High, for he is kind to those who are unthankful and wicked. You must be compassionate, just as your Father is compassionate" (Luke 6:35-36).

LIVING ON GOD'S TIME

Ishbosheth, Saul's son, was forty years old when he became king, and he ruled from Mahanaim for two years. Meanwhile, the people of Judah remained loyal to David. David made Hebron his capital, and he ruled as king of Judah for seven and a half years.

❖ 2 SAMUEL 2:10-11

We live in a fast-paced society, geared toward getting instant gratification. Having to wait makes us more impatient than ever. The same is true when we have to wait for God—it's easy to lose patience because, after all, God is able to make things happen quickly, so why doesn't he answer us "on demand"?

David was a shepherd boy when he received God's promise that one day he would become king. But that promise wasn't fulfilled until David was thirty years old (2 Samuel 5:4). During Saul's reign, David remained patient, even though he had many opportunities to take the throne by force. It took patience, discipline, and trust in God's plan—and David waited on the Lord.

Even after Saul's death, when it seemed as if the path to the throne was finally clear, the kingdom descended into civil war, divided between those following Saul's son Ishbosheth and those who followed David.

Once again, David could have resolved matters by force, defeating his enemies and, in effect, driving a permanent wedge between himself and his enemies' supporters. Instead, David waited and trusted in God. In fact, he waited *seven* more years before he was named king.

A renowned nineteenth-century rabbi taught, "Woe to the pampered one who has never been trained to be patient. Either today or in the future he is destined to sip from the cup of affliction." It is in our best interest to be patient. In Hebrew, the word *patient*, with different vowels, becomes the word *suffer*. That's because, in every trying situation, we can be patient and tranquil or impatient and suffer, depending on our faith in God. The choice is ours.

A Christian Reflection on the Messiah's Patience

Though Psalm 131 does not name a specific moment in David's life when he composed this stirring song of confidence, it fits most neatly and illustrates the time when he demonstrates his great patience as he waits to receive the promise of kingship. Apparently, his patience did not come without a struggle: "I have stilled and quieted myself" (Psalm 131:2, NIV). But David could quiet himself because he put his full confidence in God to take care of him and to fulfill his promise of kingship. David's descendant Jesus Christ (the Messiah to Christians) also stilled his heart as he faced the specter of the cross in the Garden of Gethsemane (Matthew 26:36-46). He calmed himself in confidence that God could raise him from the dead. God's people should cultivate the same confident patience as David and Jesus, knowing that God is in control.

BEING A PROMISE KEEPER

One day David asked, "Is anyone in Saul's family still alive—anyone to whom I can show kindness for Jonathan's sake?" ❖ 2 SAMUEL 9:1

Are you a promise keeper? Most of us probably would say yes. But what if no one would ever know whether you had kept a promise or not? What if it had been years since the promise was made? Would you still keep that promise?

David did. Years after his best friend, Jonathan, had died, David chose to honor a promise he had made to him years earlier. If you recall, Jonathan had made a covenant with David, saying, "Treat my family with this faithful love, even when the LORD destroys all your enemies from the face of the earth" (1 Samuel 20:15).

The promise was made when the two were young men and David was fleeing for his life from Jonathan's father, King Saul. Now David was king of Israel and had united the kingdom after settling a civil war between those loyal to Saul and those loyal to David. If anything, David could have followed a common practice and wiped out any remaining members of Saul's family to protect his throne.

Moreover, Jonathan would never know whether David kept his promise. But David was a man of his word. He summoned a servant of Saul's to inquire whether there were any relatives left to whom he could show kindness for the sake of his promise to Jonathan.

So Mephibosheth, Jonathan's son and Saul's grandson, was brought to David. The young man, who had been disabled in a childhood accident, was greatly afraid, but David reassured him, "Don't be afraid! . . . I intend to show kindness to you because of my promise to your father, Jonathan" (2 Samuel 9:7). In keeping his promise, David showed respect for Jonathan by extending mercy and compassion to Mephibosheth.

Keeping one's promises when others know is one thing. Keeping a promise when no one else would know the difference reveals a person of integrity.

A Christian Reflection on the Ultimate Promise Keeper

The apostle Paul points to Jesus as the ultimate promise keeper in that he fulfills the promises made by God through his redemptive actions: "Jesus Christ, the Son of God, does not waver between 'Yes' and 'No.' . . . For all of God's promises have been fulfilled in Christ with a resounding 'Yes!' And through Christ, our 'Amen' (which means 'Yes') ascends to God for his glory" (2 Corinthians 1:19-20). In other words, because God keeps his promises to us, we should keep our promises to others. Let our "Yes" be "Yes."

THE POWER OF POWER

The next morning, David wrote a letter to Joab and gave it to Uriah to deliver.
The letter instructed Joab, "Station Uriah on the front lines where the battle is fiercest.
Then pull back so that he will be killed." ❖ 2 SAMUEL 11:14-15

Whether we realize it or not, we all have the power to influence those around us. We have the power to make things happen—or to stop them from happening. Our words carry power. Even our body language can convey powerful messages to influence others.

We can use that power and influence for good or selfish purposes. King David used his power mostly for good, but at times, he used his power to pursue his own ends.

Most of us know the story of David and Bathsheba. When David saw Bathsheba, he wanted her—and he used his power as king to summon her. After he slept with Bathsheba and she became pregnant, David used his power to cover up the affair.

He summoned her husband, Uriah, home from the battlefield so that he would sleep with his wife, Bathsheba, but Uriah was too honorable to take such pleasure while his men were fighting. When David's plan failed, he used his power as king to order Uriah to the front lines of the battle where he would most certainly be killed in action. And Uriah was.

The passage concludes, "But the LORD was displeased with what David had done" (2 Samuel 11:27). Thankfully, the story doesn't end here, and as we read in Psalm 51, David repented of his sin and was forgiven.

Jewish tradition teaches that every person has enormous power in his or her ability to speak. As it says in Proverbs 18:21, "The tongue can bring death or life." Every time we speak, we influence others. We can spread faith, love, and light, or we can bring despair, hate, and darkness. It's an awesome power that we must use wisely.

David's story is a compelling reminder of what happens when we use our power and influence for our own purposes, rather than God's. Let his story challenge us to use whatever power and influence we have to do good and honor God.

A Christian Reflection on the Power of Influence

As Rabbi Eckstein has noted, we all have influence, whether we know it or not. The question is how we will influence others. Paul admonishes us to live like those who love God, not like those whose "minds are full of darkness" (Ephesians 4:18). Rather than living for our own desires, Paul says that we should "let the Spirit renew [our] thoughts and attitudes" and "put on [our] new nature, created to be like God—truly righteous and holy" (Ephesians 4:23-24). In this way, not only will we benefit, but we will be a positive influence on those around us.

FACING THE CONSEQUENCES

David confessed to Nathan, "I have sinned against the LORD." Nathan replied, "Yes, but the LORD has forgiven you, and you won't die for this sin. Nevertheless, because you have shown utter contempt for the LORD by doing this, your child will die."
❖ 2 SAMUEL 12:13-14

Learning from our mistakes is not pleasant. Hopefully, when we experience the painful consequences of our actions, we will remember what caused those circumstances and avoid making the same mistakes.

As we repent and change, God promises to forgive us. But that doesn't mean the consequences go away. David discovered this the hard way.

After David sinned with Bathsheba and arranged to have her husband killed in battle, God sent Nathan the prophet to confront David. When David repented, God forgave him, but David still had to bear the consequences of his sinful actions.

The child conceived from David and Bathsheba's sinful relationship died as a consequence of David's sin. But their second son was Solomon, who succeeded David as king and built God's holy Temple.

One of the most hopeful lessons from this time in David's life is that, despite his sins, David wasn't disqualified from service. God didn't dismiss David as unworthy to serve him anymore. In fact, David served God faithfully for many more years. And as we have learned in other lessons from David's life, he was considered by God "a man after [God's] own heart" (1 Samuel 13:14).

David loved God, but he was a sinner like all of us. And God used him anyway. Isn't that reassuring? The lesson for us is clear: In spite of our imperfections, God can still use us.

In Ecclesiastes 7:20 (NIV 1984), we read, "There is not a righteous man on earth who does what is right and never sins." We may have thought that to be righteous means to be completely without sin. But, as the verse teaches, a "righteous man" isn't right all the time; but he constantly corrects himself. He rights his wrongs—and that's what makes him righteous.

A Christian Reflection on God's Using Broken Vessels

From Abraham to Moses to David, the Hebrew Bible is filled with stories of people who served God though they were far from perfect. The New Testament is no different. Take the apostle Peter as an example. Peter was one of the first to declare that Jesus was the Messiah (Mark 8:27-30), but on the eve of the Crucifixion, Peter also infamously denied being one of Jesus' disciples. Nonetheless, God used Peter in mighty ways to spread the gospel and build up the early church, as the book of Acts amply illustrates. God's people aren't perfect, but when we fail, we need to repent, knowing that God forgives us and can still use us for good.

Sabbath Reflections

What new truth about David's life as king of Israel did you learn from this week's devotions?

How has this truth affected your faith?

How will you apply this truth to your daily life?

Your Key Verse for the Week:

❖ OTHER REFLECTIONS

THE ANTIDOTE FOR FEAR

The LORD is my light and my salvation—so why should I be afraid? The LORD is my fortress, protecting me from danger, so why should I tremble? ❖ PSALM 27:1

Fear is a dark cloud that enshrouds and paralyzes us. Fear prevents us from trying something new or taking a risk. It imprisons us and sometimes causes us to let opportunities pass us by. At times, we have all been victims of our fears—fear of failure, rejection, sickness, loneliness, the unknown.

David certainly had plenty of reasons to be afraid. His enemies, including King Saul, were constantly after him. He faced death on the battlefield. He knew the pain of rejection and loneliness. But David also knew that the remedy for fear was always with him—God.

In Psalm 91:15, God says, "I will be with them in trouble." When we are in trouble, God himself is right there beside us. This is why David could be fearless. As he says in Psalm 23:4, "Even when I walk through the darkest valley, I will not be afraid." Why? "You are close beside me."

In Psalm 27:1, David again writes, "Why should I be afraid?" David knew that the light of God's salvation would dispel the darkness of fear. God as his stronghold would provide him with something to hold on to during difficult times. David could remain confident even when his enemies' armies marched against him, because God was his Rock and Protector.

David could live with such confidence because he had learned to wait patiently. He waited years for the fulfillment of God's promise that he would be king, while his enemies continued to attack him. It couldn't have been easy, but David never faltered in trusting God or believing that God was with him.

What fears are keeping you awake at night? What dark cloud is preventing you from seeing clearly and stepping out in faith? Like David, turn to God as your light and your stronghold. Wait patiently and confidently before him. You *will* see God's goodness.

A Christian Reflection on Casting Out Fear

David found peace in his relationship with God, and so can we. According to the apostle John, "Perfect love expels all fear" (1 John 4:18); namely, the love of God. According to Paul, "Nothing can ever separate us from God's love," not even our "fears for today nor our worries about tomorrow" (Romans 8:38). According to the Bible, there is only one legitimate fear, and that is the "fear of the LORD"—not a fear that makes us run away, but rather a reverence or awe that draws us closer to the one who made us and sustains us (Proverbs 1:7; see 2 Corinthians 7:1).

THE FREEDOM TO OBEY

I will walk in freedom, for I have devoted myself to your commandments.
❖ PSALM 119:45

The celebration of Independence Day is a good time to reflect on the many freedoms enjoyed in the United States—freedom of religion, freedom of speech, freedom of the press, freedom to cast ballots—freedoms secured by the Founding Fathers.

While celebrating those freedoms, it's also important to remember that true freedom ultimately comes from God. According to the Bible, freedom comes from obeying God's commands: "I will keep on obeying your instructions forever and ever. I will walk in freedom, for I have devoted myself to your commandments" (Psalm 119:44-45).

Here's how the Scriptures describe the Ten Commandments that Moses brought down from Mount Sinai: "These tablets were God's work; the words on them were written by God himself" (Exodus 32:16). The *Talmud* teaches that this verse, with a slight change of vowels, would read, "The words on them were 'freedom' given by God himself." The Sages conclude, "There is no free man, except for one who lives within the Bible."

God gives us freedom, not so we can run wild, but so we can run within the safety of his prescribed laws and wisdom. Contrary to what we might expect from words like *laws*, *precepts*, and *obedience*, following God's laws does not restrain us. Rather, God's commandments free us to be what God has called us to be. In other words, by living God's way, we have the freedom to fulfill his plan for our lives.

We ought to view God's commands not as burdensome but as a joy! As the psalmist describes God's Word, it is *pleasant* and *delightful*—not the typical adjectives one might use in describing laws.

So, as we celebrate our freedoms, let's be sure to take a moment to consider the pleasant way of life God has set for us in his Word. Let us give thanks to the Lord for the true freedom we all enjoy that comes from obeying his commands and living within his Word.

A Christian Reflection on God's Law and Freedom

Christians often think that the law leads to slavery, not freedom. They might think of Paul's words in Galatians 5:1: "Christ has truly set us free. Now make sure that you stay free, and don't get tied up again in slavery to the law." But Paul is not saying that the law is bad; after all, the law expresses God's will. He is speaking against those in the church who argue that our relationship with God depends on our obedience to the law rather than our faith in Christ. Those who try to earn their salvation truly do find themselves enslaved. God made us so we are happiest and most free when we obey his law.

TOGETHER WE STAND

A person standing alone can be attacked and defeated, but two can stand back-to-back and conquer. Three are even better, for a triple-braided cord is not easily broken.
❖ ECCLESIASTES 4:12

If you have ever moved from one location to another—whether it's your office, your apartment, or an entire household—you know the value of having extra hands to help you. Some tasks are just easier with someone sharing the workload.

Solomon recognizes this truth when he writes, "Two people are better off than one, for they can help each other succeed" (Ecclesiastes 4:9). When two work together, not only can they accomplish much, but they also support and help each other when they get tired. Knowing you are not alone can make all the difference in getting the job done—or in enduring a difficult situation.

Natan Sharansky, a bold defender of Israel and champion for freedom, discovered this when he was imprisoned for nine years in the former Soviet Union. While in prison, Sharansky became friends with some Christian inmates who had been arrested for teaching their children the Christian faith.

"One of my best friends in prison was a Christian," Sharansky recalls, "who, like me, was deprived of his rights to keep his religious books in the cell. We went on hunger strikes and were fighting the enemy together. And when we got back our books, we were reading our religious books together."

Together, they fought for what they believed in and supported one another.

Christians and Jews share the same values of freedom, democracy, and human rights. And we share the same biblical heritage, love for God's Word, and love for the land of Israel. With so much in common, our efforts can be multiplied by working together to achieve our shared goals.

Alone, Israel could be overwhelmed and overpowered, but with the help of like-minded supporters—and with the help of our God—we can defend ourselves and make a difference in individual lives.

A Christian Reflection on Working Together

As Christians, we have been "grafted in" to "Abraham's tree" (Romans 11:17), and thus we have much in common with our Jewish brothers and sisters. We should work together for our common causes, especially to preserve our freedom to worship God. Of course, friendship does not mean we always agree on all issues or on the methods we use to achieve our common goals. Even so, we must never lose sight of the fact that Jews and Christians share many common goals. Let's continue to fight together for these important principles, and when we disagree, let's do so in love and in the spirit of mutual support.

SETTING BOUNDARIES

"See this pile of stones," Laban continued, "and see this monument I have set between us. They stand between us as witnesses of our vows. I will never pass this pile of stones to harm you, and you must never pass these stones or this monument to harm me."
❖ GENESIS 31:51-52

Robert Frost, in his poem "Mending Wall," penned the now-famous lines, "Good fences make good neighbors." Based on a popular seventeenth-century proverb, it points to a simple truth: Properly set boundaries can help maintain peaceful coexistence.

This principle is also biblical. As you may recall from the story of Jacob, he had worked for his uncle Laban for many years. Over the years, Jacob was so successful in building his own herds that some jealousies arose. So Jacob took his family, along with all his possessions and flocks, and left Laban. But Laban chased after Jacob, accusing him of stealing the household idols.

To prevent future confrontations—and the fear of having to look over their shoulders all the time—the two men made a boundary marker out of a pile of stones. It served as a reminder that God was watching what happened between them. As Laban said, "May the LORD keep watch between us to make sure that we keep this covenant when we are out of each other's sight" (Genesis 31:49).

It also served as a boundary that both agreed they would not cross with intent to harm one another: "They stand between us as witnesses of our vows. I will never pass this pile of stones to harm you, and you must never pass these stones or this monument to harm me" (Genesis 31:52).

Boundaries are important in our personal lives, as well. For example, we may need to set boundaries on how we interact with difficult people by limiting the time we spend with them or by interacting with them only in group situations. When both people are clear on the expectations, relationships can improve.

Good fences *can* make good neighbors, as long as they don't become walls that isolate us and prevent communication.

A Christian Reflection on Fences

The book of Acts records a remarkably honest episode in which Paul and Barnabas—close friends and coworkers—had a falling out that erected a barrier in their relationship. Barnabas wanted his cousin, John Mark, to accompany them on their missionary trip to Galatia. Paul, however, didn't want to take the young man because John Mark had previously let them down. The result was that Paul teamed up with Silas and went to Galatia, while Barnabas and John Mark went to Cyprus (see Acts 15:36-41). Though the argument was unfortunate, if Paul had not set up the "boundary," it would have hindered their missionary efforts. Now two important and effective teams were working at the same time.

OUR COMMON GROUND

I will certainly bless you. I will multiply your descendants beyond number, like the stars in the sky and the sand on the seashore. Your descendants will conquer the cities of their enemies. And through your descendants all the nations of the earth will be blessed—all because you have obeyed me. ❖ GENESIS 22:17-18

"*Kol hatchalot kashot*," claim the rabbis. "All beginnings are difficult." And beginning to foster more favorable relations and better understanding between two groups of people who have been estranged from each other for almost two millennia is no exception.

Indeed, the chasm between Christians and Jews has often been deep and acrimonious. Historically, our interactions, more often than not, have been fraught with misunderstanding, intolerance, and yes, even bloodshed.

Though much remains to be done, in recent years we have been able to make significant steps in bringing about a genuine reconciliation between the two faith groups. And we have done so by honest and fresh dialogue and by focusing on our shared heritage and values.

In God's covenant with Abraham, he promised to make Abraham into "a great nation" (Genesis 12:2). That nation would be Israel, God's chosen people. God also promised Abraham that "all the families on earth will be blessed through you" (Genesis 12:3). Today, that promise is at least partially fulfilled in the Christians who, though they are Gentiles rather than Jews, believe in the God of Israel—and the core of that faith was passed on to them through the Jews.

The differences between Jews and Christians need not divide us. As the prophet Malachi said, "Are we not all children of the same Father? Are we not all created by the same God? Then why do we betray each other, violating the covenant of our ancestors?" (Malachi 2:10). We can accept our differences with tolerance and respect. We need not allow those differences to cause us to break faith with one another.

Let's begin with our common ground. The roots of our faith grow deep, and those roots are shared by both Jews and Christians.

A Christian Reflection on Common Ground

Christians and Jews worship the same God; Christians do not reject the Hebrew Scriptures, which, after all, were the Scriptures of Jesus and his disciples. This common ground provides a solid basis for mutual respect and appreciation. Of course, while we acknowledge our commonalities, we should not ignore our differences, which center primarily on the person of Jesus, whom we recognize as the Messiah, the "one Mediator who can reconcile God and humanity" (1 Timothy 2:5). This difference, though, is no reason for pride, but for humility and a spirit of love toward our fellow human beings.

A PLACE OF SIGNIFICANCE

Jacob's sons did as he had commanded them. They carried his body to the land of Canaan and buried him in the cave in the field of Machpelah, near Mamre. This is the cave that Abraham had bought as a permanent burial site from Ephron the Hittite.

❖ GENESIS 50:12-13

For God's people, the Holy Land offers many places of significance where we can connect with our spiritual family. One of the most revered places for Jews is the Cave of the Patriarchs in Hebron, where Abraham and Sarah, Isaac and Rebekah, and Jacob and Leah are buried. It is a holy site rich in our faith tradition.

As early as Genesis 14:13, we find Abraham "living near the oak grove belonging to Mamre." When his wife, Sarah, died, Abraham went to his neighbors, the Hittites, and said, "Here I am, a stranger and a foreigner among you. Please sell me a piece of land so I can give my wife a proper burial" (Genesis 23:4). So Abraham purchased a cave for her burial just east of Mamre.

When Abraham died, "his sons Isaac and Ishmael buried him in the cave of Machpelah, near Mamre . . . where he had buried his wife Sarah" (Genesis 25:9-10). Thereafter, Mamre became the family burial site, even down to Abraham's grandson Jacob (Genesis 50:12-13).

Today, this location, two miles north of Hebron, is known as the Cave of the Patriarchs, or the Tomb of the Patriarchs. It lies in the West Bank, so a visit to this biblical holy site is conducted under the watch of armed guards. Despite the risks, a trip to the Tomb of the Patriarchs can be awe-inspiring as one soaks in the significance of this ancient holy site. Sitting next to the graves of Abraham, Sarah, and Jacob, reciting Psalms and reading Scripture, one feels an overwhelming sense of God's presence and his divine love.

Such places inspire and strengthen our faith and give us hope for the future. Where are those places for you?

A Christian Reflection on Holy Places

I remember my first trip to the Tomb of the Patriarchs as a seminary student in 1976, and the awe I felt at being at the burial place of the patriarchs and matriarchs of our faith. My special interest in studying the Hebrew Bible blossomed during that trip as I experienced firsthand the land where God made his presence known so dramatically. I also remember visiting the Garden Tomb, which, though it is not likely the actual place where Jesus was buried, contains a first-century tomb that gives the feel of the actual place. While such sites lead our emotions and thoughts to God, thankfully we can come into God's presence wherever we are.

Sabbath Reflections

What new truth about the bond between Christians and Jews did you learn from this week's devotions?

How has this truth affected your faith?

How will you apply this truth to your daily life?

Your Key Verse for the Week:

❖ OTHER REFLECTIONS

HIS SPECIAL POSSESSION

Save your people! Bless Israel, your special possession. Lead them like a shepherd,
and carry them in your arms forever. ❖ PSALM 28:9

If you want to know what a person treasures most, watch how he or she cares for a particular possession. I used to have a neighbor who spent countless hours tending and caring for his lawn. It began in the spring with a detailed regimen of fertilizer and grass seed. Then it continued into the summer with careful—and constant—watering, proper applications of weed killers, and of course, mowing two, even three, times a week!

The result? A beautifully manicured lawn that was the envy of the neighborhood. Now, I'm sure this man cared for other things in his life, but there was no doubt in the mind of anyone who passed by his house that his lawn was a treasured possession.

For any reader of the Hebrew Bible, there should be no doubt what, or more appropriately, who, was God's special possession—the people of Israel.

If you really want confirmation of the value that God places on his special possession, you need only consider how he cared for his people.

Psalm 28 describes God as giving his people strength and as being "a safe fortress for his anointed king" (Psalm 28:8). He cared for his people like a shepherd. He carried them "in [his] arms forever" (Psalm 28:9). This same word picture is depicted in Isaiah 40:11: "He will feed his flock like a shepherd. He will carry the lambs in his arms, holding them close to his heart."

What a beautiful picture of God's eternal care for his people, Israel. I think we see evidence of God's care today as he continues to preserve and protect Israel.

A Christian Reflection on God's Special Possession

Israel is indeed God's special possession. Paul points this out to a predominantly Gentile Christian audience in the city of Rome: "Since Abraham and the other patriarchs were holy, their descendants will also be holy" (Romans 11:16). Of course, God dearly loves all his human creatures, created in his image, though marred by their sin. His continuing love for humanity is powerfully expressed by the apostle John: "God showed how much he loved us by sending his one and only Son into the world so that we might have eternal life through him" (1 John 4:9).

LOOK IN THE MIRROR

I will require the blood of anyone who takes another person's life. If a wild animal kills a person, it must die. And anyone who murders a fellow human must die. If anyone takes a human life, that person's life will also be taken by human hands. For God made human beings in his own image. ❖ GENESIS 9:5-6

Take a look in the mirror. What do you see? Perhaps a better question is, Who do you see? Do you see only your reflected image, or do you see someone who is *made in the image of God?*

Sometimes, the mirror gets foggy. Some days we can be discouraged by a lack of progress and wonder if we have any value as a person. At other times, our self-worth fluctuates with the balance in our bank account, our popularity, or our success at work.

Yet, whenever we look for our worth in possessions, popularity, or achievements, we realize how hollow our lives can be when based on ever-changing criteria. Instead, our value as a person should be based on the truth that each of us is made in God's own image. For this reason alone, we can feel positive about ourselves.

The Sages teach that because God created us in his own image, we can—and should—reflect his character in our lives. They point to Exodus 34, where Moses lists "thirteen attributes of God" as a road map to becoming like our Creator. When we emulate qualities such as "slow to anger and filled with unfailing love" (Exodus 34:6), we demonstrate that we are made in the image of God.

Knowing that we are made in God's image helps us live with confidence as people of great worth. It also helps us to recognize the intrinsic value of others—because, like it or not, that pushy person in line behind us or the loud person sitting next to us is made in God's image as well.

Our challenge is always to remember the truth of who we are each time we interact with another person. How we interact with others and reflect God's character will actually help others to see their God-image, as well.

A Christian Reflection on Human Dignity

The first three chapters of Genesis tell the wonderful story of God's creation of human beings in his image, followed by a story of human rebellion and sin against their Creator. The story of Adam and Eve reminds us that we are all sinners. Yet we must never lose sight of the fact that we are created in the image of God and reflect his glory. As Paul taught the church in Corinth, we will reflect God's image and glory as we understand the truth and allow it to transform us. "All of us who have [turned to the Lord] can see and reflect the glory of the Lord. And the Lord—who is the Spirit—makes us more and more like him as we are changed into his glorious image" (2 Corinthians 3:17-18).

LOOKING THE OTHER WAY

Share your food with the hungry, and give shelter to the homeless. Give clothes to those
who need them, and do not hide from relatives who need your help.
❖ ISAIAH 58:7

What is your typical reaction when you walk down the street and see a homeless person? Sadly, I think the answer for most people is to look the other way. In other words, we do exactly what the prophet Isaiah admonishes us *not* to do.

The Hebrew expression Isaiah chooses—*Lo titalaim*—is nuanced and beautiful: "From your flesh you shall not avert your eyes." But isn't that what we often do? We pretend not to see the plight of the poor because it is much more comfortable to look away than to look into their eyes and see their needs. Poverty makes us uncomfortable because we are faced with a choice: Will we look away, or will we get involved?

God warns us: "Do not hide from relatives who need your help," because we are all made in the image of God. We share a common bond of humanity. By ignoring the needs of someone, we harden our hearts to that which makes us human—the image of God as expressed in compassion toward others.

We may even pray that God would bless such people and meet their needs, but how can God meet their needs if we do not extend our hands to help? God has blessed us so that we can be a blessing to others, as he tells us in Genesis 12:3.

Indeed, Isaiah's description of a true fast—feeding the hungry, clothing the naked, providing shelter for the poor—is at the very heart of The Fellowship's Isaiah 58 ministry and our other humanitarian efforts. It is just one way that we can connect with and help those who are hurting and in need.

A Christian Reflection on Reaching Out

Jesus set the tone for his ministry when he preached from Isaiah 61:1-2 in the synagogue in his home village of Nazareth: "The Spirit of the LORD is upon me, for he has anointed me to bring Good News to the poor. He has sent me to proclaim that captives will be released, that the blind will see, that the oppressed will be set free, and that the time of the LORD's favor has come" (Luke 4:18-19). He then announced, "The Scripture you've just heard has been fulfilled this very day!" (Luke 4:21). Jesus came to bring the Good News to the poor and oppressed and disabled, and he enlists his followers today to alleviate the misery of those less fortunate.

ALL FOR ONE, ONE FOR ALL

Are we not all children of the same Father? Are we not all created by the same God?
Then why do we betray each other, violating the covenant of our ancestors?
❖ MALACHI 2:10

Throughout history, Jews have experienced so much persecution that we have a real concern for our collective well-being. Experience has taught us that it is necessary to care for each other as a people.

The bonds of kinship that Jews feel for one another cross geographical and political boundaries, transcend denominational differences, and span diverse cultural backgrounds and race. When one part of our body hurts, our entire body feels the pain and moves to alleviate it.

The prophet Malachi spoke of this need for God's people to care for each other: "Are we not all children of the same Father? Are we not all created by the same God? Then why do we betray each other, violating the covenant of our ancestors?" (Malachi 2:10). This verse was addressed to the Jews living in Judah and spoke to their need to keep faith with one another.

Yet, because one God created us all, there is also a broader application to this verse, a universal call to the unity of humanity. We are called, as members of the human family, to look out for the needs of others—to love our neighbors as ourselves.

But how do we do that? What can one person do to alleviate the great suffering that exists today?

The answer, I believe, is found in an ancient rabbinic adage, written roughly at the time of Jesus: "If I am not for myself, who will be for me? If I am only for myself, what am I? And if not now, when?"

This powerful phrase provides guidance for us in responding to others' needs as well as our own. It challenges us to look for ways to make our homes, our communities, and the world a better place to live. And it calls us to respond immediately.

A Christian Reflection on Care for Church and Community

The book of Acts describes the early Christians as a close-knit community that helped one another in times of need: "All the believers met together in one place and shared everything they had. They sold their property and possessions and shared the money with those in need" (Acts 2:44-45). The result was a vibrant and growing community of God (see Acts 2:47). Thus, the New Testament puts an emphasis on first helping those within the household of faith; but our obligation doesn't end there. It extends beyond to all who are created in the image of God.

LOVING OTHERS AS OURSELVES

Do not seek revenge or bear a grudge against a fellow Israelite, but love your neighbor as yourself. I am the LORD. ✦ LEVITICUS 19:18

As God's people, we are called to care for each other, but how do we do that? Where do we begin?

I believe the answer can be found in the first phrase of the ancient rabbinic adage: "If I am not for myself, who will be for me?" That may sound rather self-centered, but the biblical command to "love your neighbor as yourself" is found in both Judaism and Christianity. This was part of God's law given at Mount Sinai; it was repeated by Jesus as part of the greatest commandments—to love God and love our neighbors (see Matthew 22:34-40).

Does this mean we love ourselves to the point that we are totally engrossed in our needs and desires? I don't think so. Judaism suggests that there is a fine line between the unworthy trait of narcissism and a healthy consideration for oneself.

After all, how can we love others as ourselves if we don't love ourselves first? And how can we love God if we do not believe in his abundant love for us?

In Proverbs 11:17, we read, "Those who are kind benefit themselves" (NIV). While this may be understood to mean that when we are kind to others, we benefit as well, the Sages teach another meaning. They explain the verse this way: "Those who are kind take care of themselves." One who is kind to his or her own body and soul will bestow kindness on others.

As the second part of the adage teaches, "If I am only for myself, what am I?" We must balance caring for ourselves and others like us with reaching out with God's compassion and love to those who are different from us. God says, "Do not take advantage of foreigners who live among you in your land. Treat them like native-born Israelites, and love them as you love yourself" (Leviticus 19:33-34).

A Christian Reflection on Proper Love of Self

Many of us struggle to love ourselves. We know full well our inadequacies. Additionally, the Bible, in both Testaments, teaches we are all sinners. Thankfully, that is not the end of the story. The message of the gospel is that "God loved the world so much that he gave his one and only Son, so that everyone who believes in him will not perish but have eternal life" (John 3:16). The "world" here is not some abstraction, but refers to you, me, and every individual of whatever race and nationality. What greater basis for self-esteem can we ask for?

"ONE BY ONE BY ONE"

The generous will prosper; those who refresh others will themselves be refreshed.
❖ PROVERBS 11:25

Just pick up the newspaper, or watch the news. Flooding in one part of the world. Devastating earthquakes in another. Drought causing famine in yet another. Tornadoes, wars, terrorist attacks, disease, crime, poverty. The problems in our world are crushing.

We may want to help, but we are overwhelmed to the point of inactivity. After all, what can one person do to make a difference?

I believe the rhetorical question from the ancient rabbinic adage draws out the answer: "If not now, when?" In other words, the time to act is *today*. Not tomorrow or sometime in the future. *Now.*

Mother Teresa was once asked how she intended to carry out her mission to alleviate human suffering when it is so widespread. Her response has always stayed with me: "One by one by one."

The *Talmud* teaches, "It is not upon you to complete the task, but you are not free to idle from it." God doesn't expect us to solve all the world's problems, but he does expect us to do what we can.

We may not be able to end world suffering, or even lessen the pain in our communities. But we can do our part so that others may be inspired to do theirs, and still others to do theirs, and so on.

It is that kind of chain reaction that Judaism seeks and promotes—as Jews become better Jews, and Christians become better Christians, we will encourage each other.

As the writer of Proverbs states, "Do not withhold good from those who deserve it when it's in your power to help them. If you can help your neighbor now, don't say, 'Come back tomorrow, and then I'll help you'" (Proverbs 3:27-28).

The call is clear: If we have the time and ability to help someone in need, then we must act now. In doing so, in taking even one small step, we can begin the chain.

A Christian Reflection on Acting Now

We can think of all kinds of excuses to delay or avoid helping those in need, and it is true that all the money in the world will not eradicate suffering and want. But we can all make a difference even if we have just a little. Indeed, Jesus praised the poor widow who gave two small coins because it represented a substantial sacrifice on her part and showed that, though her means were small, she wanted to make a difference for God (see Mark 12:41-44). No matter how little you have, take a step of faith and help another person today.

Sabbath Reflections

What new truth about responsibility for one another did you learn from this week's devotions?

How has this truth affected your faith?

How will you apply this truth to your daily life?

Your Key Verse for the Week:

❖ OTHER REFLECTIONS

CALM IN THE STORM

The LORD gives his people strength. The LORD blesses them with peace.
❖ PSALM 29:11

In Psalm 29, David attributes the awesome power of a storm to God's control over nature. David must have witnessed a terrifying storm!

He describes the cedars of Lebanon—favored for their great size and strength—as breaking off and shattering (Psalm 29:5). He describes the voice of God in the thunder as shaking the mountains, including Mount Lebanon and Mount Sirion (Hermon), and then rolling across the land to shake the Desert of Kadesh (Psalm 29:6, 8). The storm was so terrifying that everyone in the Temple cried "Glory!" to God in reverence and awe of his great power (Psalm 29:9).

Seven times, David attributes this storm to "the voice of the LORD" (Psalm 29:3-9). This is more than a poetic metaphor for thunder. God's voice spoke the world into existence. At his bidding, the heavens open up to unleash a furious storm. But the God who makes the storms rage and the mountains quake also brings the peace after the storm.

David the psalm writer uses the image of a storm to remind God's people to stand in awe of God's power: "Honor the LORD for his glory and strength" (Psalm 29:1). Then he concludes that the awesome power God demonstrated in the storm is available to work on behalf of his people, for "the LORD gives his people strength" (Psalm 29:11). Likewise, as God calms the storm, "the LORD blesses them with peace" (Psalm 29:11).

Whether we need God's power or his peace today, we will find what we need in him—the God who both creates and calms the storms.

A Christian Reflection on Stilling the Storm

In Luke 8, we read that one day Jesus and his disciples were in a boat when a horrible storm struck and threatened to overwhelm them. Desperate in their fear, the disciples woke up the napping Jesus, who immediately "rebuked the wind and the raging waves" (Luke 8:24). He then challenged his anxious disciples by asking, "Where is your faith?" (Luke 8:25). That's a good question for us, as well. Where is our faith when the storms of life threaten us? Like the disciples, we need to trust God as the only one who can calm the storm.

KING OF THE HILL

Jacob loved Joseph more than any of his other children because Joseph had been born to him in his old age. So one day Jacob had a special gift made for Joseph—a beautiful robe. But his brothers hated Joseph because their father loved him more than the rest of them. They couldn't say a kind word to him. ❖ GENESIS 37:3-4

Remember the childhood game "king of the hill"? One child was designated "king," and then tried to hold the high ground as others tried to knock him or her down. At times, adults do the same thing, only it's not a game.

When some people see another person succeed, they may try to detract from that person's success. We might hear someone say, "Oh, he needs to be taken down a notch." Such attempts may devalue the one in high position, but they do nothing to elevate the other person.

This certainly was the case in the story of Joseph. He was Jacob's favorite, and his brothers hated him for it. In fact, the Bible says they were so jealous of Joseph that they "couldn't say a kind word to him." They hated him so much that they plotted to kill him, until Judah intervened and they decided to sell Joseph into slavery instead.

Joseph's brothers were so jealous that they tried to eliminate him. They reasoned that if their father's favorite were no longer there, Jacob would look upon *them* with greater favor. But when they lied to Jacob and told him that Joseph had been killed, Jacob was grief-stricken and refused to be comforted. Their plan failed.

The jealousy of Joseph's brothers was rectified later in the love for Joseph's sons, Manasseh and Ephraim. When Jacob blessed them, Joseph placed Jacob's right (stronger) hand on the older boy and his left (weaker) hand on the younger child. But Jacob switched the blessing. "Jacob crossed his arms" (Genesis 48:14), honoring Ephraim, the younger child. Amazingly, Manasseh wasn't jealous. This is why, every week, Jewish parents bless their children to be "like Ephraim and Manasseh," full of love and empty of jealousy.

The success of others need not diminish our own worth. Applaud the achievements of others, knowing that your worth and your honor are secure in God's eyes.

A Christian Reflection on the Dangers of Envy

Joseph's brothers envied him and brought suffering on him, on their own families, and even on themselves. Envy is an emotion that can eat away at our souls and cause tremendous relational harm. The Gospel writers note that Jesus was arrested out of envy (see Matthew 27:18; Mark 15:10). Jesus listed envy among those "vile things" that come from within and defile us (see Mark 7:20-23), as do the other New Testament writers (see Romans 1:29; Galatians 5:21; James 4:5). The next time you feel envy for another person's position or possessions, remember that your treasure is in heaven and that God is your portion.

GOD'S RECIPE FOR SUCCESS

He took Joseph and threw him into the prison where the king's prisoners were held,
and there he remained. But the LORD was with Joseph in the prison and showed him
his faithful love. And the LORD made Joseph a favorite with the prison warden.
❖ GENESIS 39:20-21

If you go to Amazon.com and type in the word *success*, more than 120,000 titles pop
up! Success is important to us. We strive for it, and at times go to great efforts to
achieve it. Yet, as hard as we try, sometimes success seems to elude us. We look at
the success of others and wonder when it will be our turn. When will we have our
moment to shine?

Joseph may have felt that way. After having a privileged childhood and being spoiled
by his father, he was sold into slavery by his brothers. It probably seemed as if his dreams
of success had been traded for a life of bondage.

In Egypt, however, "the LORD was with Joseph, so he succeeded in everything he
did" (Genesis 39:2). Having risen to a position of authority in the service of a high-
ranking Egyptian official, his life seemed back on track. Joseph once again was doing
well. Then he was wrongly accused of sexually assaulting the master's wife and was
thrown in prison. Even in prison, "the LORD was with Joseph . . . and showed him his
faithful love" (Genesis 39:21). Consequently, Joseph became a favorite with the prison
warden.

How could Joseph be so successful in such difficult circumstances? What was
the secret to his success? The biblical narrative makes it clear: "The LORD was with
Joseph." God was in control of both the ups and the downs of Joseph's life.

It's one thing to trust God when things are going well. But when we are reduced
to the low places of life, we are tempted to think that God has abandoned us and we
look to our own efforts. At those times, we must remember that God is in control, no
matter what.

A Christian Reflection on Success

Like Joseph's early life, Paul's life was far from ideal. He suffered beatings, whippings,
stonings, and imprisonment on several occasions. Far from succumbing to anger or
depression, Paul remained mindful of God's presence in his life and stayed faithful
to him. In fact, in his letter to the Philippians, which he wrote in jail, Paul expresses
joy that God's work was being fulfilled: "I want you to know, my dear brothers and
sisters, that everything that has happened to me here has helped to spread the Good
News. For everyone here, including the whole palace guard, knows that I am in chains
because of Christ" (Philippians 1:12-13).

ROLL THE CREDITS!

Pharaoh said to Joseph, "I had a dream last night, and no one here can tell me what it means. But I have heard that when you hear about a dream you can interpret it." "It is beyond my power to do this," Joseph replied. "But God can tell you what it means and set you at ease." ❖ GENESIS 41:15-16

Whom do you thank when you experience success or accomplish a great task? Your parents? Your family? All those who helped you along the way? God?

If we're honest, we are prone to forget that all our blessings—including whatever measure of success we enjoy—come from God. Everything we have, everything we are, and all we achieve is grounded in what God does for us.

Joseph didn't forget. At every step of the way, God had given Joseph success. Joseph had been sold into slavery, but God granted him success in the service of one of Egypt's highest officials. After Joseph was wrongly accused and put in prison, God granted him success and he was placed in charge of other prisoners. God enabled him to explain the dreams of two fellow prisoners, and though a long wait ensued, one of them remembered Joseph when Pharaoh had a troubling dream.

Even as Joseph stood before Pharaoh and was asked if he could interpret the king's dreams, what did he say? "It is beyond my power to do this." You might think, *What? Joseph, you're blowing your chances here! Now is your opportunity to get out of jail free, and you're saying you can't do it?*

Joseph knew better than to take credit for the ability to interpret dreams. He wisely gave God the glory, saying, "God can tell you what it means and set you at ease."

Herein lies the secret to Joseph's success: He relied totally on God and took no credit for himself. Joseph did not let previous success go to his head. Rather than inflating his own ego with a track record of success, he gave all the credit to God. May we also remember to give credit where credit is due: to the God who makes *all* our successes possible.

A Christian Reflection on Relying on God

Paul endured much suffering on behalf of the gospel. He traveled extensively and worked hard to bring the Good News to countless numbers of people. Did he take credit for the establishment of churches in places such as Corinth? No, he gave God praise, and he criticized those who said "I am a follower of Paul" by asking, "Was I, Paul, crucified for you? Were any of you baptized in the name of Paul?" (1 Corinthians 1:12-13). Paul advocated what Jeremiah 9:24 urges: "If you want to boast, boast only about the LORD" (1 Corinthians 1:31).

YOU CAN BANK ON IT!

*During those years, Joseph gathered all the crops grown in Egypt and stored the grain
from the surrounding fields in the cities. He piled up huge amounts of grain like sand on
the seashore. Finally, he stopped keeping records because there was too much to measure.*
❖ GENESIS 41:48-49

What do you trust enough to stake your reputation, your livelihood, or your life on?
If we're honest, the answer is not much. Relationships fail, our financial situation can
change, and longtime job security is a thing of the past. But what about God's promises?

God's promises are like a check he has written to us, and his promissory note is so
trustworthy that we can "take it to the bank" with full confidence. When God says it,
he means it.

Joseph had that kind of confidence in God. When he interpreted Pharaoh's dreams,
Joseph didn't doubt that there would be seven years of abundance followed by seven
years of famine. Based on that confidence, Joseph recommended stockpiling the abundance for the years of famine.

Joseph may have seemed foolish to others. All signs pointed to continued plenty.
Indeed, the Bible says the crops produced so much that Joseph "stopped keeping
records because there was too much to measure." But Joseph knew that the abundance
would end—because God had said so.

And then, true to his word, God brought seven years of famine. Thanks to Joseph's
foresight, however, Egypt had plenty of food stored up. People from all over the world
came to Egypt to buy grain—including Joseph's brothers.

We may not have dreams like Pharaoh, and we may not know whether our future
holds years of prosperity or shortage, but we can rely on God's Word, the Bible. God's
promises are faithful and true.

Listen to what God says in Numbers 23:19: "God is not a man, so he does not lie.
He is not human, so he does not change his mind. Has he ever spoken and failed to
act? Has he ever promised and not carried it through?" Just as God has fulfilled every
promise until now, he will continue to do so forever. Make no mistake; when God says
it, he means it. Bank on it.

A Christian Reflection on the Certainty of God's Promises

Paul reminds us that God keeps his promises: "Remember that Christ came as a servant to the Jews to show that God is true to the promises he made to their ancestors"
(Romans 15:8). God made good on his promises, including that of a Messiah in Jesus
Christ. Remembering that God has fulfilled his past promises gives us a sure hope that
he will fulfill future promises, though at times, circumstances make us doubt it. Gain
hope by reading about those who held fast to the promises of God even though "none
of them received all that God had promised. For God had something better in mind
for us" (Hebrews 11:39-40).

NOTHING PERSONAL

"Please, come closer," he said to them. So they came closer. And he said again, "I am Joseph, your brother, whom you sold into slavery in Egypt. But don't be upset, and don't be angry with yourselves for selling me to this place. It was God who sent me here ahead of you to preserve your lives." ❖ GENESIS 45:4-5

When it comes to long-standing family feuds, none is perhaps as famous as the animosity between the Hatfields of West Virginia and the McCoys of Kentucky. The bad blood between the two families lasted for more than twenty-five years and claimed the lives of more than a dozen family members on both sides.

Some people have been known to hold a grudge for their entire lives over some trivial offense. Though we may not take things to such an extreme, we sometimes get offended and are slow to forgive.

After Joseph's brothers sold him into slavery, we can only imagine how Joseph felt decades later when his brothers suddenly appeared before him, begging for food during the years of famine. How easily Joseph could have made them pay for how they had treated him in their youth.

But Joseph, because of his deep trust in God throughout his lifetime, was able to lift himself above attitudes of revenge. Rather than blaming his brothers for all the bad in his life, Joseph recognized God's hand in it all. He knew that God had orchestrated the events of his life to bring both Joseph and his brothers to this point.

So, rather than punish his brothers, Joseph graciously assured them that God had sent him to Egypt so that he could help them in their hour of need—and, in effect, preserve the people of Israel.

In Leviticus 19:17, we are commanded, "Do not nurse hatred in your heart for any of your relatives." That's pretty hard to do when someone has hurt you badly! But Joseph shows us how to move away from hatred and toward healing.

It's not easy to treat with kindness those who have wronged us. Yet, when we see the situation from God's perspective and believe his hand is at work, we can graciously extend mercy and love.

A Christian Reflection on Turning the Other Cheek

Jesus offers a radical perspective on how to respond to someone who has wronged us: "If someone slaps you on the right cheek, offer the other cheek also" (Matthew 5:39). Jesus not only taught it, but he lived and died it: "He did not retaliate when he was insulted, nor threaten revenge when he suffered. He left his case in the hands of God, who always judges fairly" (1 Peter 2:23). When people hurt us, our first impulse is to hurt them back. Rather than lashing out, we should reflect on the example that Joseph and Jesus give us and "turn the other cheek."

Sabbath Reflections

What new truth about the life of Joseph did you learn from this week's devotions?

How has this truth affected your faith?

How will you apply this truth to your daily life?

Your Key Verse for the Week:

❖ OTHER REFLECTIONS

A FALSE SECURITY

When I was prosperous, I said, "Nothing can stop me now!" Your favor, O LORD,
made me as secure as a mountain. Then you turned away from me, and I was shattered.
❖ PSALM 30:6-7

When things are going well, we feel much like David did in Psalm 30: "When I was prosperous, I said, 'Nothing can stop me now!'" David was obviously at the top of his game when he wrote Psalm 30, and his sense of security made him feel invincible. Nothing was going to stop him!

How quickly David had forgotten the source of his true security. In fact, the Hebrew word for "secure," *selew*, implies a careless ease. Secure in his fortune and God's favor, David apparently had forgotten to trust in God and began to become self-focused—self-sufficient, self-confident, and self-reliant.

David had become lax, until God hid his face from him—an expression meaning that God had removed his blessing and protection from David. The results for David were devastating: "Then you turned away from me, and I was shattered." Immediately, David cried out to God and begged for mercy (see Psalm 30:8-10).

We, too, may get careless about our faith. We may allow our possessions, our education or careers, our sense of well-being, even our families or friends to distract us. When this happens, the urgency to pray or spend time with God is lessened. We may be lulled into a false sense of security.

And when the unthinkable happens, we, like David, are crushed.

Thankfully, David offers us the antidote to becoming overconfident. In the last verses of the psalm, after God has restored David and turned his "mourning into joyful dancing," David vows that "I will give you thanks forever" (Psalm 30:11-12).

When we continually turn to God with grateful hearts and thank him for what he has done in our lives, we will keep our focus where it belongs—on God, not on ourselves.

A Christian Reflection on Spiritual Complacency

How easy it is to grow complacent when things are going well. In the parable of the ten bridesmaids (see Matthew 25:1-13), Jesus warns his disciples about the danger of distractions that lead to complacency. The ten young women were responsible for meeting the bridegroom before the marriage feast. Only five were wise enough to bring extra oil; so when the bridegroom was delayed, five were out of oil. They had to run off and buy more. When they returned, the marriage feast had begun and they were not allowed to enter. Through this parable, Jesus encouraged his disciples—and us—to remain spiritually diligent, focusing on the bridegroom, Jesus himself.

NONMATERIAL BLESSINGS

The people of Israel must keep the Sabbath day by observing it from generation to generation. This is a covenant obligation for all time. It is a permanent sign of my covenant with the people of Israel. For in six days the LORD made heaven and earth, but on the seventh day he stopped working and was refreshed.

✦ EXODUS 31:16-17

American society is based on the premise of our unalienable rights to life, liberty, and the pursuit of happiness. The underlying belief is that anyone can achieve the "American dream" if he or she works long enough and hard enough.

But would it shock you to hear that those same beliefs and material blessings may also be at the root of what is eroding the moral fabric of our society? This is the argument made by former Soviet dissident Aleksandr Solzhenitsyn during his famous Harvard University commencement speech in 1978.

In Solzhenitsyn's view, the reason for the moral decay prevalent in Western society was our obsession with nationalistic humanism, a philosophy that regards humanity as the center of everything that exists. Western society, he maintained, was based on a dangerous philosophy that replaced worship of God with worship of humanity and our material needs as exemplified by the "American dream."

Said Solzhenitsyn, "We have lost the concept of a Supreme Complete Entity which used to restrain our passions and our irresponsibility. We have placed too much hope in political and social reforms, only to find out that we were being deprived of our most precious possession: our spiritual life."[5]

We can do much to stem this moral unraveling by returning to the faith values and roots that are reflected in honoring the Lord on his day. By observing the Sabbath, we can reaffirm the centrality of the family, the home, and the synagogue or church in our lives.

By observing the Sabbath, we bear testimony to the existence of a Supreme Being who loves us and is concerned for our welfare. Through the Sabbath, we can build a nation and civilization with a deep moral character, a strong spiritual backbone, and a profound sense of justice, community, and fellowship.

A Christian Reflection on a Day of Rest

"Don't let anyone condemn you for what you eat or drink, or for not celebrating certain holy days or new moon ceremonies or Sabbaths" (Colossians 2:16). Though the New Testament makes it very clear that the Sabbath is not a legal requirement for Christians, a day of rest and worship is a matter of wise living and demonstrates that we have our priorities in the right place. We were not made to work 24/7, and if we do, it is likely we have made work or money or success an idol that threatens the place of God in our lives. A Sabbath rest is important for us as individuals, families, religious communities, and a nation.

SABBATH BLESSINGS

Keep the Sabbath day holy. Don't pursue your own interests on that day, but enjoy the Sabbath and speak of it with delight as the LORD's holy day. Honor the Sabbath in everything you do on that day, and don't follow your own desires or talk idly. Then the LORD will be your delight. ❖ ISAIAH 58:13-14

What would you be willing to do to have a life filled with unlimited joy, blessing, and abundant provision for your needs? Would you take one day out of your week and devote it entirely to God? That's really all it takes. However, these blessings that are promised to those who observe the Sabbath are what we call "conditional promises."

God's three conditions have to do with dedication, delight, and devotion. God says he will reward our dedication to observe the Sabbath, and he will reward our delight. Finally, if we "honor the Sabbath in everything [we] do on that day, and don't follow [our] own desires or talk idly," God says he will reward our devotion to the Sabbath.

In return, God promised his people that they would receive three blessings: the blessing of fulfillment or satisfaction that comes from being focused on God; spiritual blessings, as indicated by his statement, "I will give you great honor"; and abundant provision, as evidenced by the statement, "I will . . . satisfy you with the inheritance I promised to your ancestor Jacob" (Isaiah 58:14).

The Sabbath is a way to express our love for God by submitting our desires to him, if only for one day. As we incorporate the Sabbath into our daily lives and routines, we will discover that putting God first, above our own agenda, is not a burden but the path to joy in the Lord.

A Christian Reflection on Sabbath Joy

Life is hectic and full of distractions; it is spiritually healthy to devote one day a week to focus on God, though not as an excuse to forget God the other six days of the week. Christian tradition, going back to the time of the New Testament (see Acts 20:7; 1 Corinthians 16:2), identifies the first day of the week, Sunday, as the Lord's Day and the time for corporate worship and individual reflection on the blessings of God. Now that Jesus has come, we celebrate the first day of the week and work the other six in anticipation of our final Sabbath rest (see Hebrews 4:1-11).

A DAY FOR KEEPING AND REMEMBERING

Observe the Sabbath day by keeping it holy, as the LORD your God has commanded you. ❖ DEUTERONOMY 5:12

Did you know that keeping the Sabbath involves two key components—*remembering* the Sabbath (see Exodus 20:8) and *observing* the Sabbath (see Deuteronomy 5:12)?

In the Jewish tradition, these biblical accounts describe the Sabbath in very different terms. The first account, from Exodus—*"zakhor et yom hashabbat"*—reminds us to "remember" the Sabbath, a term that has positive connotations in Hebrew. The second command—*"shamor et yom hashabbat"*—tells us to "observe" the Sabbath by keeping it holy. This command has a negative connotation and alludes to the negative commands in observing the Sabbath, such as laws prohibiting creative work.

Why the dual nature of Sabbath observance? According to the rabbis, when God gave the Ten Commandments, he spoke both words together—*shamor* and *zakhor*—in order to teach us that we sanctify the Sabbath only as we observe both its negative and positive commandments.

While Jews observe the various prohibitions of the day—the "shalt nots"—such as abstaining from lighting a fire or doing business, we also rejoice in the spirit of the Sabbath by observing its positive dimensions, such as studying the *Torah*, praying, eating the festive meals, and spending time with family and friends.

Without the positives, the Sabbath would become a day of don'ts and legalism. Without the negatives, the day loses an aspect of its holiness that comes from the discipline of obeying God's commands. We need both elements to bring the desired balance and proper attitude that allow us to enter fully into God's rest and blessing.

We *remember* God's ordained day of rest by focusing on him and spending time in worship and fellowship with family and others. We *keep* God's Sabbath by taking time out from our busy routines and setting boundaries around that day.

A Christian Reflection on Remembering and Observing the Lord's Day

As our previous reflections have noted, observing the Sabbath is not a legal requirement for Christians; it is, however, a matter of wisdom and promotes our spiritual growth. Whether we remember and observe the Sabbath also reveals what is most important to us. The author of Hebrews had to chastise some believers who neglected corporate worship, pointing out that they lost an opportunity to be encouraged and to offer encouragement to others: "Let us not neglect our meeting together, as some people do, but encourage one another" (Hebrews 10:25).

ONCE AND FOR ALL

He who is the Glory of Israel will not lie, nor will he change his mind, for he is not human that he should change his mind! ❖ I SAMUEL 15:29

It's human nature that we change our minds so often. Because of this propensity, we might assume that God is the same way. But God doesn't change his mind. The prophet Samuel said, "He who is the Glory of Israel will not lie, nor will he change his mind, for he is not human that he should change his mind!" (1 Samuel 15:29).

Some people think that God changed his mind about Israel and turned to the Gentiles after the time of Jesus. First of all, Jesus, who was a Jew, said, "Don't misunderstand why I have come. I did not come to abolish the law of Moses or the writings of the prophets. No, I came to accomplish their purpose. I tell you the truth, until heaven and earth disappear, not even the smallest detail of God's law will disappear until its purpose is achieved" (Matthew 5:17-18).

Second, Paul made it clear that God never has and never will reject his people, Israel: "I ask, then, has God rejected his own people, the nation of Israel? Of course not! I myself am an Israelite, a descendant of Abraham and a member of the tribe of Benjamin" (Romans 11:1). And Paul affirmed that God does not change his mind: "God's gifts and his call can never be withdrawn" (Romans 11:29).

We serve a God who keeps his promises. He does not change his mind. The promises God makes to his people are eternal. We can trust in them implicitly.

If God were in the habit of changing his mind, we would never be able to please him, because the conditions would be constantly shifting. But we serve a God who is constant and steadfast. He has given us clear instructions to follow, and we can rest assured that he won't change his mind.

A Christian Reflection on God's Persistent Love

Can God change his mind? Not according to Samuel (see 1 Samuel 15:29). Interestingly, God did "change his mind" about the judgment he was going to bring on Nineveh, thanks to their repentance (Jonah 3:10), but this change of mind moves from judgment to mercy. When God promises mercy, he does not change his mind arbitrarily to judgment. We, however, need to be careful that we don't "change our minds" regarding God. As the author of Hebrews writes, "Be careful then, dear brothers and sisters. Make sure that your own hearts are not evil and unbelieving, turning you away from the living God" (Hebrews 3:12).

OUR TRUE IDENTITY

*"Now if you will obey me and keep my covenant, you will be my own special treasure
from among all the peoples on earth; for all the earth belongs to me. And you will be
my kingdom of priests, my holy nation." This is the message you must give to the people
of Israel.* ❖ EXODUS 19:5-6

One of the most prevalent misunderstandings between Christians and Jews is how
members of the other community define themselves. It may come as a surprise for
Christians to learn, for example, that Jews tend to view most non-Jews as Christians
(except, of course, if they belong to another religion). Jews, for the most part, are
unaware that Christianity is not something you are born into, but is a faith that one
personally and consciously accepts.

Judaism, on the other hand, is something we are born into. Every child born of
a Jewish mother is a member of the Jewish community. Even those Jews who don't
practice the faith remain a part of the group. Being Jewish, therefore, is not so much
accepting a faith system, as is true with Christians, but being part of a covenantal
community that one is born into.

We understand this from our biblical roots. When the Israelites gathered at
Mount Sinai, God made a covenant with them. They were bound together, with God,
as his covenant people. This covenant is a perpetual heritage that all Jews are part of,
whether they accept it or not.

God also gave Israel the distinction of being "my own special treasure." Out of all
the nations of the earth, God declared that the Jewish people "will be my kingdom of
priests, my holy nation." These distinctions form the context of what it means to be
born into the Jewish community.

Christians and Jews perceive their faiths differently. We define our identities in
different ways, but we share a common heritage of faith in God. So remember that
your identity is more than what you do, what you look like, and even where your family comes from. It includes your understanding of your relationship with God.

A Christian Reflection on Where We Find Our Identity

Peter wrote to believers who were suffering in order to remind them of their special
identity in God. He begins by telling them (and us) that they are "living stones that
God is building into his spiritual temple" (1 Peter 2:5). The Temple was a place where
God made his presence known in the world—and so, according to Peter, are God's
people. But not only are we his spiritual temple, we're also "his holy priests" or his
"royal priests" because we offer "spiritual sacrifices that please God" (1 Peter 2:5, 9).
Peter calls believers in Jesus "a chosen people . . . a holy nation, God's very own possession" (1 Peter 2:9, citing Deuteronomy 7:6 and Exodus 19:4-6).

Sabbath Reflections

What new truth about remembering and keeping the Sabbath did you learn from this week's devotions?

How has this truth affected your faith?

How will you apply this truth to your daily life?

Your Key Verse for the Week:

❖ OTHER REFLECTIONS

THE REMEDY FOR REJECTION

Because of all my enemies, I am the utter contempt of my neighbors and an object
of dread to my closest friends—those who see me on the street flee from me.
❖ PSALM 31:11, NIV

David certainly felt the pain of rejection at many points in his life, and in Psalm 31, he pours out the pain of one who has been despised, rejected, defamed, and persecuted. We can feel the depth of David's angst as he writes, "I am dying from grief; my years are shortened by sadness" (Psalm 31:10).

When feelings of rejection overwhelm us, it's tempting to withdraw from others, including God. Our inclination is to look inward and focus on our pain and our sense of injustice about our circumstances. Instead, we should look at how David responds.

In the midst of his lament, David breaks out into praise: "I will be glad and rejoice in your unfailing love, for you have seen my troubles, and you care about the anguish of my soul" (Psalm 31:7), and, "Praise the LORD, for he has shown me the wonders of his unfailing love" (Psalm 31:21). Notice that David praises God in *anticipation* of God's deliverance and in assurance of his love.

How could he do that? I think it is because David had committed his life to God. He entrusted his spirit to God (see Psalm 31:5) and therefore had complete confidence that God would care for him—no matter what the outcome. David writes, "But I am trusting you, O LORD, saying, 'You are my God!' My future is in your hands" (Psalm 31:14-15). Because of his ongoing relationship with God and his past experiences, David knew that God was utterly faithful and worthy of all trust.

As we commit ourselves fully to God, we can have that same confidence in his protection and love as David did.

A Christian Reflection on Rejection

The New Testament tells Christians that they will face rejection because of their faith. Jesus warned his disciples that there will be those who refuse to welcome them (see Luke 9:5) when they preach about the Kingdom of God. In those moments, Jesus' followers must remember that they follow in the footsteps of their Savior, who, as Peter writes, was "rejected by people." In the same verse, though, Peter says that Jesus was "chosen by God for great honor" (1 Peter 2:4). Christians, too, can find comfort in knowing that, though we might be rejected by people, we are precious to God.

THE DARKEST HOUR

*Cry aloud before the Lord, O walls of beautiful Jerusalem! Let your tears flow like a
river day and night. Give yourselves no rest; give your eyes no relief.*
❖ LAMENTATIONS 2:18

One of the most sorrowful days of the Jewish calendar occurs on the ninth day of the
month of Av, or *Tisha b'Av*. On this day in 586 BC, the First Temple was destroyed and
the Jewish people were exiled to Babylon. Ironically, or providentially, the Second
Temple was destroyed on the very same day by the Romans in AD 70.

Throughout Jewish history, this day has been marked by other tragedies—the final
revolt against the Romans was crushed in AD 135; the expulsion of the Jews from
Spain was decreed in 1492; and in 1942, the Nazis began deporting Jews from Poland's
Warsaw Ghetto to the death camps. *Tisha b'Av* has come to embody all the suffering
that the Jewish people have endured over the centuries.

The various customs and laws surrounding this observance—refraining from eating meat or drinking wine, prohibitions against celebrations—are designed to create within us the same kind of solemn mood experienced by someone mourning the
death of a close family member. We are to feel the depth of grief and sadness that has
marked this day throughout history.

In Jerusalem, thousands go to the Western Wall to pray and read the book of
Lamentations. My wife and I join hundreds of others in a place overlooking the
Western Wall and the Old City. There is a real sense of shared history in being
together on that day.

Together, we gain strength in our own faith and are encouraged to look toward the
future with hope. We remember the words of Jeremiah, also found in Lamentations,
that speak to a brighter future: "Yet I still dare to hope when I remember this: The
faithful love of the LORD never ends! His mercies never cease. Great is his faithfulness; his mercies begin afresh each morning" (Lamentations 3:21-23).

A Christian Reflection on Lamenting

As we consider the many atrocities suffered by our Jewish brothers and sisters, we feel
deep sadness. For those perpetrated in the name of Christianity, we feel shame and ask
forgiveness. Of course, not all suffering and pain are in the past. Jews and Christians
today suffer persecution as they stand boldly for their faith. God invites us to bring
our pain to him. Even Jesus, facing death on a Roman cross, confessed his grief to his
disciples: "My soul is crushed with grief to the point of death" (Mark 14:34). As we
share our pain with God, he ministers to us and restores our souls: "He himself will
redeem Israel from every kind of sin" (Psalm 130:8).

COMFORT MY PEOPLE

Comfort, comfort my people, says your God. ❖ ISAIAH 40:1

Why do we set aside a day specifically to remember a series of tragedies and loss that have befallen the Jewish people? Why would we want to remember such terrible tragedies as the destruction of the First and Second Temples, the expulsion of the Jews from Spain, or the deportation of the Jews from the Warsaw Ghetto in Poland by the Nazis?

We find an answer in the *Talmud*: Those who don't mourn over the loss of the Temple will not merit seeing it rebuilt. Or, to put it positively, those who remember past sufferings and learn from them will ultimately merit seeing the rejoicing that comes from restoration.

All of us, at different times of our lives, will go through periods of suffering, pain, loneliness, or despair. Why would we want to remember such times? I think one reason is that we'll be able to appreciate more the blessings and the happiness we do experience following those times of darkness.

There's a tradition in Judaism that says the Messiah was born on *Tisha b'Av*. What is the meaning of that? While not meant literally, it points to the possibility of redemption that is present in the midst of despair and suffering. In fact, it will be birthed out of our tragedies.

So, yes, we are to remember the suffering. Yes, we are to mourn. Yes, we sit on the ground and grieve for something that happened thousands of years ago to our Jewish ancestors. We read Lamentations.

But as we remember and mourn the past, we also have hope in the birth of redemption, that God will comfort us and deliver us. We attest that redemption will sprout forth from the very depths of our suffering and despair.

A Christian Reflection on Comfort for the Afflicted

Lamentations presents a picture of God's people as a "man of affliction." The author, Jeremiah, has suffered horribly. Even in the midst of his suffering, Jeremiah expresses hope in the fact that "no one is abandoned by the Lord forever" (Lamentations 3:31). Here indeed is the source of our comfort. According to the book of Revelation, there will come a time when "God's home is now among his people! He will live with them, and they will be his people. God himself will be with them. He will wipe every tear from their eyes, and there will be no more death or sorrow or crying or pain. All these things are gone forever" (Revelation 21:3-4).

THE BLAME GAME

Lead me by your truth and teach me, for you are the God who saves me. All day long I put my hope in you. ❖ PSALM 25:5

Since the beginning of time, humans have played the "blame game." When God asked Adam if he had eaten the forbidden fruit, Adam replied, "It was the woman you gave me who gave me the fruit, and I ate it" (Genesis 3:12). And when God confronted the woman, she said, "The serpent deceived me. . . . That's why I ate it" (Genesis 3:13).

We've been playing this game ever since—at times over petty matters, but also with larger issues, such as who is responsible for creating the situation in the Middle East.

Ever since the United Nations proposed a partition of Israel, this question has been a tricky, political time bomb. It's often reported, and in some circles widely accepted, that Israel created the current Palestinian problem by forcibly expelling thousands of Palestinians from their homes.

This position ignores the fact that many Palestinians left their homes voluntarily. Others left believing their leaders' assurance of a quick Arab victory against the "Zionist invaders" and that they would be able to return home quickly. Seldom mentioned is the fact that Israel's leaders encouraged many of these fleeing Arabs to stay. It is even written in Israel's Declaration of Independence that "full and equal citizenship" is guaranteed for all people—Arab and Jew alike.

Clearly, the blame for today's Palestinian refugee problem cannot simply be laid at Israel's feet. The Arab states that refused to accept Israel's existence must bear a share of the responsibility for this tragedy.

What is desperately needed is God's light to shine on the truth, and in good time it will. In Proverbs 12:19, we read, "Truthful words stand the test of time, but lies are soon exposed." The days of lies are numbered. In contrast, the truth will endure forever.

In these confusing times, may God work in and through us to seek the truth in all situations and respond with his unfailing love.

A *Christian Reflection on Blaming Others*

Blaming others is simply a way of avoiding our own fault and the guilt that arises from it. When Paul addressed the Colossian church, he reminded them of their past: "You were [God's] enemies, separated from him by your evil thoughts and actions" (Colossians 1:21). But he does not leave them in the past; he goes on to proclaim that God "has reconciled you to himself through the death of Christ in his physical body. As a result, he has brought you into his own presence, and you are holy and blameless as you stand before him without a single fault" (Colossians 1:22).

EXCUSES, EXCUSES

This command I am giving you today is not too difficult for you to understand, and it is not beyond your reach. It is not kept in heaven, so distant that you must ask, "Who will go up to heaven and bring it down so we can hear it and obey?" It is not kept beyond the sea, so far away that you must ask, "Who will cross the sea to bring it to us so we can hear it and obey?" No, the message is very close at hand; it is on your lips and in your heart so that you can obey it. ❖ DEUTERONOMY 30:11-14

"It's too hard." "I can't do that." "I don't know how to do that." How many times have we heard those excuses from our children when faced with a difficult or unpleasant task? If we're honest, we sometimes use excuses like these when it comes to following God, don't we?

"I would obey God if I knew what he wanted." "I'm so busy right now—it's really difficult to find time to read my Bible." "How does God expect me to obey *all* these rules? It's too hard!" Do any of these sound familiar?

In Deuteronomy 30:11-14, Moses gives the people final instructions before entering the Promised Land, and he obviously is anticipating the people's excuses. Notice what he says: What God commands is "not too difficult" or "beyond your reach." No one has to search for it; it doesn't take special knowledge or ability to understand. No, says Moses, "the message is very close at hand; it is on your lips and in your heart so that you can obey it."

In other words, they have no excuses. God's laws are clearly written in the Bible. They are evident in the world around us. Obeying them is reasonable, sensible, and beneficial. It is not too difficult or burdensome.

For Jews, obeying God's laws is the means to redeeming or "fixing" the world. Like our ancestors at Sinai, Jews of every generation must "do everything the LORD has commanded" (Exodus 19:8), which means obeying God's Word and seeking holiness in our lives. If we do so, not only are we personally cleansed, but Israel is transformed into a "kingdom of priests" and "a holy nation" (Exodus 19:6).

A Christian Reflection on Not Making Excuses

As the psalmist proclaims, "The LORD looks down from heaven on the entire human race; he looks to see if anyone is truly wise, if anyone seeks God. But no, all have turned away; all have become corrupt. No one does good, not a single one!" (Psalm 14:2-3, quoted in Romans 3:10-13). The good news is that God's grace in Jesus transforms our hearts (see Romans 7:14-25) and allows us to heed his words: "If you love me, obey my commandments" (John 14:15). We have no excuses for not obeying him; but, as John reminds us, we also know that "if we confess our sins to him, he is faithful and just to forgive us our sins and to cleanse us from all wickedness" (1 John 1:9).

AT YOUR COMMAND

[Moses] took the Book of the Covenant and read it aloud to the people. Again they all responded, "We will do everything the LORD has commanded. We will obey."
❖ EXODUS 24:7

At one time or another, we probably have all been recipients of a "honey-do" list—a list of chores that a loved one has drawn up for us to do. If you have ever been the recipient of such a list, you know the proper response: "Sure, honey, I'll do it—as soon as I can."

As the people of Israel stood at the foot of Mount Sinai, they were the recipients of God's to-do—and not-to-do—list. As Moses read to the people all the teachings and regulations that the Lord had given to them, they responded as one voice: "We will do everything the LORD has commanded. We will obey."

Isn't that a beautiful response? All the people, unified in their purpose and desire to respond as God's chosen people, agreed to everything God had told them to do. In fact, the Jewish people's response to God's covenantal love and his imparted will is performing an act of *mitzvah*, or obeying his commands. Our very acceptance of God's lordship over our lives requires and involves our adherence to God's commands.

The *mitzvot* (plural of *mitzvah*, or commandments) are the vehicles through which the Jewish people are transformed into a kingdom of priests and a holy nation. This is how we as a people can obey the command from God to be holy because he is holy. Daily, we pray, "For they [the *mitzvot*] are our lives and the length of our days and upon them we will meditate day and night."

Rather than seeing the law as burdensome and punitive, given to us by a God who doesn't want us to have any fun, we see his rules and regulations as the outpouring and expression of his love and concern for us. To such love, there is only one proper response: *obedience*.

A Christian Reflection on Obedience

Jesus issued the followed challenge to his followers: "If you love me, obey my commandments" (John 14:15). What are Jesus' commandments? They are also Moses' commandments, about which Jesus says, "If you ignore the least commandment and teach others to do the same, you will be called the least in the Kingdom of Heaven. But anyone who obeys God's laws and teaches them will be called great in the Kingdom of Heaven" (Matthew 5:19). Is this burden too heavy? Not according to Jesus. He tells his disciples, "My yoke is easy to bear, and the burden I give you is light" (Matthew 11:30).

Sabbath Reflections

What new truth about the Jewish tradition of mourning did you learn from this week's devotions?

How has this truth affected your faith?

How will you apply this truth to your daily life?

Your Key Verse for the Week:

❖ OTHER REFLECTIONS

A VICTORY CRY

May we shout for joy when we hear of your victory and raise a victory banner in the name of our God. ✣ PSALM 20:5

David, the author of Psalm 20, faced numerous challenges throughout his life. As a young shepherd boy, he went head-to-head with the giant Goliath. David spent dozens of years running from the murderous intent of King Saul. As king of Israel, he finally subdued Israel's archenemy, the Philistines, and defeated other hostile neighbors. David even had to defend his throne from his own son Absalom.

Whatever the challenge he faced, wherever the battlefield, David knew victory was possible only with God's help. Just as David prepared his army for the battlefield with the proper armor and weapons, he also prepared spiritually.

Psalm 20 is David's prayer for victory before taking to the battlefield.

Consider what David asked: for God to answer his people in their distress; to protect them; to grant them support and give them the desires of their hearts; to succeed with all their plans; and to grant all their requests. Only then would they be able to shout for joy.

Now look at what David knew: God gives victory; God answers from his heavenly sanctuary; and God will bring the enemy to their knees while giving the Israelites the strength to rise up and stand firm. David had complete and total confidence approaching the battlefield because he knew God was on the side of the Israelites.

We might not be preparing for the battlefield, but Psalm 20 can help us face life's greatest challenges. Use it as *your* cry for victory—ask God to answer you in your distress, to protect you, and to grant you support and the desires of your heart.

As David reminds us, "Some nations boast of their chariots and horses, but we boast in the name of the LORD our God" (Psalm 20:7).

A Christian Reflection on Boasting

David had many victories over significant obstacles in his life, but he did not boast in his own strength or wisdom, but rather in the Lord. In a similar way, Paul warns Christians about boasting in themselves and redirects them to boast only in the God who saves them. In 1 Corinthians, he reminds his readers that "God has united you with Christ Jesus. For our benefit God made him to be wisdom itself. Christ made us right with God; he made us pure and holy, and he freed us from sin. Therefore, as the Scriptures say, 'If you want to boast, boast only about the LORD'" (1 Corinthians 1:30-31, paraphrasing Jeremiah 9:24).

AGREE TO DISAGREE

Finally Abram said to Lot, "Let's not allow this conflict to come between us or our herdsmen. After all, we are close relatives! The whole countryside is open to you. Take your choice of any section of the land you want, and we will separate. If you want the land to the left, then I'll take the land on the right. If you prefer the land on the right, then I'll go to the left." ❖ GENESIS 13:8-9

Some people might call them "irreconcilable differences," while others may simply "agree to disagree." The difference in how we view disagreements can be found in whether we are self-centered or love-centered. A self-centered approach to differences is unyielding. A love-centered approach accepts differences and is willing to work around them.

We see a love-centered approach to differences in the biblical story of Abraham and his nephew, Lot. Abraham and Lot had traveled to the new land that God had shown them. Along the way, both men had become very rich, so much so that their great numbers of people, flocks, and herds made it difficult to live on the same land. Tensions rose.

To preserve the peace, Abraham suggested that they go their separate ways, giving Lot first choice of land. Lot chose the most fertile portion, and Abraham willingly settled for second best. Sometimes, seeking peace means putting the good of others before our own.

In Jewish tradition, there were two schools of thought that disagreed with each other on practically everything. The House of Shammai was dedicated to truth and took a strict approach in deciding issues of law. The House of Hillel, on the other hand, championed love and often took a more lenient stance. Ultimately, Jewish law follows the House of Hillel. Why? Because Hillel always quoted Shammai's opinion before giving his own. He gave respect to the other man first.

Conflict is inevitable, but how we deal with it can preserve the peace. We don't have to let our differences do damage. We can learn from Abraham and remember to take a love-centered approach when dealing with differences in our relationships. When we give up some of our personal desires to defer to the needs of someone else, we will be rewarded with relationships that are peaceful, amicable, and more fulfilling.

A Christian Reflection on Putting Others First

The story of Abraham and Lot is quite amazing. Abraham could have demanded that Lot take the worst part of the land. But Abraham responded to their differences in love and put Lot first. Paul calls on the Philippians to work together in spite of their differences. His formula for successful relationships? "Don't be selfish; don't try to impress others. Be humble, thinking of others as better than yourselves. Don't look out for your own interests, but take an interest in others, too" (Philippians 2:3-4). If they follow his instructions, then they will have "the same attitude Christ Jesus had" (Philippians 2:5).

CONSTANT VIGIL

The land you will soon take over is a land of hills and valleys with plenty of rain—
a land that the LORD your God cares for. He watches over it through each season
of the year! ❖ DEUTERONOMY 11:11-12

One of the most repeated comments I hear from those on The Fellowship's Journey
Home Tour is how they experienced God's presence while in Israel in such a different
way than in any other place in the world. And I think that's true for both Christians
and Jews visiting the Holy Land.

It's not just the history of the land, where God has worked so many wonders
through and for his people, Israel. And it's not just the sacredness of the many sites,
such as the Temple, the Mount of Olives, or the Mount of Beatitudes. Nor is it, for
Christians, the knowledge that this is the birthplace of Christianity.

As the Bible tells us, God is uniquely present in Israel, more so than in any other
place in the world.

From before the time God's people took possession of the Promised Land, God
told them that he cared for this land in a special way: "The eyes of the LORD your God
are continually on it" (Deuteronomy 11:12, NIV).

Of course, God is everywhere in the world. We don't need to worry that we must
go to Israel to feel God's presence. However, God's presence is there in a unique way
because he cares so much for the land and his people.

This is why Jews, wherever we are in the world, face Israel when we pray. In Israel,
we face Jerusalem. And in Jerusalem, we face the Western Wall, where the Temple was
located. It's not so much that we worship a particular place, but we worship God, who
is so clearly present in that place.

Wherever we are today, however, we can rest in the knowledge that God is present
everywhere. God is not restricted to one place, one temple, one city, or one country.
God is right where we are, right now.

A *Christian Reflection on Finding God's Presence*

Having traveled to Israel many times, I agree with Rabbi Eckstein that one can feel
God's presence in the land of Israel in a unique way. That said, how wonderful it is
that we do not have to go to Israel to worship God or to be in his presence. Indeed,
God makes his presence known to us in the most intimate fashion. Jesus said that after
he entered his glory, the Spirit would come and would live within us. Our bodies are
temples of the Holy Spirit (see 1 Corinthians 6:18-20); he makes his presence known
to us every day and in every place.

WEEK 32 // DAY 4

ASK FIRST

The whole community of the LORD demands to know why you are betraying the God of Israel. How could you turn away from the LORD and build an altar for yourselves in rebellion against him? ❖ JOSHUA 22:16

Sometimes, when differences occur, it is easier to engage in a monologue of accusations rather than a meaningful dialogue seeking to understand the situation as perceived by each side. Yet, when we take the time to explore the facts and understand the feelings of those involved, it can go a long way toward maintaining peace and trust in a relationship.

We find this principle at work in the Bible as the eastern tribes of Israel returned to their land. When Reuben, Gad, and the half-tribe of Manasseh built an altar on the east side of the Jordan River, the rest of Israel feared they were starting their own religion, and they began to prepare to go to war against their brothers.

Before they did so, however, in accordance with God's laws they summoned the priest Phinehas and sent him to find out what was going on (see Joshua 22:10-34). Open discussion revealed that the altar was a memorial, rather than a place of sacrifice, so war was avoided. Seeking clarification maintained peace and unity in Israel. And so there was a happy ending to a potentially grave situation.

Second-guessing the intentions or motives of others often leads to trouble. Many conflicts can be resolved if we calmly initiate a discussion with an aim toward understanding the other person or group.

The differences between Christians and Jews are many. But often the misunderstandings that occur between the two groups could be avoided by simply asking questions rather than making assumptions based on our own preconceived ideas. Everyone welcomes honest questions more than ignorant accusations.

As we seek to understand one another, God will bless our relationships with a measure of his grace to soften the rough edges of disagreement.

A Christian Reflection on Rushing to Judgment

We are often too quick to judge other people's motives and actions. We should be careful not to rush into judgment against other people, remembering what Jesus taught: "Do not judge others, and you will not be judged. Do not condemn others, or it will all come back against you" (Luke 6:37). This warning does not mean that we should not confront others if they sin, but it does mean we should neither be quick to judge nor ever simply condemn others. If they are sinning, then we should approach them recognizing our own sin (see Luke 6:42). Respectful dialogue is a necessity for fruitful relationships.

AN EXPRESSION OF LOVE

Two people are better off than one, for they can help each other succeed. If one person falls, the other can reach out and help. But someone who falls alone is in real trouble.
❖ ECCLESIASTES 4:9-10

We all go through seasons when we struggle and the daily demands of life overwhelm us. It's times like these when having a friend to help us is most needed and appreciated. As the Beatles sang, "I get by with a little help from my friends."

Solomon recognized this truth thousands of years earlier when he wrote, "Two people are better off than one, for they can help each other succeed." Helping one another in times of need is one way we demonstrate love to each other.

Loving God and loving others is at the core of what we call Judeo-Christian values. The *Torah* teaches that we are to "love the LORD your God with all your heart, all your soul, and all your strength" (Deuteronomy 6:5). Jesus called this the "first and greatest commandment," and then he quoted Leviticus 19:18 as the second greatest commandment: "Love your neighbor as yourself" (Matthew 22:37-40).

These values have given the free world its strength, making both America and Israel beacons of hope because of our commitment to creating an ethical society based on moral values. It is a society built on the foundation of loving God and loving others.

Loving others begins with each one of us. We don't have to travel far to find someone to help. We can look for ways to help those we come in contact with each day—at home, in our neighborhoods, at work.

We can also extend our care for others as we become involved in ministries and groups that provide aid and help to suffering people around the world. In providing humanitarian support to needy Jews throughout the world, The Fellowship offers Christians tangible ways of loving their Jewish brothers and sisters.

A Christian Reflection on Helping One Another

According to Leviticus 19:18, we are to love our neighbor. But who is our neighbor? That is the question posed to Jesus by an expert in the law (Luke 10:29). That question prompted Jesus to tell the story of the Good Samaritan (see Luke 10:29-37). When a Jewish man was beaten as he traveled to Jericho, it was a "despised Samaritan" who stopped to help him. The law expert had to acknowledge that the Samaritan had acted like a true neighbor to the man in need, despite their ethnic and religious differences. Who is our neighbor, and to whom should we extend our help? Everyone.

WEEK 32 // DAY 6

SURVIVING ON FAITH

We hoped for peace, but no peace came. We hoped for a time of healing, but found only terror. ❖ JEREMIAH 8:15

Although these words from the book of Jeremiah were written thousands of years ago, fear of enemy attacks is as much a reality for many living in Israel today as it was then.

Like their ancestors, the people of Israel today have hoped for peace, but instead have encountered terror. We read about it—and experience it—on almost a daily basis. For years, innocent people living in southern Israel have been targeted by terrorist attacks from nearby Gaza.

As the prophet Jeremiah writes, "The snorting of the enemies' warhorses can be heard all the way from the land of Dan in the north" (Jeremiah 8:16). Just as then, no one in Israel feels safe anymore. Although terror attacks and war have been plaguing Israel since the day of her establishment in 1948, it is not a reality that any of us can get used to.

Living under such conditions requires daily faith. It forces us to trust God for life and safety from one moment to the next. We realize that life goes on, and so we carry on with "normal" life, despite the many obstacles and enemies we face.

For Israel, even in times of attack, "normal" means pursuing justice, participating in a strong community, and living out our faith in God. In the book of Habakkuk we read, "The righteous will live by his faith" (Habakkuk 2:4, NASB). Faith can be life-giving. When we live with faith, we are strengthened. When we act according to our faith, we become righteous. And when we pray with faith, God answers our prayers.

Next time you pray, remember the people of Israel. Lift up your voice to God to grant protection to the elderly, children, and families who are enduring the terror and the fear of having nowhere safe to run.

A Christian Reflection on Praying for Jerusalem

Christians today should heed the call of the psalmist: "Pray for peace in Jerusalem. May all who love this city prosper. O Jerusalem, may there be peace within your walls" (Psalm 122:6-7). The psalmist cites as motivation the welfare of "family and friends." The inhabitants of Israel are indeed our friends and deserve our prayers and support. Pray that the forces that want to harm and even destroy Israel will be thwarted and have a change of heart. Pray that the violence will end and that Jews and Palestinians will live together in peace.

Sabbath Reflections

What new truth about resolving conflict and our role in helping others did you learn from this week's devotions?

How has this truth affected your faith?

How will you apply this truth to your daily life?

Your Key Verse for the Week:

❖ OTHER REFLECTIONS

FIGHTING OUR ENEMIES

See how many enemies I have and how viciously they hate me! ❖ PSALM 25:19

Having enemies is nothing new for God's chosen people. From the time that Moses led the people out of Egypt, the Israelites have been surrounded, attacked, and perse- cuted by enemies. So it should not come as any surprise that even today our enemies continue to attack us not only with weapons and terrorist attacks but also with words and lies.

King David knew something about enemies. Did you know that seventy-two of the Psalms—almost half the book—speak about enemies? Before becoming king, David spent nearly half his adult life on the run from his enemy, King Saul. After he took the throne, David was attacked by his own son Absalom.

We can learn from David about how to face our enemies. David knew that bat- tling our enemies can consume us. We can quickly lose focus and allow the tactics and the lies of our enemies to cause us to despair. We can become so preoccupied with the circumstances of our particular battle that we forget that we have the greatest source of hope, comfort, and protection—God.

David never forgot that. Even as he prayed for relief from his enemies, David focused on the one who could provide that for him. In the opening lines of Psalm 25, David writes, "O LORD, I give my life to you. I trust in you, my God!" Despite having enemies who hated him, David remembered that it was God who would guide him, who would release him from the snare of his enemies, and who would relieve him of his anguish.

David had the certainty of faith that God was ultimately in control and that God alone could deliver him—and Israel—from trouble. Even in the face of such opposi- tion and trouble, David affirmed, "My eyes are always on the LORD" (Psalm 25:15).

A Christian Reflection on Intimidation

When the apostle Paul writes to the people in the Philippian church, who were being persecuted, he tells them, "Don't be intimidated in any way by your enemies" (Philippians 1:28), but rather "live as citizens of heaven, conducting yourself in a man- ner worthy of the Good News about Christ" (Philippians 1:27). They should consider the struggle a privilege because they suffer for Jesus, and they are "standing together with one spirit and one purpose, fighting together for the faith, which is the Good News" (Philippians 1:27). We, too, should not be intimidated by those who want to hurt us, but rather realize that God is our protector.

FACE THE MUSIC

When you want a piece of land, you find a way to seize it. When you want someone's house, you take it by fraud and violence. You cheat a man of his property, stealing his family's inheritance. But this is what the LORD says: "I will reward your evil with evil; you won't be able to pull your neck out of the noose. You will no longer walk around proudly, for it will be a terrible time." ❖ MICAH 2:2-3

When we tell people it's time to "face the music," we're letting them know that they have to face the unpleasant consequences of their actions. This is exactly the message that God sent to the people of Judah through the prophet Micah.

The people clearly deserved God's judgment. God had provided each family with a plot of land in Israel—an "inheritance" from the Lord—so there was no reason for anyone to seize the land of another. Yet, in Judah, the rich and powerful were defrauding others and taking their land. This was not only a sin against those whose land they stole but also against God, defiling the gift of land he had given to each of his children.

The proposed judgment fit the crime. Those who took land from others would see their own land taken away on the day Judah was conquered by foreigners. The day would come when the people would certainly have to face the music.

While Micah's chastisement was harsh, it was also founded in a deep love for the people of Judah and a desire for them to repent and turn from their wickedness back to God. The people would suffer for their actions, but God also promised, "Someday, O Israel, I will gather you; I will gather the remnant who are left. I will bring you together again like sheep in a pen, like a flock in its pasture" (Micah 2:12).

Micah's message is an important one for us today, as well. There may be times in our lives when we have to face the music for our actions and accept God's discipline. As difficult as that may be, Micah's message also reminds us that our God is loving and compassionate. Though he disciplines his children, God also will forgive when we turn to him sincerely and with truly repentant hearts.

A Christian Reflection on God's Discipline

The author of Hebrews compares God's discipline of his followers with the discipline that a loving father displays toward his children (see Hebrews 12:5-13). A father who disciplines his children when they do wrong is loving, not negligent; the same can be said for God, who does not let his people wallow in their sin, but prods them back to "a peaceful harvest of right living" (Hebrews 12:11). The author of Hebrews writes, quoting Proverbs 3:12, "The LORD corrects those he loves, just as a father corrects a child in whom he delights" (Hebrews 12:6).

JUSTICE AND MERCY

But as for me, I am filled with power—with the Spirit of the LORD. I am filled with justice and strength to boldly declare Israel's sin and rebellion. ❖ MICAH 3 : 8

Sometimes, especially when the news is bad, we hear only what we want to hear and tune out the rest. The people of Judah during Micah's time were certainly guilty of that.

While Micah continued to warn the people about God's pending judgment, false prophets reassured the people, saying, "Is not the LORD among us? No disaster will come upon us" (Micah 3:11, NIV). The people gladly believed there would be no consequences for their actions, because of God's mercy.

Micah alone stood against this false teaching. He declared to the people, "But as for me, I am filled with power—with the Spirit of the Lord. I am filled with justice and strength to boldly declare Israel's sin and rebellion." Because of the leaders' failure to deliver God's true—and urgent—message to his people, Jerusalem would be reduced to rubble. The great Temple of Solomon would be destroyed.

What an image. The Promised Land "plowed like an open field; Jerusalem will be reduced to ruins! A thicket will grow on the heights where the Temple now stands" (Micah 3:12).

While God is certainly merciful, sometimes I wonder whether we doubt there will be consequences for our actions because we want to hear only about his mercy. We forget that the Bible teaches that God is also a God of justice and there will be due penalties for our sins.

Micah's message was a sobering one for the people then, as it is for us today. Though God never left his people without comfort, nor will he do so today, it is wise for us to remember that God will hold all of us accountable for our behavior, whether we acknowledge it or not.

When we humbly confess our sins, we will meet God's mercy.

A Christian Reflection on Consequences

God's people need to avoid the dangers of "easy believism"—the idea that all it takes is an intellectual affirmation of God and a belief in the saving work of Jesus for people to be right with God. In other words, easy believism says that there is no need to fear bad consequences for our behavior. The author of Hebrews warns believers who continue to sin: "It is a terrible thing to fall into the hands of the living God" (Hebrews 10:31). And Paul was glad when the Corinthian church felt distress when he confronted them concerning their sin. Why? "Because the pain caused you to repent and change your ways" (2 Corinthians 7:9).

A SHARED PROPHECY

But you, Bethlehem Ephrathah, though you are small among the clans of Judah, out of you will come for me one who will be ruler over Israel, whose origins are from of old, from ancient times. ❖ MICAH 5:2, NIV

Micah, the passionate prophet of God, had a difficult message to deliver to the people of Judah. But he fervently and forcefully delivered God's message of pending judgment, unwavering in the face of false prophets and the people's refusal to listen.

Yet in the midst of Micah's harsh condemnation come words of hope in one of the most glorious prophecies of Israel's restoration for a new—and eternal—ruler: "But you, Bethlehem Ephrathah, . . . out of you will come for me one who will be ruler over Israel. . . . He will stand and shepherd his flock in the strength of the LORD, in the majesty of the name of the LORD his God. And they will live securely, for then his greatness will reach to the ends of the earth" (Micah 5:2, 4, NIV).

Bethlehem, of course, refers to King David, whose father was Jesse of Bethlehem, and out of whose line the Messiah would descend. This is a frequently repeated theme in Scripture, since God promised David that he would have an heir on the throne of Israel forever. My Christian friends will no doubt recognize this verse as one of the biblical passages pointing to the birth of Jesus in Bethlehem.

Now, while Christians believe that the Messiah has already arrived in the person of Jesus, fulfilling Micah's prophecy, Jews, of course, are still awaiting the Messiah's arrival. It is important to note, though, that both beliefs—Christian and Jew—have their basis in the same prophecy.

This is a shared belief that many might not realize, but which I believe is another step toward building bridges of understanding between the two faith groups. Out of the same prophecy, we both look to a future hope and peace, as Micah records, "And he will be the source of peace" (Micah 5:5).

A Christian Reflection on the Messiah's Birthplace

Jews and Christians both cite Micah's prophecy in reference to the Messiah, who will bring hope and peace. Bethlehem, just a few short miles south of Jerusalem, was David's birthplace, and thus the Messiah would come from David's descendants and be the ultimate fulfillment of the promise that God gave David that "your house and your kingdom will continue before me for all time, and your throne will be secure forever" (2 Samuel 7:16). According to Matthew 2:1, "Jesus was born in Bethlehem in Judea, during the reign of King Herod," in fulfillment of Micah 5:2 as noted by the leading priests and teachers of the religious law.

WHAT GOD EXPECTS

Should we offer him thousands of rams and ten thousand rivers of olive oil? Should we sacrifice our firstborn children to pay for our sins? No, O people, the LORD has told you what is good, and this is what he requires of you: to do what is right, to love mercy, and to walk humbly with your God. ❖ MICAH 6:7-8

It can be difficult to work (or live) with someone who is a perfectionist. It's frustrating to give everything we have and then be told it's not good enough. In exasperation we might exclaim, "What more do you want from me?"

In Micah 6, God is clearly unhappy with his people. He asks why they have grown tired of him (see Micah 6:1-3).

In the people's response, we can hear their frustration. Sure, they were making sacrifices to false gods, but they always gave the required sacrifices to the God of Israel at the Temple. What more did God want? In bitter sarcasm, they suggest offering thousands of rams—or even their firstborn children—in an effort to satisfy God.

Micah tells the people that God has already shown them what he requires. It was simple. God wanted them "to do what is right, to love mercy, and to walk humbly with your God" (Micah 6:8).

The real problem was that people had separated their service in the Temple from what they did in their daily lives. This dualism enabled them to engage in unjust behavior while under the illusion that they were still obeying God. Micah argues that God is not interested in the physical act of sacrifice. God wants obedience that comes from the heart and engages all aspects of life.

Deuteronomy 6:5 implores us to love God "with all your heart, all your soul, and all your strength." Moreover, we are to teach God's Word to our children, speak about his laws at home, on the road, when we go to sleep, and when we wake (see Deuteronomy 6:7). God is meant to be integrated into every aspect of life.

Whenever we separate religion from the other aspects of our lives, we make a grave mistake. Faith is not something we add on to our lives; it encompasses our lives. Everything we do should be a reflection of our faith.

A *Christian Reflection on "Sunday-Only Christians"*

Micah's words speak to both Christians and Jews to remind us that faith encompasses our whole lives, not just what we do in church. Christians need to beware of falling into the trap of being "Sunday-only Christians," going through the motions in church every week and then acting and thinking like everyone else during the week. God is the one who made us and sustains our lives. Jesus died on the cross for our sins and makes our lives worth living. He deserves our wholehearted and constant devotion.

HOPE FOR THE HOPELESS

As for me, I look to the LORD for help. I wait confidently for God to save me, and my God will certainly hear me. ❖ MICAH 7:7

After preaching to the people about God's pending judgment throughout much of his message, Micah opens his final chapter with these despairing words: "How miserable I am! . . . The godly people have all disappeared; not one honest person is left on the earth" (Micah 7:1-2).

Micah recounts Israel's sins and the people's transgressions: the immorality of Judah's judges and officials; the dishonesty of neighbors and friends; and the widespread treachery that led to discord within their own households among family members. In short, he confirms that Judah would be punished and led into Babylonian captivity.

Yet God's punishment would not be forever. In an eloquent statement of faith that is both personal and on behalf of his people, Micah proclaims, "As for me, I look to the LORD for help. I wait confidently for God to save me, and my God will certainly hear me" (Micah 7:7). In faith, Micah reminds himself and the people that they must be patient in their punishment because God would bring his people through the dark times (Micah 7:9); and that eventually, their enemies would be punished (see Micah 7:10).

Micah's unfailing confidence in the Lord was clear as he spoke of God's provision in times of turmoil and of God's ability to hear us even when we have gone astray. Yes, Israel would suffer for her transgressions, but God's final act on behalf of his people would be to remove those transgressions from his sight and forgive them completely.

Let Micah's message of hope and redemption in the midst of turmoil and impending disaster reassure us in facing the struggles and trials of our own lives: God is compassionate; he does not stay angry with us; and he delights in showing mercy and forgiveness as we come to him with repentant hearts.

A Christian Reflection on the Compassion of Jesus

In Micah, and throughout the Hebrew Bible, we find countless manifestations of God's compassion toward his sinful people. When we turn to the New Testament, we see Jesus acting with the same measure of divine compassion. As he traveled through Israel, he observed that the people were "confused and helpless, like sheep without a shepherd," and "he had compassion on them" (Matthew 9:36). Paul mirrored his Lord's compassion for the Philippians: "I love you and long for you with the tender compassion of Christ Jesus" (Philippians 1:8). Likewise, Paul calls on them—and through them, us—to also reflect Christ's compassion for others.

Sabbath Reflections

What new truth about the prophet Micah's life and message to the children of Israel did you learn from this week's devotions?

How has this truth affected your faith?

How will you apply this truth to your daily life?

Your Key Verse for the Week:

❖ OTHER REFLECTIONS

A FIRM FOUNDATION

The king trusts in the LORD. The unfailing love of the Most High will keep him from stumbling. ❖ PSALM 21:7

Sometimes events in our lives leave us shaken: A company where you have worked for the past twenty-five years asks you to leave because of downsizing. A spouse tells you over breakfast that "this isn't working out." Such times not only test our ability to cope—they also test our faith.

Throughout the Bible, we find men and women who have had their faith shaken. Joseph was sold into slavery by his own brothers and later imprisoned under false accusations. Hannah cried out in her barrenness for a child. Certainly David went through numerous trials—his repeated cries for relief fill the pages of the Psalms.

All these people, however, overcame their circumstances and emerged victorious. Joseph became second in command to Pharaoh. Hannah gave birth to a son. David defeated his enemies. Though shaken, they never faltered. Though tested, they remained faithful. Their trust was firmly planted in the "unfailing love of the Most High."

In Jeremiah 17:7, we read, "Blessed is the one who trusts in the LORD" (NIV). This verse is more than directions for how to become a blessed person; it provides the definition of a blessed person. A blessed person is someone who trusts that everything that happens is from the Lord with love. He or she knows that it's all God, and so it's all good, and thus he or she feels blessed.

Despite the human tendency to trust in one's own strength, David did not do that. He knew that everything he had was a gift from God. And because "the king trusts in the LORD," David knew that God's love would protect and sustain him. While events in his life might leave him shaken, God would not let him fall.

At times it might not feel as if God is there at all. But consider all the good gifts you have. Perhaps you will discover that in the end, it's *all* a gift—from our loving God.

A Christian Reflection on Trust in the Midst of Turmoil

Jesus knew that the cross awaited him. In the garden of Gethsemane, he confessed, "My soul is crushed with grief to the point of death" (Matthew 26:38), and he prayed to his heavenly Father, "Let this cup of suffering be taken away from me" (Matthew 26:39). Still, he submitted himself to his Father's will because he trusted him. Death came, but then so did the resurrection. Paul, an ardent follower of Christ, shared in Jesus' suffering. Indeed, he faced death daily (see 1 Corinthians 15:31), but his faith stayed strong because he realized that "nothing [not even death] can ever separate us from God's love" (Romans 8:38).

STAIN REMOVER

Purify me from my sins, and I will be clean; wash me, and I will be whiter than snow.
❖ PSALM 51:7

Often when we sin, we try to cover it up—like an ugly stain on a clean shirt. We try to disguise our misdeeds or blot them from our memory. But the truth is, no matter what we do, we know our sin is there.

We see this in Psalm 51, written after David committed adultery with Bathsheba and conceived a child with her. David tried to cover up his sinful behavior by enticing Bathsheba's husband, Uriah, to sleep with her. When that failed, David sent Uriah to the front lines of battle, where he was killed.

David quickly married Bathsheba, but the stain of his sin remained. When the prophet Nathan confronted him (see 2 Samuel 11–12), David penned Psalm 51 as a prayer asking God for forgiveness.

Consider the language David uses in seeking God's forgiveness. He implores God to "have mercy on me," "blot out the stain," "wash me," and "purify me" (Psalm 51:1-2). And because David acknowledged his sin and repented of it, God mercifully forgave him, so that David was washed clean of his sin.

The good news is that God offers us the same forgiveness. No sin is so great that we cannot bring it before God. We don't have to cover up our blemishes; we can receive God's forgiveness and cleansing.

Usually, when we offend somebody, we can receive forgiveness, but the damage has been done and the relationship is tainted. Not so with God. As we read in Hosea 14:2, 4, God says, "Bring your confessions and return to the LORD. . . . Then I will heal you of your faithlessness; my love will know no bounds." When we repent, it's as if the sin never happened; God's love for us is just as great as ever.

Then can we rejoice, as David did, when God restores to us a "clean heart" and "the joy of [our] salvation" (Psalm 51:10, 12).

A Christian Reflection on Forgiveness of Our Sin

Paul provides an interesting comparison and contrast between Adam and Christ in Romans 5. He looks back to Adam's sin as the time when sin and death entered the world. People don't die because of Adam's sin, but Adam's transgression illustrates that human beings are rebellious sinners who deserve death. Though Adam introduced sin and death into the world, Jesus brought "God's grace and his gift of forgiveness" (Romans 5:15). Though "Adam's sin led to condemnation, . . . God's free gift leads to our being made right with God, even though we are guilty of many sins" (Romans 5:16).

THE GOOD, THE BAD, AND THE UGLY

A friend is always loyal, and a brother is born to help in time of need.
PROVERBS 17:17

Making friends today is often as easy as a click on Facebook, yet we often feel more alone than ever. We may have seven hundred online friends, but do we really feel cared for? A true friend is more than a number that we point to.

"A man of many companions may come to ruin, but there is a friend who sticks closer than a brother" (Proverbs 18:24, NIV 1984). In other words, it's the quality, not the quantity, of our relationships that will make a difference in our lives.

One of the greatest evidences of true friendship is loyalty—standing by our friends during difficult times. We see that modeled for us in the friendship of David and Jonathan. Nothing—not even the throne—came between them.

A true friend sticks with us during the good, the bad, and the ugly. It's easy to call someone a friend when things are going well. But a genuine friend is there when you really need it. We find out during those tough times who our true friends are, don't we? They are the ones still standing with us when everyone else has left.

The Sages ask, "Which is the best path for a person to pursue?" Of five suggestions, one of them is "a good friend." Choosing good friends is critical for getting where we need to be in life. Recognizing who our true friends are is even more important.

In recent years, I think many Jews in Israel have been surprised to discover that their true friends have been Christians throughout the world. At The Fellowship, we have repeatedly seen Christians come to the aid of suffering Jews throughout the world with generosity, compassion, and prayers.

I have been so grateful to God for this bond, and I am proud to call Christians my friends who love at all times; my brothers and sisters who were "born to help in time of need."

A Christian *Reflection* on *True Friendship*

True friends love each other. We find the standard for that kind of love in 1 Corinthians 13:4-7: "Love is patient and kind. Love is not jealous or boastful or proud or rude. It does not demand its own way. It is not irritable, and it keeps no record of being wronged. It does not rejoice about injustice but rejoices whenever the truth wins out. Love never gives up, never loses faith, is always hopeful, and endures through every circumstance." True friends bring the best out of each other, build each other up, and point each other toward God in love.

LOVE IN ACTION

But if there are any poor Israelites in your towns when you arrive in the land the LORD your God is giving you, do not be hard-hearted or tightfisted toward them. Instead, be generous and lend them whatever they need. ❖ DEUTERONOMY 15:7-8

When Christians in the French village of Le Chambon-sur-Lignon agreed to take in five thousand Jews to protect them from the Germans during World War II, it was a genuine act of love. The pastors of the Pentecostal church there urged everyone in their congregations to offer safe haven for one Jew. So five thousand lives were saved because two pastors—just two men—believed that Christian love meant taking action.

We see this same principle—that real love for others involves action—in the laws that God gave to the people of Israel at the foot of Mount Sinai. In Deuteronomy 15, God tells the Israelites how they are to care for the poor among them—to be generous, lend whatever is needed, and share resources.

Love is meant to be practical. It means helping others. When we see a need, our first response must be to ask ourselves, *What can I do to help?* The answer may be easy, or it may require some degree of sacrifice, as was the case with the Christians of Le Chambon-sur-Lignon.

In Hebrew, the word *love* is *ahavah*. The Sages point out that the root of the word—*hav*—means "to give." This is because love is inextricably bound to *action*. The more we give, the more we will love; and the more we love, the more we must give.

Although our acts of love may not save lives, they can change lives. Reaching out to others in love not only meets practical needs but can break down walls of resistance and help others feel loved. And when we act in love, it opens our hearts and changes us, too.

Let us keep our eyes open for opportunities to express love to others through practical expressions of provision, protection, or personal care. It's possible that our acts of love will change a life, perhaps even our own.

A Christian Reflection on Acting in Love

Of course, Jesus taught the principle of "love in action" to his disciples when he instructed them to feed the hungry, clothe the naked, provide shelter for the homeless, and visit the sick and those in prison (see Matthew 25:35-36). The apostle John reminded the early church of this same truth when he encouraged them, saying "Dear children, let's not merely say that we love each other; let us show the truth by our actions" (1 John 3:18). It's one thing to talk about loving our neighbors as ourselves, but it's quite another to put our words into action and demonstrate that love in tangible, meaningful ways.

A HOPE AND A FUTURE

[God] ensures that orphans and widows receive justice. He shows love to the
foreigners living among you and gives them food and clothing.
❖ DEUTERONOMY 10:18

It doesn't take much to understand God's heart for the fatherless and for widows.
Throughout the Hebrew Bible, we find God exhorting and encouraging his people to
care for orphans, widows, and foreigners.

For example, in Deuteronomy 24:17, God instructs the Israelites to provide justice
for widows and orphans. He also tells the people to leave the remains of the harvest
behind so the fatherless and widows can eat (Deuteronomy 24:19-22).

Isaiah the prophet also conveyed God's message to his people: "Learn to do good.
Seek justice. Help the oppressed. Defend the cause of orphans. Fight for the rights of
widows" (Isaiah 1:17). Clearly, God "ensures that orphans and widows receive justice"
(Deuteronomy 10:18).

One of the many blessings of being associated with a ministry like The Fellowship
is that we see firsthand how the generosity of Christians in America is helping
orphans throughout Israel. For example, The Fellowship-sponsored Beit Shanti Youth
Home, known as Shanti House, has helped more than twenty-four thousand Israeli
youths fight homelessness, poverty, and despair. It is a safe haven where distraught and
abandoned young people come to know that God loves them and that there is hope
for the future.

Shaul, one young resident at Shanti House, said, "After my father beat me so bad
that he broke three of my ribs, at the age of fourteen I ran away and lived on the
streets for five months. Shanti House was the only place that took me in and provided
me with a future."

As Psalm 146:9 reminds us, "The LORD protects the foreigners among us. He cares
for the orphans and widows." God is the hope and the help of the fatherless and the
needy. But he uses us, his obedient people, to minister and provide that care.

A Christian Reflection on Care for Orphans

The New Testament describes all of us as orphans; but according to the apostle Paul,
we are orphans who have been adopted: "You received God's Spirit when he adopted
you as his own children. Now we call him, 'Abba, Father'" (Romans 8:15). Apart from
God, we are orphans, but God has adopted us, so we have a "Daddy." This experience
should warm our hearts toward the pain felt by those with no parents. Throughout
the Bible, God urges us to care for the vulnerable. "Pure and genuine religion in
the sight of God the Father means caring for orphans and widows in their distress"
(James 1:27).

A TALE OF TWO TREES

I am like an olive tree, thriving in the house of God. I will always trust in God's unfailing love. I will praise you forever, O God, for what you have done. I will trust in your good name in the presence of your faithful people. ❖ PSALM 52:8-9

Two trees of the same variety can be planted in different soils, and based on the quality of the soil, one will flourish and the other will wither and die. Trees have no choice in the matter—they must live where they are planted. We, however, can choose where we put down our roots. Some people choose to be rooted in faith; others put down roots in the soil of disbelief and evil ways.

Using the imagery of trees, David says to the wicked that the Lord "will pull you from your home and uproot you from the land of the living" (Psalm 52:5); but of himself, he says, "I am like an olive tree, thriving in the house of God" (Psalm 52:8). In this case, the "uprooted tree" refers to Doeg the Edomite, who had betrayed David (see 1 Samuel 21–22).

David had found refuge with Ahimelech the priest. When Doeg reported this to Saul, the angry king ordered his men to kill the priests, but they refused. Only Doeg agreed. He killed eighty-five priests and everyone else who lived in the town.

A man like Doeg would be uprooted because he did not trust in God. But David was like an olive tree, one of the longest-living trees, flourishing and prospering as he trusted in God's unfailing love.

Jeremiah 17:7-8 provides us with a similar imagery: "Blessed are those who trust in the LORD. . . . They are like trees planted along a riverbank, with roots that reach deep into the water." Well-rooted trees never suffer from drought, their leaves are always fresh, and they consistently produce fruit. Such is the power of a deeply rooted faith.

If we want to flourish, we will plant ourselves deep in God's Word and his ways.

A Christian Reflection on Planting in Rich Soil

In one of his most famous parables, Jesus talks about a farmer who sows seed in order to grow a crop. Some seed fell on a footpath, where the birds ate it. Other seed fell on rock, where it withered for lack of water. Still other seed got overwhelmed by thorns. However, some seed fell on fertile ground, and "this seed grew and produced a crop that was a hundred times as much as had been planted!" (Luke 8:8). Jesus later identified the seed as "God's word" (Luke 8:11). What does the rich soil represent? People with receptive hearts who are rooted in God's Word and obey him. Such people will live fruitful lives.

Sabbath Reflections

What new truth about acting in love did you learn from this week's devotions?

How has this truth affected your faith?

How will you apply this truth to your daily life?

Your Key Verse for the Week:

❖ OTHER REFLECTIONS

FOR MEMBERS ONLY

Who may climb the mountain of the LORD? Who may stand in his holy place?
❖ PSALM 24:3

Before joining any kind of organization, questions typically come up: Who is allowed to join? What qualifications are needed in order to enjoy the benefits of that group? What are the membership requirements?

It seems that David, in Psalm 24:3, is asking similar questions of God: "Who may climb the mountain of the LORD? Who may stand in his holy place?" Psalm 15:1 also asks, "Who may worship in your sanctuary, LORD? Who may enter your presence on your holy hill?"

David's questions reminded worshipers that, although everyone may attend worship at the sanctuary, not everyone will receive God's blessings or will enjoy the status of righteousness. Indeed, in a recurring theme throughout the Hebrew Bible, God expects his people to welcome their privileges from the heart and to reflect that in their behavior.

So what is required? David lists the following: clean hands (the Hebrew word can also be translated "innocence"), a pure heart, and a desire to trust and follow God rather than idols and false gods. A person who meets those requirements is the one who will receive blessings from God and who will be regarded by others as having "a right relationship with God their savior" (Psalm 24:5).

This type of "membership requirement" is expressed elsewhere in Scripture: "Those who lead blameless lives and do what is right, speaking the truth from sincere hearts" (Psalm 15:2); "The sacrifice you desire is a broken spirit" (Psalm 51:17); "The LORD detests the sacrifice of the wicked, but he delights in the prayers of the upright" (Proverbs 15:8).

How is your membership standing?

A Christian Reflection on Membership in God's Family

Who deserves membership in God's family? On one level, *nobody*. As Paul states, "No one can ever be made right with God by doing what the law commands. The law simply shows us how sinful we are" (Romans 3:20). How does anyone join, then? Paul writes, "We are made right with God by placing our faith in Jesus Christ" (Romans 3:22). But that does not mean that God's people can continue to sin. Again, Paul testifies, "Since we have died to sin, how can we continue to live in it?" (Romans 6:2).

THE ROYAL DANCE

David danced before the LORD with all his might, wearing a priestly garment. So
David and all the people of Israel brought up the Ark of the LORD with shouts of joy
and the blowing of rams' horns. But as the Ark of the LORD entered the City of David,
Michal, the daughter of Saul, looked down from her window. When she saw King
David leaping and dancing before the LORD, she was filled with contempt for him.
❖ 2 SAMUEL 6:14-16

When David finally was able to bring the Ark of the Covenant back to Jerusalem, it was an incredibly joyous occasion. Imagine the scene described for us in Scripture: "David danced before the LORD with all his might, wearing a priestly garment. So David and all the people of Israel brought up the Ark of the LORD with shouts of joy and the blowing of rams' horns."

Yet, curiously, the following verse describes how this wonderfully joyful scene upset Michal, King David's wife: "When she saw King David leaping and dancing before the LORD, she was filled with contempt for him." Apparently, Michal felt that it was inappropriate for a king to let loose in public and that his behavior diminished him in the eyes of his subjects.

There are many different ways to serve God. Some people are exuberant—singing, clapping, and even dancing. Then there are those who choose to worship more quietly, or even thrive on silence. There are also those who *want* to dance and sing, yet somehow can't bring themselves to do so for fear of what others might think of them. That mind-set has no place in truly authentic service to God.

Our need to please others can take away from our service in other ways. Perhaps we were quiet when we knew we should have spoken up. Or we may have shied away from taking a stand for a good but unpopular cause. To fully serve our Creator, we need to live our lives as King David did—"leaping and dancing before the LORD." That means saying and doing the things that please God, even if it makes our family and friends uncomfortable.

Resolve to be as fearless as King David. Humble yourself in front of men, and you will find that you stand as royalty before God.

A Christian Reflection on Exuberant Worship

The author of Hebrews writes, "Since we are receiving a Kingdom that is unshake-able, let us be thankful and please God by worshiping him with holy fear and awe" (Hebrews 12:28). Proper worship of God is exuberant. If you find worship boring and you feel unengaged, something is wrong. Perhaps you are forgetting whom you worship. God is our Creator and Redeemer. He is all-powerful and the coming Judge. He guides us and takes care of us. He is "a devouring fire" (Hebrews 12:29). Such a God deserves more than our mere presence.

FOR GOD'S SAKE

When King David was settled in his palace and the LORD had given him rest from all the surrounding enemies, the king summoned Nathan the prophet. "Look," David said, "I am living in a beautiful cedar palace, but the Ark of God is out there in a tent!"

❖ 2 SAMUEL 7:1-2

After years of war, peace prevailed over David's kingdom. Yet, as he got settled, he had an uncomfortable thought: "I am living in a beautiful cedar palace, but the Ark of God is out there in a tent!" How could David enjoy his palace while the Ark of God was housed in a tent?

Did the Ark care? Does God really need a house?

It reminds me of my friend who, as a child, was baffled by a Jewish tradition performed at the *Pesach* (Passover) *Seder*. At one point, Elijah the Prophet is invited to join the *Seder*; those present stand while one person opens the door for him to "enter." My friend thought that this was utterly ridiculous. If Elijah was a spirit, like a ghost, couldn't he just come straight through the walls?

As an adult, my friend understands that the act of opening the door for Elijah is not for Elijah. It is for the benefit of those present at the *Seder*. Tradition teaches us that Elijah will appear immediately before the messianic times arrive. By opening the door and getting up to greet him, the participants demonstrate that they play an active role in bringing about redemption.

Similarly, while God certainly does not need a home, nor is it possible to contain the Almighty in any one place, the act of building a house of God is intended for our sake. When a community makes it a priority and invests in building a house of worship that they are proud to attend, it reinforces the centrality of God in every aspect of their lives.

We put our money into what we value most. If you want to know what you really care about, look at where you spend your money. Your expenditures will match your priorities.

A Christian Reflection on Putting Faith into Action

The saying "Put your money where your mouth is" is not in the Bible, but the principle is. As James reminds us, "Faith by itself isn't enough. Unless it produces good deeds, it is dead and useless" (James 2:17). The faith that saves us manifests itself in good deeds. James also says, "Suppose you see a brother or sister who has no food or clothing, and you say, 'Good-bye and have a good day; stay warm and eat well'—but then you don't give that person any food or clothing. What good does that do?" (James 2:15-16). Do you put your money where your mouth is?

FAIL TO BE GREAT

David confessed to Nathan, "I have sinned against the LORD."
2 SAMUEL 12:13

When we think of great individuals, we typically think of those who have accomplished important things and who have succeeded in reaching their goals. Greatness is mastery and flawlessness. According to Scripture, however, one man's greatness is defined by failure.

Here are the words that transformed King David into one of the greatest men of all time: "I have sinned against the LORD." This was David's response when the prophet Nathan confronted him with the sin the king had committed with Bathsheba. Bathsheba was married at the time, and though King David did not personally kill her husband, Uriah, he did have him sent to the front lines of battle, where he was killed. King David's greatest and defining moment is the confession he voices as soon as his sin comes to light. Jewish tradition teaches that it was his ability to admit his mistake that made King David worthy of everlasting kingship.

Everyone makes mistakes, but our mishaps are not what define us. It is our response to our lowest moments that transforms us into better or lesser beings. If we own up to our mistakes and take responsibility for them, we can learn from them. Ironically, our failures can end up becoming our greatest catalysts for positive growth.

Take Thomas Edison, for example. He failed a thousand times before he successfully invented the life-changing lightbulb. When asked how he felt about failing so many times, Edison replied, "I didn't fail one thousand times. The lightbulb was an invention that had 1,001 steps." Greatness is born out of failure. More specifically, mistakes provide us with the opportunity to become great. The choice is ours.

How would your relationships be different if every time you wronged someone you owned up to it? Three little words—"I was wrong"—might be the best gift you can give.

A Christian *Reflection on Dealing with Our Sin*

Both David and Saul sinned, but God removed Saul from the throne and placed David there, promising David that his descendants would follow him on the throne (see 2 Samuel 7). The difference between the two kings was David's willingness to own up to his sin, confess it, and repent. Repentance restores our relationship with God, which is why Paul grieves over the Corinthians when he tells them, "You have not repented of your impurity, sexual immorality, and eagerness for lustful pleasure" (2 Corinthians 12:21). Repentance is not something we do once, but many times over the course of our lives, knowing that God readily forgives us.

TELLING TIME

[David's] advisers were amazed. "We don't understand you," they told him. "While the child was still living, you wept and refused to eat. But now that the child is dead, you have stopped your mourning and are eating again." David replied, "I fasted and wept while the child was alive, for I said, 'Perhaps the LORD will be gracious to me and let the child live.' But why should I fast when he is dead? Can I bring him back again? I will go to him one day, but he cannot return to me."

❖ 2 SAMUEL 12:21-23

King David's servants had a big problem. Their mighty and powerful king had spent seven days on his knees weeping, fasting, and begging the Almighty to heal his sick infant. He was inconsolable. Now, the king's baby had died. How could they possibly tell him? If he was in such a terrible state when the baby was sick, what might he do now that the baby was gone?

When David noticed his servants whispering to one another, he figured out that his child had died. His reaction absolutely stunned them. King David got up, bathed, changed his clothing, prayed, and ate. The men could not understand how the king could feel better when his circumstances had clearly changed for the worse.

King David explained to them, "I fasted and wept while the child was alive, for I said, 'Perhaps the LORD will be gracious to me and let the child live.' But why should I fast when he is dead? Can I bring him back again? I will go to him one day, but he cannot return to me."

King David is teaching us that there are times in our lives when we must do all that we can to effect change. Yet there are also times when there is nothing left to do but accept God's will and move on. Sometimes it's not easy to know which response is appropriate. However, other times, when we take a moment to examine our situation, it is painfully obvious which response is necessary.

How might life be different if we focused our energy on the areas on which we have influence? How much more peace would be in our lives if we accepted the things that we cannot change?

A Christian Reflection on Accepting God's Will

In this fallen world, we will all experience loss in many forms. We may lose a friend or relative to death, a spouse to divorce, or our health to sickness. Of course, we would be unfeeling if we did not experience disappointment or pain when events like these happen to us. On the other hand, there comes a time when we have to move on, as David did after the loss of his child. It's not that we ever completely forget, but when God chooses not to answer our prayers, we should not stay buried in our grief. When suffering loss, pray to God to give you the ability to move on with life.

IN CASE OF EMERGENCY

Morning, noon, and night I cry out in my distress, and the LORD hears my voice.
❖ PSALM 55:17

Since grade school, we all have been trained in what to do in case of an emergency. But what's our plan when it comes to those types of emergencies that we can't avoid simply by planning an escape route? How do we cope with situations like betrayals, false accusations, broken relationships, devastating losses, or illnesses?

In Psalm 55, David faces an emergency situation. His words express the depth of his despair: "Please listen and answer me, for I am overwhelmed by my troubles. My enemies shout at me, making loud and wicked threats. . . . My heart pounds in my chest. The terror of death assaults me. Fear and trembling overwhelm me, and I can't stop shaking" (Psalm 55:2-5).

Some biblical scholars believe this psalm was written during the rebellion of David's son Absalom. Certainly, the emotions expressed point to the betrayal of a person close to David: "Instead, it is you—my equal, my companion and close friend" (Psalm 55:13-14).

So what did David do? How did he cope with such emotional pain and distress? David's "emergency drill" was to pray "morning, noon, and night" (Psalm 55:17). He turned to God in his despair, confident that God would hear his prayers and deliver him: "But I will call on God, and the LORD will rescue me" (Psalm 55:16).

Praying continually throughout the day not only is a good idea during the difficult times in our lives but is also a good way to keep our priorities straight throughout the day. No matter what we may be facing today, King David invites us to "give your burdens to the LORD, and he will take care of you" (Psalm 55:22).

A Christian Reflection on Being Prayerful

At the end of his letter to the church in Thessalonica, Paul instructs them to "never stop praying" (1 Thessalonians 5:17). What does it mean to pray 24/7? I believe Paul is calling us to a constant communication with God. Not that we have to pause, close our eyes, fold our hands, and talk out loud, but we should be in touch with God constantly, in good times as well as bad. That said, we should also have times every day when we are in focused and intentional prayer. How wonderful it is that we have access to the very throne room of God, where we can bring him our praise and our requests!

Sabbath Reflections

What new truth about David's sin and repentance did you learn from this week's devotions?

How has this truth affected your faith?

How will you apply this truth to your daily life?

Your Key Verse for the Week:

❖ OTHER REFLECTIONS

THE PERFECT REFRESHMENT

The instructions of the LORD are perfect, reviving the soul. ❖ PSALM 19:7

How do you refresh yourself? A brisk walk outdoors? Maybe listening to music or watching a favorite TV program? Perhaps a quick nap or a long, soothing bath? What about reading God's Word?

That's what refreshed King David! God's law revitalized David's soul. It prepared him for each day. It energized him and enabled him to deal with his circumstances. It made him wise and gave him insight. Moreover, it brought him joy.

God's words, conveyed in the *Torah*, were precious to him, "more desirable than gold" and "sweeter than honey" (Psalm 19:10). From Scripture, David was able to discern what was right and what was wrong. He had insight into his hidden faults and sinful ways (see Psalm 19:12). For David, there was no better pastime than to read and meditate on God's Word.

Is that how we view the Bible? Maybe at times we do. But more often than not, reading God's Word is merely an item on our to-do list. Dutifully, we get up in the morning (or maybe set aside time at night) and open our Bibles and try to wade through the passage for that day. Sometimes we might get a nugget of truth or a word of encouragement from our reading. Sometimes we're challenged by what we read.

But *joy*? Do we come away from our reading with joy in our hearts?

Think of how much richer we are than even King David. For not only do we have the Law (the *Torah* for the Jew), but we also have the Psalms, the books of wisdom, and the wonderful stories of the heroes, the prophets, and the people of the Bible to inspire us, guide us, warn us, and encourage us.

Consider what you can do in opening up your Bible so that you, like David, will be refreshed and find joy in God's holy and perfect Word.

A Christian Reflection on the Power of God's Word

God's Word has real power, for as James says, "It has the power to save your souls" (James 1:21). God's Word can save us, but not magically. James goes on to say, "Don't just listen to God's word. You must do what it says. Otherwise, you are only fooling yourselves. . . . But if you look carefully into the perfect law that sets you free, and if you do what it says and don't forget what you heard, then God will bless you for doing it" (James 1:22, 25). Refreshment for your soul begins with reading God's Word and obeying it.

THE ROCK

I wait quietly before God, for my victory comes from him. He alone is my rock and my salvation, my fortress where I will never be shaken. ❖ PSALM 62:1-2

If you have ever visited the Holy Land, one thing becomes quickly apparent—there are a lot of rocks! The hillsides, the long, winding road leading up to Jerusalem, the craggy landscape surrounding the Dead Sea, all are dominated by rugged terrain—and rocks.

So when David was looking for a way to describe the protection he experienced from his loving Father, he used an illustration and metaphor that would be familiar— God as a rock, the source of our protection.

In the Hebrew Bible, God is frequently referred to as "the Rock of Israel" (Genesis 49:24), "the Rock" (Deuteronomy 32:4), and "the towering rock of safety" (Psalm 61:2). Furthermore, God assured his people that, to those who feared him as holy, he would be a sanctuary, but to those who do not fear the Lord, "he will be a stone that makes people stumble, a rock that makes them fall" (Isaiah 8:14).

In Psalm 62, David finds rest in God's protection, knowing that his salvation from his enemies comes from God alone. David knew firsthand what it was like to hide in caves and seek shelter in rocky, mountainous regions, as he fled from his enemies on many occasions. With this knowledge, he affirmed that God was his rock, his place of refuge and protection. He did not hide himself in the shelter of the rocks, but in the shelter of the Rock.

Though we may find shelter and protection in our homes, God is ultimately our protection. There is no greater rest than knowing that we are under God's protection. Whenever we are afraid, we can turn to the Rock, as David did.

A Christian Reflection on God as Our Rock

The early Christians certainly had confidence that God protected them in the midst of the resistance and persecution they experienced. After all, Jesus prayed to the Father, "Now protect [my followers] by the power of your name" (John 17:11). Later, the apostle Paul bore witness to King Agrippa that "God has protected me right up to this present time" (Acts 26:22). God's protection is not merely a thing of the past; his protection extends to all who seek it.

A SPECIAL HOMECOMING

[The Lord said,] "What's more, I am with you, and I will protect you wherever you go. One day I will bring you back to this land. I will not leave you until I have finished giving you everything I have promised you." ❖ GENESIS 28:15

For centuries, the Holy Land has been a beacon of light to the children of Israel. Throughout history, it has been the hope and dream of exiled and dispersed Jews to one day return to the land of their forefathers. Even today, we are witnesses to the ongoing *aliyah*—or emigration to Israel—of Jews from around the world who are choosing to return to their biblical and historical home.

I, myself, was nearly fifty when I made *aliyah* in response to where I felt God was calling me. Still, after ten years of living in Israel, every time I return home after traveling, I feel a swell of inspiration and a sense of peace as the plane finally lands at Ben Gurion Airport. I am home.

But a flight I took recently had special meaning for me as I had the honor and privilege of accompanying my parents, Rabbi Simon and Belle Eckstein, as they made *aliyah*. At the ages of ninety-one (my father) and eighty-four (my mother), they decided to spend their final years in the land of their spiritual forefathers.

For me, this is not only a source of pride in my parents' willingness to relocate at this stage in their lives, but I also see it—as I do all *aliyah*—as the fulfillment of biblical prophecy. The Bible tells us that God told Abraham that the people of Israel would go into exile in Egypt (see Genesis 15). But God promised that "after four generations your descendants will return here to this land" (Genesis 15:16).

I am so grateful to God for my parents' example. They have taught me that it is never too late to fulfill your life's dream and to trust in God to guide you all your days.

A *Christian Reflection on* Aliyah

One of the differences between Christianity and Judaism concerns the connection between our religions and the land. Not that Israel is unimportant to Christianity. It is the place where God made his presence known in a special way and acted to redeem his people throughout history. But Christians worldwide do not feel the same call as our Jewish brothers and sisters to return to Israel. On the other hand, we certainly admire those who decide to return to Israel. We rejoice along with our Jewish friends in seeing ancient prophecy fulfilled in our lifetimes.

A SIGN OF RESPECT

Remember this and keep it firmly in mind: The LORD is God both in heaven and on earth, and there is no other. If you obey all the decrees and commands I am giving you today, all will be well with you and your children. I am giving you these instructions so you will enjoy a long life in the land the LORD your God is giving you for all time.
❖ DEUTERONOMY 4:39-40

In Western culture, a man shows respect by removing his hat. In polite society, men are expected to remove their hats when inside a home, at church, or in a restaurant. And it is considered respectful for men to remove their hats when being introduced to someone.

But did you know that in the Jewish tradition, a man shows respect by *putting on* a hat? Of course, I am referring to the traditional Jewish head covering, known as a *kippah* in Hebrew, though many know it by the Yiddish term, *yarmulke*.

Though there is no clear biblical precedent for wearing a *kippah*, Jewish tradition identifies it as a sign of respect and a reminder that God is above us at all times. It increases our awareness that all our actions are witnessed by God above. When we wear a *kippah*, we are more mindful of how we conduct ourselves. A person wearing a *kippah* should think twice about being rude to a waiter or cutting in line at the store.

The Deuteronomy passage reminds us not only that God is above us, but that when we keep God's commands, it will go well with us. These are the same concepts that we keep in mind when we wear a *kippah*. By acknowledging that God is Lord of all, we align our lives to live according to his ways. The ultimate sign of respect for God is not whether one wears a *kippah*, but whether one obeys God.

Wearing a *kippah* may not be a tradition for everyone, but we can always keep in mind that God is above us, watching all we do. As we become more aware of God's presence in our lives, we will be prompted to do the right thing.

A Christian Reflection on Displaying Allegiance

Though Christians don't wear *kippahs*, we, too, should be constantly aware that God is present in our lives and that we represent God in the world. Some Christians do have items that publicly identify themselves as followers of God, such as a cross on a necklace or a T-shirt sporting a Scripture verse. Others don't have any external signs of their faith, and ultimately, that is not what's most important. As Jesus taught, "Your love for one another will prove to the world that you are my disciples" (John 13:35).

HELPING HANDS

They share freely and give generously to those in need. Their good deeds will be remembered forever. They will have influence and honor. ❖ PSALM 112:9

In the Jewish faith, there is a strong mandate to care for others and for ourselves that is expressed in this ancient rabbinic adage: "If I am not for myself, who will be for me? If I am only for myself, what am I? And if not now, when?"

This powerful maxim is a clear call to us to balance caring for our families with caring for others, and to act when we have the opportunity to do so for those less fortunate. This principle has a biblical foundation as well.

From Israel's beginnings, God established an organized system of caring for the poor. Every third year, a tithe was given for the helpless, hungry, or poor. It was the responsibility of everyone to care for the less fortunate—families were to help other family members; towns were to help members of their community (see Deuteronomy 14:22-29).

Helping the poor, in fact, was an important part of possessing the land. As God instructed the people, "Give generously to the poor, not grudgingly, for the LORD your God will bless you in everything you do" (Deuteronomy 15:10).

This is an important message for us today as well—and a critical one for friends of The Fellowship. Recent reports indicate that more Israelis of all ages are falling victim to a grinding poverty. Indeed, out of thirty-five countries in the Organization for Economic Cooperation and Development (OECD), Israel is second only to Mexico in its level of poverty. More than one in every five children in Israel lives in poverty.

God has called each of us to do what we can to help those less fortunate—wherever we may find them—in our homes, our communities, or even across the world. Let us consider what each of us can do to honor and obey God by caring for his children.

A Christian Reflection on Helping the Poor

As Jesus told the rich man, "If you want to be perfect, go and sell all your possessions and give the money to the poor, and you will have treasure in heaven. Then come, follow me" (Matthew 19:21). While Jesus' demand for him to sell "all his possessions" probably was directed to that individual to expose his idolatry of riches, Jesus does want us all to be generous with the poor. Indeed, right from the start the church also had systems in place to care for the needy (see Acts 6:1-7). And Paul devoted much of his energy to gathering a gift to give to the poor in Jerusalem (see Romans 15:25-30).

HUNGRY TO SHARE

[God said,] "No, this is the kind of fasting I want: Free those who are wrongly imprisoned; lighten the burden of those who work for you. Let the oppressed go free, and remove the chains that bind people. Share your food with the hungry, and give shelter to the homeless. Give clothes to those who need them, and do not hide from relatives who need your help." ❖ ISAIAH 58:6-7

If you buy lunch for $7, five times a week, that's approximately $140 per month. And if you buy a specialty coffee every weekday morning, at $3 each, that's $60 per month.

While I enjoy lunch and coffee as much as anyone, I want to illustrate that sometimes we can find areas where we can make sacrifices for the purpose of helping others. This is the point that God makes in Isaiah 58.

Though fasting can be spiritually beneficial, it serves to help only the one doing it. And while we can spend countless hours studying the Scriptures, we can miss the boat if we think this is true worship.

Through Isaiah, God wanted to teach his people that fasting doesn't just mean giving up something as a sign of devotion. True devotion to God also involves helping others in need. The type of fast that honors him is one where someone gives up something to share with another.

The Day of Atonement, *Yom Kippur*, is a fast day. God calls it "a day to deny yourselves" (Leviticus 23:27), and Jews abstain from five things: eating, drinking, marital relations, washing, and wearing leather shoes. But the point of this fast isn't to feel bad—it's to become better, more compassionate people. It makes us more sensitive to those who may be homeless, hungry, or lonely.

We all need a reminder, now and then, that we are truly blessed. Even if we have trouble paying the bills, we have so much to be thankful for—our homes, food to eat, and modern comforts. Many people live without these things. We can do something about poverty, and God says that doing so is a way to please him.

The question for each of us is what would we be willing to sacrifice for God to help meet the needs of others? Giving up something, even something small, can make a huge difference.

A Christian Reflection on Fasting

In his Sermon on the Mount, Jesus encourages fasting as a spiritual discipline and gives these instructions about the proper way to fast: "When you fast, comb your hair and wash your face. Then no one will notice that you are fasting, except your Father, who knows what you do in private. And your Father, who sees everything, will reward you" (Matthew 6:17-18). Even so, Jesus, like Isaiah, pointed out that fasting alone does no good. He tells the rich man that, though he fasted, he needed to "give . . . money to the poor." Only then would he "have treasure in heaven" (Luke 18:22).

Sabbath Reflections

What new truth about displaying allegiance to God did you learn from this week's devotions?

How has this truth affected your faith?

How will you apply this truth to your daily life?

Your Key Verse for the Week:

❖ OTHER REFLECTIONS

WHAT'S YOUR SOURCE?

I cry out to God Most High, to God who will fulfill his purpose for me.
❖ PSALM 57:2

In today's information-driven culture, the Internet has become our number one go-to resource. Type a word into any search engine, and instantly you have at your fingertips hundreds of articles about that topic. But when it comes to getting information about life, hope for getting through difficulties, and encouragement for the days ahead, we need another resource. For thousands of years, and for millions of people, that resource has been God's Word, and the Psalms in particular. For Christians and Jews alike, the Psalms are recited in public worship and cried out in private prayer; they are expressions of the heart and soul of humanity in the context of our relationship to God.

More important, the Psalms give us insight into the character of God himself. Through them, we see God as Creator, Sustainer, Healer, and Redeemer. They are a testimony of his overwhelming power and sovereignty over the world. They tell of his goodness and assure us that he is worthy of our trust and has the right to judge us.

The Psalms are our source of wisdom, thanksgiving, comfort, hope, and encouragement, no matter what our circumstances. Consider David's words in Psalm 57:2: "I cry out to God Most High, to God who will fulfill his purpose for me." Do you know where David was when he wrote those words? In a cave, on the run from King Saul, who wanted to kill him. Yet, despite his situation, David knew the source of his hope, his deliverance, and ultimately, his purpose.

Whatever it is that you need most today, consider your Source. Go to him, and then you can say along with King David: "My heart is confident in you, O God; my heart is confident. No wonder I can sing your praises!" (Psalm 57:7).

A Christian Reflection on the Psalms

Unfortunately, it's true that many Christians tend to avoid the Old Testament, but the Psalms prove an exception to this rule. The Psalms help us express our own emotions, thoughts, and desires to God. But even more, they reveal God to us. He is our shepherd, our king, our warrior, and more. Fourth-century theologian Athanasius called the Psalms "an epitome of the Old Testament," and Jesus himself told his disciples that the Psalms anticipated his coming (Luke 24:44). Daily reading from the book of Psalms helps us understand ourselves better and brings us into the very presence of God.

THE CALL OF THE TRUMPETS (FOR *ROSH HASHANAH*)

On the first day of the seventh month hold a sacred assembly and do no regular work.
It is a day for you to sound the trumpets. ❖ NUMBERS 29:1, NIV

On *Rosh Hashanah*, the key ritual is the sounding of the trumpet, or in Hebrew, the *shofar*. During this observance, the *shofar* is sounded in three different ways, representing three messages we are meant to understand about this holiday.

The long, singular *tekiah* blast reminds us of royalty. When a king enters a place, trumpets are blown to signal his presence. Similarly, on *Rosh Hashanah*, the King of the World is present. Every year on *Rosh Hashanah*, we recognize that the Lord, our God, is King, and we acknowledge his dominion over the world.

The three-part *shevarim* sound closely resembles the sound of weeping. This distinctive blast reminds us that life, and everything we hold dear, hangs by a single thread held by the Master of the universe. It could all disappear in the blink of an eye. That's why we cry. Yet our brokenness leads us to wholeness when we pray to God, seeking his blessing for another year. We remember that he is our loving Father and that he will answer our prayers.

The nine, short *teruah* blasts are reminiscent of an alarm, and their purpose is to awaken us from our slumber. All year long we get caught up in the humdrum of life. Once a year, we make it a point to wake up and remember that we are here for a specific purpose. During the High Holy Days, we reassess our lives and make any necessary alterations.

Together, the three distinct types of *shofar* sounds point us to a deeper understanding of the holiday. *Rosh Hashanah* literally means the "head of the year" because on that day we define which way our year is headed. When we recognize that God is the King who directs our lives and we adjust our lives to reflect that truth, we will have set the New Year in the right direction.

A Christian Reflection on the Last Trumpet

When the New Testament speaks of the appearance of the Son of Man and his angelic army, it is preceded "with the mighty blast of a trumpet" (Matthew 24:31). Paul tells us that "it will happen in a moment, in the blink of an eye, when the last trumpet is blown. For when the trumpet sounds, those who have died will be raised to live forever. And we who are living will also be transformed" (1 Corinthians 15:52). Next time you hear a trumpet, think of the future coming of your divine King.

WHERE ARE YOU? (FOR *ROSH HASHANAH*)

Give the following instructions to the people of Israel. On the first day of the appointed month in early autumn, you are to observe a day of complete rest. It will be an official day for holy assembly, a day commemorated with loud blasts of a trumpet.
❖ LEVITICUS 23:24

Most people familiar with *Rosh Hashanah* will tell you that it commemorates the creation of the world. And they would be somewhat correct. More specifically, the first day of the Hebrew month of *Tishrei*, on which we celebrate *Rosh Hashanah*, correlates with the sixth day of creation. On that day, God completed the creation of the world with his final act: the creation of man.

On that day not only did Adam meet his spouse, he also had his first run-in with God after Adam and his new wife ate from the forbidden tree. When they realized what they had done, Adam and Eve tried to hide from God; but nothing is hidden from the Almighty.

And what does God say to them in the Garden? "Where are you?" (Genesis 3:9). But God already knows the answer. His question really is, "Where are you spiritually?" In other words: "Somewhere between the time that I created you and now, you veered off the path of righteousness. Take a look at where you are and find your way back."

"Repentance" in Hebrew is *teshuvah*, but the word has other meanings as well. *Teshuvah* means "to return," and it also means "answer." This is because our answer to God's question, "Where are you?" is to return to the path of righteousness.

Rosh Hashanah is a time of deep introspection. Out of all God's creations, humans are the only ones who have the ability to reflect on their lives and do something about them. And when we do take those steps to make our world a better place, we raise humanity up to a higher level.

That's why we celebrate the New Year with introspection that leaves us knowing more than ever who we are and where we need to go, not with parties that leave us in a drunken stupor so that we forget who we are.

A Christian Reflection on Repentance

When John the Baptist started preaching in the wilderness, his message was simple and clear: "Repent of your sins and turn to God, for the Kingdom of Heaven is near" (Matthew 3:2). When the author of Hebrews speaks of "the fundamental importance of repenting from evil deeds and placing our faith in God" (Hebrews 6:1), he indicates that repentance and faith are two fundamental building blocks of a relationship with God. Repentance means turning from our sin and turning to God, and it is something we need to do daily.

RESOLUTIONS THAT LAST (FOR *ROSH HASHANAH*)

It is a land the LORD your God cares for; the eyes of the LORD your God are
continually on it from the beginning of the year to its end.
❖ DEUTERONOMY 11:12, NIV

When the Bible tells us that God's eyes are always on the land, the simplest explanation is that God pays special attention to the land of Israel. However, Jewish Sages teach that there is another lesson for us.

They explain that the word *land* refers to the entire earth and everyone who lives on it, and God's "eyes" refer to a time of judgment. "The beginning of the year to its end," they explain, refers to the judgment that takes place on the Jewish New Year. On that day, according to the Jewish tradition, God decides the fate of every living creature for the year ahead.

But something else happens on that day too. While God decides our lot for the next year, we also make important decisions about the year to come, called our New Year's resolutions.

The rabbis point to a nuance in our verse that isn't obvious in English, but jumps out in the original Hebrew. The beginning of the year is called *the* year, but the end of the year is called *a* year. As the rabbis explain, we call the beginning of every year "the year," as in, "This will be the year that I lose twenty pounds," and so on. But, explain the rabbis, at the end of the year, the enthusiasm wears off. We realize that this year is "a year" like any other.

The verse contains a warning for us, as well as a suggestion. God's eyes are *continually* on the land—from the first day of the year to the last. It makes no difference to God whether it is the first day or the last day of the year. He is there 100 percent of the time, doing his job every day. And that's how we need to live every day—like it's our first and our last.

A Christian Reflection on "Being There" 100 Percent

Because God is there for us 100 percent of the time, we need to show up 100 percent of the time as well. Jesus made this point in the parable of the ten bridesmaids (see Matthew 25:1-13). The ten were to be ready with lit torches in order to escort the bridegroom to the wedding. Only half were prepared with enough oil to keep the torches lit; the other five, who were not ready when the bridegroom showed up unexpectedly, were left out of the festivities. We need to be ready 100 percent of the time to greet Jesus, our Bridegroom, when he returns.

TREMBLING WITH JOY (FOR *ROSH HASHANAH*)

Serve the LORD *with reverent fear, and rejoice with trembling.* ❖ PSALM 2:11

On *Rosh Hashanah*, "the Day of Judgment," we believe everybody stands before God in judgment. The previous year is taken into review, and decisions are made regarding the year to come.

It is always hard to know how to relate to *Rosh Hashanah*. On one hand, it is a day of joy and celebration. We dress in our finest clothing and share delicious meals with family and friends. On the other hand, we spend time in prayer, contemplating that we are being judged by the Master of the Universe. That's a scary thought!

The psalmist captures our ambivalence with words that the *Talmud* associates with *Rosh Hashanah*: "Serve the LORD with reverent fear, and rejoice with trembling." Well . . . which is it? Are we rejoicing, or are we trembling? It seems difficult to do both at the same time.

I understood the words of the psalm writer when I went through a profound experience—I moved. Anyone who has moved houses knows that it's no picnic. Moving to Israel, where everything is tiny compared to supersized America, also means downsizing. We had to make decisions about every item we owned. Do we really need it? Does it serve a good purpose?

The process of decluttering one's life and assessing one's worldly possessions is downright painful. But at the same time, it is incredibly liberating. It's painful, but joyful.

Now I could understand the Day of Judgment. On *Rosh Hashanah*, we tremble, knowing that we are being judged. We are forced to take stock of our inner worlds: Do I really want to behave this way? We take note of all the junk cluttering our minds and interfering with our souls, and we throw it out!

And you know what? It feels good to go through such a thorough cleansing. We feel lighter, clearer, and—yes—joyful.

A Christian Reflection on Fear and Joy

Fear and joy seem to be opposite emotions, but the New Testament also urges God's people to experience both. On the one hand, we should listen to Paul when he says, "Work hard to show the results of your salvation, obeying God with deep reverence and fear" (Philippians 2:12). Such an attitude will encourage us to "live clean, innocent lives as children of God, shining like bright lights in a world full of crooked and perverse people" (Philippians 2:14-15). The result? Joy, according to Paul, who concludes by saying, "You should rejoice, and I will share your joy" (Philippians 2:18).

THE SECRET OF THE *SHOFAR* (FOR *ROSH HASHANAH*)

Happy are those who hear the joyful call to worship, for they will walk in the light of your presence, LORD. ❖ PSALM 89:15

My friend Jonathan was pulled over by the police for talking on the phone while driving. As the officer began scolding Jonathan and explaining that he had earned himself a sizable fine, Jonathan's wife tried making excuses. The officer seemed to anticipate an argument, and his voice only got louder and stronger.

Finally, Jonathan said something that stopped the officer midsentence. He said, "You're right. Hand me the ticket." The officer's mouth hung open, as if he had suddenly forgotten how to talk. In the end, the officer's demeanor completely changed and he issued a warning, but no ticket.

Tradition teaches that when we blow the *shofar* on *Rosh Hashanah*, God our King, who is sitting on his throne of judgment, gets up and takes the seat of compassion. With just one piercing sound, the day is transformed from a day of stern judgment into a day of merciful compassion. Why?

In ancient days, a Jewish trial began with the sounding of the *shofar*. So when we blow the *shofar*, it is as if we are willingly starting our own trial. We initiate the judgment. It's as if we are saying to God, "Hand me the ticket. I know I'm guilty." As we recognize the things we've done wrong and accept our verdict, God switches his mode from judgment to compassion.

The psalmist writes, "Blessed are those who have learned to acclaim you, . . . LORD" (Psalm 89:15, NIV). The Hebrew word for "to acclaim you" in this verse is *teruah*. *Teruah* is also the name of the nine-note "wake up!" shofar blast. So our Sages interpret this verse to mean, "Blessed are those who know the secret of the *shofar* blast." The "secret" is that it unleashes God's mercy.

A Christian Reflection on Judgment and Mercy

God's love and mercy save us from the judgment we rightly deserve because of our sin. As Paul points out, "When we were utterly helpless, Christ came at just the right time and died for us sinners" (Romans 5:6), and "God showed his great love for us by sending Christ to die for us while we were still sinners" (Romans 5:8). The result? "Since we have been made right in God's sight by the blood of Christ, he will certainly save us from God's condemnation" (Romans 5:9). Though we should rejoice in that fact, we must also remember that we are called to a life of repentance and obedience.

Sabbath Reflections

What new truth about the observance of Rosh Hashanah, *the Jewish New Year, did you learn from this week's devotions?*

How has this truth affected your faith?

How will you apply this truth to your daily life?

Your Key Verse for the Week:

❖ OTHER REFLECTIONS

WHERE ARE YOU LOOKING?

Whom have I in heaven but you? I desire you more than anything on earth.
❖ PSALM 73:25

Why do evil people prosper? Most of us have wrestled with this age-old question. For people of faith, the answer depends on where we're looking.

In Psalm 73, the psalmist grapples with this issue. At first, he is perplexed by what he sees: The arrogant and wicked have no struggles; they are healthy, prosperous, and free from the burdens most people carry. Based on this observation, the psalmist wonders why he bothers keeping his heart pure and trying to do the right thing in God's eyes. He writes, "I tried to understand why the wicked prosper. But what a difficult task it is!" (Psalm 73:16). Sound familiar?

The psalm writer gains a new perspective after entering God's sanctuary. As he spends time in worship and focusing on God and his Word, he finally realizes that God, indeed, does see all and know all. God knows all about the wicked and will deal with them accordingly: "Truly, you put them on a slippery path and send them sliding over the cliff to destruction" (Psalm 73:18).

In the end, what sustains the psalmist from despairing over the wicked is focusing on God. In doing so, he discovers that his knowledge of God is all he really needs. Indeed, he writes, "Whom have I in heaven but you? I desire you more than anything on earth." With that knowledge, the psalmist was able to confidently conclude, "God remains the strength of my heart" (Psalm 73:26).

When we are confronted with life's injustices—whether big or small—we need to remember that our God in heaven is totally in control and will bring about his justice in his time. We have all we need in him—the one who *is* our strength and our portion.

A Christian Reflection on Suffering

How we deal with suffering is a reflection of what we believe. The apostle James gives us another way to look at our trials: "Dear brothers and sisters, when troubles come your way, consider it an opportunity for great joy" (James 1:2). Why would he say that? Because our troubles can teach us perseverance, allow us to develop patience, strengthen our faith, and help us grow deeper in our relationship with God. As we are tested and our faith matures, James says, "You will be perfect and complete, needing nothing" (James 1:4).

AT ONE-MENT

Aaron will then present as a sin offering the goat chosen by lot for the LORD. The other goat, the scapegoat chosen by lot to be sent away, will be kept alive, standing before the LORD. When it is sent away to Azazel in the wilderness, the people will be purified and made right with the LORD. ❖ LEVITICUS 16:9-10

On the Day of Atonement (*Yom Kippur*) in biblical times, two goats were brought before the high priest. Lots were cast to determine which goat would be sacrificed to the Lord and which would be sent into the wilderness, bearing the sins of the people. After the first goat was slaughtered and sacrificed to God, the other was set free in the desert. However, when the free goat came to a cliff, he was pushed off.

What does this seemingly bizarre practice have to do with the personal changes we aim for on *Yom Kippur?* The question comes down to this: Which goat would you rather be—the one freed, or the one sacrificed?

It would seem that the goat chosen for the wilderness received the better deal. The other goat was immediately sacrificed, whereas the second goat was released to the wilderness, free to roam. It was only at the last moment, when the goat realized he was about to meet his end, that he saw things differently.

Jewish tradition teaches that the two goats symbolize ways of living. The first goat represents those who choose to dedicate their lives to God. They nullify their will to his and give up their ego for the sake of God's name.

The second goat represents those who choose to live wild and free. These people look at those serving God and pity them. Yet at some point, often just before they die, they consider that maybe they have been wrong all along. We all die eventually, but only some will have filled their lives with meaning.

Atonement means that we are cleansed of our sins when we choose to be "at one" with God. That's why we might say "at one-ment." On *Yom Kippur,* we make this critical decision: Do we live our lives in a wilderness of nothingness, or do we live a life filled with meaning and godliness? If we choose "at one-ment," we will achieve atonement.

A Christian Reflection on Atonement

The New Testament presents Jesus as the ultimate sacrifice that achieves atonement between God and his people. Indeed, he is both the sacrifice *and* the priest who offers the sacrifice of himself on the cross. According to Hebrews, he is different from the other priests, like Aaron, who had to offer a sacrifice for their own sins before offering sacrifices for the people of Israel (see Hebrews 5:3; Leviticus 16:11). Instead, Jesus became "a merciful and faithful high priest in service to God . . . that he might make atonement for the sins of the people" (Hebrews 2:17, NIV).

THE PLEDGE

On the tenth day of the appointed month in early autumn, you must deny yourselves.
Neither native-born Israelites nor foreigners living among you may do any kind
of work. This is a permanent law for you. ❖ LEVITICUS 16:29

What does it mean to deny ourselves?

As part of our *Yom Kippur* observance, we don't eat or drink, wash our bodies, beautify ourselves with cosmetics, engage in marital relations, or wear leather shoes. The Bible refers to these observances when it says, "You must deny yourselves."

Why is deprivation a crucial component of *Yom Kippur*?

There was once a rabbi who wanted to raise money for the needy. He knocked on the door of a wealthy donor, and when the man answered, the rabbi asked him to step outside. In spite of the cold, the man obliged. The rabbi started talking, and he would not stop. The donor suggested that they take the conversation indoors—once, twice, three times—until the rabbi finally agreed to enter the warm home.

Once inside, the rabbi explained: "I came to ask you for a donation to buy warm coats for the poor. But first I wanted you to feel what it's like to be cold. Now that you are sensitive to the need, I know you will give to your greatest capacity."

Yom Kippur works in much the same way. On this most holy day, we pledge to be better people. But in order to make our pledge more significant, we sensitize ourselves to the needs of others and decide what we can do to make this a better world.

When we deny ourselves food and drink, we identify with those who are hungry. When we abstain from physical intimacy, we remember those who are lonely. When we cannot wash up or use cosmetics, we begin to imagine what it's like for those who have no place to go for a warm shower.

When we deny ourselves ordinary comforts, we walk in someone else's shoes. That experience should shape our plans for the year to come.

A Christian Reflection on Denying Oneself for Others

Paul reprimands the Corinthians for losing sight of the needy: "Already you have all you want! Already you have become rich!" (1 Corinthians 4:8, NIV). Paul then refers to himself and the other apostles when he says, "To this very hour we go hungry and thirsty, we are in rags, we are brutally treated, we are homeless" (1 Corinthians 4:11, NIV). No wonder he led the effort to raise money for the poor in Jerusalem (see 2 Corinthians 8–9). Paul urges us to serve others with the same attitude as Jesus, who "made himself nothing by taking the very nature of a servant" (Philippians 2:7, NIV).

ATONEMENT FOR (ALMOST) EVERYTHING

On that day offerings of purification will be made for you, and you will be purified
in the LORD's presence from all your sins. ✦ LEVITICUS 16:30

Scripture tells us that *Yom Kippur* is a day of atonement for all our sins. But we need to read the fine print. The Sages explain that while God can forgive us for the wrongs we have done in our relationship with him, when it comes to our relationships with other people, we need to ask *them* for forgiveness.

That's why *Yom Kippur* is a time of asking forgiveness—from God and from the people around us. If we are to walk away from this holy day completely cleansed, we recognize that we need forgiveness from everyone we may have hurt. It's not easy to do, but *Yom Kippur* reminds us that it's worth it.

True story: One morning, Shmulik had a heated argument with his wife, which he concluded by walking out and slamming the door behind him. His wife, Rivka, was visibly hurt. Fifteen minutes later, the phone rang. "Hi, Rivka. It's Shmulik. I'm heading into the tunnel, and I just wanted to say that I love you and I'm so sorry for what happened before."

Why the sudden change of heart?

Shmulik and Rivka live in a small town in Israel, and during the difficult years of the *Intifada*, the road from their town to Jerusalem became extremely dangerous and many innocent people lost their lives in sniper attacks. People started calling the tunnel on that road the Tunnel of Love, because when you entered the tunnel, you realized what's really important in life. Your fervent wish was to make it home alive and see your loved ones again, because nothing matters more in life.

Yom Kippur is very much like that tunnel. The time to repair hurt relationships is *now*—before it's too late. It's hard to ask for forgiveness, but even harder to live without it.

A Christian Reflection on Asking Forgiveness

In the Sermon on the Mount, Jesus affirms the necessity of asking forgiveness from a person against whom one has sinned. It is not enough just to ask God for forgiveness. It is important to seek forgiveness from the person whom we have hurt. Indeed, according to Jesus, "If you are presenting a sacrifice at the altar in the Temple and you suddenly remember that someone has something against you, leave your sacrifice there at the altar. Go and be reconciled to that person. Then come and offer your sacrifice to God" (Matthew 5:23-24).

ACCEPTING YOUR MISSION

Jonah got up and went in the opposite direction to get away from the LORD. He went down to the port of Joppa, where he found a ship leaving for Tarshish. He bought a ticket and went on board, hoping to escape from the LORD by sailing to Tarshish.

❖ JONAH 1:3

Jonah is the prophet of second chances. One of the relevant messages from the book of Jonah is that repentance is always possible. That's why the book of Jonah is part of the traditional Scripture readings during *Yom Kippur*.

God called upon Jonah to go to Nineveh and tell the wicked people to repent or face God's judgment. Instead, Jonah ran in the opposite direction, trying to evade God's commandment. He boarded a ship, and when a storm threatened to destroy the vessel, Jonah was thrown overboard to save the other men. He was swallowed by a great fish and remained there until he prayed to be released and accepted his divine mission. Jonah preached to the city of Nineveh, and the people repented.

If the evil people of Nineveh could repent, so can we. But there is another message: Jonah's journey is everyone's journey.

We are all born with a divine mission—something only we can do. But often we are afraid to accept our task. Like Jonah, we try to evade it. We try to escape our mission in life by distracting ourselves with other things. Yet something inside of us always remains unfulfilled.

My friend David lives in the holy city of Safed, studying Jewish mysticism and making beautiful art based on his learning. But his life didn't always look this way. Twenty-five years ago, David became very ill. Until he found himself lying in a hospital bed, David had been living a normal life. But it wasn't the life he was meant to live.

David knew that something had to change. Like Jonah in the big fish, David knew that he could live out his mission, or die trying to escape it. Once he was well, David completely changed his life. And he hasn't looked back since.

Yom Kippur is the day on which each of us can relive Jonah's journey and consider whether we are running away from God's divine mission for us or toward it.

A Christian Reflection on Accepting Our Mission

Acts 9 tells the story of Paul's accepting God's commission for his life. After Paul had persecuted the early church, God removed the blinders from his eyes and set him on a path to be the apostle to the Gentiles. Few of us will have as dramatic a journey as Jonah or Paul, but we all need to examine our lives prayerfully before God and ask him to make clear to us how he would have us spend our lives in order to build up his Kingdom here on earth. In this way, we will find true meaning and satisfaction in life.

SHALOM, SHALOM!

"I have seen what they do, but I will heal them anyway! I will lead them. I will comfort those who mourn, bringing words of praise to their lips. May they have abundant peace, both near and far," says the LORD, who heals them. ❖ ISAIAH 57:18-19

For many, *Yom Kippur*, the holiest day of the Jewish year, is the *only* day of holiness on their yearly agenda. They may not make it to daily or even weekly services during the year, but like Christmas is for Christians, on the Day of Atonement, just about everyone is in attendance. It's the one time a year that even the most distant soul checks in with God. And God offers him a special greeting.

One of the readings during *Yom Kippur* comes from the book of Isaiah. God says "Peace, peace, to those far and near" (Isaiah 57:19, NIV). In Hebrew, the word *peace* is *shalom*. *Shalom* is also the word used to greet someone. So, another way of understanding the verse is that God is greeting everyone with an enthusiastic "*Shalom!*"

Question: If two of your friends showed up at your door—one with whom you are very close and one with whom you don't have much to do—whom would you be happier to see? Obviously your closer friend. But when two people show up to synagogue on *Yom Kippur*—one who attends regularly, and one who only comes yearly—God is more excited to see the person who has less to do with him. In our verse, God mentions those "far" before he mentions those who are "near." Those most distant from God are greeted first.

When we read Isaiah's words on *Yom Kippur*, they deliver an encouraging and relevant message to those in attendance. No matter how distant we may feel, or how far we may have strayed from the path of righteousness, God is still overjoyed to see us.

God never writes anyone off, and it's never too late to return to the Lord. On the contrary, our heavenly Father anticipates our arrival with joy in his heart and a warm greeting on his lips: "*Shalom, shalom!*"

A Christian Reflection on Returning to the Lord

Jesus relates the parable of the prodigal son, about a father (representing God) who enthusiastically welcomes home his wayward son—even after this son had wasted his inheritance on wild living. The older, dutiful son is filled with resentment at this special treatment, but the father tells him, "We had to celebrate this happy day. For your brother was dead and has come back to life! He was lost, but now he is found!" (Luke 15:32). It is never too late, but now is better than later to enjoy a rich relationship with God.

Sabbath Reflections

What new truth about the observance of Yom Kippur, *the Day of Atonement, did you learn from this week's devotions?*

How has this truth affected your faith?

How will you apply this truth to your daily life?

Your Key Verse for the Week:

❖ OTHER REFLECTIONS

THE BUCKET LIST

LORD, remind me how brief my time on earth will be. Remind me that my days are numbered—how fleeting my life is. You have made my life no longer than the width of my hand. My entire lifetime is just a moment to you; at best, each of us is but a breath.
❖ PSALM 39:4-5

Several years ago, Jack Nicholson and Morgan Freeman starred in the film *The Bucket List*, a comedy about two terminally ill men who decide that they still have a long list of goals they both want to achieve before "kicking the bucket." So the unlikely pair (one a billionaire, the other a blue-collar worker) break out of the hospital armed with a checklist that includes sky-diving, playing the poker tables in Monte Carlo, and racing the fastest machines on four wheels.

While the film's intent was to make us laugh at their antics and be touched by the unlikely friendship that develops between the two, the film also underscored a hard truth: Life for all of us is terminal. Our days are numbered and our lives are fleeting. As David writes in Psalm 39:5, "At best, each of us is but a breath."

In light of this truth, David realizes the futility of those who chase after possessions and wealth: "We are merely moving shadows, and all our busy rushing ends in nothing. We heap up wealth, not knowing who will spend it" (Psalm 39:6). He clearly sees life in light of eternity: "My entire lifetime is just a moment to you."

How do we respond in the face of our mortality? We can become depressed—or we can see the brevity of our lives as an opportunity to realign our priorities. We can accept the challenge of knowing our days are brief and fleeting by examining what is most important to us—and to God.

Indeed, we can choose to live our lives as "moving shadows," or we can invest ourselves in godly pursuits. As David said, "Lord, where do I put my hope? My only hope is in you" (Psalm 39:7).

A Christian Reflection on Storing Up Treasures

The New Testament trumpets what the Old Testament (see Daniel 12:1-3) only hints at: This brief life is not the end of the story. Even so, the hope of eternal life does not change the fact that our priority should be spiritual, not material, wealth. After all, Jesus himself said, "Don't store up treasures here on earth, where the moths eat them and rust destroys them, and where thieves break in and steal. Store your treasures in heaven, where moths and rust cannot destroy, and thieves do not break in and steal. Wherever your treasure is, there the desires of your heart will also be" (Matthew 6:19-21). Where is your treasure?

A DECLARATION OF DEPENDENCE (FOR *SUKKOT*)

Enter his gates with thanksgiving; go into his courts with praise. Give thanks to him and praise his name. ❖ PSALM 100:4

At Thanksgiving, Americans traditionally gather around a table laden with turkey and all the fixings to give thanks for their material blessings. But did you know that for thousands of years the Jewish people have been celebrating a time of thanksgiving to God for all his many provisions?

We call our celebration *Sukkot*, and though it is rich with spiritual meaning, it was actually agricultural in origin. The Feast of Ingathering was a day of thanksgiving for the fruit harvest, which ended around the time *Sukkot* is celebrated, and for God's provision through nature in the year that had just passed.

For Jewish people, even today, Thanksgiving Day is eclipsed by this biblical festival. As we build the *sukkah* structures (booths), we are reminded of God's past provisions and protection, as well as how dependent we still are on him for our daily needs. From that knowledge springs forth gratitude—the same gratitude expressed for the harvest, for God's presence with the Israelites those many years ago.

Sukkot is a day of joy and thanksgiving, but it is also a time of humility. Thus, it mirrors the true nature of thanksgiving—because anyone who says "thank you" is expressing not only joy and happiness but also an acknowledgment that these good things came from an outside source—from the one being thanked.

While it is wonderful to have these special times set aside specifically to focus on our many blessings and to give God thanks, as people of faith, we should regularly offer our thanks as an act of obedience, in our words of worship, and as a declaration of utter dependence on God.

Remember that all we have comes from him and not as a result of our own success. Then, with hearts filled with joy and humility, let us say, "Thank you."

A Christian Reflection on Sukkot

As John records in his Gospel, Jesus celebrated *Sukkot* in Jerusalem, highlighting his Jewish roots and upbringing. While his brothers mocked him, taunting Jesus to use the festival as an opportunity to perform miracles for all to see, Jesus instead attended the Festival, using it as an opportunity to teach. On the last day of the Festival, during a climactic water ritual, Jesus announced, "Anyone who is thirsty may come to me! Anyone who believes in me may come and drink! For the Scriptures declare, 'Rivers of living water will flow from his heart'" (John 7:37-38).

THE TRUE MESSAGE OF *SUKKOT*

For seven days you must live outside in little shelters. . . . This will remind each new generation of Israelites that I made their ancestors live in shelters when I rescued them from the land of Egypt. ❖ LEVITICUS 23:42-43

What possible reason could God have for commanding his people to live in small huts (*sukkot*)?

Leviticus 23 seems to provide the reason. The purpose of living in *sukkot* for the duration of the holiday is to commemorate God's kindness in bringing the Jews out of Egypt. Simple enough, right?

As it turns out, the ancient rabbis of the *Talmud* were actually split into two camps when it came to interpreting this verse and answering the question of how the *sukkot* are supposed to remind us of the Exodus.

One camp answered that the *sukkot* are literal booths. In other words, we are commanded to construct makeshift huts because, during the Exodus, our forefathers *also* constructed huts so they could take shelter during their travels. In building huts on the holiday of *Sukkot*, then, we are simply reenacting the biblical drama.

The second camp, however, believed that the *sukkot* refer to the Clouds of Glory (*ananei ha-kavod*), which appear at crucial junctures in biblical stories. Indeed, the Clouds of Glory, for the ancient rabbis, represented an emotional, sensory reminder of God's mastery over the world.

When we build *sukkot*, then, we are not simply reminding ourselves of the human ingenuity required to sustain life through years of traveling through the desert. Instead, we are acknowledging that without God's help and kindness, no amount of human know-how or ability would be worth anything. All our successes are possible only through God's support.

This is the true message of *Sukkot*. It is a day on which humanity fully concedes its fundamental dependence on the will of God, and on which we give thanks for all the kindnesses he has done for us.

A Christian Reflection on Submitting to God's Will

While *Sukkot* reminds us that we are fully dependent on God's will for everything good that happens, we all know how difficult it is to submit to someone, even to God. We want to be our own bosses. We want to set our own agendas. The author of Hebrews, however, reminds us that we are God's children; like wise children, we must submit to our Father even when he disciplines us. Like any good father, God disciplines us for our own good. Thus, "since we respected our earthly fathers who disciplined us, shouldn't we submit even more to the discipline of the Father of our spirits, and live forever?" (Hebrews 12:9).

FAMILY MATTERS

Everyone who had returned from captivity lived in these shelters during the festival, and they were all filled with great joy! The Israelites had not celebrated like this since the days of Joshua son of Nun. ❖ NEHEMIAH 8:17

After construction of the Second Temple was completed, the leaders of the Jewish people, especially Ezra and Nehemiah, decided to build on this physical accomplishment by setting corresponding spiritual goals, culminating in the Jewish people's recommitment to God's Word, as recorded in the *Torah*.

As Nehemiah 8:17 describes, the achievement of this recommitment represented a spiritual high point that had not been reached since the earliest days of the Jewish people's existence, shortly after the Exodus and sojourn in the desert.

Intriguingly, the very first act undertaken during this spiritual revival was the national celebration of *Sukkot*. Why *Sukkot*? Of all the holidays, of all the commandments in the *Torah*, why was *Sukkot* mentioned first among all the laws the Jewish people honored during the days of Ezra and Nehemiah?

Perhaps the answer lies in the nature of *Sukkot* itself. On this holiday, Jews are commanded to retreat from their homes into makeshift huts for the entirety of the holiday. Naturally, these huts are not nearly as elaborate or spacious as our normal houses.

As a result, the entire family—sometimes even including grandparents, aunts, uncles, cousins, or grandchildren—crowds into a small space. It ends up being a wonderful family time. During the rest of the year, everyone is busy doing his or her own thing, but *Sukkot* is a time to gather together and reconnect.

One of the first principles Ezra and Nehemiah wanted to highlight during this spiritual revival was the importance of family. They understood that to build a proper connection to God, one must first appreciate the importance of family as our built-in support system and companions in faith.

Sukkot offers all of us the opportunity to reconnect with our loved ones and to strengthen the natural ties that already bind us.

A Christian Reflection on Family

Jesus taught, "If anyone comes to me and does not hate father and mother, wife and children, brothers and sisters—yes, even their own life—such a person cannot be my disciple" (Luke 14:26, NIV). Was Jesus against family values? Reading this verse in isolation might give that impression, but of course we should not read his words apart from his other teachings. Elsewhere, Jesus affirms the importance of honoring parents (see Mark 7:9-13) and marriage (see Matthew 5:31-32; 19:1-9). He also valued children (see Luke 9:46-48; 18:15-17). So how do we reconcile his teaching on family? Family was important and valuable, but even more important is our relationship with God. Jesus knew that a relationship with God was crucial for a strong family.

THE SHARING *SUKKAH*

Jacob, on the other hand, traveled on to Succoth. There he built himself a house and made shelters for his livestock. That is why the place was named Succoth (which means "shelters"). ❖ GENESIS 33:17

During *Sukkot*, Jews all across the world fulfill God's command recorded in the Bible to spend seven days living in makeshift huts known as *sukkot* (singular, *sukkah*). Did you know that *Sukkot* is also the name of a place in the Bible?

And while Jacob's constructions of shelters for his livestock occurred many years before the Exodus and God's command to observe the holiday *Sukkot*, I believe the "shelters" in the Genesis passage have something to teach us about the holiday of *Sukkot*.

Jacob's actions teach us about the essential nature of the *sukkot* that Jewish people build at this time of year. After all, Jacob's actions are actually quite remarkable. Here is Jacob, traveling with his family as well as all his animals. The whole experience must have been wearying, and at night, the job of putting up shelters so that both he and his family could sleep safe and sound under a roof must have been even more tiring. The last thing Jacob would have wanted at the end of the day is more work.

And yet the verse tells us that Jacob *also* made shelters for his animals. Indeed, Jacob was such a kind and loving person that he even worried about the well-being of his animals, who depended upon him for food and protection. Putting up those extra *sukkot* represents an exemplary act of kindness.

The Bible, in this verse, may actually be hinting at the true purpose of the holiday of *Sukkot*. On *Sukkot*, each Jewish family builds a hut—a *sukkah*—that is meant not only to hold that one family but also to host guests, friends, and all who wish to join in the celebration. The holiday of *Sukkot*, in other words, is about sharing what is yours with others. *Sukkot* is about kindness and about going the extra mile for another . . . even when doing so might be inconvenient.

A Christian Reflection on Going the Extra Mile

In the New Testament, Jesus and his disciples repeatedly taught about the need to share with others and to show them kindness, even in a material way. Indeed, the phrase "going the extra mile" comes from Jesus' teaching to share not just with those like ourselves but even with those who try to exploit us. During the Roman occupation of the first century, Roman soldiers used to demand that people carry their gear for a mile. Rather than resisting, Jesus taught that "if a soldier demands that you carry his gear for a mile, carry it two miles" (Matthew 5:41).

EVERYTHING FOR THE BEST

Be joyful at your Feast—you, your sons and daughters, your menservants and maidservants, and the Levites, the aliens, the fatherless and the widows who live in your towns. ❖ DEUTERONOMY 16:14, NIV

The *Talmud* relates the story about the great Sage, Rabbi Akiva, who was traveling through a forest. As darkness began to fall, Rabbi Akiva decided to settle down for the night. Before falling asleep, he lit a candle so that he would be able to see; he set down a rooster next to him to wake him up in the morning; finally, he tied up his trusty donkey on which he rode during the day.

As nightfall arrived, a strong wind came and blew out the candle; then, animals of prey snatched up his rooster and donkey and ate them. Alone in the darkness, and without any way of traveling onward, Rabbi Akiva could have panicked. Instead, he smiled and observed, "Everything the Merciful One does is for the best," and promptly went to sleep.

After waking in the morning, Rabbi Akiva traveled on foot to the next town. Upon his arrival, the townspeople informed him that in the night a band of murderous thieves had passed through the very forest where Rabbi Akiva had slept.

Although the townspeople were able to defend themselves, Rabbi Akiva would have been utterly helpless had the thieves chanced upon him asleep. Of course, since his bright candle had been put out and his noisy animals had been taken from him, Rabbi Akiva had gone undetected. God was watching out for him the whole time!

It's true that this sort of relentless optimism is difficult to achieve even temporarily, let alone all the time. On *Sukkot*, however, God specifically commands us to be joyful. More than any other time of the year, *Sukkot* is a time for rejoicing, for happiness, and for optimism. Indeed, while it's difficult to be as full of joyful conviction as Rabbi Akiva *all the time*, God is telling us that attaining this level at least for a short while is a worthy goal for all of us.

A Christian Reflection on Optimism

It's hard to be optimistic when considering our personal problems, not to mention the world's problems. But God's people should be positive-minded because we know God is in control. Even bad things that happen to us can be good for us, as we learn from the story of Rabbi Akiva or from the biblical story of Joseph, who was sold into slavery and thrown into jail—horrible events that eventually put him in a position to help God's people survive a devastating famine. To keep a positive outlook, we need to remember that "God causes everything to work together for the good of those who love God" (Romans 8:28).

Sabbath Reflections

What new truth about the observance of Sukkot, the Feast of Shelters, did you learn from this week's devotions?

How has this truth affected your faith?

How will you apply this truth to your daily life?

Your Key Verse for the Week:

❖ OTHER REFLECTIONS

TELLING OTHERS YOUR STORY

He lifted me out of the pit of despair, out of the mud and the mire. He set my feet on solid ground and steadied me as I walked along. He has given me a new song to sing, a hymn of praise to our God. Many will see what he has done and be amazed. They will put their trust in the LORD. ❖ PSALM 40:2-3

When we tell others how God has blessed us or has been faithful in his promise to us, it bolsters our faith and encourages others to trust in him as well. Throughout the Psalms, David does exactly this, sharing his faith journey and all that the Lord has done for him.

In Psalm 40, we find David waiting patiently for God to come and help him. And as God comes to his rescue and lifts David out of the "mud and the mire" and sets him on "solid ground," David is filled with gratitude and praise.

He writes, "He has given me a new song to sing, a hymn of praise to our God." David can't help but share his story with others. Throughout the psalm we find him bursting to tell others about his God: "I have told all your people about your justice" (Psalm 40:9); "I have talked about your faithfulness and saving power" (Psalm 40:10). Wanting everyone to know about God's faithfulness, David says, "O LORD my God, you have performed many wonders for us. Your plans for us are too numerous to list" (Psalm 40:5). God's mercy and love are not reserved only for David, but for all who trust in him.

And because of David's story, "many will see what he has done and be amazed" (Psalm 40:3).

We may not be as eloquent as David, but we certainly have our own story to tell of God's faithfulness and his love for us. Sharing our stories with others can be just the encouragement a hurting friend may need to hear today.

A Christian Reflection on Giving Testimony

Every week, my church sets aside time for people in the congregation to talk about what God is doing in their lives. Some share how God has saved their marriage; others share struggles they presently face and ask the congregation to pray for them. Not only do we share our stories in church but also in everyday conversation. I have a friend who from time to time will simply ask me, "What is God doing in your life?" Why does he want to hear my story, and why do I want to hear his? His story encourages me and builds me up in my faith, and my story encourages him and builds him up in his faith (see 1 Thessalonians 5:11).

A REASON TO REJOICE

How joyful are those who fear the LORD and delight in obeying his commands.
❖ PSALM 112:1

Every year around this time, Jews celebrate *Simchat Torah*, which literally means "rejoicing in the *Torah*." It is a celebration of the completion of reading through the *Torah*
over the previous year. In the Jewish tradition, every Sabbath in synagogues around
the world, Jews participate in public readings of the *Torah*, which comprises the first
five books of the Bible. We begin with Genesis chapter 1 and finish with the closing
words in Deuteronomy. When the annual cycle of readings is completed, it's time to
celebrate! Then we begin the yearly cycle all over again.

It is a joyous celebration. All the *Torah* scrolls are taken out of the Ark and carried around the sanctuary seven times. There's singing and dancing, and everyone is
involved, from our eldest members to our children, who lead the procession.

Simchat Torah not only demonstrates our love for God's Word and our grateful-
ness to God for giving us the gift of the Bible, but it also is a reminder that learning
and studying God's Word never ends—it is a lifelong process because there is always
more to understand. In fact, the Hebrew term for a great *Torah* scholar is *talmid chakham*,
which means "wise student."

In Psalm 112, the psalmist gives us plenty of reasons to celebrate when we "delight"
in God's Word. Consider just a few of the reasons he gives: Our children will be
successful and an entire generation will be blessed (see Psalm 112:2); we will enjoy
prosperity and a reputation of righteousness (see Psalm 112:3); we will not be fearful
because we trust in the LORD (see Psalm 112:7); and we will enjoy honor and influence
(see Psalm 112:9).

Take some time this week to reflect on and celebrate the many benefits you have
received from spending time in God's Word.

A Christian Reflection on Disciplined Scripture Reading

While Christians, unfortunately, do not have a formal celebration of Scripture read-
ing such as the *Simchat Torah*, we should engage in a regular schedule of Bible reading
in order to grow in our faith by learning more about God, ourselves, and our world.
If you have never read through the Bible in a year, there are some helpful One Year
Bibles available to guide your reading. Of course, we should not approach reading the
Bible as a legalistic duty, but once you start reading it regularly, it will be hard to stop!
Strive to be like Apollos, "who knew the Scriptures well" (Acts 18:24).

OUR SPIRITUAL COMPASS

Joyful are people of integrity, who follow the instructions of the LORD. Joyful are those who obey his laws and search for him with all their hearts. ❖ PSALM 119:1-2

Since ancient times, when travelers relied on the stars and sun to navigate, our ability to plot a course has vastly improved. Today, cars equipped with GPS systems allow us to input an address and then be guided turn by turn with a computerized voice of our choosing.

No doubt new and even more sophisticated technologies will be developed to make finding our way even easier in the years ahead. But if you are looking for directions for life, the ultimate guidance system has been the same for thousands of years. For Jews and Christians alike, God's Word is the definitive source of wisdom, hope, inspiration, and encouragement for every situation.

The Bible is, perhaps, the greatest point of commonality we have as Jews and Christians. Beyond being a historical record of the nation of Israel and the Jewish people, the Scriptures have provided a spiritual compass for *both* Jews and Christians for thousands of years. Jews and Christians share a love and reverence for the *Tanakh* (the Hebrew Bible, or what Christians refer to as the Old Testament).

In fact, we more than likely agree that the key to preserving our biblical values—both in the home and in our society—is in studying God's Word. We cannot expect the next generation to exemplify and live out our biblical values if we don't live them out ourselves. As people of God, we need to reorient ourselves to our spiritual compass and immerse ourselves in his Word.

When we make God and the Bible the center of our lives, we will be rewarded with the divine guidance described by the prophet Isaiah: "Your own ears will hear him. Right behind you a voice will say, 'This is the way you should go,' whether to the right or to the left" (Isaiah 30:21). That is the ultimate GPS: *God's Positioning System!* Who wouldn't want that?

A Christian Reflection on Trusting Scripture

In the New Testament, one of the most well-known verses reminds us that Scripture is indeed God's very Word to his people: "All Scripture is inspired by God and is useful to teach us what is true and to make us realize what is wrong in our lives. It corrects us when we are wrong and teaches us to do what is right" (2 Timothy 3:16). Since the New Testament was not completed at the time of Paul's statement to Timothy, the primary reference here is to the Old Testament (*Tanakh*). Today Christians believe that both Testaments are God-inspired words to guide our lives.

MY PRIZED POSSESSION

The laws of the LORD are true; each one is fair. They are more desirable than gold, even the finest gold. They are sweeter than honey, even honey dripping from the comb.
❖ PSALM 19:9-10

If your house were on fire, which possessions would you grab and save? Whatever your answer, undoubtedly you would grab the items of most value to you.

In Psalm 19, David reveals what is most valuable to him—God's Word. In describing God's laws, David says they are worth more than gold and are sweeter to the spirit than the very best honey. No doubt this is what David would most likely rescue from the fiery flames.

In the Jewish tradition, we show how much we value God's Word by the way we treat the Bible. We kiss the *Torah* if it falls on the floor; we bury it in a cemetery when it is old and torn; and we always treat the name and Word of God with respect.

This is the concept of holiness—what we call *kedusha* in Hebrew—that the Bible emphasizes. In fact, while the Bible tells us to do many things—observe the Sabbath, honor our parents, and so forth—in only one instance does it command us to a state of *being*—to be holy. God says, "You must be holy because I, the LORD your God, am holy" (Leviticus 19:2).

What is holiness? To be holy means to be separate, set apart, special. The Sabbath is holy because it is separate from all other days. A synagogue is holy because it is designated for worship. Although a *Torah* is but an animal hide, once we allocate it for God's Word, it becomes holy and must be treated accordingly.

How does a person become holy? In Exodus 19:5-6 we read: "Now if you obey me fully and keep my covenant, then out of all nations, you will be my treasured possession. . . . You will be for me a kingdom of priests and a holy nation" (NIV). When we dedicate ourselves to God and his Word, we become holy—and also his most prized possession.

A Christian Reflection on God's Call to Be Holy

In 1 Peter 1:16, the apostle cites God's call in Leviticus to "be holy because I am holy." Paul describes holiness as a status conferred on us: "[God] made you holy by means of Christ Jesus" (1 Corinthians 1:2). In other words, Jesus is the one who set us apart. And if we are set apart, then we must act accordingly. As Peter says, "Think clearly and exercise self-control. . . . You must live as God's obedient children. . . . You must be holy in everything you do, just as God who chose you is holy" (1 Peter 1:13-15).

THE HIGHEST GOAL

Your word is a lamp to guide my feet and a light for my path.
❖ PSALM 119:105

What are your goals? Maybe one of them is losing ten pounds this year, or exercising five hours each week. Maybe it's to cross off a few items on your "bucket list." Or maybe your goals are more financially oriented—to save fifty dollars every paycheck, or pay off your debt by the end of the year.

What about your spiritual goals?

In the Jewish tradition, studying the Bible is one of the loftiest spiritual pursuits we can undertake. Our love for God is linked with our love for his Word. Each day we pray, "With an eternal love hast Thou loved Thy people, the house of Israel; *Torah*, commandments, good deeds, and laws hast Thou imparted to us. Therefore, O LORD our God, when we lie down and when we rise up, we will ponder thy laws and rejoice in the words of the *Torah* and commandments. For they are our lives and the length of our days and upon them we will meditate day and night."

Studying the Bible orders our daily lives and gives us the focus and inspiration we need each day. It is the *Torah* (which literally means "teachings") that brings solace, inner strength, and spiritual fulfillment to the Jew, in good times and in bad. It is the *Torah* that guides our path, shapes our character, and links us with God. It is the *Torah* that enables us to truly know God.

By immersing ourselves in the sacred act of Bible study, we can come to better understand both the content and the source of that divine Word. For this reason, Jewish education (the study of the *Torah*) is one of the most important *mitzvot*, or religious duties, in all the Jewish faith.

Simply put, it is our highest goal for our spiritual lives.

A Christian Reflection on Scripture Study

When Paul preached in Berea, a city in southwestern Macedonia, the Bereans responded by "search[ing] the Scriptures day after day to see if Paul and Silas were teaching the truth" (Acts 17:11). Why did they turn to the Scriptures? Because they knew that was where God revealed himself to people. If Paul and Silas's message lined up with what the Bible said about God, then the Bereans could trust them. The Scriptures reveal who God is and who we are and guide us in our daily lives. We grow in spiritual maturity as we read and study God's Word and apply it to our lives.

AN EVERLASTING COVENANT

But despite all this, I will not utterly reject or despise them while they are in exile in the land of their enemies. I will not cancel my covenant with them by wiping them out, for I am the LORD their God. For their sakes I will remember my ancient covenant with their ancestors, whom I brought out of the land of Egypt in the sight of all the nations, that I might be their God. I am the LORD. ❖ LEVITICUS 26:44-45

People often ask, "Hasn't God's covenant with Israel ended now that he has reached out to the Gentiles?" This is a sad misunderstanding, dating back to early Christendom in the third century. At that time, Christians began to be infected with "triumphalism," the belief that God was finished with the Jewish people.

Neither the Hebrew Bible nor the Christian New Testament teaches this. God's everlasting covenant with Israel cannot be broken. "Understand, therefore, that the LORD your God is indeed God," Moses writes in Deuteronomy 7:9. "He is the faithful God who keeps his covenant for a thousand generations and lavishes his unfailing love on those who love him and obey his commands." God will keep his covenant to a thousand generations! Civilization is nowhere near a thousand generations old.

But what about the New Testament? Some people believe that the "new covenant" *replaced* the "old covenant." First of all, God has made many covenants with his people, including Adam, Noah, and Abraham. God's new covenants have never replaced or abolished previous covenants. To do so would be to break his covenants, which we know God cannot do.

Jesus himself said, "Don't misunderstand why I have come. I did not come to abolish the law of Moses or the writings of the prophets. No, I came to accomplish their purpose" (Matthew 5:17). And the apostle Paul writes, "Has God rejected his own people, the nation of Israel? Of course not!" (Romans 11:1). So, not even the New Testament teaches that God has finished with his people.

If God could break his promises to the Jewish people, how could you trust *any* of his promises? You can be sure that God will keep his promises to Israel and to you.

A Christian Reflection on an Everlasting Covenant

Paul in his letter to the Galatians recognizes that one covenant does not replace the other. He points out that when God entered into a covenant with Israel through the mediation of Moses (see Exodus 19–24), the covenant with Abraham was not canceled (see Galatians 3:17-18). Rather, these covenants *build* on each other. Paul goes on to say that all these old covenants find their fulfillment in Christ, even making the startling claim that Jesus was the promised "seed" from the Abrahamic promise. The question isn't whether we are Jewish or Gentile—Paul, after all, was a Jew, a point he emphasizes in Romans 11:1—but where we place our faith and how we respond to God's law.

Sabbath Reflections

What new truth about studying God's Word did you learn from this week's devotions?

How has this truth affected your faith?

How will you apply this truth to your daily life?

Your Key Verse for the Week:

❖ OTHER REFLECTIONS

BUILDING A NEW TRUST

Even my best friend, the one I trusted completely, the one who shared my food,
has turned against me. ❖ PSALM 41:9

Nothing hurts more than the betrayal of a friend. David certainly knew this type of pain when he wrote, "Even my best friend, the one I trusted completely, the one who shared my food, has turned against me." At the time, David had been surrounded by enemies who were spreading false rumors about him. But it was his friend's betrayal that caused the most pain.

Who among us has never experienced a deceitful betrayal by someone we thought we could trust? We have all felt that kind of pain. It can make us extremely cautious, even skeptical of the motives of others who claim to be our friends.

Throughout history, Jews have been hurt by Christians many times in many different ways. It has been a relationship fraught with animosity, even fratricide. And for thousands of years those feelings of mistrust and betrayal have become entrenched.

So when Christians today offer to help Jews, Jews have sometimes responded with skepticism, wondering about the underlying motives of these offers. Thankfully, we have witnessed these deep-seated feelings of mistrust beginning to erode as Christians have reached out to Jews in tangible ways, gradually overcoming that skepticism with a new history of love and concern.

Gradually, Jews are starting to respond to this Christian generosity with new levels of trust. Just as Christians are reaching out to Jews with tangible acts of love, Jews are beginning to extend the hand of friendship back to Christians. The gap of skepticism and mistrust is being bridged by compassion and love.

Indeed, that has been my heart and vision in forming The Fellowship—to promote unity between our two great faith communities and to provide meaningful, tangible ways for Christians and Jews to show love and compassion to one another.

A Christian Reflection on Rebuilding Trust

Christians have much to repent of in our relationship with our Jewish brothers and sisters. But more than words, we Christians need to show our love and affection to Jews by our actions. As Jesus pointed out, "Just as you can identify a tree by its fruit, so you can identify people by their actions" (Matthew 7:20). Talk is indeed cheap, so supporting an organization like The Fellowship that serves the needy is a tangible expression that will help rebuild trust with our Jewish friends.

YOUR SPIRITUAL CORE

May my tongue stick to the roof of my mouth if I fail to remember you, if I don't make Jerusalem my greatest joy. ❖ PSALM 137:6

Every organization has a core principle that shapes and guides the group's mission. For the Red Cross, it's saving lives. For the Boy Scouts, it's training young men as future leaders. At Nike, it's the trademark motto, "Just do it."

For the Jewish people of biblical times, it was the Temple that truly bound Jewish hearts to the land of Israel. The Temple became the spiritual center, the core, of the Jewish faith, always in Jerusalem. And it has remained so.

In spite of countless occupations, periods of exile, and wars, the Jewish people have vowed throughout the centuries never to forget Jerusalem. Whether it was the remnant that kept a physical presence in Jerusalem or those who carried Jerusalem in their hearts, the Jewish people have been a part of Jerusalem continuously.

We see that core ideal expressed beautifully in the words of Psalm 137. Here the psalmist is writing of life in exile. He wept when remembering Zion and suffered when his captors demanded that he sing songs of joy. The connection to Jerusalem, though, enabled him to persevere. He promised, "If I forget you, O Jerusalem, let my right hand forget how to play the harp" (Psalm 137:5).

For more than two millennia, the Jewish people have clung to the memory of Jerusalem. In fact, customs were put into practice to keep that memory alive. For example, at weddings, when we are most joyous, a glass is broken under the wedding canopy to commemorate Jerusalem's destruction. A wall in every home is dedicated to Jerusalem. We turn toward the direction of Jerusalem every time we pray, and we conclude our holidays proclaiming, "Next year in Jerusalem!"

What keeps you centered when you are isolated or in the midst of difficult situations? How do you keep your spiritual focus from causing you to despair or give up? How can you "never forget" what God has done for you?

A *Christian Reflection on Jesus and the Temple*

Before the coming of Jesus, the Temple represented God's presence on earth. Now Christ is the center of our faith that keeps us focused on God. The beginning of the Gospel of John announces, "The Word became human and made his home among us. He was full of unfailing love and faithfulness. And we have seen his glory, the glory of the Father's one and only Son" (John 1:14). Though Christians disagree over whether a future third Temple will be built in Jerusalem, all know of the powerful picture of heaven presented as a New Jerusalem in which there will be no Temple because "the Lord God Almighty and the Lamb are its temple" (Revelation 21:22).

PRAY FOR JERUSALEM

Pray for peace in Jerusalem. May all who love this city prosper.
❖ PSALM 122:6

Prayer is such a vital part of our spiritual lives. We see this evident throughout Scriptures—from Isaac's servant who prayed for success in finding his master a wife, to Hannah's heartfelt prayer for a son, to the three young men in the fiery furnace who boldly prayed for God to rescue them.

In Psalm 122, we see David urging his readers to pray not for themselves, not for a family member, but for an entire city—Jerusalem. He wasn't seeking his own peace and prosperity; he was praying for his brothers and sisters living there, that *they* would prosper, that *they* would experience peace.

Why did David urge his readers to pray for Jerusalem? You might imagine that he was seeking peace for Jerusalem so that his job as king of Israel would be easier. What leader wouldn't want peace within his country, city, or town? But that was not the motivation behind David's prayer. Rather, he was praying for the peace of Jerusalem for the sake of his "family and friends," and "for the sake of the house of the LORD our God" (Psalm 122:8-9). David's concern was for others and, ultimately, for God's reputation and for God's glory to be reflected to Israel's neighbors and enemies.

Part of Jews' daily prayer, the *Amidah*, pleads, "Return to Your city Jerusalem, in mercy, and establish Yourself there as you promised," and "Blessed are you, Lord, builder of Jerusalem." Like David's prayer, the focus is on God and asking him to return to Jerusalem as he has promised—for his name's sake.

As we come before God in prayer throughout this week, let us be reminded of David's prayer, and seek that which will bring glory to God.

A Christian Reflection on Prayer for the Church

The New Testament authors often urge their readers to pray for the church as the assembled believers, and for the world, that they might know the glory of God. But we often feel inadequate in our prayers and question whether God listens to our distracted mumblings. Paul, however, assures us that even when we stumble in praying, "the Holy Spirit prays for us with groanings that cannot be expressed in words. And the Father who knows all hearts knows what the Spirit is saying, for the Spirit pleads for us believers in harmony with God's own will" (Romans 8:27).

GIVE ME SHELTER

From the ends of the earth, I cry to you for help when my heart is overwhelmed.
Lead me to the towering rock of safety. ❖ PSALM 61:2

When unexpected storms hit, we know we should take immediate shelter; but when we are away from home, in unfamiliar territory, finding that shelter presents a more difficult challenge.

Where do we go to find shelter? How quickly can we get there? It's a situation that can leave us feeling unprotected, vulnerable, and helpless.

David felt all these emotions when he wrote Psalm 61. He may have been on the run from King Saul, or from his own son, the rebellious Absalom. Whatever the situation, David found himself unprotected and far from familiar shelter.

So what does he do? He cries out to God, "Lead me to the towering rock of safety, for you are my safe refuge, a fortress where my enemies cannot reach me" (Psalm 61:2-3). David longed to be in the shelter of God's tent, the Tabernacle; he yearned to be "safe beneath the shelter of [God's] wings" (Psalm 61:4).

For David, true security was found only in God's presence, in the assurance of God's promises, and in the protection of his unfailing love and faithfulness.

We, too, can be assured that no matter where we are, no matter what circumstances we find ourselves in, God is there. It doesn't matter whether we are surrounded by familiar sights and faces. Even in a strange location, God offers us shelter under his wings.

In Leviticus 23:42, we are commanded, "For seven days you must live outside in little shelters." Once a year, during the holiday of *Sukkot*, we live in shelters that are required to be temporary structures—flimsy and vulnerable. We do this in order to remember that there is only one true shelter in life: almighty God.

God will never abandon us. Whether we are secure in our situation or left vulnerable in times of uncertainty and difficulty, we can be assured that he will be our rock of safety, our strong tower against our foes.

A Christian Reflection on God as Our Shelter

During his earthly ministry, Jesus expressed his desire to protect people with the striking image of a mother hen: "How often I have wanted to gather your children together as a hen protects her chicks beneath her wings, but you wouldn't let me" (Matthew 23:37). Even when facing the cross, Jesus prayed for his followers: "Holy Father, you have given me your name; now protect them by the power of your name so that they will be united just as we are" (John 17:11). God protects us, and it is to him that we should go for protection in the midst of the chaos of life.

A UNIVERSE OF LOVE

When the LORD began to speak through Hosea, the LORD said to him, "Go, marry a promiscuous woman and have children with her, for like an adulterous wife this land is guilty of unfaithfulness to the LORD." ❖ HOSEA 1:2, NIV

Albert Einstein once said that the most important decision we will ever make is whether we believe that the universe is friendly or hostile. From that one decision, says Einstein, all others follow.

So, is the universe friendly? The book of Hosea answers that question, and the answer is one that even Einstein never imagined.

The book begins with one of the most unusual commandments God ever gave to a human. Hosea is commanded to seek out an unfaithful woman, marry her, and start a family with her. The *Talmud* gives us some background that led up to this command.

According to Jewish tradition, God came to Hosea and said, "Your children have sinned." To which Hosea replied, "So exchange them for another people." When a similar statement was made to Moses, he replied, "My children? Are they not Your children too?" That should have been Hosea's response as well. But he didn't understand the relationship between God and his children.

God wanted Hosea to understand how he related to Israel, so he commanded Hosea to marry a prostitute. Hosea and his wife, Gomer, become an allegory for God's love of unfaithful Israel. Hosea lived God's pain when his love went unreciprocated. He experienced God's frustration when Gomer left him for another man. Hosea now understood why God would stop at nothing to win Israel back, and he began to grasp the depth of God's unending love.

As Hosea learned, God's love is so great that even when his children are completely disloyal, his love for them never wanes. Everything he does is in order to win them back. Even when Israel is punished, it's only in order to guide her back into the arms of the one who loves her.

No, the universe is not hostile. It's not even unfriendly. The message of Hosea is that the universe is a place of love! God is madly in love with his children. And that means that everything that happens—the good and the bad—happens out of love.

A Christian Reflection on God's Amazing Love

For Christians, the greatest example of God's overwhelming love for the world is, of course, Jesus. Paul reminds us of that when he writes, "God showed his great love for us by sending Christ to die for us while we were still sinners" (Romans 5:8). Not only did God pay the highest price possible—the sacrifice of his only Son—but he also did this "while we were still sinners." That's amazing love, indeed!

THE GIFT OF NOTHING

Therefore I am now going to allure her; I will lead her into the wilderness and speak tenderly to her. ❖ HOSEA 2:14, NIV

Of all the places I might take my wife on a second honeymoon, the desert is the last place I would choose! But when God speaks about reconnecting with his estranged nation, that's exactly where he plans to take his bride. The desert, according to the Lord, is the perfect place to rekindle the flames of love. Why?

A cute book came out a number of years ago called *The Gift of Nothing*. It is about a cat named Mooch who wants to get a present for his canine friend, Earl. But Mooch can't think of anything to give Earl, who already has everything. After thinking it over, Mooch finds a big box, wraps it up, and gives Earl "nothing." Earl is confused, and looking into the empty box, he says, "There's nothing here!"

"Yes!" says Mooch. "Nothing . . . except me and you." The story ends by saying, "Mooch and Earl enjoyed nothing. And everything."

This clever little story reminds us that sometimes, less is more. Things can be distracting and disorienting. Nothingness helps us focus on what really matters. The desert is the perfect place for God to connect with his people. The Hebrew word for desert is *midbar*. It is almost exactly the same as the word *midaber*, which means "one who speaks." The Sages tell us that this is because in the desert we are able to hear the one who speaks.

This explains why God began his relationship with Israel in the desert, after taking them out of Egypt. It was in the desert that God gave the *Torah* to the Israelites. And it is in the desert, God tells us in Hosea, that he will reconnect with his nation once again.

We, too, need to find ways to create a desert in our lives so that we can enjoy *nothing*. And everything.

A Christian Reflection on the Desert

The desert, or wilderness, also plays a significant role in the New Testament. Just as God led the Israelites into the desert to test them, the Holy Spirit led Jesus into the wilderness to be tested by Satan (see Matthew 4:1-11). During his ministry, Jesus often retreated to the wilderness where he could be alone with his Father "for prayer" (Luke 5:16). Later, John tells us that Jesus took his disciples into the wilderness before approaching Jerusalem for the final time (John 11:53-54). In the desert, Jesus found encouragement and strength to face the troubling times ahead—and so can we.

Sabbath Reflections

What new truth did you learn from this week's devotions?

How has this truth affected your faith?

How will you apply this truth to your daily life?

Your Key Verse for the Week:

❖ OTHER REFLECTIONS

THE GOOD OLD DAYS

My heart is breaking as I remember how it used to be: I walked among the crowds of worshipers, leading a great procession to the house of God, singing for joy and giving thanks amid the sound of a great celebration! ❖ PSALM 42:4

Often, we look back with fondness to "the good old days." Maybe those were simpler times because we had fewer responsibilities; or we were just launching a new venture and everything was exciting; or technology seemed simpler, so life was slower and less complicated.

There are plenty of reasons to recall the good old days.

In Psalm 42, the writer fondly recalls the good old days and how it used to be: "I walked among the crowds of worshipers, leading a great procession to the house of God, singing for joy and giving thanks." But now, for whatever reason, the psalmist feels alienated from God. Although he thirsts for God (see Psalm 42:2), God seems far away.

So what does the psalm writer do? He remembers. He remembers when he went to the Temple to worship God. He remembers God's kindness to him: "I will remember you—even from distant Mount Hermon, the source of the Jordan, from the land of Mount Mizar" (Psalm 42:6). And he finds comfort in those memories of when he felt close to God and experienced God's presence in his life.

According to Jewish tradition, a person is required to remember the Exodus from Egypt every day of his life. As Deuteronomy 16:3 says, "As long as you live you will remember the day you departed from Egypt." We remember the Exodus so that we will be encouraged by the redemption of the past and given hope for redemption in the future. Remembering is inspiring.

As we recall the people and events that God used to shape our lives in the past, we can gather the strength to face the present.

A Christian Reflection on Remembering

When the present is full of trouble and the future looks bleak, it is often helpful to look to the past to see God's hand. Not only should we remember the good days when our relationship with God was more vital, but we can also look to the past to see other pivotal moments when God saved his people out of their troubles. Christians can look back to the Cross and the Resurrection, when God raised Jesus from the dead. Remembrance is often the key to finding confidence and hope in the midst of a troubled present.

BY MY SPIRIT

Then he said to me, "This is what the LORD says to Zerubbabel: It is not by force
nor by strength, but by my Spirit, says the LORD of Heaven's Armies."
❖ ZECHARIAH 4:6

One of the "can't miss" stops on any tour to the Holy Land is a visit to the Knesset,
the Israeli parliament. Standing outside this historic building is a massive *menorah*,
a seven-branched candelabrum that has long been a symbol of Judaism.

The *menorah* is first mentioned in the commands that God gave to Moses for the
construction of the Tabernacle. Its purpose was to provide light inside the Tabernacle
and later inside the Temple in Jerusalem.

Following the return of the exiled Jews from Babylon to Jerusalem, the *menorah* also became a representation of the Spirit and anointing of God. The prophet
Zechariah was shown a vision of a *menorah* and an angel said to him, "This is what the
LORD says to Zerubbabel: It is not by force nor by strength, but by my Spirit, says the
LORD of Heaven's Armies" (Zechariah 4:6).

Thus, Zerubbabel, the leader of the newly restored Jewish nation, was led by the
Spirit of God, represented by the *menorah* with its seven lamps, and was given guidance
and favor in rebuilding the nation of Israel. The *menorah* also plays a central role in the
miraculous story of *Hanukkah*, which celebrates the victory of the Jews over their Greek
oppressors and the miracle of the single flask of olive oil that kept the *menorah* lit for
eight days.

When the modern State of Israel was founded in 1948, the *menorah* was chosen as
the nation's emblem, symbolizing the continuity and eternality of the Jewish people.
But I am even more proud that the verse Israel's forefathers chose to inscribe on our
national symbol is the same verse as the one given to Zechariah: "Not by might nor by
power, but by my Spirit" (NIV).

The menorah stands as a visible reminder that God, not ourselves, is the one who
leads us, empowers us, and protects us.

A Christian Reflection on the Spirit's Power

As Jesus anticipated his death, he comforted his disciples by telling them they would
receive the Spirit to comfort them and lead them into the truth: "When the Spirit
of truth comes, he will guide you into all truth" (John 16:13). Not only will the
Spirit comfort Jesus' followers, the Spirit will be the source of our strength when
we face inevitable conflict in a hostile world. Paul even mentions "the sword of the
Spirit" (Ephesians 6:17) as part of our arsenal against "all strategies of the devil"
(Ephesians 6:11). Along with Zerubbabel, we learn that it is "not by might nor by
power, but by my Spirit."

A YOUNG GIRL'S LEGACY

Remember the LORD your God. He is the one who gives you power to be successful,
in order to fulfill the covenant he confirmed to your ancestors with an oath.
❖ DEUTERONOMY 8:18

Anne Frank is one of the most renowned and most discussed Jewish victims of the Holocaust, mainly due to the publication of her diary, which became one of the world's most widely read books and the subject of various plays and films.

Anne received a journal for her thirteenth birthday, in June 1942. Less than a month later, her family was forced to move to a secret hiding place built into the stairwells of her father's office building. Her diary recounts the changes resulting from the Nazi Germany occupation. She describes the relationships between herself and her family; the Van Pels family, who later joined the Franks in hiding; as well as the faithful employees who took care of the families' needs. She wrote about her faith and her observations of human nature.

In a poignant and prescient statement, Anne wrote of her dreams to become a journalist and express herself through words: "I want to be useful or bring enjoyment to all people, even those I've never met. I want to go on living even after my death! And that's why I'm so grateful to God for having given me this gift, which I can use to develop myself and to express all that's inside me!"

The Franks were eventually captured and sent to Auschwitz. Anne was later transferred to Bergen-Belsen, where she died of typhus in 1945, just weeks before the camp was liberated. Still, her legacy has lived on. Through her diary, her words have endured and have affected the lives of millions who have met Anne only through the printed page. Anne's dreams did come true in ways she never imagined.

God has gifted each one of us with unique abilities and opportunities to accomplish his purposes. It is up to each of us to make the most of those gifts and our time here on earth—just as Anne did.

A Christian Reflection on Calling

God gave Anne Frank the gift of writing and used her to educate others about the horrors of anti-Semitism. God has a calling for each of us, and we need to ask and pray constantly about where God wants to use us to further his Kingdom here on earth. Not many will have the broad influence of Anne Frank, but God can use us all to influence others to faith and good works. Paul's prayer for the Thessalonians can then be a prayer for all of us: "We keep on praying for you, asking our God to enable you to live a life worthy of his call" (2 Thessalonians 1:11).

A PLACE OF PRAYER

On the holy mountain stands the city founded by the LORD. He loves the city of Jerusalem more than any other city in Israel. ❖ PSALM 87:1-2

Standing in the Old City of Jerusalem, the Western Wall is considered one of the holiest sites in all of Judaism. It is the only remnant from the Second Temple, and Jews all over the world direct their hearts and prayers toward this remnant of their biblical heritage.

For many Jews, the Wall represents not only every Jew's yearning to return home to Israel but also their right to return there. Even during the many years of the Jews' exile from their biblical homeland, the Western Wall remained our most visible landmark in the city. The Jewish claim to Jerusalem was never forgotten because our ancestors' handiwork—the lone remaining wall of the Temple—stands as a testament to our right to the City of David.

For Jews, the Western Wall is a visible reminder of God's presence, his protection, and his provision for his people over the centuries. Standing at the Wall today, one can almost imagine the scent of the sacrifices that were offered in that very spot thousands of years ago by King Solomon, and taste the tears of the thousands of people who came to the Temple daily, praying and begging God for divine guidance and help.

At the Wall today, thousands of people, Jews and Christians alike, bring their prayers scrawled on scraps of paper and stick them into chinks in the Wall. It remains a place of prayer. Even though the Temple no longer exists, we believe it is still the place where God's presence dwells in a unique way.

The Western Wall is a beautiful and wonderful reminder to all people of faith that the God of Abraham, Isaac, and Jacob keeps his promises—past, present, and future. No matter where we are in the world, we can be confident in that truth as we come to our Father in prayer.

A Christian Reflection on God's Future Promises

We indeed marvel as we observe how God has been faithful in fulfilling his past promises. Because he has kept his promises in the past, we have certain hope that he will fulfill his future promises as well. In the apostle Peter's second letter, he reminds us that God "has given us great and precious promises. These are the promises that enable you to share his divine nature and escape the world's corruption" (2 Peter 1:4). What are these promises? That Christ will come again (see 2 Peter 3:4). For this reason, "we are looking forward to the new heavens and new earth he has promised, a world filled with God's righteousness" (2 Peter 3:13).

THE GOD WHO FIGHTS FOR US

Oh, please help us against our enemies, for all human help is useless.
With God's help we will do mighty things, for he will trample down our foes.
❖ PSALM 60:11-12

When King David wrote this psalm, he mentioned several enemy nations: Moab lay directly to the east, Edom to the south, and Philistia to the west. The Israelites were also fighting against the forces of Aram to the north. God's people were surrounded. Sound familiar?

In 1967, Israel was surrounded by enemy nations: Egypt, Syria, and Jordan. The three largest nations bordering Israel to the north, south, and east were staging military operations against her. The mood in Israel was somber. Once again, God's people were under siege.

Throughout their history, the people of Israel have come to the battlefield against their enemies, and God has always come through, sometimes in miraculous ways. So it was with the confidence of David that we also prayed during those dark days: "With God's help we will do mighty things, for he will trample down our foes" (Psalm 60:12).

In the Six-Day War of 1967, Israel accomplished what the world deemed impossible. The tiny nation of Israel launched a preemptive strike that destroyed the entire Egyptian Air Force as it sat on the tarmac. Even though Israel's small army was divided across three fronts, they were able to take control of Jordan's West Bank and the Jordanian sector of Old Jerusalem, uniting that city once again. They also wrested control of the Golan Heights from the Syrians.

The only plausible explanation is that God answered our prayers and looked favorably upon his people by giving us aid against our enemies. Our own military might and strategies would have amounted to little were it not for the help of God fighting on our behalf.

Whatever battle you might be facing today, remember that we have a God who fights for us. We can have confidence that "with God's help we will do mighty things."

A Christian Reflection on God the Warrior

In the New Testament, God continues to fight for his people, but here his battle is against the spiritual "powers" and "authorities" (Ephesians 6:10-20). He provides the weapons we need against such a foe. As Paul tells the Corinthians, "We are human, but we don't wage war as humans do. We use God's mighty weapons, not worldly weapons, to knock down the strongholds of human reasoning and to destroy false arguments. We destroy every proud obstacle that keeps people from knowing God. We capture their rebellious thoughts and teach them to obey Christ" (2 Corinthians 10:3-5).

SOUR MILK

*God looks down from heaven on the entire human race; he looks to see if anyone is truly
wise, if anyone seeks God. But no, all have turned away; all have become corrupt.
No one does good, not a single one!* ❖ PSALM 53:2-3

Anyone who has ever opened a jug of milk that has gone beyond its expiration date
realizes it immediately! Sour milk has a pungent odor and unpleasant taste. There
is only one way to deal with sour milk—throw it away. So, it is interesting to note in
Psalm 53 God's assessment of the human race. David writes that God surveyed the
human race "to see if anyone is truly wise, if anyone seeks God" (Psalm 53:2) and
discovered that "all have turned away; all have become corrupt" (Psalm 53:3). The
Hebrew word for "become corrupt" is *alah*, which literally means "soured," like milk.
God looked down from heaven and saw that the human race had gone sour.

Like spoiled milk, the human race had deteriorated to the point of needing to
be discarded; but unlike sour milk, there is hope for restoration for humanity. David
looked forward to a day when restoration would come: "Who will come from Mount
Zion to rescue Israel? When God restores his people, Jacob will shout with joy, and
Israel will rejoice" (Psalm 53:6). In God's plan, even a human race that had become
spoiled like milk could be restored. There is hope!

As we consider the condition of our world today, we might very well come to the
same conclusion as David does in Psalm 53—that all have become corrupt. But, as
David notes, we also can turn to God for restoration. David describes the evildoers
as those who "wouldn't think of praying to God" (Psalm 53:4), so the remedy for our
condition as soured milk is to call upon God in prayer.

When we turn to him, God will surely change our hearts and turn toward us. We
can find our present hope in our relationship with a God who cares about us now.

A Christian Reflection on Being Made Right with God

In Romans 3:9-12, Paul quotes Psalm 53:1-3 (also Psalm 14:1-3) and strings this passage together with others to make the point that "all people, whether Jews or Gentiles,
are under the power of sin." Paul does not tell his readers this to make them feel bad
about themselves but to point to the solution: "We are made right with God by placing
our faith in Jesus Christ. And this is true for everyone who believes, no matter who we
are" (Romans 3:22).

Sabbath Reflections

What new truth about the impact of the Western Wall on the Jewish faith and tradition did you learn from this week's devotions?

How has this truth affected your faith?

How will you apply this truth to your daily life?

Your Key Verse for the Week:

❖ OTHER REFLECTIONS

FOLLOW GOD'S LIGHT

Send out your light and your truth; let them guide me. Let them lead me to your holy mountain, to the place where you live. ❖ PSALM 43:3

Maybe you've seen the TV commercials in which the main characters are assisted in some way by large, flashing signs. Don't you sometimes wish there were large flashing signs from God telling you whether to take the new job or what career path to follow?

In Psalm 43:3, the writer appears to be asking for that type of guidance from God. He prays, "Send out your light and your truth." This imagery brings to mind the pillar of fire that God used to lead his people through the wilderness. The psalmist may have desired such an obvious means of guidance from God.

Like his ancestors did, the psalmist wants God's light to guide him to a specific place. He prays for guidance to "your holy mountain, to the place where you live," the source of "all my joy" (Psalm 43:4).

According to Jewish tradition, Adam, the first man, discovered fire on the first Saturday night. That was a very dark night for Adam—he was allowed to stay in the Garden for the Sabbath, but was expelled just after it ended. God sent Adam fire, as if to say, "Whenever you sit in darkness, I will send you light." As Micah 7:8 says, "Though I sit in darkness, the LORD will be my light."

As we seek God's guidance for our lives, we can trust that his light and truth will guide us. We may not see a pillar of fire or a flashing sign, but God and his Word will light the path for us. His truth and trustworthiness will not lead us astray.

If we commit ourselves to obeying and knowing God's truth as found in his Word, the other details of our lives will become clear when the time is right. God will not leave us in the dark. Then, like the psalmist, we can praise God, who is the source of all our joy.

A Christian Reflection on Finding God's Will

God reveals his will through his Word. Granted, God's Word does not give us specific guidance to questions such as whom we should marry or what job to take, but it does encourage us to marry someone with whom we share our most important values, especially our faith, and to take a job where we feel we can make a difference for God and others. As we seek to obey God's Word, he will lead us in the right direction. It may not be without problems and pain, but we can be assured that "God causes everything to work together for the good of those who love God and are called according to his purpose for them" (Romans 8:28).

REMEMBER WELL

[Joshua] told them, "Go into the middle of the Jordan, in front of the Ark of the LORD your God. Each of you must pick up one stone and carry it out on your shoulder— twelve stones in all, one for each of the twelve tribes of Israel. We will use these stones to build a memorial. In the future your children will ask you, 'What do these stones mean?'" ❖ JOSHUA 4:5-6

Outside Jerusalem stands a living memorial to the six million Jews who perished during the Holocaust. The Forest of Martyrs contains four-and-a-half million pine trees, one for every adult who died; nearby stand a million and a half cypress trees, one for every Jewish child who was murdered by the Nazis.

This memorial is a powerful reminder of the terrible price the Jewish people paid for the hatred of others. The Jewish people vow to never forget so that such horrific events will never happen again.

When the Israelites finally crossed the Jordan River into the Promised Land, the first thing they were told to do was to build an altar of rocks so that when their children asked them what the stones meant, they could answer, "They remind us that the Jordan River stopped flowing when the Ark of the Lord's Covenant went across."

Why was it so important for the people to remember their past? Because it was this past history that the next generations would build their faith upon. It would help them remember the stories that would guide them as they settled in the Promised Land.

According to Jewish tradition, there are "Six Remembrances" that we must recall every day: We remember the Exodus, because it gives us hope for redemption; Mount Sinai, because it reminds us of our mission; the nation Amalek, because it reminds us to fight evil; the golden calf, because it reminds us to avoid sin; Miriam, because she reminds us to watch our speech; and finally, the Sabbath, because it reminds us that God is our Creator and Sustainer.

Remembering our past helps us move forward. We are encouraged by remembering how God has helped us. Remembering our past mistakes can help us avoid the wrong path again. Remembering helps us be thankful during hard times because we know how God has provided for us in the past.

A Christian Reflection on Remembrance

Faith is indeed built on remembrance of what God has done in the past. For Christians, the greatest act of remembrance is the death and resurrection of Jesus. Remembering Christ's work gives us confidence to live in a difficult present and to hope for the future. When Paul was imprisoned in Rome, he encouraged Timothy to "remember that Jesus Christ, a descendant of King David, was raised from the dead" (2 Timothy 2:8). Paul called this "the Good News I preach" (2 Timothy 2:8) and testified that it gave him the strength he needed to endure his present suffering (see 2 Timothy 2:10). What do you remember when life becomes hard?

THE MIRACLE WORKER

No pagan god is like you, O Lord. None can do what you do! . . . For you are great and perform wonderful deeds. You alone are God. ❖ PSALM 86:8, 10

Do you believe miracles still happen?

If we took a look below the surface, we might see that God works miracles every day. With every birth of a child, we witness the miracle of new life. From the letters of our many donors we hear about the miracles of God's timely provision, whether it comes in the form of an unexpected check, the recovery of a loved one from a devastating illness, or reconciliation with an estranged friend.

The greatest miracle that I believe we have all witnessed is the birth of the State of Israel and the continuing ingathering of God's people back to their homeland. True, there are those who see these events as an amazing occurrence that came about because of the courage, training, and initiative of the Israeli army. While that is a correct estimation, this perspective fails to take into account the words of Moses: "The LORD your God is going with you! He will fight for you against your enemies, and he will give you victory!" (Deuteronomy 20:4).

Throughout the nation of Israel's history—from the fall of Jericho's mighty walls, to Gideon's routing of the Midianites with only three hundred men, to the countless victories David won on the battlefield—God has repeatedly intervened and delivered his people. The very existence of the Jewish people—despite centuries of persecution—bears witness to a God who is directly involved in human history, who is concerned about its direction, and who cares deeply about the welfare of his children.

Witnessing the miracle of Israel should be an encouragement to us all that the Lord is interested in our lives and is acting on our behalf. Indeed, as the psalm writer says, "No pagan god is like you, O Lord. . . . For you are great and perform wonderful deeds."

A Christian Reflection on God's Uniqueness

Some people say, "All religions are the same and they all point to the same God." This viewpoint could not be more wrong. The God of the Bible is utterly unique; the God whom Israel worshiped was the one who created the universe. He created everything that exists, whether animate or inanimate, human or spirits like angels. Though this God is not a part of Creation (he is transcendent), he stays involved with his creatures (he is immanent). Ultimately, the pagan gods are figments of human imagination, so another key difference is that the God of the Bible does "perform wonderful deeds." This unique God deserves our worship and devotion.

HOLY PARTNERS

[Abraham said,] "Will you sweep away both the righteous and the wicked? Suppose you find fifty righteous people living there in the city—will you still sweep it away and not spare it for their sakes?" ❖ GENESIS 18:23-24

Sometimes, when things happen in life that leave us bewildered, we wonder where God is in these circumstances. Certainly, there are times in our lives when we question God's presence, his justice, even his love. There are times we beseech God for help, for an answer to prayer, and the answer comes back "No."

The Jewish view is that it's appropriate to question God, to challenge his justice and fairness. It's okay to ask why.

Remember when God announced his plans to destroy Sodom and Gomorrah? Abraham challenged God, saying, "Will you sweep away both the righteous and the wicked? Suppose you find fifty righteous people living there in the city—will you still sweep it away and not spare it for their sakes?" (Genesis 18:23-24).

After God responds that he would spare the city for fifty innocent people, Abraham amazingly continues to bargain with God. What about forty? Thirty? Twenty? And to each, God says, yes, he would spare the city. Finally, Abraham asks if God would destroy the city if there were only ten righteous people.

At this point, I'm waiting for God to really give it to Abraham. But he doesn't. In his graciousness and in his mercy, God respects Abraham's questions and says, yes, he would spare the entire city for ten righteous people.

Through this exchange, God showed Abraham—and us—that asking for anything is allowed, with the understanding that God's answer comes from his perspective and not ours. In the Jewish view, we are holy partners with God, not just his subjects. We have the right to question his justice and love just like Abraham did—but then we must accept God's will as sovereign.

God welcomes your questions, your doubts. Trust his answer, even if it is not in harmony with your expectations.

A Christian Reflection on Questioning God

Christians are often reluctant to come to God with doubts and questions. The author of Hebrews, however, reminds us that Jesus, our High Priest, understands our weaknesses and so we can "come boldly to the throne of our gracious God" (Hebrews 4:16). And indeed Abraham, Job, and Jeremiah all provide examples, for Christians as well as for Jews, about how to approach God in this bold way. Indeed, the laments of the book of Psalms—Psalms 69, 77, 88—provide models of prayers when we have questions and even difficulty with God. God doesn't want our empty words of praise; he wants our honest prayers.

HEIRLOOMS OF FAITH

He issued his laws to Jacob; he gave his instructions to Israel. He commanded our
ancestors to teach them to their children, so the next generation might know them—
even the children not yet born—and they in turn will teach their own children.
❖ PSALM 78:5-6

It was a brief conversation that I had quickly forgotten. But not my eldest daughter. As I was saying good-bye to her after dropping her off at college, I told her to remember what her great-grandparents went through to come to this country and to give their son—my father, her grandfather—the opportunities of a good education.

But their greatest hope and prayer for their son was that he observe the Sabbath wherever he was, because that is the key to Jewish life. My father passed that legacy of faith to me, and now I was reminding my daughter to do the same. Years later, my daughter told me that this brief, five-minute conversation had the strongest influence on her and inspired her to keep the Sabbath during her college years.

God commanded his people to share with each generation the stories of his faithfulness, to teach their children his law and his mighty acts so that they will not forget all that God has done for them. The same is true for us today.

Passing on heirlooms of faith is the most important thing that we can do for our children. At times, we do this with intention when we instill biblical values through religious education. Or we share our faith journey with our children and tell them the stories of God's faithfulness to us through the years.

More often than not, we pass along our faith through daily conversations with our children, through our actions and our deeds, through how we treat our neighbors and others. Our children are constantly watching us and seeing how what we do matches with what we tell them. Our lives are a living textbook for our children of what we value most.

What are our children or grandchildren learning from us today?

A Christian Reflection on Passing on the Faith

The *Tanakh* emphasizes the importance of teaching children to love and obey God. Besides Psalm 78, we think of Moses telling the Israelites to "repeat [God's commands] again and again to your children" (Deuteronomy 6:7), and of Proverbs 22:6, which tells parents to "direct your children onto the right path, and when they are older, they will not leave it." The New Testament also emphasizes this. After all, the gospel promise is "to you, and to your children" (Acts 2:39). Paul instructs fathers to "not provoke your children to anger by the way you treat them. Rather, bring them up with the discipline and instruction that comes from the Lord" (Ephesians 6:4).

WHAT'S YOUR RESPONSE?

I am the LORD, the God of all the peoples of the world. Is anything too hard for me?
❖ JEREMIAH 32:27

At Mount Sinai, God confronted Moses from the burning bush. In that instant, Moses' life, the course of Israel's history, and indeed, world history, were altered forever. But for a moment, the fate of the Israelites truly hung in the balance.

God told Moses that he had heard the cries of his people enslaved by the Egyptians and he was going to send a deliverer—Moses! And what was Moses' response? "Who am I to appear before Pharaoh? Who am I to lead the people of Israel out of Egypt?" (Exodus 3:11). Even after God assured Moses that he would go with him, Moses still protested. He even pleaded with God to send someone else.

All Moses could see was himself—his weaknesses, his lack of speaking skills, his fears of rejection and failure. Moses was so concerned about his own inadequacies that he didn't trust in God's ability to help him. He couldn't imagine that God would be able to overcome his deficiencies to accomplish this great task.

It's easy to read this account from the Bible and judge Moses for doubting God. But we shouldn't be so hasty, should we? Doesn't God speak to us, whether through his Word, a message from a sermon, our circumstances? Isn't God calling us to accomplish something for him? And don't we often respond like Moses, saying, "We're too weak; we aren't capable; ask someone else"?

Thankfully, God understands our fears, our deep sense of inadequacies. And he responds just as he did with Moses, and later, through the prophet Jeremiah: "I am the LORD, the God of all the peoples of the world. Is anything too hard for me?"

As he did with Moses, God promises to be with us, to help us with whatever task he has given to us.

A Christian Reflection on the Great Commission

The Gospel of Matthew concludes with a call to the disciples, which the church through the ages has understood as directed to all Christ's followers: "I have been given all authority in heaven and on earth. Therefore, go and make disciples of all the nations, baptizing them in the name of the Father and the Son and the Holy Spirit. Teach these new disciples to obey all the commands I have given you." Like Moses, we can think of many excuses why we can't follow through on Christ's commission. For this reason, Jesus concludes by assuring us, "I am with you always, even to the end of the age" (Matthew 28:18-20).

Sabbath Reflections

What new truth about passing on your faith did you learn from this week's devotions?

How has this truth affected your faith?

How will you apply this truth to your daily life?

Your Key Verse for the Week:

❖ OTHER REFLECTIONS

HOPE FOR THE FUTURE

O God, we have heard it with our own ears—our ancestors have told us of all you did in their day, in days long ago. ✦ PSALM 44:1

When facing a difficult task or a tough situation, it helps to know that someone has successfully gone through something similar. Knowing about past experiences can help us navigate future difficulties.

In Psalm 44, the psalm writer—and the people of Israel—are in a bad place. They have retreated before their enemies and have been plundered by their foes (Psalm 44:10); they are mocked and disgraced before their neighbors (Psalm 44:13). Worse yet, it feels as if God himself has turned his back on them: "You have covered us with darkness and death" (Psalm 44:19).

Israel had been defeated by her enemies, despite her faith (Psalm 44:17) and obedience (Psalm 44:18). And though the psalmist could not understand what was happening, he did not give up hope. Why? Because he remembered what God had done for the people of Israel in "days long ago" (Psalm 44:1).

The psalmist recounts, "You drove out the pagan nations by your power and gave all the land to our ancestors. You crushed their enemies and set our ancestors free" (Psalm 44:2). He knew that it was God who had secured victory for his people and not their own strength: "Only by your power can we push back our enemies; only in your name can we trample our foes" (Psalm 44:5).

Because of that knowledge, the psalm writer is confident that God will answer their prayers and rescue them because of his unfailing love (Psalm 44:26).

When we go through difficult times, it is easy to become discouraged and think that God has abandoned us. But we need to remember how God has delivered us in the past and trust that he will once again restore us.

Remembering the past can help us face the future with confidence.

A Christian Reflection on Turning to the Past for Hope

The basis for Christian hope is firmly rooted in a past event, the resurrection of Jesus. Paul makes this point while refuting those who deny there is a resurrection of the dead. As he points out, if there was no resurrection of the dead, then Christ was not raised, and if Christ was not raised, then "all who have died believing in Christ are lost!" (1 Corinthians 15:18). But as Paul affirms, "In fact, Christ has been raised from the dead. He is the first of a great harvest of all who have died" (1 Corinthians 15:20). Thus, Jesus is our sure ground of hope as we face an uncertain future.

THE FEAR FACTOR

But when I am afraid, I will put my trust in you. I praise God for what he has promised. I trust in God, so why should I be afraid? What can mere mortals do to me?
❖ PSALM 56:3-4

Several years ago, *Fear Factor*, a popular TV show, opened with these chilling words: "Imagine a world in which your greatest fears become a reality." During the show, contestants were confronted with a series of challenges that involved facing their most primal fears, such as being enclosed in small spaces or being thrown into a pit crawling with spiders or snakes.

Most of us would not voluntarily choose to face our fears, but nearly all of us grapple with fear on a daily basis. Fear is a natural human emotion, but we can let it overwhelm us until we are paralyzed.

Psalm 56 was written by David when he fled from Saul and hid among the Philistines. When the Philistines recognized David, he was afraid for his life, so he pretended to be insane, even drooling, so that the king would think he was no threat (see 1 Samuel 21:10-15). That's when David wrote, "I trust in God, so why should I be afraid? What can mere mortals do to me?" (Psalm 56:4).

David freely admitted that he felt fear, but he did not let that fear control his thoughts and actions. Instead, he took his fear to God and reaffirmed that when he is afraid, he will trust in God.

We tend to feed our fear so that our problems and anxieties grow larger and larger. But when we admit our fear to God, we feed our faith instead of our fears.

In Psalm 2:11 we read, "Serve the LORD with reverent fear, and rejoice with trembling." How can we rejoice while trembling? What kind of joy can be found in fear? The answer depends on what, or rather whom, we fear. The adage goes, "He who fears many, fears any; but he who fears One, fears none." When we fear only one God, instead of many men, we can trust that everything will be all right. And that's a reason to rejoice!

A Christian Reflection on Facing Fear

If it weren't for God, there would be plenty to fear in the world. But as Paul points out, "If God is for us, who can ever be against us? Since he did not spare even his own Son but gave him up for us all, won't he also give us everything else?" (Romans 8:31-32). Even if we experience "trouble or calamity, or are persecuted, or hungry, or destitute, or in danger, or threatened with death" (Romans 8:35), Paul says we should not fear, because "despite all these things, overwhelming victory is ours through Christ, who loved us" (Romans 8:37).

THIRSTING FOR GOD

O God, you are my God; I earnestly search for you. My soul thirsts for you; my whole body longs for you in this parched and weary land where there is no water. I have seen you in your sanctuary and gazed upon your power and glory. ❖ PSALM 63:1-2

Our bodies need water regularly to live. Without it, we wouldn't be able to survive very long. It is this essential need for a life-giving source that David refers to in Psalm 63. Except David's need is not just physical; it's also spiritual.

David wrote this psalm during a time when he was in the wilderness of Judah, seeking refuge, after his son Absalom had launched a rebellion against him. While in this "parched and weary land," David most likely experienced a physical thirst, but even more critical for him was his spiritual thirsting for God.

David longed for someone to ease his loneliness and his suffering. He yearned for God's protection and his unfailing love. No wonder he cried out, "O God, you are my God; I earnestly search for you. My soul thirsts for you."

Can we relate? Have there been times when we have longed for God's presence? Perhaps we have cried out, as David did, "My God, I desperately need you!"

In Amos 8:11, we read, "The time is surely coming . . . when I will send a famine on the land—not a famine of bread or water but of hearing the words of the LORD." The Sages explain that in the end times there will be a dearth of spirituality that will cause a hunger for God.

The good news is that, just as God provided water for the physical needs of his people while they wandered in the desert for forty years, he also provides "living water" for those who trust him.

Through the prophet Isaiah, God offers us this invitation: "Is anyone thirsty? Come and drink—even if you have no money!" (Isaiah 55:1). God offers each one of us what we need to sustain our souls, as long as we, like David, seek him: "Seek the LORD while you can find him. Call on him now while he is near" (Isaiah 55:6).

A *Christian Reflection on Spiritual Thirst*

Jesus recognized the spiritual thirst of the Samaritan woman he met at the community's watering hole. In an interesting interplay between physical and spiritual thirst, Jesus tells her, "If you knew the gift of God and who it is that asks you for a drink, you would have asked him and he would have given you living water" (John 4:10, NIV). Jesus then presents himself as the provider of this spiritual water as he again contrasts it with physical water: "Everyone who drinks this water will be thirsty again, but whoever drinks the water I give them will never thirst" (John 4:13-14, NIV). How are you trying to quench your thirst?

FOR SUCH A TIME

If you keep quiet at a time like this, deliverance and relief for the Jews will arise from some other place, but you and your relatives will die. Who knows if perhaps you were made queen for just such a time as this? ❖ ESTHER 4:14

The account of Queen Esther is one of the most stirring portrayals of courage and willingness to take a stand against evil in the Bible. After uncovering a plot to kill all the Jews in the country, Esther's cousin Mordecai pleads with her to intervene on behalf of the Jews before her husband, King Xerxes. Esther is faced with a difficult choice.

If she refuses to say anything, the Jewish people will surely perish. If she does speak up, however, she risks death, because no one was allowed to enter the king's presence without being summoned. Who can forget Esther's inspiring words as she made her decision: "I will go in to see the king. If I must die, I must die" (Esther 4:16).

Both Mordecai and Esther were in a unique position to save the Jewish people. They could have refused to do anything and save themselves. But they saw they had an opportunity to make a difference, and they acted.

During another time in history when the Jews once again faced annihilation, there were individuals, groups, and even an entire village that recognized they had an opportunity to make a difference—and they acted. We call these brave souls the Righteous Gentiles, non-Jews who risked their lives to save Jews during the Holocaust.

The people of Le Chambon-sur-Lignon, a Protestant village in southern France, offered a haven for Jews fleeing from the Nazis. As they said, "Things had to be done, and we happened to be there to do them. It was the most natural thing in the world to help these people."

We may never be asked to put our lives on the line in the way that Esther or the Righteous Gentiles did, but we can commit to stand against injustice, anti-Semitism, and prejudice in our own communities. It may make all the difference.

A Christian Reflection on Making a Stand for Justice

How can we recognize a Christian? According to the apostle John, "Since we know that Christ is righteous, we also know that all who do what is right are God's children" (1 John 2:29). Taking a stand for justice and against prejudice is the right thing, the righteous thing, to do. Esther and the Righteous Gentiles are good examples of those who reflect their heavenly Father by doing the right thing in the face of injustice. Jesus pronounces blessings on "those who hunger and thirst for justice" (Matthew 5:6). Where can you take a stand for justice in your community?

OUR REFUGE

The LORD is my rock, my fortress and my deliverer; my God is my rock, in whom I take refuge, my shield and the horn of my salvation. He is my stronghold, my refuge and my savior—from violent people you save me. I called to the LORD, who is worthy of praise, and have been saved from my enemies. ❖ 2 SAMUEL 22:2-4, NIV

King David knew something about finding a safe haven and being protected. For years, on the run from the jealous King Saul, David sought safety in the caves and hills outside Jerusalem. He sought protection from his enemies on the battlefield and from within his own family. But David found his ultimate refuge in God.

In 2 Samuel 22:2-4, David writes a praise song in gratitude for the countless times God has delivered him from his enemies and from Saul. Its words are nearly identical to those in Psalm 18 and may have been written toward the end of David's life, during a time of peace. You can imagine David looking back and reflecting on God's gracious provision for him throughout the many trials and difficulties in his life.

Look at the many ways David characterizes God's protection in the first two lines: God is a rock, which cannot be moved by anyone who wants to harm us. He is a fortress, a shield, a stronghold, the "horn of [our] salvation" (2 Samuel 22:3, NIV). Finally, God is a refuge, a place of safekeeping, where we are free from harm.

In the early days of the Zionist movement, a political expression of the Jewish desire to return to Israel, an argument broke out between two factions. One side favored accepting Uganda's offer of a temporary refuge for persecuted Jews. The other side refused, saying only one place was truly a safe haven for Jews—Israel.

For the Jewish people, the only place of refuge, of safety, is Israel. It is the place we call home, where we are free from persecution, from pogroms, from anti-Semitic laws. It is the one place where we are free to worship our Rock, our Shield, our Fortress, and the Horn of our Salvation.

A Christian Reflection on God Our Refuge

Our promise-keeping God is our place of protection, our refuge from trouble. That is the message of the author of the book of Hebrews. He says that God has taken an oath that he will bless us and protect us. His message is a wonderful reminder for those under persecution for their faith: "God has given both his promise and his oath. These two things are unchangeable because it is impossible for God to lie. Therefore, we who have fled to him for refuge can have great confidence as we hold to the hope that lies before us" (Hebrews 6:18).

HOME SWEET HOME

I will rejoice over Jerusalem and delight in my people. And the sound of weeping and crying will be heard in it no more. ❖ ISAIAH 65:19

Israel for the Jew is more than a mere abstraction or antiquated theological proposition. It is more than just a geographic location. It is the Promised Land, the heart and lifeblood of the Jewish people. It is "a land that the LORD your God cares for. He watches over it through each season of the year!" (Deuteronomy 11:12). God's love for the land of Israel is intertwined with his special love for the people of Israel: "I will rejoice over Jerusalem and delight in my people" (Isaiah 65:19).

What I didn't fully realize is that Christians share this love for Israel. I finally understood this during a trip to Israel I made when I was twenty-six. Although I had been to the Holy Land many times, this was the first time I had visited with a group of Christians. At the time, I was a newly ordained rabbi from New York, and my roommate was a seventy-five-year-old Baptist minister from rural Virginia. We couldn't have been more different!

As I stepped out onto our hotel balcony to say my morning prayers, I was moved to tears looking out over Jerusalem. Imagine my surprise when I came back to the room one night and found my roommate kneeling, tears streaming down his face, as he thanked God for enabling him to fulfill his lifelong dream of visiting the Holy Land. Over and over again, he said, "Lord, thank you. I am luckier than Moses. He only *saw* the Holy Land. I have *walked* in it."

I was profoundly moved. I, a young Jew, had been emotionally and spiritually stirred by being in Israel. This elderly Baptist minister was no less affected. I realized then that a profound link existed between him and me, between Christians and Jews. Because of this realization, it has been my calling and my life's work to build bridges of understanding between Christians and Jews.

A Christian Reflection on the Holy Land

Indeed, both Christians and Jews feel deeply connected to the land of Israel. God gave the land to Israel in fulfillment of the promise to Abraham (see Genesis 12:1-3). As one walks around the land, the stories of the Bible come alive. For Christians, it is also the place where Jesus walked, taught, and ministered. He died, was raised, and ascended into heaven from this land. Though our ultimate promise is in the New Jerusalem, where God "will wipe every tear from their eyes" (Revelation 21:4), our love for the land of Israel and Jerusalem binds the hearts of Jews and Christians together.

Sabbath Reflections

What new truth about the Jewish and Christian connection to the Holy Land did you learn from this week's devotions?

How has this truth affected your faith?

How will you apply this truth to your daily life?

Your Key Verse for the Week:

❖ OTHER REFLECTIONS

THE APPLE OF YOUR EYE

Keep me as the apple of your eye; hide me in the shadow of your wings.
❖ PSALM 17:8, NIV

The apple of my eye is _____. How did you fill in that blank? Did you think of a person? Or was it an object? Typically, when we talk about someone or something being the apple of our eye, we are referring to someone we cherish, something that is important to us.

The phrase, which was first used in the Bible, comes from a Hebrew expression that literally means "little man of the eye," and it refers to the tiny reflection of yourself that you can see in other people's pupils. To be the apple of someone's eye means that you are being gazed upon and watched closely by that person. Your very image is dancing in the eyes of that person!

So when David asks God to "Keep me as the apple of your eye" in Psalm 17, he is asking God to keep an eye on him and not lose sight of him. David asks God to regard him as one would a cherished child. And as the apple of God's eye, David also seeks shelter in God, asking for his protection: "Hide me in the shadow of your wings."

David knew, even as he was making these heartfelt requests, that God would answer his prayer. He was confident that God would show him the "wonders of your great love" (Psalm 17:7, NIV) and that he would be vindicated before his enemies.

We can have the same confidence that David had. We, too, can be assured that God hears our prayers. We can know that he will answer them. And because we are the apple of his eye, we know that he will protect us. As cherished ones in his sight, God will guide us through whatever circumstances life throws at us.

A *Christian Reflection on Living by Faith*

The New Testament reminds us that we are loved by God and protected by him: "Through your faith, God is protecting you by his power until you receive this salvation, which is ready to be revealed on the last day for all to see" (1 Peter 1:5). But what does that mean? Bad things still happen to us. We and our loved ones get sick and die; our enemies seem to prevail. But that is the short-term view. We will be there on the "last day," and we will see with clearer eyes just how God cared for us through our lives, in spite of the pain and difficulty. For now, we live by faith.

FOLLOW THAT LEADER?

*The shepherds of my people have lost their senses. They no longer seek wisdom
from the LORD. Therefore, they fail completely, and their flocks are scattered.*
❖ JEREMIAH 10:21

During the time of Jesus, one of the most powerful Jewish sects was the Sadducees.
As leaders, they were most concerned about power and position. Their power and
authority stemmed from their control of the Temple. Most of the priests at that time
were Sadducees—a position that had been passed down from father to son, rather
than attained by merit. Without accountability, many had become corrupted.

In addition, the Sadducees were the political liaisons to the hated Roman Empire.
They tended to be wealthier and more aristocratic than the other Jewish groups.
Josephus, a respected and noted historian of that time, recorded that the Sadducees
"have none but the rich on their side." They had a general disregard for commoners,
and in turn, the common people didn't hold them in high regard.

This group, probably more than any other, had the greatest opportunity to influence the existing power structure for the benefit of others. They were wealthy, well
connected, and powerful. As priests, they also had a responsibility to the people to
lead them in a way that honored and reflected God. Yet they failed miserably to lead
the people in a godly way and to use their influence positively. Rather than using their
position and their authority for the good of others, they used it to benefit themselves.
Rather than glorify God, they glorified themselves. When the Temple was destroyed
in AD 70, the Sadducees lost their power base and dwindled into obscurity.

God has given each one of us a unique position and opportunity to influence and
help others—whether it's at home, in the workplace, or in our neighborhoods. We
have a responsibility to use the positions and opportunities entrusted to us to help
others and work for *their* benefit—not our own.

A Christian Reflection on Shepherds of God's Flock

The Christian church has had its share of bad leaders—bad shepherds who care more
about themselves than the people that they are supposed to lead. Jude devotes a sizable chunk of his short letter to exposing leaders who acted like "shameless shepherds
who care only for themselves" (Jude 1:12). In contrast, Jesus is "the great Shepherd of
the sheep" (Hebrews 13:20; see also John 10:11-18) and a model for all leaders today.
His type of leadership is that of a servant, willing to wash the feet of the people, even
willing to die on their behalf.

A LEGACY OF LEARNING

*Teach me your decrees, O LORD; I will keep them to the end. Give me understanding
and I will obey your instructions; I will put them into practice with all my heart.*
❖ PSALM 119:33-34

Previously, we looked at one of the three main Jewish sects at the time of Jesus'
ministry—the Sadducees. This group, even though the most powerful, left a legacy
of failed leadership, putting their own interests and position ahead of those they
supposedly served and led.

The Pharisees offer us a much different picture—and legacy. (And yes, this *is* the
group that Jesus sparred with the most.) More than any other group, the Pharisees
tended to be open-minded, judicious, and democratic. Predominantly from the
rural and middle classes, the Pharisees were not linked to Rome and were loved and
respected by the common people.

Many of the religious ideas and institutions this group helped establish, such as the
concept of the synagogue and the rabbi, have guided Jewish life since the destruction
of the Temple in AD 70. When the Temple was destroyed, gone was the chief function of the priestly class, paving the way for the emergence of the rabbi as the central
authority figure in Jewish life.

The establishment of the rabbi added a whole new dimension to Judaism.
Whereas before, the priesthood was attained through one's ancestry, now any Jewish
male could potentially earn the role of a rabbi through his piety and his knowledge of
the *Torah* and Jewish law. In fact, the Pharisees emphasized the need for *all* Jews—not
just the priests and rabbis—to study the Bible for themselves. God's Word became
available and open to whoever sought it and wanted to learn from it.

That is a legacy that Christians and Jews continue to enjoy today. We don't have
to be ordained rabbis or pastors in order to read the Bible and study it. We can simply
read for ourselves what God wants us to know and how he wants us to live.

A Christian Reflection on the Priesthood of All Believers

All Jews and Christians have the responsibility and privilege to read and study the
Bible. We don't need special training, and we do not require the help of specialists.
Indeed, rather than having a special category of "priests" necessary to help us know
God and his Word, Peter tells us, "You are his holy priests" (1 Peter 2:5), a statement
that is the foundation to the idea of the priesthood of all believers. That said, there is
still a place for those who devote their lives to the study and teaching of God's Word
(rabbis, ministers, biblical scholars) to provide the resources to deepen our understanding of the Word.

ALL IN THE FAMILY

For the sake of my family and friends, I will say, "May you have peace."
❖ PSALM 122:8

Most Christians recognize the Pharisees as the group that Jesus argued with the most. So would it surprise you to know that many biblical scholars believe that Jesus himself was brought up as a Pharisee?

Many scholars believe that Jesus grew up as a member of the Pharisees because he shared their belief on the issue of the resurrection of the dead, which the Sadducees denied. He also denounced war and violence, just like Paul, who clearly identified himself as a Pharisee. Moreover, I think the fact that Jesus argued the most with the Pharisees is more proof that he himself was one.

Why? Because if he were raised a Pharisee and continually found their practices faulty or objectionable, might he not be more concerned about a "family matter" than an issue from a group he had no association with? Just as parents are more concerned about their *own* wayward child than the child down the street, so Jesus might have had a greater concern for his own wayward Jewish brothers and sisters.

Whatever Jesus' reasons for criticizing the Pharisees, it seems most likely that he spent a lot of time with them during the formative years of his short life. And it might help explain why Christianity—the faith that developed out of Jesus' original followers—and Judaism—the faith that continued to develop from a long line of Pharisees—actually share much in common.

Through my many years working with Christians, I have discovered that Bible-believing Christians are among the Jewish people's and Israel's greatest friends. My prayer is that we both will continue to break down the barriers that are between us, while respecting the distinctives and differences of our faith.

A Christian Reflection on Jesus the Pharisee

Though we know Jesus was a Jew, we are less certain about which sect he affiliated with. We do know that he appeared to have two main problems with the Pharisees. One, he felt that they didn't practice what they preached. He told his disciples that the Pharisees were "the official interpreters of the law of Moses. So practice and obey whatever they tell you, but don't follow their example" (Matthew 23:2-3). The second problem is that the Pharisees did not accept Jesus as the Messiah. Nevertheless, we share much in common with the modern heirs of the Pharisees, and we need to focus on these similarities to break down the barriers between us. Yet we also must respectfully recognize the differences between us, the largest of which remains the central role of Jesus.

UNITED UNDER GOD

Let me be united with all who fear you, with those who know your laws.
❖ PSALM 119:79

At the close of the first century, only two Jewish groups had survived—the Pharisees, whose contributions of the synagogue, the rabbi, and *Torah* study became the foundation of modern Judaism; and the believers in Jesus, who founded Christianity. As Gentiles increasingly comprised the newly emerging churches, Christianity effectively ceased being a Jewish movement.

The resulting division between Christianity and Judaism led to thousands of years of conflict, animosity, and fratricide. For many Jews, even today, Jesus and the cross are not viewed as symbols of love and compassion but as reminders of oppression and persecution.

Thankfully, over the past several decades, Jewish views of Jesus have shifted dramatically. More historically accurate, favorable, and less polemical Jewish views of Jesus have emerged. Jews today more readily acknowledge Jesus' Jewishness, his great moral teachings, his kindness, compassion, and love toward others. Many Jews acknowledge that Jesus brought salvation to the Gentiles. As the relationship between Christians and Jews has strengthened and improved, there has been a fundamental shift from the hostile view that Jews historically had about Jesus and his ministry.

As a young rabbi with the Anti-Defamation League, I was sent to help raise public opposition to a planned march by a neo-Nazi group in Skokie, Illinois, in 1977. At the time, this Chicago suburb had the largest population of Holocaust survivors in the United States. As I went door to door, I was shocked to discover that it was the Christians who were the most vocal and most supportive of our efforts.

As I began to explore that relationship further, I was overwhelmed by the expression of Christian love shown not only to me but also to the Jewish people and to Israel. That experience shaped my life's work, causing me to launch a ministry to help build bridges of understanding between the two groups.

A Christian Reflection on Mutual Respect and Support

As the gospel was extended to the Gentiles, there was conflict among Christians as well as with Jews on such issues as circumcision and kosher diet. Of course, the leading cause of disagreement between Jews and Christians had to do with Jesus' claim that he is the Messiah. That said, the violence that erupted between Jews and Christians is scandalous, and the atrocities committed by Christians against Jews over the years is horrific and cannot be justified, only repented. While acknowledging our differences, we should love and support each other deeply as brothers and sisters.

TRUE LOVE

Hatred stirs up quarrels, but love makes up for all offenses.
❖ PROVERBS 10:12

The Sages tell the following story of a young man who visited his rabbi and became so overwhelmed with emotion that he cried out, "Rabbi, I love you dearly!" The rabbi, both touched and amused by the young man's sincerity, asked him, "Tell me, my son, you say that you love me, but where do I hurt? What ails me?"

Perplexed, the young man replied, "But Rabbi, I don't know where you hurt. But nevertheless, I love you dearly!" The rabbi then replied, "How can you say you love me when you do not even know where I hurt and what brings me pain?"

Indeed, how can we love someone we don't truly understand?

This touching story illustrates well the place where Christians and Jews must begin a dialogue together. We need to explain to each other who we are and what we believe—and to share with one another what brings us joy and what brings us pain.

That has been the underlying mission and purpose of our founding of The Fellowship—to initiate dialogue and build bridges of understanding. As we learn from one another, we strive to identify the common ground we share, in hopes that this, in turn, will lead to joint efforts and cooperation.

Though many inroads have been made in the past three decades, much remains to be done. We will make mistakes, and sensitivities between the two faith communities will undoubtedly be trampled. But if we move together in a spirit of love and understanding, much can be forgiven and much can be accomplished.

It is my hope and prayer that our efforts will move us along in our common search, not only for wisdom but also for how we might better deepen our bonds of love with one another and strengthen our relationship with God and devotion to him.

That's true love.

A Christian Reflection on True Love

One of the most famous passages in the New Testament is Paul's statement on love in 1 Corinthians 13. Paul was likely informed by Proverbs 10:12 when he wrote, "Love is patient and kind. Love is not jealous or boastful or proud or rude. It does not demand its own way. It is not irritable, and it keeps no record of being wronged. It does not rejoice about injustice but rejoices whenever the truth wins out. Love never gives up, never loses faith, is always hopeful, and endures through every circumstance" (1 Corinthians 13:4-7).

Sabbath Reflections

What new truth about the main Jewish religious groups during Jesus' time on earth did you learn from this week's devotions?

How has this truth affected your faith?

How will you apply this truth to your daily life?

Your Key Verse for the Week:

❖ OTHER REFLECTIONS

OUR ETERNAL REFUGE

A river brings joy to the city of our God, the sacred home of the Most High. God dwells in that city; it cannot be destroyed. From the very break of day, God will protect it.
❖ PSALM 46:4-5

As any visitor to Jerusalem can tell you, the city has no river running through it. There is only one major spring in the city, Gihon, which has been gurgling since before King David's time. So it may seem curious that Psalm 46 refers to a river that "brings joy to the city of our God." Certainly, the "city of our God" refers to Jerusalem, but what is this river?

Undeniably, it was God's very presence that, like a river, sustained the people's lives and protected them. We know that God's glory, *Shekhinah*, filled the Temple at the time of King Solomon (see 1 Kings 8:10-12). God's acknowledged presence among the people gave them the confidence that he, indeed, would be their "refuge and strength, always ready to help in times of trouble" (Psalm 46:1).

According to the psalmist, Jerusalem would not fall because God was present within her and would protect her (see Psalm 46:5). Years after this was written, however, the city did fall. The prophet Ezekiel records that, because of the idolatry practiced in the Temple (see Ezekiel 8), God's *Shekhinah* glory departed from the Temple (see Ezekiel 10). Sadly, Jerusalem later fell to the Babylonians (see 2 Kings 25), and the Temple was destroyed.

Yet, today, God remains our refuge and help, even in the midst of terrible trials and disasters. He is our eternal protection and can provide us the strength we need in any circumstance, as long as we turn to him in obedience and faith. God will be the sustainer of our lives as long as we make him our center and do not allow the idols of this world to take his place.

God is our river that brings us joy.

A Christian Reflection on the Water That Brings Joy

Psalm 46 brings to mind the glorious picture of the New Jerusalem, a metaphor of the new heavens and the new earth that will come at the end of the age. The angel showed the apostle John "a river with the water of life, clear as crystal, flowing from the throne of God and of the Lamb. It flowed down the center of the main street. On each side of the river grew a tree of life, bearing twelve crops of fruit, with a fresh crop each month. The leaves were used for medicine to heal the nations" (Revelation 22:1-2). What a marvelous picture of our future hope!

BEING A GOOD SAMARITAN

Then a despised Samaritan came along, and when he saw the man, he felt compassion for him. Going over to him, the Samaritan soothed his wounds with olive oil and wine and bandaged them. Then he put the man on his own donkey and took him to an inn, where he took care of him. ❖ LUKE 10:33-34

Sometimes when we witness someone else in trouble, we take action. We stop and assist a stranded motorist, or carry groceries for a young mom. And sometimes we don't. Maybe we're in a hurry, or maybe we feel uncomfortable about offering help, so we look the other way.

But does our busyness or discomfort excuse us from helping others? No. The Bible makes it clear that we are to help others in need. As God commanded the Israelites, "Do not seek revenge or bear a grudge against a fellow Israelite, but love your neighbor as yourself. I am the LORD" (Leviticus 19:18).

When teaching about this command, Jesus relied on the power of story—what Jews call *midrashim*—to illustrate this principle. He drew upon an experience familiar to his audience (traveling the treacherous road to Jerusalem) in the parable about the Good Samaritan.

Jesus described a Jewish man who was beaten, robbed, and left by the side of the road. Of the three people who passed by, only one stopped to help the man— a Samaritan, the hated enemy of the Jews. Jesus told this story in response to a question regarding what it means to "love your neighbor as yourself," from Leviticus. By helping the desperate man, the Samaritan loved his neighbor as himself.

In Exodus 23:5, God commands: "If you see that the donkey of someone who hates you has collapsed under its load, do not walk by. Instead, stop and help." Loving your neighbor applies to both friends and enemies alike. In fact, the Sages comment that if we see two donkeys buckling under their loads—one belonging to a friend and one to an enemy—we must help our enemy first!

Loving our neighbor as ourselves means showing mercy to others no matter who they are. It means giving of our time, our efforts, and our resources to help *all* people.

A Christian Reflection on Loving Our Neighbor

The instruction to "Love your neighbor as yourself" is one of the most frequently cited statements in the New Testament, not only by Jesus (see Matthew 19:19; 22:39; Mark 12:31; Luke 10:27), but by others as well. Paul urges believers, "Owe nothing to anyone—except for your obligation to love one another. If you love your neighbor, you will fulfill the requirements of God's law" (Romans 13:8). As James reminded the church in Jerusalem, "It is good when you obey the royal law as found in the Scriptures: 'Love your neighbor as yourself'" (James 2:8). Such repetition throughout Scripture underlines the importance of the command.

AN ARMY OF COMPASSION

The officers of the army must address the troops and say, "Has anyone here just built a
new house but not yet dedicated it? If so, you may go home! You might be killed in the
battle, and someone else would dedicate your house. . . . Has anyone here just become
engaged to a woman but not yet married her? Well, you may go home and get married!
You might die in the battle, and someone else would marry her."
❖ DEUTERONOMY 20:5, 7

It's hard to focus on our jobs when we are worrying about a sick family member or
other pressing private concerns. While we try not to let our personal problems affect
our work, it's not always easy. So when an employer comes alongside us and takes the
time to help us, it can make all the difference.

This care and compassion is played out daily in the Israeli Defense Force (IDF).
All young Israelis are required to serve in the army—men from ages eighteen to
twenty-two, and women from eighteen to twenty-one—and though they know the
importance of serving in the army, they often do so at the expense of their families
and their personal needs.

Those in charge of training and working with the soldiers know the realities and
hardships of enlistment. For some soldiers, it means forfeiting the income that would
help support their families. For newly arrived immigrants (*oleh*), it often means being
on their own for the first time in a new country without any social support or family
network.

Thankfully, compassion toward soldiers is a longstanding, biblical tradition in
Israel. In Deuteronomy 20, army officers were instructed to show compassion toward
those who had genuine needs at home. There was very good reason for this. If a soldier among them became fearful (of leaving behind a new bride, for instance) or discouraged, it would affect the others. The rule was, "Is anyone here afraid or worried?
If you are, you may go home before you frighten anyone else" (Deuteronomy 20:8).

By taking care of the needs of soldiers, including the needs of their families, the
army ensures that soldiers won't be distracted in their service. As it says in the Bible,
"Indeed, he who watches over Israel never slumbers or sleeps" (Psalm 121:4).

A Christian Reflection on the True Source of Victory

What do we learn about God from Deuteronomy's provision that those newly married or those afraid may be exempt from military service? We learn that when God is
involved in the battle, a large army is unnecessary. Think of Gideon, whom God commanded to pare his army of thirty-two thousand down to three hundred men. When
they won the battle against the Midianites (see Judges 7), they knew for certain that
their victory was not the result of their own strength and resources but because of God.
We read in 2 Corinthians 12:9, "My power works best in weakness." In our battles in life,
we need to fight with the knowledge that our strength is in God and not in ourselves.

BUILDING BRIDGES OF FORGIVENESS

O LORD, God of heaven, the great and awesome God who keeps his covenant
of unfailing love with those who love him and obey his commands, listen to my prayer!
Look down and see me praying night and day for your people Israel. I confess that
we have sinned against you. Yes, even my own family and I have sinned!

❖ NEHEMIAH 1:5-6

For more than two thousand years, the relationship between Christians and Jews has been marked by mistrust and animosity. For the past thirty years, I have devoted my life's work and mission to breaking down those walls and helping Christians and Jews better understand one another and the common ground we share.

It may take a lifetime, but the efforts we make today will gradually bring us closer together. One step we can take is to confess our collective sins against others.

We can learn from Nehemiah's example as he prayed on behalf of the sins of his people. He didn't have any connection with the Jews whose sin had led to the Exile, but he confessed their sins as a collective failure against God. He didn't have any connection with the Jews who had returned from Exile nearly a hundred years earlier and had failed to restore Jerusalem, but Nehemiah confessed their sins as a collective failure against God.

Jews are accustomed to the concept of collective responsibility and corporate prayer. That is, when a Jew prays, it is frequently phrased as "we" rather than "I" to recognize that we share in the collective burdens and blessings of the Jewish people. To Christians influenced by Western individualism, this is often an unfamiliar concept.

This is why so many Christians don't feel a connection to the past sins committed by Christians against Jews in various parts of history. But if Christians were to begin to reach out to Jews by asking forgiveness for the sins committed against Jews in the name of Jesus throughout history, it would begin to help Jews trust Christians today.

The question shouldn't be, Who made this wrong? Rather, we should ask ourselves, What can we do to make it right?

A Christian Reflection on Corporate Prayer

It is appropriate for Christians to ask Jews for forgiveness because of the atrocities committed against the Jews in the name of Jesus. It is also true that Christians often think very individualistically, and in that way, we distance ourselves from these sins. We should freely confess our sins to those whom we (as individuals and as a group) have harmed, as well as to God. As the apostle James reminds us, "Confess your sins to each other and pray for each other so that you may be healed. The earnest prayer of a righteous person has great power and produces wonderful results" (James 5:16).

BE A BLESSING

I will make you into a great nation. I will bless you and make you famous, and you will be a blessing to others. I will bless those who bless you and curse those who treat you with contempt. All the families on earth will be blessed through you.
❖ GENESIS 12:2-3

Imagine if Abraham had first considered the cost when God called him to leave his home and move to an unknown land. Suppose he had said, "What if I don't like it there? What if I get lost? What if I lose all my cattle and sheep on the way? How will I make a living? What if my family doesn't want to move?"

Of course, God made some incredible promises to Abraham if he did obey and go: He would make Abraham into a great nation; Abraham would be blessed and his name would be great. Those are some compelling reasons to obey, don't you think?

Then we come to God's second command to Abraham: "Be a blessing" (Genesis 12:2). Many translations render this more as a prediction—"You will be a blessing"—but in the Hebrew it literally means, *"Be a blessing."*

Abraham was called to be a conduit of blessings, not just a recipient. We tend to think of *receiving* blessings. We even pray for God to bless us. But how often do we seek to bless others?

God's two commands are related in a sequential way. Abraham couldn't be a blessing unless he first left to go where God was sending him. As Abraham obeyed the first command, God was able to bless him. Then, as a result of God's blessing, Abraham could obey the second command to *be* a blessing.

Sometimes we can't see how we can bless others. But if we obey God, we often find ourselves in a position to be a blessing. God loves to bless people, so when we are obedient and available to him, we take the first step toward allowing God to work in and through our lives to bless others.

A Christian Reflection on Being Blessed and Blessing Others

The New Testament offers an illustration that teaches God's followers to bless others even as they themselves are blessed (see John 13:1-20). During Jesus' final meal with his disciples before facing the cross, he got up from the table and removed his robe, placed a towel around his waist, and began washing the disciples' feet. This act was considered demeaning, a task some people would not even let their slaves perform. Yet, through this humble service, Jesus blessed his disciples, instructing them to "wash each other's feet," and telling them that "now that you know these things, God will bless you for doing them" (John 13:14, 17).

A PATH TO RECONCILIATION

The LORD detests the proud; they will surely be punished. Unfailing love and
faithfulness make atonement for sin. By fearing the LORD, people avoid evil.
❖ PROVERBS 16:5-6

Pride damages relationships. When one person is hardened by pride, the relationship
suffers. It becomes more difficult to demonstrate mutual love, openness, and trust.
When pride has damaged a relationship, it takes love and faithfulness over the course
of time to restore the relationship to a healthy state.

The same is true concerning relationships between groups of people, and particularly between Christians and Jews. Throughout history, Christians have committed
many wrongs against Jews in the name of Jesus. Of course, Christians today are not
personally responsible for what Christians did to Jews in the past, but it is important
for Christians to acknowledge history and extend a hand of reconciliation to Jews today.

To deny the wrongs of the past is prideful, and as the Bible teaches, "The LORD
detests all the proud of heart" (Proverbs 16:5, NIV). Though Christians are not responsible for the sins of their heritage, to deny the sins of the past is to be blinded by pride.

Today's passage in Proverbs teaches us an important path to reconciliation:
"Unfailing love and faithfulness make atonement for sin." As Christians acknowledge
the wrongs of the past, they can foster reconciliation with Jews by demonstrating love
and faithfulness to Jews over time.

My close friend Pastor Jack Hayford says, "I can't accept the beautiful things from
my heritage without accepting responsibility for the failures of my heritage." He demonstrates his heart while addressing a Jewish congregation and asking forgiveness for
the past history of the church's persecution of the Jews.

Much work remains to be done, but I believe we are making great strides in mending the brokenness between our two great faith communities and building a new
foundation based upon our shared heritage and love for God.

A Christian Reflection on Accepting Correction

Why is pride so dangerous and humility so important? If one is prideful, he or she
won't listen to the correction of others and thus is doomed to repeat the mistakes of
the past. As Proverbs 12:1 puts it, "To learn, you must love discipline; it is stupid to
hate correction." Only pride would have us deny the atrocities that Christians perpetrated against Jews in the past; indeed, the proper response is repentance. When we
are truly sorry and repentant for our sins, it can lead the way to changed attitudes and
behavior. As Paul writes, "The kind of sorrow God wants us to experience leads us
away from sin and results in salvation" (2 Corinthians 7:10).

Sabbath Reflections

What new truth about forgiveness and reconciliation did you learn from this week's devotions?

How has this truth affected your faith?

How will you apply this truth to your daily life?

Your Key Verse for the Week:

❖ OTHER REFLECTIONS

KING OVER ALL

God is the King over all the earth. Praise him with a psalm. God reigns above the nations, sitting on his holy throne. ❖ PSALM 47:7-8

For students of American history, the idea of serving a king is actually negative, in the sense that the United States was birthed from a revolt against the English king and his tyrannical rule. So when we read about the kingship of God in the Psalms and of God sitting on his throne, we often struggle with what it means.

We need to understand that, in biblical times, kings had complete authority. They could confiscate property, enslave entire groups of people, wage war for personal gain, and collect taxes without any vote on the matter. They had, in fact, complete power over life and death. And they demanded absolute loyalty from their subjects.

So when God is referred to as *King*, it is not a mere title or the position of a figurehead; his position is one of true authority and power.

Psalm 47 is known as one of the kingship or enthronement psalms, celebrating God's universal reign over all the earth. It is believed that this psalm was performed annually, along with a set of rituals that acted out the enthronement of God as king over all the earth. Such a reenactment created a vivid image in the minds of the participants, reminding them that God reigned supreme, not only over Israel but over all the earth.

This truth is as relevant today as it was during David's time. God sovereignly controls the course of human events. As such, he is rightfully declared King over all the earth because he rules over all the nations. His authority exceeds and supersedes the authority of any human king, president, dictator, or other ruler. But unlike any earthly ruler, God rules with justice, righteousness, and mercy.

A Christian Reflection on Worshiping the King

The wise men following the star asked Herod, "Where is the newborn king of the Jews? We saw his star as it rose, and we have come to worship him" (Matthew 2:2). Jesus was that newborn king, the Messiah or "anointed one," referring to the ancient practice of anointing a new king with oil to symbolize God's spirit on him. As the New Testament opens with the wise men seeking Jesus to worship him as king, so it ends with "the song of Moses, the servant of God, and the song of the Lamb," which praises God as king: "Great and marvelous are your works, O Lord God, the Almighty. Just and true are your ways, O King of the nations" (Revelation 15:3).

THE REAL DEAL

The LORD had said to Abram, "Leave your native country, your relatives, and your father's family, and go to the land that I will show you. I will make you into a great nation. I will bless you and make you famous, and you will be a blessing to others."
❖ GENESIS 12:1-2

As people of faith, we are sometimes asked, "How do you know God's promises are real and can be trusted?" Good question—and I think we can find the answer in God's call and promise to Abraham (originally called Abram).

Abram was living in Ur when God called him to a covenantal relationship with him. God promised that Abram would become a great nation and that *all* the nations of the world would be blessed through him. What a remarkable set of promises!

Of course, Abram's half of the bargain required significant sacrifice and obedience. He had to leave his home and go to a foreign land. Uprooted from his home and comfort, Abram traveled to the land of Canaan, where he built an altar and worshiped the Lord. There, he and his wife, Sarai, lived, awaiting fulfillment of the promise of an heir, the beginnings of a great family.

To some, it might have appeared that God had abandoned his promise to Abram, as he and Sarai remained childless for decades. Nevertheless, later events in Abram's life demonstrated God's unwavering faithfulness. When Abram was one hundred years old, he and Sarai finally had the son they were waiting for—Isaac. Years after Isaac's birth, Isaac's son Jacob, also called Israel, became the father of the twelve tribes that would become the nation of Israel.

God, indeed, fulfilled his promise to Abraham to make him into a great nation. Through God's covenant with one man, the rest of the world was also blessed. God kept his promises, and history was radically altered. God's blessing spread to Abraham's descendants and is still in force today.

In 1 Samuel 15:29, the prophet tells us, "He who is the Glory of Israel will not lie, nor will he change his mind." The God of Israel does not lie. Just as he has kept promises in the past, he will fulfill all promises in the future.

That's how we know that God's promises are the real deal.

A Christian Reflection on the Faith of Abraham

In the letter written to Hebrew Christians struggling in their faith, the author encourages them by pointing out great examples of faith such as Abel, Enoch, Noah, Moses, and of course, Abraham. This great faith hero not only believed that God was who he said but also that God would do what he said: "Faith is the confidence that what we hope for will actually happen; it gives us assurance about things we cannot see" (Hebrews 11:1). When your faith wavers, remember Abraham. God will fulfill his promises to you as well.

THE PROMISE KEEPER

Abram believed the LORD, and the LORD counted him as righteous because of his faith.
❖ GENESIS 15:6

Next time you're at the beach, scoop up a handful of sand. In essence, you are holding an object lesson of God's promise to Abram.

God didn't promise Abram wealth or fame. God promised him a nation, a people who would be so great in number that they would rival the stars in the sky or the grains of sand on the seashore (see Genesis 22:17). It is a promise that Jews have held on to through thousands of years. It is a promise that has connected us—physically and spiritually—to our homeland, Israel.

Remember when God gave that promise to Abram? In Genesis 15, Abram had no children, and he was beginning to despair of ever having an heir. God came to Abram in a vision and comforted him; he renewed the promise he had given earlier: "Look up into the sky and count the stars if you can. That's how many descendants you will have!" (Genesis 15:5).

How did Abram respond? "Abram believed the LORD, and the LORD counted him as righteous because of his faith." It was his belief that made Abram right with God. The fulfillment of God's promise did not rest on what Abram did—or did not do—but on Abram's faith in the one who gave the promise.

That's true for us, as well. We can do all the right things—go to worship, engage in Bible study, act charitably toward others—but ultimately that's not what makes us right with God. Rather, it is the combination of both our faith and our actions—our holy deeds—that brings us closer to God.

At the end of the book of Ecclesiastes, King Solomon says, "Here is now my final conclusion: Fear God and obey his commands, for this is everyone's duty" (Ecclesiates 12:13). Judaism maintains that both reverence and obedience are essential. Following God's commands is fundamental, but our service is incomplete without faith.

A Christian Reflection on the Faith That Saves

Three times the New Testament quotes Genesis 15:6 in support of the idea that faith, not our good deeds, is the bedrock of our relationship with God (Romans 4:3; Galatians 3:6; James 2:23). Abraham was a role model for us. Paul puts it this way: "When God counted him as righteous, it wasn't just for Abraham's benefit. It was recorded for our benefit, too, assuring us that God will also count us as righteous if we believe in him, the one who raised Jesus our Lord from the dead" (Romans 4:23-24). God saves us by his grace; when we put our faith in him, we demonstrate that faith through our obedience to his will.

RESTORATION WORK

When the LORD brought back his exiles to Jerusalem, it was like a dream! We were filled with laughter, and we sang for joy. And the other nations said, "What amazing things the LORD has done for them." ❖ PSALM 126:1-2

The work of restoration and renewal takes place all around us. We see it as people labor to rebuild their homes after the devastation of floods, hurricanes, and earthquakes. Forests that have been ravaged by fires grow back over time. Old homes are refurbished because of their historical or sentimental value. Through the power of modern medicine, health is restored and broken bones are repaired.

One of the more amazing—indeed, miraculous—examples of restoration is happening in the State of Israel, thanks to the support and generosity of our Christian friends. Over and over again, we see God continuing to bring his people, the Jews, back to their land, fulfilling the covenant he made with Abraham thousands of years ago.

Like the author of Psalm 126, our mouths are filled with laughter and our hearts rejoice because of the amazing things God has done for us. God, indeed, has restored our fortunes. He has taken our tears and turned them into joy.

God's ability to restore life, to bring good from tragedy, to bring joy out of grief, is often beyond our ability to comprehend. But God's power is evident to all who believe and call him Lord. Even when we are burdened with sorrow or crippled with grief, we can turn to him and trust that he will work to restore us.

Then we will be able to experience what the psalmist describes: "Those who plant in tears will harvest with shouts of joy. They weep as they go to plant their seed, but they sing as they return with the harvest" (Psalm 126:5-6).

If you are weighed down today with worries and beset with troubles that seem overwhelming, remember that even if it doesn't appear so, God is at work bringing about that great harvest of joy.

A Christian Reflection on Turning Weeping into Rejoicing

The Bible is filled with stories and testimonies of how God brings joy out of tragedy. For Christians, the ultimate realization of this theme is Jesus himself, whose "criminal's death on a cross" (Philippians 2:8) gave way to resurrection and exaltation, as "God elevated him to the place of highest honor and gave him the name above all other names" (Philippians 2:9). For this reason, our own pain will change to joy because death no longer has its sting (see 1 Corinthians 15:54-57) and all our tears will be wiped away (see Revelation 7:17; 21:4).

WORTH THE WAIT

Don't be afraid, for I am with you. Don't be discouraged, for I am your God. I will strengthen you and help you. I will hold you up with my victorious right hand.
❖ ISAIAH 41:10

How long are we willing to wait for something? The answer depends on what we're waiting for, doesn't it? If it's lunch from a fast-food establishment, ten minutes may be too long. If it's saving for a new home, we may be willing to wait several years. If it's news following a loved one's surgery, then waiting for an hour seems like an eternity. If it's our career, we might be willing to wait a lifetime to achieve our ultimate goals.

But what about thousands of years? For Jews, waiting has been woven into the very fabric of our history and our faith. The people of Israel waited four hundred years for a deliverer to rescue them from bondage in Egypt. They waited for nearly one hundred years, exiled in a foreign land, before they were allowed to return to their beloved Jerusalem. And once again exiled and dispersed to "the ends of the earth," they waited nearly two millennia to return to the land promised to Abraham, Isaac, and Jacob.

How is such waiting possible? Why did we never give up hope that one day we would return to our homeland? I think part of the answer lies in the prophet Isaiah's words: "I have called you back from the ends of the earth. . . . For I have chosen you and will not throw you away" (Isaiah 41:9). Not only are we a people who wait, we are a people of faith. We depend on and trust in God, who has promised that he has not rejected us and that he is with us always.

The same is true for all people of faith. We should not fear or grow weary of waiting, because we know that God is with us. He has established a relationship with us, and he gives us assurance that he will strengthen and help us through whatever we face.

A Christian Reflection on Waiting

According to Paul, God's people "wait with eager hope for the day when God will give us our full rights as his adopted children, including the new bodies he has promised us" (Romans 8:23). Paul previously described how the Creation had been subject to God's curse (see Romans 8:20), an allusion to Genesis 3 that describes the alienation and frustration that entered the world in response to human sin. But the message of the Bible is that God will redeem the world from sin and death, and we look forward with certain hope to that future day. In the meantime, "the Holy Spirit helps us in our weakness" (Romans 8:26) as we wait for that glorious future day.

WITH GOD'S HELP

I look up to the mountains—does my help come from there? My help comes from the LORD, *who made heaven and earth!* ❖ PSALM 121:1-2

Imagine if you, where you live right now, were surrounded by enemies committed to your total destruction. How would it feel to live with that tension and fear, 24/7?

Welcome to life in the State of Israel, a country no bigger than the state of New Jersey. Throughout her history, Israel has been surrounded by enemies who share one goal—her destruction. Within a day of modern Israel's inception as a nation, five of her "neighbors" declared war on her and attacked from all directions. We were outnumbered twenty to one, yet we prevailed.

Perhaps we shouldn't be surprised by this. We need only recall the biblical accounts of Gideon and the Midianites, when three hundred Israelites routed their much stronger enemy. Or how Nehemiah and the people rebuilt the wall around Jerusalem in fifty-two days, despite opposition from their enemies. Over and over again, we see the people of Israel succeed despite being outnumbered, outmanned, and out-equipped.

The one thing we were never without, however, was God. Remember what God told Gideon: "With these 300 men I will rescue you and give you victory over the Midianites" (Judges 7:7). And when Nehemiah and the people completed the rebuilding project in record time, the nations around them realized that "this work had been done with the help of our God" (Nehemiah 6:16). The prophet Zechariah reminds us of this as well, in God's message to his people: "It is not by force nor by strength, but by my Spirit" (Zechariah 4:6).

There was opposition to God's plans in biblical times; there is opposition to God's plan for his people today. But what people of faith can depend upon is that God's Word will endure. He cares for his people and will deliver them from all opposition.

A Christian Reflection on the Final Victory

If we looked at the world with human eyes, we might conclude that evil people are in control. But, Paul reminds us, "we don't wage war as humans do. We use God's mighty weapons, not worldly weapons, to knock down the strongholds of human reasoning and to destroy false arguments" (2 Corinthians 10:3-4). In Revelation 19:11-21, we are given a picture of the conclusion of history when Jesus will lead God's heavenly army to rescue his people and bring justice to those who are evil. The Bible gives us a vision that probes deeper than our eyes can see when it tells us that, in reality, God is in control and he will have the final victory.

Sabbath Reflections

What new truth about God's promises did you learn from this week's devotions?

How has this truth affected your faith?

How will you apply this truth to your daily life?

Your Key Verse for the Week:

❖ OTHER REFLECTIONS

CITY OF THE GREAT KING

How great is the LORD, how deserving of praise, in the city of our God, which sits on his holy mountain! It is high and magnificent; the whole earth rejoices to see it! Mount Zion, the holy mountain, is the city of the great King! ❖ PSALM 48:1-2

The first glimpse of the holy city of Jerusalem is an awe-inspiring sight for new-comers; even for me, though I call Israel home, the vista never fails to take my breath away. I am overcome with emotion as I look out on God's holy city. It is confirmation to me, yet again, of God's continuous care and love for his people.

So, when I read Psalm 48—a celebration song about God's holy city—it is not hard for me to identify with the psalm writer. I can envision Jerusalem's lofty beauty that "the whole earth rejoices to see." But its greatest feature is that God himself "is in Jerusalem's towers, revealing himself as its defender" (Psalm 48:3).

The psalmist and the people knew that it was God who had secured the city and had protected them from their enemies. Because of his presence, their enemies fled in terror and were destroyed. God's power and protection demonstrate his faithfulness and unfailing love for his holy dwelling place and his people.

The people rejoiced in God's goodness as they walked around the city and observed her ramparts and her citadels, which were unharmed because God had protected and preserved them. As they walked, they were encouraged to share stories of God's goodness and provision with the next generation.

In some ways, this reminds me of how we celebrate Jerusalem Day, *Yom Yerushalayim*, in Israel. One of the favorite traditions is to walk to the Western Wall, the holiest site in Jerusalem. Tens of thousands of people walk to the Old City, where they join together in celebration and prayer. In doing so, we remind one another that this very place remains God's holy city and that he will continue to protect Jerusalem.

A Christian Reflection on the City of God

Since the time of David, Jerusalem has been the place where God has made his presence known to his people. According to the New Testament, God still makes his presence known in that city, but not exclusively. The splitting of the veil of the Temple at the time of Christ's crucifixion signified the spreading of God's presence through all the earth (see Matthew 27:51). It is not that Jerusalem is no longer a special place. It is. But we don't have to go to Jerusalem to be in God's presence. Seeing Jerusalem also reminds us of the future, because God's heavenly Kingdom is pictured as a New Jerusalem in Revelation 21 and 22.

PRAISE FROM A CAVE

I will thank you, Lord, among all the people. I will sing your praises among the nations.
For your unfailing love is as high as the heavens. Your faithfulness reaches to the clouds.
❖ PSALM 57:9-10

It's easy to praise God when things are going well, but how about when life is falling apart? Do you remember to praise God when you are hurried, harried, and half out of your wits?

When David wrote these words from Psalm 57, he was hiding from Saul in a cave. Yet, in the midst of his difficult situation, he praised God. David lifted his eyes above his circumstances and put his focus on God. He knew that God was "over all the earth" (Psalm 57:5), so God could see and control everything that happened.

Out of the darkness, David said he would "wake the dawn" with his songs (Psalm 57:8). Not only would he praise God from the shelter of the cave, but he would ultimately praise God "among all the people" (Psalm 57:9). David wanted to declare God's praise in public so that others would know of God's faithfulness.

At times, life can make us feel like hiding in a cave. It can seem so overwhelming that we want to escape the pressure. But in those moments, it is important to lift our eyes above our circumstances and praise God, who is above it all. Moreover, as we lift our voices to him in praise, our situation doesn't seem as dark anymore.

In Psalm 92:2 we read, "It is good to proclaim your unfailing love in the morning, your faithfulness in the evening." The Sages explain that the morning represents times in our lives that are sunny, when God's love is obvious. But the evenings describe the dark times when God seems hidden. It is then that we must proclaim God's faithfulness—both to ourselves and to others.

As we praise God in the midst of our circumstances, we should follow David's example and tell others what God is doing in our lives. As we share our stories, we can encourage others who might be struggling as well.

A Christian Reflection on Praise in the Midst of Adversity

Paul was sitting in a prison cell when he penned his letters to the Ephesians and the Philippians. He was imprisoned because of his faith and ministry: "Everyone here, including the whole palace guard, knows that I am in chains because of Christ" (Philippians 1:13). But was Paul depressed? No, he rejoiced and praised God in prison. In particular, he rejoiced because he knew that the Good News about Jesus was being heard (see Philippians 1:15-19). Like David and Paul, consider God's greatness and goodness in spite of your circumstances, and join them in praising him.

WHAT'S YOUR WORTH?

What are mere mortals that you should think about them, human beings that you should care for them? Yet you made them only a little lower than God and crowned them with glory and honor. ❖ PSALM 8:4-5

Did you know there is a website called humansforsale.com? Based on your answers to questions concerning such criteria as your athletic ability, education, income level, weight, appearance, and sense of humor, the site will calculate a dollar amount of what you are worth.

While this site is definitely tongue-in-cheek, it does raise the question: How much do you think you are worth? More important, what criteria would you use to determine your worth?

If we're honest, too often we assess our worth by standards similar to those on the website—looks, abilities, income, popularity. And we assess others according to the same benchmarks. Is it any surprise that many of us walk around with self-esteem issues?

Thankfully, King David offers us another yardstick by which to measure our worth—God's! In Psalm 8, we discover God's measure of humans—he has made us "only a little lower than God." He has crowned us "with glory and honor." God entrusted us with his Creation, putting us in charge of everything. Truly, we are highly valued in God's eyes.

This truth was inherent from the very beginning. When God created humans, he first created one. As it says, "God created man" (Genesis 1:27, NKJV). The Sages explain that this teaches us that every person must say: "The world was created just for me!" Each person has a special contribution to make, and there never was, nor will be, anyone just like you or me. There is a specific mission that only one person can do. Just like God, we are singular—unique, divine creations.

As we understand that we have great worth *because* we have been created in God's image, we will then see others in the same light. Just as we are worth much to God, so is our neighbor, our coworker, our family member—and we must treat them accordingly.

A Christian Reflection on Our True Value

Psalm 8 reminds us of our true value. We are crowned with glory and honor, just a little lower than God. After all, we are created in God's image, and therefore reflect who he is. True, sin has marred our created nature, but sin has not changed the fact that we are created in the image of God. As we turn to God, we "reflect the glory of the Lord. And the Lord—who is the Spirit—makes us more and more like him as we are changed into his glorious image" (2 Corinthians 3:18). So, when he returns, "we will be like him, for we will see him as he really is" (1 John 3:2). Here is where we find our true value, in our relationship with God.

PERFECT HARMONY

How wonderful and pleasant it is when brothers live together in harmony!
❖ PSALM 133:1

Too often, it is very difficult to love other people, even people who are close to us. Sometimes, even our own family members are difficult to love. And then we talk about loving someone who belongs to a community of people with whom we have a two-thousand-year history of estrangement and hostility? That's a lot to ask, don't you think?

King David reminds us in Psalm 133 what a wonderful thing it is when brothers—and sisters—live together in unity. David uses images and adjectives such as *refreshing* and *precious* to describe this harmony. What he forgot to mention is how difficult such unity and harmony is to achieve!

For the past thirty years, I have spent my life attempting to build bridges of understanding, accord, and—yes—even love between Christians and Jews. Such love can be costly. It requires us to look past some of our long-held prejudices and fears and relate to individuals, rather than assigning qualities and assuming people are a certain way because they belong to a particular group.

It requires us to make a supreme effort to understand one another and learn who we truly are. We share a rich heritage of faith, and we must endeavor—even strive—to know one another. If we truly attempt to discover the sources of each other's joy and pain, then real love between our communities becomes a possibility—and perhaps, with God's help, a reality.

Only then will we be able to achieve that refreshing and precious harmony that David writes about. That doesn't mean there won't be differences of opinion, just as there are many notes in a musical chord. But it does mean that we will sing one song of praise and worship to our God, who is faithful through all generations to his people.

A Christian Reflection on Living in Harmony

The New Testament envisions the people of God drawn from many different backgrounds. We come from different nations, different economic and social strata, men and women, boys and girls. Accordingly, there is plenty of room for disagreement, but the hope of the gospel is that we will all unite around the worship and praise of God. Paul voices this desire in Romans 15:5-6: "May God, who gives this patience and encouragement, help you live in complete harmony with each other, as is fitting for followers of Christ Jesus. Then all of you can join together with one voice, giving praise and glory to God, the Father of our Lord Jesus Christ."

IN HIS IMAGE

God said, "Let us make human beings in our image, to be like us. They will reign over the fish in the sea, the birds in the sky, the livestock, all the wild animals on the earth, and the small animals that scurry along the ground." ❖ GENESIS 1:26

Both the Jewish and Christian traditions affirm that we are created in God's image. But when it comes to what that means, and in particular, how it relates to our sinfulness, Christians and Jews must part ways.

Christians believe that as a result of Adam's sin, humanity is *fallen*—that is, shackled by a sinful nature. Humans are incapable of redeeming themselves. But through an act of grace, Christians believe that God sent Jesus to die for our sin so that those who believe in him will be saved and given eternal life.

By contrast, Jews view sin as human action, not an inescapable part of our nature. We believe that man has both the ability and the duty to change his ways and initiate forgiveness through repentance.

In the Jewish view, man is created from "the dust of the earth," but he is also an "inspired being," "breathed into" by God. In Genesis 1:26, we read, "God said, 'Let us make human beings in our image, to be like us.'" The Sages ask, "Who is God talking to? Who is the 'us'?" They explain that God is speaking to the earth and the Spirit. God tells them both to combine in order to form man, who is like the earth, but who is also like the Spirit of God. As a result, humanity is of immense worth and acts as a partner with God in perfecting the world.

Here, I believe our faiths intersect again, because both Judaism and Christianity uphold the intrinsic value of life and the worth of each individual as God-created and God-imbued. That fundamental belief should influence how we view ourselves and others and how we treat our fellow human beings.

As important as it is to discuss and recognize our differences, it is equally important to seek out and celebrate our commonalities. We are, after all, made in God's image.

A Christian Reflection on the Nature of Sin

While some Christians believe we inherit a sinful nature from Adam, it is probably better to think of the story of Adam's rebellion as an example of what we all do. That is, apart from God, we put ourselves first and choose to sin. Nowhere in the Bible is our guilt attributed to Adam's sin, but rather to our own personal sin. Granted, Adam's sin introduced sin and death into the world, but "death spread to everyone, for everyone sinned" (Romans 5:12). Christians believe that everyone is a sinner (see Romans 3:9-20, citing passages from Psalms and Isaiah) and needs God's grace to change. Christians look to Jesus Christ and his death and resurrection as the agent of that change.

FIXING THE WORLD

O Israel, hope in the LORD; for with the LORD there is unfailing love.
His redemption overflows. ❖ PSALM 130:7

Some people like to fix things, whether it's a leaky faucet, a crooked picture, or a broken relationship. But what about fixing the world?

Some might laugh at that idea. Others might think that such a thing is impossible. Still others might say, "That's not my job." But to the Jews, fixing the world *is* our job. God requires us to narrow the gap between our broken reality and the messianic ideal.

We call this concept *tikun olam*, which means "fixing or redeeming the world." It is as core a principle in Judaism as salvation is to the Christian faith. *Tikun olam* presumes three underlying principles: the broken nature of our world, the inherent potential for goodness in humanity and the world, and our ability, through holy living, to restore completeness to ourselves and the entire world.

Though it's true that redemption of the world can't be fully achieved until the messianic age is ushered in, we are to do our part in fixing the world by following God's Word. In the Jewish tradition, we are active partners with God in bringing about its redemption.

This principle is illustrated during the Passover meal, when tradition requires us to open the door for Elijah the prophet, who is destined to appear just before the messianic age. Of course, Elijah doesn't really walk in; only his spirit does. So why do we open the door? The opening of the door is symbolic; it teaches us that Elijah and the messianic age won't just appear—we have a role to play. We must "open the door" by fixing the world.

Though this is a difficult concept to grasp, and it differs greatly from the Christian core belief of personal salvation, I think we can agree that doing whatever we can to "fix" our particular corner of the world is a good thing. Perhaps that might mean righting an injustice, helping the poor, or offering kindness to a stranger.

A Christian Reflection on Tikun Olam

"God saved you by his grace when you believed. And you can't take credit for this; it is a gift from God. Salvation is not a reward for the good things we have done, so none of us can boast about it. For we are God's masterpiece. He has created us anew in Christ Jesus, so we can do the good things he planned for us long ago" (Ephesians 2:8-10). This passage reminds us that although personal salvation is at the core of our religion, it does not end there. God redeemed us so we can participate in his putting right the broken world—that is, "we can do the good things." It's true that our religion is not based on works, but it inevitably leads to them.

Sabbath Reflections

What new truth about the differences between Christian and Jewish beliefs did you learn from this week's devotions?

How has this truth affected your faith?

How will you apply this truth to your daily life?

Your Key Verse for the Week:

❖ OTHER REFLECTIONS

YOU CAN'T TAKE IT WITH YOU

Don't be dismayed when the wicked grow rich and their homes become ever more splendid. For when they die, they take nothing with them. Their wealth will not follow them into the grave. ❖ PSALM 49:16-17

Several years ago, a popular bumper sticker proclaimed: "He who dies with the most toys wins!" The phrase was a tongue-in-cheek suggestion that "winning in life" means accumulating the most "stuff."

The writer of Psalm 49, however, has a very different outlook when it comes to our final end. He says that how much (or how little) wealth one amasses in life makes no difference in the end. "They cannot redeem themselves from death by paying a ransom to God" (Psalm 49:7). In the end, our money, our possessions—yes, even our most prized toys—are of no value, "for when they die, they take nothing with them" (Psalm 49:17).

It's a sobering reminder that, at death, we all will be empty-handed before God.

Though this may be a depressing thought, Psalm 49 can also be viewed as a wake-up call for how we consider our money and our possessions. The truth is that our tendency is to trust in our toys. We tend to look at our wealth as protection from the harsh realities of life and to provide security for an uncertain future. But, as the psalmist points out, such security is an illusion: "They will die, just like animals" (Psalm 49:12).

Rather than focusing on investing in earthly treasures, the psalmist recommends investing in godly pursuits. We should regard our worldly wealth as a gift received from God to be shared with others. As we bless others with our resources, God promises that he will bless us.

The psalm writer concludes, "But as for me, God will redeem my life. He will snatch me from the power of the grave" (Psalm 49:15). Our true hope and our real security lies with a gracious God.

A Christian Reflection on True Treasure

James, the brother of Jesus, blasted the rich for ignoring those whom they cheated: "Your wealth is rotting away, and your fine clothes are moth-eaten rags. Your gold and silver have become worthless. The very wealth you were counting on will eat away your flesh like fire. This treasure you have accumulated will stand as evidence against you on the day of judgment" (James 5:2-3). The parable of the rich man and Lazarus (see Luke 16:19-31) illustrates Jesus' teaching to "store up treasure . . . in heaven!" (Luke 12:33).

WORTH THE STRUGGLE

"Your name will no longer be Jacob," the man told him. "From now on you will be called Israel, because you have fought with God and with men and have won."
❖ GENESIS 32:28

The nation of Israel was birthed from an intense struggle between Jacob and God (see Genesis 32:22-32). Camped near the banks of the Jabbok River, Jacob was entangled in a wrestling match with a "man" that lasted until dawn. Jacob refused to give up until the man blessed him. Before blessing him, the man said, "From now on you will be called Israel, because you have fought with God and with men and have won."

The twelve tribes of Israel descended from the sons born to Jacob: Reuben, Simeon, Levi, Judah, Dan, Naphtali, Gad, Asher, Issachar, Zebulun, Joseph, and Benjamin. On Jacob's deathbed, the tribes were modified somewhat and Joseph's two sons, Manasseh and Ephraim, were made heads of tribes. From that time forward, Manasseh and Ephraim are listed in place of Joseph. Collectively, Jacob's descendants became known as the children of Israel, God's chosen people.

That's quite a comeback for a man whose life was filled with deception and disappointment—from the time Jacob deceived his father, Isaac, into blessing him instead of his older twin, Esau, to his struggles with his uncle Laban in winning Rachel as his wife after first being tricked into marrying her older sister, Leah. But throughout Jacob's life, we witness his strong desire for a relationship with God. For Jacob, it was worth the struggle to remain close to God.

Sometimes, we believe life will go smoothly because of our faith in God. When disappointments or difficulties come, we sometimes retreat and believe that God has let us down—or worse, has abandoned us. That's when we need to remember Jacob's story. Like Jacob, we need to persist in pursuing God, in staying close to him. We need to wrestle with our problems and our struggles, however painful, until we overcome them with God's help.

A Christian Reflection on God's Use of Flawed Servants

Jacob was a flawed man, but God used him anyway. Why did God choose Jacob? The apostle Paul points out that the story of Jacob shows "that God chooses people according to his own purposes; he calls people, but not according to their good or bad works" (Romans 9:11-12). Peter is a similarly flawed figure in the New Testament. For example, when Jesus was arrested, Peter denied that he knew him—not once, but three times. Yet as we read the book of Acts, we see how God used Peter to build the early church. The good news is that God can use us, despite our flaws, for the purpose of building up his Kingdom.

THE LOST TRIBES

In that day the Lord will reach out his hand a second time to bring back the remnant of his people—those who remain in Assyria and northern Egypt; in southern Egypt, Ethiopia, and Elam; in Babylonia, Hamath, and all the distant coastlands.
❖ ISAIAH 11:11

How is it possible to *lose* entire groups of people? To answer that question, we need a brief history lesson. Following the death of King Solomon, the nation of Israel split into two kingdoms—the northern kingdom, Israel, and the southern kingdom, Judah. The tribes of Reuben, Simeon, Dan, Naphtali, Gad, Asher, Issachar, Zebulun, Ephraim, and half the tribe of Manasseh made up the northern kingdom. Benjamin and Judah were in the southern kingdom.

In 722 BC, the Assyrians conquered the northern kingdom of Israel, and according to Scripture, many were deported to "colonies in Halah, along the banks of the Habor River in Gozan, and in the cities of the Medes" (2 Kings 17:6). The northern tribes have not been heard from since that time.

Theories on the ten "lost" tribes abound. According to the *Encyclopedia of Judaism*, a wide range of non-Jewish tribes and groups claim descent from the Israelites, such as sections of the Nigerian Yoruba tribe in Africa. Groups in Afghanistan and Pakistan have subtribal names such as Reubeni (Reuben), Efridar (Ephraim), and Ashuri (Asher), suggesting that they come from the lost tribes.

Stories of the recent discovery and return to Israel of the *Bnei Menashe*—the Jews living in India—and the Jews of Ethiopia, support the idea that Jewish exiles from the north migrated to the "four quarters of the earth" (Isaiah 11:12, NIV), just as the Bible prophesied. And as the Scriptures also foretold, God "will reach out his hand a second time to bring back the remnant of his people."

I believe we are witnessing that today as Jews from the former Soviet Union, Africa, India, South America, and around the globe are returning to Israel.

As we witness biblical prophecy being fulfilled, we can be encouraged that the Holy One we worship is faithful to all his promises.

A Christian Reflection on Fulfilled Promises

Why do we trust God to fulfill his promises to us? Because he is a promise-keeping God and his track record is 100 percent. At the heart of the Christian faith is the belief that Jesus is the promised Messiah: "All of God's promises have been fulfilled in Christ with a resounding 'Yes!'" (2 Corinthians 1:20). For that reason, we should take the advice of the author of the book of Hebrews, who writes, "Let us hold tightly without wavering to the hope we affirm, for God can be trusted to keep his promise" (Hebrews 10:23).

A SONG FOR THE JOURNEY

I was glad when they said to me, "Let us go to the house of the LORD." And now here we are, standing inside your gates, O Jerusalem. ❖ PSALM 122:1-2

Today, when we talk about a Jewish person returning to his or her homeland, we refer to it as making *aliyah*. This word was often used to describe the pilgrimage all Jews made three times a year in biblical times to Jerusalem for the festivals of Passover, Pentecost, and *Sukkot*.

In fact, Psalms 120–134 are often called "pilgrim psalms," or "songs of ascent." These psalms were typically sung by those who journeyed to the Temple in Jerusalem for the annual festivals. Each psalm is considered a step along the journey. It begins with Psalm 120, as the pilgrim sets out from a distant land, surrounded by enemies: "How I suffer in far-off Meshech. It pains me to live in distant Kedar. I am tired of living among people who hate peace" (Psalm 120:5-6).

The journey continues in Psalm 121, as the psalm writer expresses the hope and trust he has in God's protection, day and night. Read aloud these beautiful words of God's ever-present watchfulness: "Indeed, he who watches over Israel never slumbers or sleeps" (Psalm 121:4). In Psalm 122:2, the pilgrim acknowledges his entrance into Jerusalem: "And now we are here, standing inside your gates, O Jerusalem." In the remaining pilgrim psalms, the pilgrim moves toward the Temple itself—the very spiritual center of Israel.

The psalms of ascent can also be seen as a metaphor for our own spiritual journey. Just as getting to Jerusalem, to the Temple, required an arduous, physical climb, so too does spiritual growth. If we are to grow closer to God, we must commit to hard work, long hours, introspection, and perseverance. But when we arrive, we will join with the other pilgrims who succeeded in completing the journey: "Yes, the LORD has done amazing things for us! What joy!" (Psalm 126:3).

A Christian Reflection on Our Spiritual Journey

Thinking of our spiritual journey as making *aliyah* to the Temple in Jerusalem is a powerful metaphor, particularly when we realize that the Temple represents "heaven on earth," the place where God chose to make his presence known among his people. It is interesting, though, that the description of the heavenly Jerusalem in the book of Revelation has "no temple in the city." Why? Because "the Lord God Almighty and the Lamb are its temple" (Revelation 21:22). No special holy place will be needed, because God's presence will permeate all of heaven.

A LAND PROMISED

The LORD had said to Abram, "Leave your native country, your relatives, and your father's family, and go to the land that I will show you." ❖ GENESIS 12:1

Since the time when God first called Abraham, his descendants—the children of Israel—were promised a land. But it was a long time in coming. Only after enduring four hundred years of slavery under Egyptian oppression, forty years of wandering in the desert after God rescued them, and then conquering the land were they able to call this land home.

Today, God's children are once again home in this Promised Land. But again, it was a long time coming. The Israelites were exiled from their land not once but twice, finally expelled to the four corners of the world by the Romans in AD 70.

The exiled Jews settled into new lands, but it was never home. And they were never wholly welcomed wherever they went. When persecution and organized killings ensued, many Jews returned to the land that had always been at the center of their hearts and souls—*Eretz Yisrael.*

Beginning in the 1800s through today, waves of Jews have returned to the land of Israel during times of persecution and oppression. We call these waves *aliyah,* based on a Hebrew term that means "to ascend" or "to go up" that was used to describe the Jewish pilgrims "going up" to Jerusalem to worship God (see Psalm 122:4).

"Going up" makes sense when you understand Jerusalem's location in the hills of Israel, rising above the surrounding plains. It is also the spiritual center of Israel and the place where God's presence dwelled in his Temple. When Jews return to Israel, they are returning to their spiritual center, to a land promised to them since the time of Abraham.

A Christian Reflection on Making Aliyah

As Christians, we have likened our spiritual journey to the New Jerusalem (which represents heaven, and in which there is no Temple) to the Jews' spiritual journey, *aliyah.* A second New Testament passage also uses the language of *aliyah,* but here it speaks of a present spiritual reality. We don't have to wait until heaven to have a taste of an intimate relationship with God, because "you have come to God himself, who is the judge over all things. You have come to the spirits of the righteous ones in heaven who have now been made perfect. You have come to Jesus, the one who mediates the new covenant between God and people, and to the sprinkled blood, which speaks of forgiveness instead of crying out for vengeance like the blood of Abel" (Hebrews 12:23-24).

ON THE SHOULDERS OF NATIONS

This is what the Sovereign LORD says: "See, I will give a signal to the godless nations. They will carry your little sons back to you in their arms; they will bring your daughters on their shoulders." ❖ ISAIAH 49:22

As I heard the Scriptures read in synagogue when I was a child, I often puzzled over this particular verse in Isaiah. What could it possibly mean that God would signal other nations to carry his sons and daughters back to their homeland, Jerusalem? How was that going to happen?

The verse comes in the context of other promises God made to his people: "I would not forget you! See, I have written your name on the palms of my hands" (Isaiah 49:15-16). God promised that he would never forget Israel, his people. Just as he did during the time of the Exodus, God heard his people's cries and promised to restore them.

Such beautiful promises! These words have been a source of comfort for the Jewish people, not only during the exile to Babylon but also to Jews who have been scattered throughout the earth since AD 70. But the question was always, How was God going to use the nations to bring his people back?

I think we're seeing the answer today. God is summoning Christians from among the nations—from the United States, Canada, South America, and around the world—to help bring his people back to Israel through ministries such as The Fellowship's On Wings of Eagles. Today, we are seeing Jews returning to Israel from the four corners of the earth—from the former Soviet Union, Africa, India, Yemen, Morocco—and it is faithful Christians who are carrying our sons and daughters back.

I thank God for his provision, for his moving in the hearts of so many and stirring them to answer the call. I am thankful for the partnership of my Christian friends in helping to fulfill this prophecy. We all can rejoice in serving a God who proves himself faithful over and over again to fulfill all he has promised.

A Christian Reflection on the Future of God's People

God's fulfillment of his promise in Isaiah 49 to bring Israel back to the land after their scattering among the nations encourages our firm confidence that God will fulfill all his promises. As Christians, we believe that God fulfilled his promise that the Messiah would come in the person of Jesus. But there is the further wonderful promise that Jesus will return and bring us into God's presence. When we tire and experience distress, we should remember passages such as 2 Thessalonians 1:7: "God will provide rest for you who are being persecuted and also for us when the Lord Jesus appears from heaven."

Sabbath Reflections

What new truth about the fulfillment of biblical prophecy did you learn from this week's devotions?

How has this truth affected your faith?

How will you apply this truth to your daily life?

Your Key Verse for the Week:

❖ OTHER REFLECTIONS

A SACRIFICE OF THANKS

Make thankfulness your sacrifice to God, and keep the vows you made to the Most High. Then call on me when you are in trouble, and I will rescue you, and you will give me glory. ❖ PSALM 50:14-15

We all know what it means to go through the motions—to give less than our full effort to a project, a team, or even a relationship. But do we ever think about whether we are just going through the motions in our relationship with God? Because we can't see God eye to eye, it's easy to be lulled into complacency in our relationship with him.

Yet it's very clear from Psalm 50 that not only does God notice when we are going through the motions, he also will judge us for our lack of faithfulness. In Psalm 50:8, the people clearly were obedient in bringing their sacrifices to the Temple, as God said, "I have no complaint about your sacrifices."

That wasn't the issue. Rather, it was the people's attitudes. They were just going through the motions, leading God to remind them, "I do not need the bulls from your barns or the goats from your pens. For all the animals of the forest are mine, and I own the cattle on a thousand hills" (Psalm 50:9-10).

God didn't need their stuff. What God wanted was their sacrifice of thankfulness and their trust in him. What God wanted was their hearts. God wanted their righteousness, not empty rituals.

King David understood that when he confessed and repented of his sin with Bathsheba. He writes, "You do not desire a sacrifice, or I would offer one. . . . The sacrifice you desire is a broken spirit. You will not reject a broken and repentant heart" (Psalm 51:16-17). When it comes to serving God, the essential component is our hearts.

Although the sacrificial system was abolished when the Temple was destroyed, we can be guilty of the same thing as the people in Psalm 50 when we participate in religious activity but our hearts are not wholly in it. We honor God when we obey him out of heartfelt love and true gratitude for his many blessings.

A Christian Reflection on Authentic Sacrifice

God doesn't want us to just go through the motions. He wants our full and enthusiastic worship in grateful response for everything he has done for us. Paul puts it this way: "Dear brothers and sisters, I plead with you to give your bodies to God because of all he has done for you. Let them be a living and holy sacrifice—the kind he will find acceptable. This is truly the way to worship him" (Romans 12:1). God wants our whole selves to be devoted to him. Remember that the next time you worship God. Are you giving him your all?

A SEASON OF MIRACLES

O God, your ways are holy. Is there any god as mighty as you? You are the God of great wonders! You demonstrate your awesome power among the nations.
❖ PSALM 77:13-14

This is a season of miracles and celebrations. My Christian friends celebrate the birth of Jesus at Christmas, and my Jewish brothers and sisters celebrate the spiritual and military victory during the celebration of *Hanukkah*. At the center of both of these celebrations is our God of miracles.

As the psalm writer notes, "Is there any god as mighty as you?" It's certainly a theme echoed throughout the Scriptures. After the miraculous escape from Egypt through the parting of the Red Sea, Moses and the people of Israel erupt in song: "Who is like you among the gods, O LORD—glorious in holiness, awesome in splendor, performing great wonders?" (Exodus 15:11).

Christmas and *Hanukkah* are times to remember that we worship and serve a God who is completely unique. He alone is able to perform mighty deeds for those who love him. He alone is powerful and worthy of our love and adoration. God alone is able to intervene in human history and work miracles on behalf of his people.

Remembering God's miracles and faithfulness sustained the people of Israel through their many difficulties and enabled them to act when all avenues seemed closed to them. *Hanukkah* reminds us of the importance of *bitachon*, or "trust in God." It was the Jews' trust in a loving and caring God that prompted them, the few and weak, to rise up against the many and mighty. It was their faith in the God of miracles that gave them courage to light the Temple *menorah* with the last remaining flask of pure oil. They acted because they knew that God was capable and trustworthy.

When we are faced with obstacles and overwhelming difficulties, we need to remember how God has acted on our behalf in the past and how good he has been to us. Then, we can step out and act in faith, knowing that he will continue to care for us.

A Christian Reflection on the Unique One

Time and again, the Bible rejoices in God's uniqueness. As Moses said, "There is no one like the LORD our God" (Exodus 8:10). In the dramatic opening to the Gospel of John, the writer refers to Jesus as the "unique One" (John 1:18). No one is like him. How can God be unique and Jesus be unique? John answers our question when he says that Jesus "is himself God." We are here dealing with the mystery of the Trinity, that God is one but three—three in one—the Father, Son, and Holy Spirit. To see Jesus is to see God. "He has revealed God to us."

SPIRITUAL VICTORIES!

Now I know that the LORD rescues his anointed king. He will answer him from his holy heaven and rescue him by his great power. Some nations boast of their chariots and horses, but we boast in the name of the LORD our God. ❖ PSALM 20:6-7

Like many Jewish holidays, the celebration of *Hanukkah* has multiple meanings. While it is a peaceful and happy celebration in the Jewish year, it primarily commemorates a military victory in the year 165 BC of a Jewish group called the Maccabees over their much greater and more powerful Greek and Syrian oppressors.

It was during this time that King Antiochus tried to impose his pagan beliefs on the Jewish people and make them give up their faith and practices, such as dietary observances and circumcision. He even put a statue of Zeus in the holy Temple! Finally, a group of Jews revolted against their oppressors. On the twenty-fifth day of the Jewish month of *Kislev*—which usually falls in December—they were able to defeat their enemies.

For the Jews, this was as much a spiritual victory as a military victory. In over-coming the much superior forces of their foes, they were able to regain control of the Temple, cleanse it of all foreign idols, and rededicate it to God. That's what *Hanukkah* means—rededication. Through this victory, this courageous band of Jews was able to preserve their faith for generations to come. If not for the miracle of the Jewish military defeat over the Syrian-Greek tyrants, there might be no Judaism and, subsequently, no Christianity.

The miracles of this victory—both spiritual and military—remind us of how God works in history and in our lives. The Jewish people acted against the odds, trusting in God's salvation. But they relied on God's saving grace only after exhausting their own human powers. They recognized, as did David a thousand years earlier, that while God alone gives victory, we also have a role in initiating that action. We, too, must play our part in order for God to work through us and in us.

A Christian Reflection on Pride

Due to our pride, we are often tempted to boast in ourselves. The apostle Paul wants us to know that our relationship with God has nothing to do with our inherent good-ness, our looks, our wealth, or anything having to do with us. Our relationship with God is a matter of grace. Indeed, Paul goes further and says, "God chose things the world considers foolish in order to shame those who think they are wise. And he chose things that are powerless to shame those who are powerful" (1 Corinthians 1:27). For these reasons, we can't boast about ourselves but "only about the LORD" (1 Corinthians 1:31).

A LITTLE BIT OF FAITH

*Search for the LORD and for his strength; continually seek him. Remember the wonders
he has performed, his miracles, and the rulings he has given.*
❖ PSALM 105:4-5

How much faith does it take for God to work miracles? Truly, all it takes is a willing
heart and one small step. Throughout the Scriptures, we see evidence of this. Remember
the Israelites as they prepared to enter the Promised Land, only to encounter a raging,
flood-sodden Jordan River? What did God tell them to do? Take one step forward . . .
one step into those waters, and God would do the rest.

Or what about the widow of Zarephath? In faith, she used her last handful of flour
and cooking oil to make a meal for the prophet Elijah. In return, she was the recipient
of an incredible miracle—she and her son were able to eat from an endless supply of
flour and water during a time of famine and drought (see 1 Kings 17:8-24).

The celebration of *Hanukkah* provides yet another example. When the Jews
reclaimed the Temple and wanted to relight the eternal flame, they were faced with a
dilemma: There was only enough pure oil to keep the flame burning for one day. They
could either light the flame for one day or leave the Temple unclean without the flame
until the new oil arrived.

What did they do? They trusted in God, lit the flame, and witnessed a miracle—
the lamp stayed lit for eight days until the new oil came!

Some may say, "Miracles don't happen today," but I don't believe that's true. The
very existence of Israel and the continued survival of the Jewish people is a miracle.
Every Jew brought home to the Holy Land is a miracle.

Every miracle—large or small—begins with an act of obedience. All it takes is one
small step toward God's promises to us, and then he will work.

A Christian Reflection on Moving Mountains

On one occasion, the disciples could not heal a demon-possessed boy, so they asked
Jesus why they weren't able to cast out the demon. Jesus answered, "You don't have
enough faith. . . . I tell you the truth, if you had faith even as small as a mustard seed,
you could say to this mountain, 'Move from here to there,' and it would move. Nothing
would be impossible" (Matthew 17:20). Jesus is not saying that great faith allows his
followers to do magical tricks. He is saying that great faith will allow his followers to
accomplish great things for God. Faith, or confidence, in God is what allows us to take
that first step that leads to miracles.

REDEDICATE YOURSELVES

May you be completely faithful to the LORD our God. May you always obey his decrees and commands, just as you are doing today. ❖ 1 KINGS 8:61

Hanukkah is a time of rededication. In fact, the word *Hanukkah* means "rededication." After the victory of the Maccabees over their oppressors, the people immediately began the process of cleaning out the idols from the Temple and rededicating it to God.

In the Jewish tradition, *Hanukkah* is an opportunity for us to rededicate and purify ourselves before God. We see this modeled during the dedication service when the very first Temple was completed 480 years after the Israelites had escaped from Egypt.

After seven years, the building of God's Temple in Jerusalem was completed, and King Solomon summoned everyone to assemble in Jerusalem for the dedication ceremony. But it was more than just blessing a building. It was also an opportunity for the people to rededicate themselves to God's service.

The word *Hanukkah* comes from a Hebrew word meaning "education." This is because any rededication has to be accompanied by reeducation. We learn many things throughout our lives, but they are often forgotten or set aside. During any rededication, we remember our ideals and recommit ourselves to what we stand for.

This is exactly what King Solomon did during the dedication of the Temple. He reminded the people of God's faithfulness to them. "Praise the LORD who has given rest to his people Israel, just as he promised. Not one word has failed of all the wonderful promises he gave through his servant Moses" (1 Kings 8:56). And he encouraged the people to "be completely faithful to the LORD our God [and] . . . always obey his decrees and commands, just as you are doing today" (1 Kings 8:61).

What a wonderful reminder for us as well! Solomon's prayer of dedication is as appropriate today as it was when the Temple was completed. Let us use this Season of Lights to rededicate ourselves to serving and loving God.

A Christian Reflection on Rededication

Our relationship with God is not simply the result of a one-time decision. Our life of faith is full of challenges, and we need to daily rededicate our lives to follow God. The author of Hebrews warns his readers against becoming "spiritually dull and indifferent" and encourages them "to follow the example of those who are going to inherit God's promises because of their faith and endurance" (Hebrews 6:12). Communion, or the Lord's Supper, can also be a time of formal, intentional rededication, a recommitment to "the new covenant between God and his people—an agreement confirmed with [Jesus'] blood, which is poured out as a sacrifice for you" (Luke 22:20).

WHAT'S YOUR STAND?

But Daniel was determined not to defile himself by eating the food and wine given to them by the king. He asked the chief of staff for permission not to eat these unacceptable foods. ❖ DANIEL 1:8

As we have read, the celebration of *Hanukkah* has many lessons for us. It is a reminder that we serve a God of miracles; it's a time of reflection and rededication. It is also a reminder of our need to take a stand, when necessary, against the culture.

In AD 165, King Antiochus tried to impose on the Jews the dominant Hellenistic culture—and many were seduced into following the "enlightened" ways of Hellenism. The very survival of Judaism was at stake, until a small band of Jews decided enough was enough. For three years, this group of determined Jews fought against their oppressors. They were willing to pay whatever price was necessary—including their lives—because they had resolved not to go along with the status quo.

This small group of Jews, known as the Maccabees, resolved to take a stand—and then did something about it. We find this same principle in the opening chapters of the book of Daniel, when the young Daniel and his friends were taken captive and exiled to Babylon. They were chosen to be trained in the king's service, but part of that training meant they had to eat food from the king's kitchen. To Daniel, eating that food was the first step toward dishonoring God by accepting the culture he was in.

Even though it meant defying the king's order, Daniel made up his mind to remain devoted to his principles and to God. Like the Maccabees and their brave followers, Daniel determined to do what was right and not give in to the pressures around him.

As people of faith, we often are confronted with pressure to compromise our beliefs. We face temptations daily to live like the world around us. When those temptations and those pressures arise, remember the stories of the Maccabees and Daniel. Then act as they did, and resolve to stand against the culture and obey God.

A *Christian Reflection* on Taking a Stand

The New Testament, too, warns about the seductive power of the surrounding culture that threatens to undermine our faith and obedience. John tells us in no uncertain terms, "Do not love this world nor the things it offers you, for when you love the world, you do not have the love of the Father in you. For the world offers only a craving for physical pleasure, a craving for everything we see, and pride in our achievements and possessions. These are not from the Father, but are from this world" (1 John 2:15-16).

Sabbath Reflections

*What new truth about the Jewish observance of Hanukkah did you learn
from this week's devotions?*

How has this truth affected your faith?

How will you apply this truth to your daily life?

Your Key Verse for the Week:

❖ OTHER REFLECTIONS

LET OUR LIGHT SHINE

Arise, Jerusalem! Let your light shine for all to see. For the glory of the LORD rises to shine on you. Darkness as black as night covers all the nations of the earth, but the glory of the LORD rises and appears over you. ✦ ISAIAH 60:1-2

This season is a special time of year for both Christians and Jews as we celebrate and honor the God of miracles and the God of light.

During *Hanukkah*, we celebrate the miraculous spiritual and military victories of the Jewish people over their oppressors, who were much stronger and more powerful. The events that transpired during that first *Hanukkah* point to a God who was faithful to his people to protect and preserve them. At Christmas, my Christian friends, too, celebrate a miracle—the miraculous birth of a child, the one they recognize as God's Son.

This is a season of light as well, of God intervening in human history to bring light to his people. At *Hanukkah*, we celebrate the fact that the light of the Temple *menorah* miraculously lasted for eight days—well beyond the one-day allotment of oil that the people had on hand.

My friends, I think we also can celebrate together that God has called his people of faith to be a light to the world, to shine his glory over the thick darkness. How do we do that? I think as we work together for the good of others, to help and comfort the homeless, the orphans, and the widows, we bring God's light to needy people. As we seek to understand and honor our differences, yet come together in those areas and bonds we do share, we bring a great light to the world.

I strongly believe that, as each of us in our way becomes a better Christian or a better Jew, we work together for a better world, and we make a difference for his name's sake and to bring his glory to all people everywhere.

A Christian Reflection on Not Hiding Our Light

Jesus makes it very clear to his disciples that we are to be a light in the world and that we are light by doing good deeds, helping others, and making the world better. In his Sermon on the Mount, he told his listeners, "You are the light of the world—like a city on a hilltop that cannot be hidden. No one lights a lamp and then puts it under a basket. Instead, a lamp is placed on a stand, where it gives light to everyone in the house. In the same way, let your good deeds shine out for all to see, so that everyone will praise your heavenly Father" (Matthew 5:14-16). How is your light shining today?

CHOOSE YOUR PART

Then [the king] said, "Cut the living child in two, and give half to one woman and half to the other!" Then the woman who was the real mother of the living child, and who loved him very much, cried out, "Oh no, my lord! Give her the child—please do not kill him!" But the other woman said, "All right, he will be neither yours nor mine; divide him between us!" ❖ 1 KINGS 3:25-26

King Solomon had one wish. God appeared to Solomon in a dream and invited him to ask for anything he wanted. King Solomon chose wisdom so that he could best serve God in his role as king.

Immediately afterward, two women approached the king about a dispute over a baby. The first woman claimed that the other woman had stolen her baby after accidentally killing her own child by rolling over on him during the night. The second woman denied the claim and insisted that the living child was hers.

With his newfound wisdom, King Solomon discerned the truth by offering to cut the baby in two and give each woman half. As Solomon anticipated, the true mother was revealed when one of the women pleaded with the king to give the whole child to the other woman rather than put the child to death.

When reading this story, we generally marvel at King Solomon's divine wisdom. However, when we consider the attitudes of the women in the passage, a profound message emerges: The baby's true mother teaches us that there are things more important in life than being right.

We all experience conflicts; sometimes, we are in the right and know that we can prove it. However, the question we must ask is this: *At what cost?* Obviously the life of a child is more important than being right. But so is a child's self-esteem. So is a marriage. So is a friendship. The list goes on.

In every conflict, we can choose to be like the second woman—so intent on making the other person wrong that she is willing to give up everything. Or we can be like the first woman, who focused on what was really important to her and was able to let the other person "be right" in order to preserve what she truly cared about.

A Christian Reflection on Conflict

James cuts to the quick when he talks about the motivation for conflict. "What is causing the quarrels and fights among you? Don't they come from the evil desires at war within you?" (James 4:1). If we are honest, we will recognize the truth of James's diagnosis of the reason for conflict among us. We are selfish and we want our own way. What is the solution to such conflicts? Turn from our demands and surrender to God. Ask God for what you don't have (see James 4:2) and then wait patiently for his answer.

A PLACE OF WORSHIP

But will God really live on earth? Why, even the highest heavens cannot contain you.
How much less this Temple I have built! ❖ I KINGS 8:27

At the inauguration of the Temple built for God by King Solomon, he expressed the following: "But will God really live on earth? Why, even the highest heavens cannot contain you." How in the world can an infinite God possibly be contained in a finite physical building? King Solomon makes a good point. Of course, his question is rhetorical, and he is simply teaching us a very important lesson about every place of worship for all time.

If we think that any place of worship is God's address, then we are gravely mistaken. God isn't contained to any one space. God is everywhere. As a great rabbi, the Rebbe of Kotzk, once said when asked where God is, "God is everywhere you let him in!"

So if God is everywhere, then what was the purpose of building him a home? And why do we still build places for prayer today?

Places of worship are like a pair of glasses. They are a window. They allow us to see and experience God in a way that we could not have otherwise. Although God himself is everywhere, we experience his presence more in some places than others.

In today's places of worship, and a million times more in the Temples that once stood, a person was in the presence of God in a much more concrete way than if he were anywhere else. Through this greater encounter with God, that person would be changed. His prayers would be changed. They would be more powerful and more passionate. And that is why they were more likely to be answered. Not because God is any different in a house of worship, but because *we* are different in such holy spaces, and our prayers become more aligned with God's will for us when we are more connected to him.

A Christian Reflection on Places of Worship

Many people today avoid going to places of worship, believing that the most important thing is their own personal relationship with God. Who needs other people? People can be difficult and can sometimes make worship harder. Interestingly, the New Testament sometimes speaks about the Temple as made up of people rather than stones and wood. Paul challenges the Corinthians to remember that "all of you together are the temple of God" (1 Corinthians 3:16). God is with us as individuals, but some biblical passages teach that he is present with us in a special way as we meet corporately (see Matthew 18:20).

IN GOD WE TRUST

But Elijah said to her, "Don't be afraid! Go ahead and do just what you've said, but make a little bread for me first. Then use what's left to prepare a meal for yourself and your son. For this is what the LORD, the God of Israel, says: There will always be flour and olive oil left in your containers until the time when the LORD sends rain and the crops grow again!" ❖ I KINGS 17:13-14

During a famine in the land of Israel, the prophet Elijah encountered a widow with just about nothing left. And he gave her advice that we all can benefit from in our times of need.

When Elijah met the widow, he asked her for some water and bread. She explained that she had only enough flour and olive oil to make one last meal for herself and her son. After that, she expected that they would die.

In response, Elijah said to her, "Don't be afraid! Go ahead and do just what you've said." In other words, there is no sense in worrying. Go on with your life and do what you need to do. Then Elijah gave her another set of instructions: "But make a little bread for me first. Then use what's left to prepare a meal for yourself and your son." In other words, share what you have with others.

Then comes the kicker—in return, Elijah announced a promise from God: "There will always be flour and olive oil left in your containers." With God by your side, anything is possible!

What a great message for difficult times: *Don't worry, share,* and *have faith.*

Now here's the thing: God didn't deliver twenty jars of flour to the widow the next morning. She didn't open her pantry and find twenty jugs full of oil either. The widow would not be able to *see* where her sustenance was going to come from. Instead, she would have to trust God for his provision.

In difficult times, we all like to look into our bank accounts and know that we will be okay. However, no matter how much we have in the bank today, at some point there is an end.

But there is no end to what God can do for us when we trust him.

A Christian Reflection on the Faith to Share

Whether we are poor or rich, we find it hard to share. Why? Because we put our trust in our money and believe we need it to rescue us from life's difficulties. It takes faith to give up our money to help others. Sharing opens us up to potential problems and reveals that we put our trust in God and not in our own resources. Paul speaks to the importance of faith in giving when he reminds those he is encouraging to give that "God will generously provide all you need. Then you will always have everything you need and plenty left over to share with others" (2 Corinthians 9:8).

REAL MAGIC

When Ahab got home, he told Jezebel everything Elijah had done, including the way
he had killed all the prophets of Baal. So Jezebel sent this message to Elijah: "May the
gods strike me and even kill me if by this time tomorrow I have not killed you just as
you killed them." ❖ I KINGS 19:1-2

The people of Israel had gathered at Mount Carmel for the ultimate standoff. On one
side were 450 self-proclaimed prophets of the god Baal, backed by King Ahab and
Queen Jezebel. On the other side was the lone figure of Elijah the prophet.

The challenge: to offer a sacrifice that would bring down fire from the heavens and
thus be devoured. The goal: to prove who represented the true God.

The 450 prophets went first. They built an altar, called out to Baal, and offered a
bull. But nothing happened. They performed a ritual dance. Nothing happened. They
called out louder, inflicted wounds on themselves, and "prophesied." Nothing happened.

Then it was Elijah's turn. He built a stone altar and dug a trench around it. He
placed wood on the altar and a bull on the wood. To add to the drama, he drenched
the offering, the altar, and the trench with water. Elijah invoked the name of the Lord,
and a fire immediately descended from heaven and devoured the offering, the altar,
and even the water in the trench.

The contest was won, and the nation of Israel proclaimed that the Lord is God.
The grand spectacle concluded with a thunderous rainstorm, putting an end to a
three-year drought.

So what was Jezebel thinking when, after all this, she vowed to kill Elijah the very
next day? Didn't she fear a revolt if she murdered the most popular figure in the entire
kingdom?

Jezebel planned to kill Elijah "tomorrow" because she knew that the effect of
his showmanship would already begin to wane. Jezebel understood that miraculous
moments are nothing if not followed up by daily action.

Lasting change doesn't happen in a single moment. Inspiring moments can cata-
lyze change, but they do not guarantee it. It is only when we are able to experience
God in the "everyday" that change is really possible.

A Christian Reflection on the Importance of the Everyday

In the parable of the rich man and Lazarus (see Luke 16:19-31), after the rich man
realizes his fate, he wants to warn his brothers by having Lazarus appear to them from
the dead. Surely, such an event would motivate them to change their lives. Abraham
wisely refuses, saying that the appearance of a dead man won't change their lives.
Why? Because as Rabbi Eckstein points out, the experience would wear off. Perhaps
the brothers would later think they had a bad dream brought on by something they
ate. What could create the change the rich man wanted in his brothers? Only a daily
relationship with God.

THE SOUND OF SILENCE

Give [King Ahab] this message: "This is what the LORD says: 'Wasn't it enough that you killed Naboth? Must you rob him, too? Because you have done this, dogs will lick your blood at the very place where they licked the blood of Naboth!'"
❖ I KINGS 21:19

King Ahab was known for his evil deeds, but it was the murder of an Israelite named Naboth that got him in the most trouble with God.

You see, Ahab had his eye on Naboth's vineyard. He offered to buy it from him or give him a better one in exchange. Naboth refused the offer, which made Ahab very angry. When Ahab's wife, Jezebel, heard about this, she wouldn't stand for it. She conspired with the elders of Naboth's town to set him up and make it look as if he had cursed God and the king. Her plan was carried to fruition when Naboth was framed and then stoned to death for his alleged crime. His vineyard was then free for the taking.

However, when Ahab went to claim the vineyard, Elijah was there and gave him a message from God: "The dogs will lick your blood at the very place where they licked the blood of Naboth." Ahab responded cryptically, "So, my enemy, you have found me!" In other words, "You are biased and only find me guilty because we are enemies—the truth is I didn't do it!" To which Elijah replied, "I have come because you have sold yourself to what is evil in the LORD's sight" (1 Kings 21:20).

Edmund Burke famously expressed this same principle thousands of years later: "The only thing necessary for evil to flourish is for good men to do nothing." To be silent is to concede. Ahab knew about Jezebel's evil plans, and yet he allowed her to carry them out. Even though he did not touch even so much as a single hair on Naboth's head, he was completely responsible for his murder.

We are living in times when evil has reared its ugly head once again. Overseas, and in our own backyards, there is no shortage of injustice. We must speak up. We dare not remain silent, lest we be held responsible.

A Christian Reflection on Speaking for Justice

Jesus is on the side of justice. Quoting Psalm 45, the author of Hebrews reminds us of these words concerning Jesus: "Your throne, O God, endures forever and ever. You rule with a scepter of justice. You love justice and hate evil. Therefore, O God, your God has anointed you, pouring out the oil of joy on you more than on anyone else" (Hebrews 1:8-9). He is the one who came to "proclaim justice to the nations" (Matthew 12:18) and pronounced blessings on "those who hunger and thirst for justice" (Matthew 5:6). Knowing these things, how can his followers remain silent in the face of injustice?

Sabbath Reflections

What new truth about the life of the prophet Elijah did you learn from this week's devotions?

How has this truth affected your faith?

How will you apply this truth to your daily life?

Your Key Verse for the Week:

❖ OTHER REFLECTIONS

ASK AND YOU SHALL RECEIVE

You shall have no foreign god among you; you shall not worship any god other than me.
I am the LORD your God, who brought you up out of Egypt. Open wide your mouth
and I will fill it. ❖ PSALM 81:9-10, NIV

True story: A friend of mine was feeling pretty down one day when she had one of
those encounters with a human being that leaves you feeling like you've really had an
exchange with a messenger from God. She was filling up her car at a gas station that
she hardly ever goes to when a homeless man named Daniel approached her.

Daniel handed her a rose that he had made from palm fronds he was carrying
on his back and said, "If you have a dollar, I'd appreciate it. If you don't because you
only have a credit card, that's okay. It's yours." My friend didn't have a dollar, so she
took out a twenty and folded it up so he wouldn't see what it was. But somehow, even
folded, Daniel knew that it was more than a dollar.

He said, "You know, the Almighty takes care of my needs. I never have to ask for
my needs, but if I want something, I have to ask. Today, I asked for a bath and a place
to sleep, because I didn't have either last night. And then he sent me to you."

In Psalm 81:9-10, King David shares with us the secret to getting what we want.
These verses can be broken down into three main ideas. First, "You shall have no foreign god." Don't think that anything or anybody in the world can help you like God
can. Nothing and no one is more powerful than God. Period.

Second, "I am the LORD . . . who brought you up out of Egypt." Not only is the
Lord the most powerful source in the universe, he is willing and able to wield his
power on your behalf. Just as he rescued the Jewish people from Egypt, he can and
will help you, too.

And finally, "Open wide your mouth and I will fill it." Once you put your faith
in God, all you have to do is open your mouth in prayer and ask him for what you
want. And if what you ask for is in your best interest, he will fill your request with
joy and love at exactly the right time.

A Christian Reflection on Asking and Receiving

In teaching his disciples about prayer, Jesus gave these instructions: "I tell you, keep
on asking, and you will receive what you ask for. Keep on seeking, and you will find.
Keep on knocking, and the door will be opened to you. For everyone who asks,
receives. Everyone who seeks, finds. And to everyone who knocks, the door will be
opened" (Luke 11:9-10). Persistence in prayer helps us understand our own needs and
does more to change *our* hearts and minds than God's. As we persist in prayer, we are
better able to recognize God's work in our lives.

PARTNERS WITH ZION

Wherever this Jewish remnant is found, let their neighbors contribute toward their expenses by giving them silver and gold, supplies for the journey, and livestock, as well as a voluntary offering for the Temple of God in Jerusalem. ❖ EZRA 1:4

Theodor Herzl, considered by many to be the father of the modern State of Israel, kept a diary detailing the journey he underwent trying to birth Israel. He wrote about those who helped him, and one name in particular is mentioned more than any other—the Reverend William Henry Hechler.

The greatest ally of the Jewish journalist from Vienna was an English priest. Hechler's partnership with Herzl played a fundamental role in the reestablishment of the State of Israel and the return of the Jews to their homeland.

Partnership between Jews and Gentiles for the sake of Israel goes back thousands of years to biblical times. The book of Ezra opens with a monumental declaration by Cyrus, king of Persia. Seventy years after the Jewish nation had been exiled from their homeland by the Babylonians, the Persians took control and initiated the Jewish return to their land. Not only did Cyrus grant permission for the return and rebuilding of the Temple, but he also urged local residents to donate to the cause. It was with the help of these Gentile friends that the Jewish people were able to return to Israel.

Sound familiar? Just as the initial return to Israel was only possible because of the partnership between Jews and Gentiles, today's return to Zion is the product of a Jewish and non-Jewish alliance once again.

I don't think that's an accident. God wants to give all people a chance to be involved in the rebuilding of the Holy Land. Israel may be the homeland of the Jewish people, but the Holy Land contains everyone's past, and also their future. Scripture tells us that the third and final Temple will be a house of prayer for *all* nations. So it is only fitting that every nation should have the opportunity to contribute to its making.

A Christian Reflection on Repentance, Gratitude, and Justice

On what grounds should Gentiles, and Christians in particular, contribute to Jewish restoration to the land of Israel? Though Christians debate whether a third Temple is part of God's redemptive plan, it is true that Israel contains everyone's past and is for everyone. This recognition should engender an attitude of thankfulness that evokes our thoughtful support. Further, as we have seen, Gentiles in the past have sinned against the Jews in horrendous ways, and repentance involves more than words—it involves actions. Lastly, those who follow Christ should be those who proclaim justice, which also leads us to help rebuild the Holy Land.

WHEN OPPORTUNITY KNOCKS...

Then God stirred the hearts of the priests and Levites and the leaders of the tribes of Judah and Benjamin to go to Jerusalem to rebuild the Temple of the LORD.
❖ EZRA 1 : 5

At first blush, the response to King Cyrus's declaration that the Jewish people could return to their homeland seemed positive. People left Babylon and went to Jerusalem. But who, exactly, went? Or, more important, who did *not* go? The overwhelming question remains: Why didn't every last exile immediately return to Jerusalem?

This time period is known as *Shivat Zion*, which means "the Return to Zion." One of the most important things to understand about that period is that most Jews did not participate. They chose to remain in Babylon. In fact, Jewish tradition teaches us that had the Jews come back to Israel in droves, they would have built the holy Temple and ushered in the messianic era right then and there! Why did so many Jews miss this grand opportunity?

The answer, in a word, is *comfort*. The exile lasted only seventy years, but that was enough time for the Jewish people to become comfortable in their new surroundings. Though the people never forgot Jerusalem—Jerusalem was always the dream—Babylon had become their reality. For many Jews, it was simply easier to stay.

Change, even for the good, is not easy. It requires us to leave our comfort zone and venture into the unknown. That can be hard, and change may bring about difficult consequences. But there are also consequences for resisting change, and those consequences can be tragic. More than two thousand years of human suffering could have been averted had the Jewish people embraced change and returned to Jerusalem. A fantastic opportunity was missed, and we are suffering the consequences even today. Yet we can learn from the past and change the future.

It has been said that opportunity never knocks twice on anyone's door. Next time you hear a knock at your door, run—don't walk—and answer it.

A Christian Reflection on the Knock on the Door

In the book of Revelation, the letter to the church of Laodicea contains these well-known words: "Look! I stand at the door and knock. If you hear my voice and open the door, I will come in, and we will share a meal together as friends" (Revelation 3:20). Though these words would be appropriate even for those who have no relationship with God, they are part of a letter to Christians in the church at Laodicea, who had grown lukewarm in their relationship with God. Jesus was offering to renew and revitalize that relationship. Jesus still is knocking at the door and wants to enter into a deep and meaningful relationship with all who answer.

GREAT EXPECTATIONS

Many of the older priests, Levites, and other leaders who had seen the first Temple wept aloud when they saw the new Temple's foundation. The others, however, were shouting for joy. ✦ EZRA 3:12

What a joyous moment it must have been when the foundation for the Second Temple had been completed. The Jewish people had succeeded in returning to their homeland after a seventy-year exile and now were rebuilding the Temple that the Babylonians had destroyed.

The completion of the Temple foundation was a big deal. The people blasted trumpets, clanged cymbals, and sang praises to the LORD. The joy was palpable, and sounds of celebration could be heard from afar. But not everyone was happy.

Many of the elders who had seen the First Temple before its destruction wept at the site of the new Temple's foundation. Why? Because it was obvious to them that the Second Temple paled in comparison to the first. On the other hand, those who couldn't remember or had never seen the First Temple in all its glory were ecstatic. To them, the Second Temple was the greatest accomplishment they had ever known.

Our expectations are often an invitation to disappointment. That's because our expectations are rarely met. Home renovations seldom turn out exactly like home-owners would have liked. Children are hardly ever the perfect little people their parents envisioned when they were born. The lives we live now are not always in sync with what we might have imagined when we were younger.

It doesn't really matter if things end up better or worse. When we are invested in having things turn out a certain way, we are bound to experience defeat. The trick is to shed our expectations of what should be, so that we can experience the joy of what actually is.

Don't let the beauty of the moment pass you by. Open your eyes to the reality around you—without any expectations of what you think should be. Then you, too, can shout for joy!

A Christian Reflection on Rejoicing in the Present

The apostle Paul knew that life was hard, and he was more than aware that the people he wrote to experienced grave hardships. But what does he tell them? Repeatedly, Paul tells them to rejoice. "Whatever happens, my dear brothers and sisters, rejoice in the Lord" (Philippians 3:1). How can Paul rejoice? He has hope—hope "for the day when God will give us our full rights as his adopted children, including the new bodies he has promised us" (Romans 8:23). He also knows that, even in the midst of a troubled world, we have glimpses of a future heavenly reality.

EMBRACING RESISTANCE

*The local residents tried to discourage and frighten the people of Judah to keep them
from their work. They bribed agents to work against them and to frustrate their plans.
This went on during the entire reign of King Cyrus of Persia and lasted until King
Darius of Persia took the throne.* ❖ EZRA 4:4-5

As the Jewish people progressed in building the Second Temple, they encountered
resistance from a group of Samaritans. Although the visitors purported to come in
peace and offered to help rebuild the Temple, what they really wanted to do was
thwart the construction.

They did everything they could to undermine the project. They frightened the
Jews, sabotaged their work, and told lies about them to the ruling government. And
they succeeded. Construction of the Temple was stopped. All the momentum and
joy that had accompanied the Jews on their return evaporated.

And so it is with life. One moment we are flying high with our latest plans; the
next moment we collide with a wall blocking our way. What do we do then? Do we
turn around and go back the way we came, or do we stick around until we can find
a way around the barrier?

The Jewish people stuck it out for eighteen years until they were able to continue
building the Temple. They persevered and eventually reached their goal. We can do
the same. With perseverance, we can overcome almost any obstacle. But why does
God put obstacles there in the first place? Why did he allow the Samaritans to stand
in the way?

When we want to strengthen our muscles, there is only one way: *resistance*. Go to any
gym, and the strongest individuals are working the hardest. They load on the weights
and push themselves to the limit. The more they sweat, the stronger they get.

God helps us out when we want something by making us work hard for it. When we
work hard for something, it strengthens our commitment to that goal. The more committed we are, the more likely we are to achieve and sustain that goal in the long term.

Next time you find yourself up against a wall, don't dismay. Push against the resistance. It's that very resistance that gives way to your goals.

A Christian Reflection on Being up against the Wall

The book of James tells us what to do when we run into obstacles to plans that we
know conform to God's will. Obviously, James's readers have run into troubles, so he
gives them the following advice: "Dear brothers and sisters, when troubles come your
way, consider it an opportunity for great joy. For you know that when your faith is
tested, your endurance has a chance to grow. So let it grow, for when your endurance
is fully developed, you will be perfect and complete, needing nothing" (James 1:2-4).
Has trouble come into your life? Rejoice! You have an opportunity to grow.

TOTAL DEVOTION

*This was because Ezra had determined to study and obey the Law of the LORD
and to teach those decrees and regulations to the people of Israel.* ❖ EZRA 7:10

Ezra, a great priest and teacher of Israel, was extremely blessed. When he began his
journey to the land of Israel, he had the full support of the king of Persia. The king
furnished Ezra with gold and silver, cattle for offerings, and as much food as he needed
for the way. He also authorized Ezra to govern and waived taxes for anyone working in
the Temple. This was a far cry from the previous kings, who had outlawed building the
Temple altogether.

It seems that Ezra got a huge dose of help from above. But what did he do that
allowed him such wonderful and unusual divine providence?

Judaism has an oral tradition that says, "Align your will with My Will, in order that
I will align My Will to your will" (*Ethics of our Fathers* 2:4). In other words, when we
want what God wants, then God wants what we want. When we dedicate our lives to
doing God's work and his will, we become partners with him.

The Scriptures teach us that Ezra wholly devoted his life to study, observance, and
teaching the Word of God. So it's not surprising that God took extra special care of him.
Because Ezra's world revolved around God, God made the world revolve around Ezra.

Now, this doesn't mean that everyone needs to quit their jobs and become a
teacher or scholar of the Scriptures. You can be fully committed to God's will and still
be a doctor, a business owner, a teacher, or a mother. There are always opportunities to
pass along God's Word and God's love. And of course we teach best by example—by
living the words that we teach.

As we make it our will to do God's will, his will becomes our priority, and we
become his.

A Christian Reflection on Aligning Our Will with God's Will

God does not promise to give us whatever we want, but he does want to bless us by
working through us. As we come to know God better, our desires will conform to his,
and we will find joy in being used by God to bring about his plan on earth, even if it
brings us pain. As the apostle Peter tells us, "If you have suffered physically for Christ,
you have finished with sin. You won't spend the rest of your lives chasing your own
desires, but you will be anxious to do the will of God" (1 Peter 4:1-2). As Jesus taught,
we should pray, "May your Kingdom come soon. May your will be done on earth, as it
is in heaven" (Matthew 6:10).

Sabbath Reflections

What new truth about the life of Ezra did you learn from this week's devotions?

How has this truth affected your faith?

How will you apply this truth to your daily life?

Your Key Verse for the Week:

❖ OTHER REFLECTIONS

Endnotes

1. "Israeli rower won gold—and sang 'Hatikvah' on her own," YouTube video, 2:28, from a live performance of "Hatikvah" by Israeli athlete Moran Samuel at a rowing competition in Italy, video posted by "MidEastTruth," May 2, 2012, http://www.youtube.com/watch?v= W9ppv7v1b-Q.
2. "'You've go to find what you love,' Jobs says," *Stanford Report*, June 14, 2005, text of Steve Jobs' commencement speech at Stanford University, June 12, 2005, http://news.stanford.edu/news/2005/june15/jobs -061505.html.
3. Natan Sharansky, http://www.ifcj.org/site/DocServer/Sharansky_gulag .pdf?docID=5022.
4. Moses Hess, nineteenth-century Zionist, www.cambridgeforecast.org /MIDDLEEAST/MOSES-HESS.html.
5. Aleksandr I. Solzhenitsyn, "A World Split Apart," commencement speech at Harvard University, June 8, 1978.

Scriptural Index

Topical Index

About the Authors

RABBI YECHIEL ECKSTEIN, founder and president of the International Fellowship of Christians and Jews, has devoted his life's work and ministry to building bridges of understanding between Christians and Jews, and raising broad support for the State of Israel and for the Jewish people worldwide. An ordained Orthodox rabbi, Rabbi Eckstein is an internationally respected Bible teacher and has served on the faculties of Columbia University, Chicago Theological Seminary, and Northern Baptist Seminary. To learn more about Rabbi Eckstein, The Fellowship, and its programs, please visit www.ifcj.org.

Rabbi Eckstein received Orthodox rabbinic ordination from Yeshiva University in New York. He holds master's degrees from Yeshiva University and Columbia University, where he also completed studies for his doctorate. He currently serves on the executive committee of the American Jewish Joint Distribution Committee and the Jewish Agency for Israel, where he chaired its Committee on *Aliyah* and Rescue.

Prior to founding The Fellowship, Rabbi Eckstein was national codirector of interreligious affairs for the Anti-Defamation League. In that role, he broke new ground by forging partnerships with evangelical Christians. Recognizing the potential of these strong interfaith relationships, in 1983 he established The Fellowship to help Christians and Jews begin a dialogue and work together on projects promoting the security and well-being of Jews in Israel and around the world.

In Israel, Rabbi Eckstein served as an informal adviser to then-Prime Minister Ariel Sharon, and in 2005 was appointed as official Goodwill Ambassador of the State of Israel. He has worked to build support for Israel throughout Europe, Asia, Latin America, and Australia.

In 2010, The Fellowship launched *Holy Land Moments*, a daily radio broadcast featuring Rabbi Eckstein's insights into Jewish belief and faith, Israel, and the Jewish roots of Christianity. The show, which is now heard in English and Spanish (*Momentos en Tierra Santa*), airs daily on 1,050 stations in the United States, Australia, Canada, Ireland, Japan, New Zealand, the United Kingdom, Russia, the Philippines, Israel, Africa, and throughout Latin America. More than nine million listeners hear the programs each week.

Rabbi Eckstein is married to Joelle, lives in Jerusalem, and has three daughters and five grandchildren.

DR. TREMPER LONGMAN III is the Robert H. Gundry Professor of Biblical Studies at Westmont College. He earned a BA in Religion at Ohio Wesleyan University, an MDiv from Westminster Theological Seminary, and a PhD in Ancient Near Eastern Studies from Yale University. He has authored or coauthored more than twenty books, including commentaries on Job, Proverbs, Ecclesiastes, Song of Songs, Jeremiah, Lamentations, Daniel, and Nahum. His books have been translated into seventeen languages. As a Hebrew scholar, he is one of the main translators of the popular New Living Translation of the Bible and has served as a consultant on other popular translations, including *The Message*, the New Century Version, the *Holman Christian Standard Bible*, and the *Common Bible*. He has also edited and contributed to a number of study Bibles and Bible dictionaries. Tremper and his wife, Alice, have three adult sons and two granddaughters.

International Fellowship of Christians and Jews.

Celebrating more than thirty years of blessings, the International Fellowship of Christians and Jews is dedicated to building bridges of friendship and promoting understanding between Jews and Christians, fostering broad support for Israel and her people through humanitarian assistance and life-saving aid.

The Fellowship blesses Israel and her people through four ministry programs:

On Wings of Eagles.

On Wings of Eagles helps needy Jews immigrate to the Holy Land and assists them in starting a new life.

Isaiah 58

Our Isaiah 58 ministry delivers food, clothing, medicine, and other lifesaving care to orphans, elderly Jews, and needy families in the former Soviet Union.

 Guardians of Israel

Guardians of Israel provides food, medical care, and other essentials to Israelis living in poverty, and provides relief and security to Israelis affected by terrorism and war.

 STAND for ISRAEL

Stand for Israel mobilizes churches, Christian leaders, and individuals to stand with Israel through prayer and public advocacy.

To find out more about Rabbi Eckstein, The Fellowship, and our programs, please visit www.ifcj.org.

Do-able. <u>Daily.</u> Devotions.

START ANY DAY THE ONE YEAR WAY.

Do-able.
Every One Year book is designed for people who live busy, active lives. Just pick one up and start on today's date.

Daily.
Daily routine doesn't have to be drudgery. One Year devotionals help you form positive habits that connect you to what's most important.

Devotions.
Discover a natural rhythm for drawing near to God in an extremely personal way. One Year devotionals provide daily focus essential to your spiritual growth.

It's convenient and easy to grow
with God the One Year way.

CP0500